D1083513

Conceptual Systems and Personality Organization

Conceptual Systems and Personality Organization

O. J. HARVEY, University of Colorado

DAVID E. HUNT, Syracuse University

HAROLD M. SCHRODER, Princeton University

New York · London, John Wiley & Sons, Inc.

Library of Congress Catalog Card Number: 61-15400
Printed in the United States of America

Preface

This book is an outgrowth of interaction among the three authors during the last several years. Our initial aim in these discussions was to consider overlapping aspects of each of our research projects. However, the focus of our discussions very soon turned toward an attempt to delineate some general principles which would accurately represent and integrate our ideas. The purpose of this book, therefore, is to articulate our own thinking through setting forth a general viewpoint and applying it to several diverse content areas in psychology. The aim is to apply a rather broad integrative net to problems with the hope that such application may indicate to us, as well as to the reader, areas in which investigations are required.

As a consequence of this goal the reader should not expect to find a definitive or traditional account of the diverse topics covered, which include conceptual structure, child development, training methods, attitude change, psychopathology, and personality measurement. The most central belief shared by the authors of this book is that many topics and problems in psychology, often treated separately, may be better understood and integrated if considered from a common viewpoint.

In applying our general assumptions to numerous problems, no doubt we have overextended their appropriateness. But we would agree strongly with William James that the only adequate test of a theoretical position is to bring it to bear on as many problems as possible, even until the threshold of absurdity may be attained. So this we have done, mindful of our violation of the oft-repeated "law of parsimony" as it is promulgated by psychology. We remain unsure, however, of whether "real" parsimony is better served by a minimum of inclusive theoretical assumptions or a maximum of exclusive ones. Surely it will some day become a simple truism that the theory is best which is *both* most inclusive and most exclusive, which will tell us in what ways more things are of common dimensions, and in what ways more things are of different dimensions.

This book emphasizes mediational processes, concepts or programs, as the integrative unit. It is strongly functional in orientation focusing upon the nature of adaptation to a changing environment as a consequence of differences in conceptual structure. In stressing adaptability to change we have been less concerned with the level of performance in a relatively constant environment. We recognize that this latter component, the level of performance in an unchanging environment, is an important concern in any situation in which sheer achievement or output is the major goal. However, in this view, gross level of performance is not an adequate criterion for differentiating between different levels of adaptability. Conceptual evolvement is described in terms of the increasing effectiveness of adaptability to change.

As a result of our aim and approach, we have not written with any particular circumscribed audience in mind. The book should, however, hold potential interest for persons (whether undergraduates or research workers) who share our belief about the importance of understanding psychological problems through the use of a common viewpoint. Also, we hope that some readers may find certain of our (unsupported) assertions or derivations sufficiently divergent from their own viewpoint that they will be impelled to conduct investigations to attempt to refute the hypotheses.

Like most authors we have experienced the unavoidable vexation of not being able to include relevant sources which either have appeared or have been discovered after completion of the final draft. We feel particularly unfortunate in being unable to refer to the following recent and highly relevant works: D. E. Berlyne, *Conflict, Arousal, and Curiosity*. New York: McGraw Hill, 1960; G. Miller, E. Galanter, and K. Pribram, *Plans and the Structure of Behavior*. New York: Holt-Dryden, 1960; M. Rokeach, *The Open and Closed Mind*. New York: Basic Books, 1960; and R. W. White's paper, "Competence and the psychosexual stages of development," in the *Nebraska Symposium on Motivation*, 1960.

We wish to express our appreciation to the Office of Naval Research and to the National Institute of Mental Health for supporting our research activities during the last several years. Thanks are due also to our three universities—University of Colorado, Syracuse University, and Princeton University—for providing either faculty fellowships or other means of reducing the usual academic demands which permitted a greater concentration of time for completing the book. We are especially grateful to Dr. Ralph L. Dunlap who read the entire manuscript and made numerous valuable suggestions, many of which we have incorporated. We will not attempt to list all of the many students, colleagues, assistants, and typists who have contributed in many different ways to the current work, but we appreciate their assistance.

At this point we are not certain whether to thank or admonish our wives for their support during the development of this book. However, we do deeply acknowledge their tolerance.

Since there is no senior author and no attempt to imply any differential contribution to the final outcome, the authorship listing follows an alphabetical order.

O. J. H.
D. E. H.
H. M. S.

June, 1961

Acknowledgments

We wish to acknowledge with thanks the courtesy extended by the following publishers, journals, and authors in granting permission to reprint excerpts from the indicated works:

Addison-Wesley Publishing Company for material from J. S. Bruner and R. Tagiuri in G. Lindzey (Ed.), *Handbook of Social Psychology.*

George Allen & Unwin Ltd. for material from L. Levy-Bruhl, *Primitive Mentality.*

The American Medical Association and T. Lidz, Alice Cornelison, Dorothy Terry, and S. Fleck for excerpts from an article in *Archives of Neurology and Psychiatry.*

The American Psychological Association and respective authors for material from articles in the *Journal of Abnormal and Social Psychology* by J. Bieri and E. Blacker, by J. Birren, by R. W. Brown, by A. J. Caron and M. A. Wallach, by M. Deutsch and H. B. Gerard, by J. L. Gewirtz and D. M. Baer, by A. R. Jensen, by J. C. Mark, by J. McDavid, by R. F. Peck, and by E. S. Schaefer; for material in the *Journal of Consulting Psychology* from an article by C. R. Rogers; for material in *Psychological Monographs* from an article by K. Goldstein and M. Scheerer.

The American Sociological Association and E. H. Powell for material from an article in *American Sociological Review.*

Appleton-Century-Crofts, Inc. for material from D. C. McClelland, J. W. Atkinson, R. A. Clark, and E. L. Lowell, *The Achievement Motive* and from P. M. Symonds, *The Psychology of Parent-Child Relationships.*

Basic Books, Inc. for material from Maxwell Jones, *The Therapeutic Community.*

J. and A. Churchill, Ltd. for material from an article by T. A. Lambo in the *Journal of Mental Science.*

Columbia University Press for material from K. Lewin and from J. Piaget in D. Rapaport (Ed.), *Organization and Pathology of Thought.*

The *Denver Post* for an excerpt from an article by Bob Whearley entitled "Alabaman Views Segregation as God's Will—Methodists Won't Set Integration Target Date."

Duke University Press for material from articles by J. W. Getzels and E. G. Guba and by C. G. McClintock in the *Journal of Personality.*

The Family Service Association of America for material from an article by D. W. Goodrich and D. S. Boomer in *Social Casework.*

The Free Press of Glencoe, Illinois, for material from A. F. Henry and J. Short, *Suicide and Homicide: Some Economic, Sociological and Psychological Aspects of Aggression,* and from F. Redl and D. Wineman, *Children Who Hate.*

Grune and Stratton, Inc. and respective authors and editors for material by D. P. Ausubel, *Ego Development and the Personality Disorders,* and by D. M. Levy in P. H. Hoch and J. Zubin (Eds.), *Psychopathology of Childhood.*

Hall Syndicate, Inc. for special permission to quote a caption from "Dennis the Menace" cartoon.

Harcourt, Brace and World, Inc. for material from G. Murphy, *Historical Introduction to Modern Psychology,* and from J. Piaget, *The Moral Judgment of the Child,* and *The Child's Conception of the World.*

Harper and Brothers for material from H. A. Witkin, Helen B. Lewis, M. Hertzman, Karen Machover, Pearl B. Meissner, and S. Wapner, *Personality through Perception,* from E. Hoffer, *The True Believer,* from Frances L. Ilg and Louise B. Ames, *Child Behavior,* and from G. Murphy, *Personality: A Biosocial Approach.*

D. C. Heath and Company for material from R. Ergang, *Europe from the Renaissance to Waterloo.*

Paul B. Hoeber, Inc. and the author for material from an article by S. Rado in *Psychosomatic Medicine.*

Holt, Rinehart and Winston, Inc. for material from Erich Fromm, *Escape from Freedom.*

International Universities Press, Inc. and the author for material by H. Werner, *Comparative Psychology of Mental Development* (Rev. Ed.).

The *Journal of Conflict Resolution* of the University of Michigan for excerpts from an article by R. Abelson.

The Journal Press for material from an article by R. R. Sears, J. Whiting, V. Nowlis, and Pauline Sears in *Genetic Psychology Monographs.*

The Macmillan Company for material from A. N. Whitehead, *Modes of Thought.*

The Massachusetts Institute of Technology Press and John Wiley & Sons for material from C. Cherry, *On Human Communication: A Review, A Survey, and A Criticism.*

McGraw-Hill Book Co., Inc. for material from R. Grinker and J. Spiegel, *Men under Stress,* and from K. Lewin, *A Dynamic Theory of Personality: Selected Papers.*

New York University Press for material from H. Cantril and C. Bumstead, *Reflections on the Human Venture.*

North-Holland Publishing Company for material from articles by M. D. Vernon and by R. G. Barker in the *Proceedings of the Fifteenth International Congress of Psychology, Brussels, 1957.*

W. W. Norton and Company, Inc. for material from E. H. Erikson, *Childhood and Society,* from G. A. Kelly, *The Psychology of Personal Constructs,* and from R. P. Smith, *"Where did you go?" "Out." "What did you do?" "Nothing."*

Prentice-Hall, Inc. for material from J. B. Rotter, *Social Learning and Clinical Psychology.*

Research Center for Group Dynamics of the University of Michigan for material from articles by W. G. Bennis and H. A. Shepard and by M. Haire and Willa F. Grunes in *Human Relations.*

The Ronald Press Company for material by H. S. Coffey in L. A. Pennington and I. A. Berg (Eds.), *An Introduction to Clinical Psychology,* by G. S. Klein in R. R. Blake and G. V. Ramsey, *Perception, An Approach to Personality,* by S. Rosenzweig in J. McV. Hunt (Ed.), *Personality and the Behavior Disorders,* by R. W. White, *The Abnormal Personality.*

Rutgers University Press for material from D. W. Brogan, *America in the Modern World.*

Social Forces of the University of North Carolina for material from an article by R. K. Merton.

Society for Research in Child Development, Inc. and the respective authors for material from articles by Eleanor E. Maccoby and by Lawrence K. Frank in *Child Development.*

Stanford University Press for material by E. E. Jones and J. W. Thibaut in R. Taguiri and L. Petrullo (Eds.), *Person Perception and Interpersonal Behavior.*

John Wiley and Sons for material from F. Heider, *The Psychology of Interpersonal Relations,* from M. B. Smith, J. S. Bruner and R. W. White, *Opinions and Personality,* and from J. Thibaut and H. H. Kelley, *The Social Psychology of Groups.*

The University of Nebraska Press for material by H. Levin and A. L. Baldwin in the *Nebraska Symposium on Motivation, 1959.*

The William Alanson White Psychiatric Foundation for material from articles by Ruth Benedict, by T. Tietze, and by Susan Reichard and C. Tillman in *Psychiatry*.

Yale University Press for material from D. Riesman, *The Lonely Crowd*, from Harriet Linton and Elaine Graham in I. L. Janis and C. I. Hovland et al. (Eds.), *Personality and Persuasibility*, and from J. Whiting and I. Child, *Child Training and Personality: A Cross-Cultural Study*.

We also wish to thank: A. R. Anderson and O. K. Moore and the Office of Naval Research for excerpts from an ONR Technical Report, Herbert C. Kelman for excerpts from an unpublished manuscript, and Adrien Pinard for excerpts from a paper presented in 1959 at Yale University.

Contents

1 Overview

The belief that psychological activity is the joint product of situational and dispositional factors is a basic assumption in many psychological viewpoints, whether cognitive, psychophysical, or functional. One consequence of this interdependent determination is that in order to evaluate the effect of either situational or dispositional factors, the interrelated effect of the other factor must be considered.

How can this joint effect be understood? We assume that an individual interacts with his environment by breaking it down and organizing it into meaningful patterns congruent with his own needs and psychological make-up. As a result of this interchange, perceptual and behavioral constancies develop, which stem from the individual's standardized evaluative predilections toward differentiated aspects of his external world. We will refer to such evaluative tendencies as *concepts.* In serving as modes of relatedness or connecting ties between the individual and his environment, concepts thus provide the basis for understanding the joint effect of situational and dispositional factors.

A concept is a system of ordering that serves as the mediating linkage between the input side (stimuli) and the output side (response). In operating as a system of ordering, a concept may be viewed as a categorical schema, an intervening medium, or program through which impinging stimuli are coded, passed, or evaluated on their way to response evocation. *It is with the nature and development of these subject-object ties and with facets and effects of variations in the kinds of conceptual linkages between the individual and his world that this book is concerned.* It is this bridge of relatedness *between* subject and object on which we focus rather than on either the subject or object *per se.* Many approaches have emphasized the variations in the subject (organismic variables such as age and intelligence) and variations in the nature of the objects to which the conceptual ties are anchored (for example, content areas such as the Republican party, God, and Yale). In this book, however, we are concerned with *how* the individual relates to objects through modes of subject-object connectedness that are presumably independent of the content or nature of the object. Assuming, therefore, that the structural properties of the ways the individual relates objects to himself are not contingent upon what is being related, we focus upon the variation in ways objects are conceived and upon differences in evaluative predispositons toward more or less common objects.

The distinction between the present emphasis upon subject-object relatedness and the more traditional approaches emphasizing only the object of reference is similar to the difference between "anschauung" and "attitude," respectively, made by Klein:

> The term, *Anschauung*, is preferable to "attitude" because of the rather more narrow, well-worn connotations of the latter term in American psychologies, particularly in social psychology. Attitude usually implies a quite specific *content* and a direction toward or away from an object. In this common meaning it carries no implications of formal personality structure. But our use of it is precisely in the latter sense as a genotypic principle of control, having no ties to specific content, not necessarily related to particular conflicts or stresses, and with counterparts in all forms of cognitive behavior (Klein, 1951, p. 332).

Our study of concepts, like that of "anschauung," therefore will focus upon organizational properties that are not restricted to any particular referent object, but might be directed toward any object. As the above quotation suggests, a focus upon organizational or structural aspects is likely to render fairly insignificant certain traditional distinctions, such as that between attitude and value. On a similar basis our concern with specific behavioral manifestations will be only as indices of genotypic evaluative orientations to the world. Therefore, rather than emphasize content, for example, the object of an attitude or the level of achievement, we emphasize structural components of the conceptual system underlying evaluation and response to objects and the adaptive function that these conceptual linkages serve the organism.

Let us consider the cases of an avid atheist and a zealous believer in God: in terms of many behavioral criteria or attitudinal classifications, these two persons might be viewed as opposites. This classification rests upon the phenotypic yardstick of directionality toward the referent God. If they were considered according to the more genotypic aspects of their ways of relating to God, the atheist and the zealous believer might be seen as very similar to each other, more similar in fact than either would be to a person to whom the object, God, had little personal relevance.

Once a concept develops, it serves as an experiential filter through which impinging events are screened, gauged, and evaluated, a process that determines in large part what responses can and will occur. In this functional capacity, concepts are seen as providing a transforming mechanism similar to a judgmental baseline (Sherif and Cantril, 1947) or an adaptation level (Helson, 1947), through which reality is read. In serving as a means of evaluating events, concepts therefore define the positive or negative quality of an event, which in turn is assumed to determine the nature of affective arousal.

Our concentration on concepts as the internal referents that provide the basis for relating to the environment leads to certain deliberate restrictions of this book. Omitted specifically, for example, is a detailed consideration of the operation of such internal factors as are embodied in the biogenic motives and other physiological processes. This is not to imply, of course, that these conceptual referent points that we treat are not themselves affected by physiological states and biological factors, as we indicate briefly. It is but to suggest that our focus is on the operation and effects of the more conceptual or symbolic of these internal standards.

Concrete-Abstract Nature of Concepts

The functional nature of a concept is assumed to be interdependently related to the structural characteristics of the subject-object ties. We assume that the most important structural characteristic is the degree of concreteness or abstractness. The more concrete, the more the structure is assumed to be restricted to, or dependent upon, physical attributes of the activating stimulus.

In more concrete functioning, the mediating link between input and output is more *fixed*. Such an extreme dependence upon the physical stimulus is perhaps most clearly illustrated by an organism low on the phylogenetic scale for which the stimulus takes on a compelling pressure to make a particular response. Such a taxic response as that of the moth which "has no choice" but to fly toward a light epitomizes the effects of extremely concrete structure. At the human level, concrete functioning, even in extreme cases, rarely reaches this degree of complete dependence upon external stimulation. However, there is enormous variation along the concrete-abstract dimension at the human level, as the incidence of stereotyped thinking illustrates. We are concerned with such variation throughout this book and particularly with the conditions determining a person's attainment of a given level of abstractness. In addition, we focus upon "going beyond the information given," to use Bruner's phrase (1957), and the implications of such a differential ability in cognitive, affective, and behavioral consequences in situations that confirm or refute one's conceptual standards.

Development of Concepts

The factors determining the level of concreteness-abstractness reached by an individual are considered from a developmental viewpoint. We assume that development represents progression toward greater abstractness on the concrete-abstract dimension, which results in modification in the structural nature of the subject-object ties. We will not view development in such terms as the acquisition of motor behavior or as the acquisition of bowel or bladder control, as many others have done.

The present view of development occurring along the abstractness-concreteness dimension assumes an increased availability of alternative concepts or schemata for coping with the same stimuli. Thus, as progressive development occurs, the person orders the world more relativistically and less stereotypically. In other words, he operates more in terms of multiple alternatives (within a more complex and dimensionalized space) rather than in terms of bifurcated black-white categories. As the interconnecting ties to objects become less dependent upon physical properties of the object, the individual progresses from perceiving events as entirely externally caused to attributing a causal role to his own transactions with the environment.

Learning: The Acquisition of Concepts

In contrast to many other views, learning is seen in terms of the acquisition of concepts. Thus, "what is learned" are forms of relatedness, or subject-object ties. We assume that learning occurs through a process of differentiation and integration, during which time the person breaks down the environment into parts relevant to his current conceptual structure and then integrates these parts in ways compatible with his current organization. We draw an important distinction between the learning of concepts and learning as more traditionally defined, that is, in terms of how closely the performance of the person matches some prescribed external standard of the training agent. This distinction is illustrated by Lewin's comments on "achievement concepts" as follows:

> The use of *achievement concepts* is one of the essential obstacles in the way of discovering the concretely existing Gestalt relations. Not that the

task is to subsume everything in any remotely possible relationship, but rather to establish whether and where actual Gestalt relations do or do not exist in a given case.

Let us take a training process, for example, the learning of typewriting. The learning curve rises at first quite steeply to level off later on. In time, a more or less jump-like transition from that level to a higher level takes place, and so forth. The achievement concept "typewriting" lumps all these processes together, as if they were a single action (Lewin, 1951, pp. 89–90).

If the word "concept" is substituted for "Gestalt relation" in the above quotation, then the distinction is relevant to the present position.

A person may learn to make a particular overt response demanded by the training agent without substantially modifying any of the structural features of his concepts. To use the case of the zealot again: he might, in response to effective propaganda or other methods of persuasion, shift from an "anti" position to an equally committed "pro" position toward the same object and in so doing not modify at all the structural properties of his ties to the object. Thus considering only the occurrence of specific responses as indicating learning may prevent understanding the genotypic reorganization, if any, which may parallel such overt change. It should be made clear at this point that we are not disavowing interest in behavior, for it is only through behavior that we can understand the process of conceptual functioning. Also, we are not trying to disclaim the importance of content of concepts, for it is obvious that the directionality of response tendencies toward an object, whether approach or avoidant, has social and personal significance. We only are maintaining that the relation between behavior and concept is very complex in that the same behavioral response may be associated with two or more quite different conceptual structures, and similarly that the same conceptual structure may be associated with quite different behavioral responses. One implication of this is that a single response cannot provide a valid index of the structural qualities of directing conceptual schemata. Hence multiple measures, which provide at least two points in space and time, are necessary for "mapping" or accurately inferring the conceptual structure assumed to underlie any and all responses.

If learning is viewed in terms of the acquisition of concepts, then what is learned by the person who is the object of training may differ radically from the explicit goals of the training agent. In other words, since the goal of the training agent is usually to change overt responses, he is unlikely to be aware of what forms of subject-object relatedness he is "also" teaching. For example, the dominating parent, intent upon forcing a child to be polite, will likely not be aware of the fact that what the child is "really learning" is not simply an obedient response, but rather that interpersonal relations or subject-object relatedness occurs in terms of dominant-submissive relationships. If the training agent were less concerned with the *what,* or teaching a specific response, and more concerned with the *how* of the relatedness being established, then such disparity between the explicit goals of the training agent and what is learned by the object of training would not be so great.

Concepts, Conceptual Systems, and the Self

We assume that the characteristics associated with a single concept may also be applied to groups of concepts. Let us imagine a dimension with a single concept at one extreme and the totality of a person's concepts at the other extreme. For particular purposes we may choose a unit of analysis at any point on this dimension. At the most specific extreme the unit would be the concept, and at the most general extreme the unit would be the self-system, with in-between areas representing conceptual systems. In reality, the dimension of unit specificity is hypothetical because a single concept probably never functions completely independently. We maintain that in order to understand a concept, one should place it in relation to as many independent dimensions, for example, the concrete-abstract dimension, as possible rather than employing the more traditional separation of concepts into attitudes, values, and so forth. In keeping with the present generic approach, therefore, we use the same structural dimensions to refer to all concepts, whether in describing pathological conceptual functioning (resulting from real life stress) or referring to the more normal functioning (elicited by less stressful laboratory manipulations as in conflict resolution).

From the present viewpoint, the development and functioning of a concept is assumed to be inseparable from the development and functioning of the self. We define the self as the intertwined totality of one's concepts; furthermore, it is in terms of such a conceptual matrix that one defines his existence in space and time. Although the directing and regulating function of the self has been described by many others, the following statement by Murphy is particularly relevant:

> Indeed, the self-picture has all the strength of other perceptual stereotypes and in addition serves as the chart by which the individual navigates. If it is lost, he can make only impulsive runs in fair weather; the ship drifts helplessly whenever storms arise (Murphy, 1947, p. 715).

When a single concept is viewed as a part of a larger conceptual organization, the self, it becomes apparent that not all of one's concepts necessarily have the same structural characteristics. Owing to the diversity of developmental conditions experienced in initially establishing these linkages, it is common to find individuals whose conceptual ties to certain objects (for example, religion) are more concrete, and to other objects (for example, science) are quite abstract. Thus when we speak of modes of conceptual functioning we do so in relation to certain specific areas without assuming that the same organizational tendencies would apply in *all* other areas of functioning. Although the extent of generality of structural aspects across one's total conceptual system remains empirical, it seems likely that some individuals will tend to be quite consistent in many areas whereas others will manifest much more diversity.

Conceptual Confirmation and Refutation

Confirmation and refutation of concepts are, respectively, the evaluation of a situation as being either in line with or contradictory to the directional or volitional striving (either approach or avoidant) toward the object of the concept. The experience of confirmation or refutation depends in part upon structural characteristics, such as the centrality and interrelatedness, of the concepts concerned. However, in general, confirmation results in the experience of positive affect with accompanying approach tendencies toward the perceived agent of confirmation. Conversely, refutation results generally in the experience of negative affect with accompanying avoidant tendencies toward the perceived agent of refutation.

Confirmation and refutation rarely occur in relation to a single concept. More likely is the involvement of several concepts so that simultaneous confirmation and refutation occur, producing conflict and vacillation. Faced by such circumstances, the person is assumed to attempt to resolve the conflict in a way that will maximize positive affect. If the conflict involves concepts of varying centrality, he may neutralize or modify the less central concept. If the conflict involves two or more highly central concepts, however, then the individual may resort to a more pathological resolution, which in the extreme instances may take the form of amnesia or other dissociative or disintegrative phenomena.

Much of this book is devoted to various maneuvers that function to neutralize or transform potentially refuting events into experiences that leave the self minimally threatened and maximally unaltered. Maintenance of concepts is maintenance of self. Severance of all conceptual linkages between the subject and objects to which one is related would constitute a destruction of the self, an obliteration of the spatial and temporal anchorages on which one's definition of his existence depends. Not only is man's psychological being dependent upon such stabilizing conceptual linkages to the world, but also in very extreme cases is his physiological being.

Aim and Plan of the Book

The aim of the present book is to consider a rather broad set of problem areas from the same theoretical viewpoint. To the reader who wonders what the book is about we may note that we deal with a number of seemingly diverse problem areas such as child development, attitude change, personality measurement, motivational principles, and psychopathology. However, these traditional problem areas do not actually convey what the book is about because we are not directly concerned with any one of these areas as such. Rather we are concerned with the possibility of applying a common set of principles and constructs to these various problem areas. The common thread, which we attempt to weave through these diverse areas, is that of concepts or conceptual systems. Perhaps a more accurate way of stating what the book is about would be to say that we are interested in how an individual learns to adapt to his interpersonal environment, how such a pattern of adaptation affects his reaction to contemporaneous events, and how such patterns of conceptual organization may be modified.

We share the puzzlement of the student in introductory psychology, whether it be the bewildered freshman or the only slightly less confused sophomore, as to why there should be such a lack of continuity and consistency in the chapters of an introductory textbook in psychology. Most such books have highly compartmentalized chapters with almost no integrating constructs or theoretical principles. We believe that such changing constructs and terminology for each of the several content areas are not only unnecessary but also unwise since they prevent furthering our understanding about one area through knowledge in another. Therefore, we believe that attempting to view various problem areas with the same constructs may provide a basis for some theoretical rapprochement that extends beyond mere analogy. A similar view was expressed by Lawrence Frank (1960) when he urged the use of new concepts and methods in attempting to understand the process of development:

> . . . our problem becomes that of discovering how the organism-personality persists while changing, maintains a dynamic stability, with self-correcting and self-repairing processes and the capacity to transform organic functions

and behavior into the patterned physiological activities and the symbolic behavior required for living in a symbolic cultural world and participating in a social order (Frank, 1960, p. 189).

In the chapters to follow, therefore, the reader encounters the following kinds of treatment: motivational principles viewed in terms of conceptual refutation and confirmation; child development viewed in terms of the progressive development of concepts; personality organization viewed in terms of conceptual system structure; personality measurement viewed in terms of assessing the most prevalent pattern of conceptual system functioning; attitude change viewed in terms of resolutions emanating from conceptual functioning; psychopathological reactions viewed in terms of extreme resolutions associated with the functioning of conceptual systems; and psychotherapy and education viewed in terms of modification of conceptual system organization. We attempt to apply a consistent viewpoint to all of these areas without expecting to provide any final answers.

At a practical level it is hoped such a homogeneous approach will open the possibility for bringing together areas such as diagnosis and therapy, in which at present the assessment has little or no relation to the therapeutic intervention. However, more realistically, the present work is largely an attempt to focus upon the inconsistencies or gaps that occur when the viewpoint is applied, thus highlighting areas where research is needed or where conceptual reformulation is required. It is in this sense of raising such problems and pointing out research possibilities that we submit this book to the reader. Very apropos to the intent of this book is the comment of Hoffer concerning his own work:

> The reader is expected to quarrel with much that is said in this . . . book. He is likely to feel that much has been exaggerated and much ignored. But this is not an authoritative textbook. It is a book of thoughts, and it does not shy away from half-truths so long as they seem to hint at a new approach and help to formulate new questions. "To illustrate a principle," says Bagehot, "you must exaggerate much and you must omit much" (Hoffer, 1951, p. 59).

2 Nature of Concepts

That the same external event may be evaluated differently by different persons no doubt is a timeless truism. As a phenomenon receiving experimental attention, it goes back at least to around 1820 to the work of the astronomer Bessel who termed it the "personal equation" after his recognition of the scientific implications of the fact that even reputable astronomers tended to differ in their time observations of the stellar transits (Heidbreder, 1933; Murphy, 1949; Boring, 1950). Interest of psychology in this problem was given impetus by the advent of the theory of evolution and especially by the work of Galton (Galton, 1883).

Once having entered the stream of psychology, the operation of individual differences in almost all functioning became one of psychology's most basic dogmas and pervasive assumptions. Contributing heavily to the experimental documentation of this tenet has been the wealth of research on the effects of motivational factors on cognition during the last three decades, research that stemmed from the assumption that perception and other cognitive processes are bipolarly determined (Kohler, 1929), that is, are jointly determined by external and internal factors operating interdependently (Sherif, 1935).

Among the most influential of the multiplicity of internal or dispositional factors in determining any cognitive outcome are the stored, organized effects of past experience that we have labeled concepts. It is with these internal determinants of behavior, especially as they relate to the evaluation of and response to certain interpersonal stimuli, that this book is largely concerned.

Some General Characteristics of Concepts

A concept in the most general sense is a schema for evaluating impinging stimulus objects or events. Abstracted from the experience of objects in the environing world, it represents a category of varying definitiveness and breadth along some specifiable dimension (hot-cold, good-bad, and so forth) (Harvey and Rutherford, 1958). Once a concept has evolved, it serves as a psychological yardstick in terms of which stimuli are compared and gauged, a kind of experiential filter through which objects are screened and evaluated on their way from sensory reception to ultimate response evocation.

Concepts, in their matrix of interrelatedness, serve the critical cognitive function of providing a system of ordering by means of which the environment is broken down and organized, is differentiated and integrated, into its many psychologically relevant facets. In this capacity, they provide the medium through which the individual establishes and maintains ties with the surrounding world. It is on the basis of the web of these conceptual ties that one is able to place oneself stably and meaningfully in relation to time, space, and other objects and dimensions of his psychological universe. It is on this basis, hence, that one's self-identity and existence are articulated and maintained. Threat to such ties or severance of them leads to a psychological mobilization aimed at maintaining or restoring them, efforts, which if unsuccessful may result in a major reorientation and organization of ties to the world, or more drastically, even to breakdown or destruction of the self.

Our emphasis upon this adaptive function of concepts certainly is not new nor unique. It is closely akin at the theoretical level to two major schools of thought: to the evolutionary functionalists, with their emphasis on motivation and adaptation of the organism to the environment; and to the Gestalters, with their emphasis on the organizational and cognitive determinants of behavior. More recently Kelly has stated a position that clearly stresses the adaptive importance of concepts ("constructs" as he terms them):

> Man looks at his world through transparent patterns or templets which he creates and then attempts to fit over the realities of which the world is composed. The fit is not always very good. Yet without such patterns the world appears to be such an undifferentiated homogeneity that man is unable to make any sense out of it. Even a poor fit is more helpful to him than nothing at all.
>
> Let us give the name "constructs" to these patterns that are tentatively tried on for size. They are ways of construing the world. They are what enables man, and lower animals too, to chart a course of behavior, explicitly formulated or implicity acted out, verbally expressed or utterly inarticulate, consistent with other courses of behavior or inconsistent with them, intellectually reasoned or vegetatively sensed (Kelly, 1955, pp. 8–9).

That cognitive activity cannot be considered independently of motivational factors, and vice versa, has been demonstrated amply during the last twenty years, especially in the work of the not-now-so-new "New Lookers." The importance of the individual's conceptual linkage with his environment to his very existence, however, is only now being recognized, owing largely to the dramatic effects of communist "brainwashing" and research resulting from this and other international problems, such as space travel, which has given rise to increased investigation of the effects of isolation and "sensory deprivation." Paralleling this concern with effects of subject-object severance is a return of sociologists to the kindred problems of anomie and alienation, first emphasized by Durkheim (1897) and treated more recently by others (Merton, 1949; Srole, 1956; Nettler, 1957; Powell, 1958).

Concepts Epitomize Relativity

The simplest concept is the placement of two points into a relationship that will permit a judgment of "equal," "different," or "similar." This simplest kind of inference Stern refers to as "transduction," "the transition from one concrete, isolated judgment to another coordinate, single judgment," in contrast to induction and deduction, which involve making more generalized and abstract judgments (Werner, 1957, p. 327). One of the two points is always some internal standard or referent of the receiver, and the evaluation of the second point or event is always contingent upon its interdependence with this standard. After a concept has evolved, it enters into the matrix of other internal standards—which first are more biogenic but later are more conceptual—where it serves as the referent for the experiencing of related objects or events. As the conceptual referent is altered, so is the evaluation or judgment of the impinging stimulus—both while the stimulus is present (generally called perception) and during its absence (generally labeled memory).

It probably is not too far afield to suggest that no event has psychological relevance to an individual or exists for him until he has in some way related it to an existing internal standard(s). This implies that the behavioral relevance of an object "out there" is dependent on the way it is differentiated from the booming, buzzing environment and functionally compared, consciously or unconsciously, to key internal referents operative at the moment. One consequence of this is that although relationships can be and are formed between two or more external objects the linkage is *not* directly between these objects. Instead, the relationship between them stems from and is mediated through their mutual dependence on a common internal referent that links these objects on some dimension, rendering them as similar or dissimilar. The simple judgments of two weights as "lighter," "heavier," or "equal," for example, means that both of these objects have been compared implicitly to the common conceptual standard of heaviness and that their relationship to each other is a function of the relationship of each to this common evaluative yardstick. A person reared in a hypothetical environment where gravitational pulls had been kept at zero, for instance, could not differentiate between the two objects in terms of their heaviness. He might, however, be able to make some comparative judgment along other dimensions.

Not only does an object have no psychological value until it is compared to a conceptual referent, but also the reciprocal is true. A concept operates only in the presence of objects that are relevant to it. Remove the object—a task more difficult as the abstraction ladder is ascended because of conceptual extensions of the present into the past and future—and the concept lies dormant until another relevant object appears.

Thus the dependence of object and concept on each other is reciprocal. This may be analogous to the triggering effects of "releasers" (Tinbergen, 1951) or of "sign qualities" (Werner, 1957) in eliciting instinctual response tendencies or undifferentiated relationships between object and motive in the lower level species or—for Werner—in concrete human functioning. Considering that one of the characteristics of a concept is a readiness to respond to an object and that the concept lies in disuse until the object is presented, this may be more than analogous. This interdependence may actually be akin to the triggering effects of releasers and signal qualities, with the exception—and an important exception it is—that at the lower phylogenetic and more concrete levels the response elicited by a stimulus property is much more invariant. We are nevertheless now certain, for example, that the old controversy of heredity versus environment is meaningless unless these two factors are considered in interdependence; that whatever the characteristic or potential is in one, its fruition depends on a triggering off by the environment and a reciprocal state of readiness within the organism.

This view of the interdependence of object and concept approaches in one important way the epistemological stand of Aristotle and Anaxagoras (Heidbreder, 1933), as well as that of such functionalists as Spencer (1897), James (1890), and Dewey (1896), who emphasized relationships as the irreducible elements of reality. A relationship necessitates the existence of at least two points before anything can be related. Hence a single point, A, could have no existence—for us at least, no psychological relevance—until it existed in conjunction with at least a second point, B. Both A and B after being registered by the organism must be brought into reciprocal relevance by the mediating activity of a common internal referent (C) before a relationship between them can be said to exist.

Today instead of examining the Aristotelian question of form versus matter (to which we shall return later) we are more likely, when we discuss the problem at all, to pose the question as genotype versus phenotype (Lewin, 1935). Whatever the language, the important point is that no "fact" speaks for itself. No event has psychological relevance apart from the internal standard to which it is related. The "nature" of the fact or event is dependent on its relationship to a second, a third, an *n*th "fact" or event, as these are interlinked by a common internal yardstick. As Whitehead (1938) avers:

> . . . A single fact in isolation is the primary myth required for finite thought, that is to say, for thought unable to embrace totality.
>
> This mythological character arises because there is no such fact. Connectedness is of the essence of all things of all types. It is of the essence of all types, that they be connected. Abstraction from connectedness involves the omission of an essential factor in the fact considered. No fact is merely itself. The penetration of literature and art at their height arises from our dumb sense that we have passed beyond mythology; namely, beyond the myth of isolation (pp. 12–13).

Even more directly relevant perhaps is the comment by Spencer:

> For that which distinguishes Psychology from the sciences on which it rests, is that each of its propositions takes account both of the connected internal phenomena and of the connected external phenomena to which they refer. In a physiological proposition an inner relation is the essential subject of thought; but in a psychological proposition an outer relation is joined with it as a co-essential subject of thought. A relation in the environment rises into co-ordinate importance with a relation in the organism. The thing contemplated is now a totally different thing. It is not the connection between the internal phenomena, nor is it the connection between the external phenomena; but it is *the connection between these two connections.* A psychological proposition is necessarily compounded of two propositions, of which one concerns the subject and the other concerns the object; and cannot be expressed without the four terms which these two propositions imply (Spencer, 1897, Vol. I, p. 132).

The reader should keep sharply focused on the fact that it is with the relationship or connection *between* the subject and object, a relationship we term "concept," and not on the object or subject in independence of the other that this book is concerned.

Relationship of Concepts to Other Cognitive Outcomes

In the history of psychology attempts have been made to differentiate sharply between such terms as percept, concept, judgment, and memory. Without any expectation of quieting this argument with one brief pass, it does seem appropriate, however, to suggest that the dependence on at least two points in space and time is as essential for other of the so-called cognitive processes as it is for concept formation and functioning. Perception, judgment, and any other of the varieties of discrimination are essentially acts of evaluation, of comparing two or more objects or points on some common dimension(s) that are embodied as integral facets in existing internal standards. Thinking and problem solving in general may also be seen as similar processes that represent the postulation, either explicitly or implicitly, of a relationship between two or more objects that is accompanied by some type of behavior, either overt or covert, aimed at testing the validity of the hypothesized relationship. Memory, moreover, is the endurance or change of this postulation across time as it is affected by the input of intervening sensory events through both intero- and exteroceptors. The intervening events may operate to reinforce, to make more distinct the hypothesized relationship by their being perceived as congruent with the postulation. Or these events may serve to render the postulated relationship more diffuse and uncertain owing to the failure of the events to be perceived in accord with it. A modification of the underlying or referent concept results in a necessary change in the nature of the experience of those events—in the presence of those events (perception) or in their absence across time (memory).

Concepts Are Products of Both External and Internal Factors

Stimulus and Motivational Factors Operate Interdependently

The development and functioning of concepts, like all other cognitive outcomes, are bipolarly determined (Kohler, 1929; Lewin, 1935; Sherif, 1935; Piaget, 1951); that is, concepts are jointly determined by the totality of external (situational) and internal (dispositional) factors at the given time operating in mutual interdependence. This is not to say that both sets of these cognitive determinants exercise equal weight in the final outcome. The influence exerted by each is a function of the compellingness of the external or stimulus factors and the intensity of the internal or motivational factors (Sherif, 1935; Coffin, 1941; Sherif and Harvey, 1952; Thrasher, 1954). The less compelling, or the more ambiguous the stimulus variables, the greater the influence of the motivational state in the cognitive outcome. Similarly, the more intense the motive arousal the greater its weight in the consequent psychological organization. The condition under which motives are maximally influential, then, is high stimulus ambiguity and high motivational arousal. Conversely, motivational influence in concept functioning is minimal and stimulus determinants are maximal under conditions of high stimulus structure and low motive arousal.

Thus as one cannot speak of point A in isolation of point B or C or N, one cannot speak accurately of the weight of either external or internal factors in the conceptual outcome unless the contemporaneous condition or state of the other factors is simultaneously specified.

Concepts Both Structure the Environment and Are Structured by It

Once a concept or matrix of concepts has evolved, it serves as a system of ordering through which the external world is filtered, evaluated, and responded to. At the same time, however, the very impingement of external stimuli exercises a feedback effect on the concept, either toward reinforcing or modifying it. Thus a concept influences and is reciprocally influenced by the environmental impingement. Piaget (1951) describes the evolution of the structure of thought —which is almost identical to our characterization of concepts—in the same way. Thought, according to Piaget (and concept for us), is the outcome of the reciprocal effects of "assimilation" and "accommodation," by which he means respectively the incorporation of external factors into the existing conceptual framework and the modification of the framework as a result of environmental impingement. ". . . These two aspects of thought are inseparable: thought organizes itself in adapting to objects, and thought structures objects in organizing itself" (Piaget, 1951, p. 186).

The evolvement and functioning of concepts must then be viewed in terms of some type of feedback model in which they serve as both cause and effect—or as independent and dependent variables if one wishes to choose this language—of themselves and other cognitive outcomes. Concepts serve as "cause" in the sense that, once they have evolved, they exercise a channeling or molding effect on subsequent concepts and experience. They are "effect" in the sense that they themselves represent the outgrowth of antecedent and often extremely rudimentary systems of ordering, systems which may have been no more than simple sets and other cognitively selecting predispositions that resulted from biogenic needs and physiological states. (It is these sets and physiological selectivities that initially channel impinging stimuli into some consistent psychological structure or system of ordering.)

The mutual dependence of environmental and conceptual factors in determining concepts and other cognitive outcomes implies that each stimulus impingement and its evaluation produces some modification, albeit infinitesimal, in the conceptual referent. A hypothetical consequence of this is ". . . that *no state once gone can recur and be identical with what it was before*" (James, 1890, Vol. I, p. 230). Even though the objective characteristics of the impinging object or event may remain constant, each subsequent experience of the object must be different because its preceding exposure modified the conceptual standard in terms of which it was being gauged.

Thus as James suggested,

> . . . Often we are ourselves struck at the strange differences in our successive views of the same thing. We wonder how we ever could have opined as we did last month about a certain matter. . . . From one year to another we see things in new lights. What was unreal has grown real, and what was exciting is insipid. The friends we used to care the world for are shrunken to shadows; the women, once so divine, the stars, the woods, and the waters, how now, so dull and common; the young girls that brought an aura of infinity, at present hardly distinguishable existences; the pictures so empty; and as for the books, what *was* there to find so mysteriously significant in Goethe, or in John Mill so full of weight?
>
> But what here strikes us so forcibly on the flagrant scale exists on every scale, down to the imperceptible transition from one hour's outlook to that of the next. Experience is remoulding us every moment, and our mental reaction on every given thing is really a resultant of our experience of the whole world up to that date (James, 1890, Vol. I, pp. 233–234).

The change in conceptual referents that underlie the change in evaluation and experience of the same objects need not be only in the direction suggested by James, that is, toward conceptual satiation and extinction of the accompanying response tendency. Instead of weakening the underlying concept, one may mold reality into it in such a way as to reinforce and strengthen the conceptual metering system. This latter possibility seems to receive striking confirmation, for example, in the persistence of social stereotypes. Functioning in terms of practically closed concepts, the highly prejudiced individual tends to fit his perception of the object or prejudice into the confines and dimensions of the gauging concepts in such a way that the concept is reinforced, or at least not appreciably weakened.

Concepts Develop through the Process of Differentiation-Integration

Whereas concepts represent the joint product of the interdependent operation of situational and dispositional factors, the "equilibrium between assimilation and accommodation"—to use Piaget's phrase—the psychological process through which this interaction finds expression is that of *differentiation-integration.*

Differentiation refers to the breaking of a novel, more undifferentiated, situation into more clearly defined and articulated parts. Integration is the relating or hooking of such parts to each other and to previous conceptual standards.

Differentiation-Integration Proceeds Saccadically

In spearheading the development of concepts, differentiation and integration do not proceed at a steady linear rate. Instead this process, much like visual scanning, seems to move saccadically (Carmichael and Dearborn, 1948). "The eyes when they scan the lines of a printed page, or in fact any scene, do so in a series of extremely rapid jerks (called *saccades*) between points of comparative rest (*fixation pauses*) at which they take in information" (Cherry, 1957, pp. 122–123). Conceptually, the saccades seem to operate much like "bracketing," to borrow a term from artillery, in which defined referent points, sensory or more conceptual, are placed around the extreme limits of the target or phenomenon. With these end points at the extremes serving as anchorages from which to radiate, the subject begins to make finer differentiations in between these defining limits. In conceptual development, one seems first to form gross differentiations by cognitively cutting the ambiguous or undifferentiated into large chunks. This larger chunk one might differentiate more before moving to break off another chunk, but generally one moves to the cutting of a second chunk before finely and clearly differentiating the first. In fact, it seems in most cases that it is with the aid of differentiations and referent points gained from the latter gross segment that one is able to differentiate more finely—and even veridically—the facets of the first chunk.

Underlying our hypothesis that concepts develop saccadically is the further assumption that the end points or poles of a concept operate as a kind of opposites, exercising a force or an energy that results in a conceptual outcome that parallels cell mitosis, in which the grosser parts are divided into more articulated and numerous ones. Were a force of some nature not brought to bear on a phenomenon, if that phenomenon existed only in a cocooned vacuum, then presumably no modification of it, growth or otherwise, could occur. Hence for a grossly differentiated concept to attain a state of greater differentiation and refinement we assume that its two poles must exert contradictory pulls sufficiently strong to produce evaluative alternatives other than the either-or categories characterizing the earlier stage. The concept, "good," for example, is non-existent without the opposite pole "bad," in conjunction with which it came into being. Engagement of the concept in its less differentiated form could lead only to a bifurcated evaluation: the object is all good or all bad. With further delineation into multiple facets through the reciprocal pull of the good-bad poles the engagement of the concept leads to more specific evaluations of gradations from good to bad. Later, in discussing the structural properties of concepts, we shall by elaborating the above position show how love and hate, religious zeal and atheism, for example, are more similar to each other than either is to an intermediate position of neutrality or to a position that allows for multiple evaluation.

This position is very reminiscent of the basic premise of Hegel's Logic: Every truth, every reality has three aspects or stages. The first is a preliminary or tentative affirmation (thesis), which more or less can be equated with gross differentiation; the second is a negative of the thesis (antithesis), which results in finer differentiations as a result of opposite pulls from the two; and the third is an integration of the more finely articulated parts (synthesis).

Without subscribing to his epistemology or to his postulation of a necessary end, we assume that phases much akin to those described by Hegel occur in most forms of development in the process of trying to adapt to or make sense out of any novel and relevant situation: in childhood development and socialization, in learning a new role or important skill, or in any structuring of an ambiguous and ego-involving situation.

Some Historical Notions of Stages and Phases of Differentiation-Integration

The question of stages is an ancient one, going back at least to Aristotle. It was reworked by representatives of the church during the Middle Ages and burst into full bloom in conjunction with the advent of theory of evolution.

A central theme running through the various notions of sequential stages has been, in one variety or another, that it is one of the general laws of nature that the simple tends to evolve into and become an inseparable part of a more complex, more comprehensive totality. This was one of the most essential assumptions underlying Aristotle's argument for relativity and final causality (Aristotle, translated by Hammond, 1902). All things but one—God—can be considered as either *form* or *matter*, according to Aristotle, depending on the objects or phenomena being compared and the level of the comparison. Matter was the simpler, lower level unit, whereas form was the more complex, higher level order that encompassed matter of the antecedent level. Marble, for example, was matter for the pillar of the building, and the pillar, in turn, was form for the marble. The same pillar (a subpart), on the other hand, was matter to the building (a larger totality). From here the progression of simpler into the more comprehensive, of the inclusion of matter into a next higher form, continued until the ultimate of progression, God—who was form to all and matter to nothing—was attained. In a large sense, Aristotle viewed the universe and the development of causality as a closed system. God was the end toward which all things moved in their development. This was the telelogical goal or force that made all paths point toward it.

The essential feature of Aristotle's argument was later elaborated and popularized by Thomas Aquinas in such a way that the Church dogma and science of the day were well enough reconciled so that St. Thomas' arguments were accepted by both—especially by the Church.

Notions of stages and inevitable progression of subparts or elements into larger structures found its way into physics, into chemistry, and later as crucial features of the theory of evolution. These notions emerged in their fullest strength among geologists, biologists, and social scientists. The period preceding the advent of Darwin's theory, however, saw the emergence of several notions on evolution. Goethe, in his study of botany, for example, worked out a theory of evolution. The French philosopher Fourier had built a theory of human destiny in terms of stages involving thousands of years, and Hegel had worked out the notion that civilization had gone through various stages of development in keeping with the universal Idea (Murphy, 1949).

> In the scientific thought of the period two types of evolutionary teaching went on side by side: first, the theory of the evolution of the inanimate physical universe, the study of inorganic evolution; second, the study of biological or organic evolution. Laplace developed in connection with his mechanics the theory commonly known as the *nebular hypothesis*. . . . In geology, Lyell was making investigations from 1830 to 1860 to show how rock strata were formed by a series of changes in the earth . . . Lyell enunciated the theory that the earth itself had gone through an orderly series of changes, in which a chaos of elements had gradually been superseded by differentiation and separation. . . . He had undertaken to show that the earth itself reveals stages requiring vastly greater time than the six days allowed in the Book of Genesis. As a matter of fact, Lyell was not the first nor the last, but in terms of scientific as well as popular influence he was by far the greatest, of the geological evolutionists. He prepared the way for the habit of thinking of growth in terms of changes in living organisms. Lyell's evolutionism was, indeed, a direct stimulus to the work of Charles Darwin (Murphy, 1949, pp. 111–112).

Many anthropologists, such as Morgan and Tyler, applied modified versions of evolutionary doctrine to the genesis and development of culture (Lowie, 1937). In fact such a notion was basic to the "diffusionists," those theorists who held that all cultures must have evolved, as had all biological species, from a single, common origin.

Spencer (1897) articulated the belief of sequential development into dimensions more directly relevant to psychology and brought them to bear on his survivalistic, functionalistic notions on the subject. Central to his theory of "evolutionary associationism" was the assumption that relationships, ideas, and other simpler and more complex cognitive events follow an ordered pattern in their development. Spencer maintained that from the unrelated, undifferentiated, psychologically irrelevant mass of impinging stimuli, from the booming, buzzing confusion to which James later applied notions of stages in cognitive development, the individual differentiates out facts relevant to his survival and subsequently integrates them into some type of association functional to his existence. Through this process, development progresses from the simple to the more complex. Differentiation gives rise to a more complex integration.

The belief that the organism in both its biological and conceptual development advances through stages, from the simpler to the more complex or from the more undifferentiated and concrete to the more highly integrated and abstract, occupies a central position in some of the best known works of psychology and biology: in Murphy's treatment of personality (1947); in Piaget's many writings on the developmental facets of behavior (1926, 1929, 1932, 1954); in Werner's comparative psychology of conceptual development (1957); and in Weiss' approach to biological structure and maturation (1939). One of the best known experiments in psychology is that of Carmichael (1926, 1927), showing the importance of differentiation and integration of maturational factors in levels of learning and motor attainment.

If indeed a concept is a schema or category for the placement of events and objects in relationship to existing internal referents in order that they may be experienced and evaluated, as we suggested earlier, then a concept could not exist until the unstructured environment is broken down and patterned. It becomes our assumption accordingly, much as it was of the above writers, that concepts and other cognitive outcomes develop in the order suggested by Spencer: from undifferentiation to differentiation to integration. We desire, however, to disavow for three general reasons the often implied necessity that differentiation-integration must pass through definite stages and toward invariant ends:

1. Differentiation-integration, as we view it, does not *itself* follow

necessary stages. Instead it is a *process,* as we have already indicated, by means of which the organism breaks his environing world down into parts and relates them in a way relevant to his motive system and existence. Differentiation does not necessitate integration; a discriminated aspect of a stimulus can be left in isolation and not related to others, for example, as in extremely concrete organization. The attainment of a more abstract level of functioning, as we shall suggest shortly, does, on the other hand, follow stages. It must have been preceded by differentiation and integration on a more concrete level. One does not get to a high level of abstraction without having gone through lower levels.

2. As a result of the fact that differentiation may occur in an isolated and compartmentalized way without integration, differentiation does not necessarily give rise to a more complex organization or cognitive structure. Increased complexity can only result from placement of the articulated parts in interrelatedness.

3. Differentiation and integration need not be separated by time spans. It seems to be a general, although implicit, assumption of some writers that differentiation and integration are separated by a temporal lapse. The assumption rests on logical grounds, since integration must be preceded by differentiation. However, it is also empirically plausible that differentiation and integration may occur simultaneously. Indeed any differentiation has in it an element of integration in that the way the environing situation is articulated into parts is in terms of internal standards operative at the time, rendering the individual selective toward a particular feature of his environment and reciprocally endowing particular aspects of the situation with relevance for the perceiver.

Stages of Conceptual Development

Concepts May Be Placed at Different Levels or Stages of Concreteness-Abstractness

We proposed that differentiation-integration is a process through which concepts develop and a means by which the concepts attain some level on the dimension of concreteness-abstractness. It is the levels of concreteness-abstractness at which concepts may be placed to which we propose to apply the term stages and *not* to differentiation-integration as such. The level of abstractness, in this sense, represents the *how* of differentiation and integration, how the ambiguous or undifferentiated is broken or differentiated into parts and then integrated or interrelated into a conceptual pattern.

Although differentiation-integration and concreteness-abstractness are inseparably linked, we would like to attempt a distinction by viewing the former as a psychological *process* or *activity* and concreteness-abstractness as a *resultant* or *outgrowth* of this process. This cause and effect relationship, however, like most such relationships, is reciprocal. A given level or stage of concreteness-abstractness is attained through differentiation-integration, but this same level or stage of abstractness affects both what kind of differentiations or discriminations of the environing stimuli are made and how these are subsequently organized or integrated by their being related to existing internal standards.

As a result of his biological make-up man can respond to only certain stimuli, and even these are dependent on the level of maturational development. Sound waves that surpass 20,000 to 25,000 cps are beyond the upper ranges of human auditory reception. Certain motor and other types of learning cannot develop until neurological development reaches a certain stage. The child, for example, is unable to walk, to control his elimination process, and to develop more abstract concepts until the central nervous system has gone through certain necessary stages of development.

More Specific Characterization of "Stages"

Few attempts have been aimed at delineating exactly what is meant by the term "stage" despite the frequent postulation of stages in the development of the phenomenon under consideration. Hence the criteria that can be appropriately applied to distinguish between stages are also lacking.

The most frequent use of the term "stage" seems to refer to a more or less constant rate of some index of performance or behavior—maturational, motor, linguistic, social, and others—over a time span of varying lengths. A marked change in the rate or curve of performance, in terms of whatever manifestation is being indexed, is taken to represent both the beginning and terminating points of a given stage. A given stage exists as long as, and to the extent that, constancy of the behavioral index is maintained, whether the rate of performance or development is ascending at a fairly constant rate, maintaining a plateau at a fairly constant rate, or descending at a fairly constant rate. Some writers would prefer to speak only of the more or less level *plateaus as stages* and the ascending or descending of rates of performance toward or away from this as *transition.* Thus if the total picture of the behavior were being looked at, one technically could equate stage with state and accordingly speak of stages of transition, of plateaus or levels, of ascendancy or decline. Furthermore, the temporal length of the fairly constant rate, whatever its direction, and the magnitude of the change in the developmental index that is taken to mark the beginning and terminating ends of a stage can—and do—vary as a function of the behavioral manifestations under observation and the instruments employed in the observations. The what and the how of observation, of course, vary in turn with the problem and the theoretical approach of the observer; in the absence of fixed criteria, they are defined by him.

Our use of the term "stage" in the present book refers to levels of cognitive functioning on what we assume to be a continuous dimension of concreteness-abstractness. As we repeatedly stress, no level is absolutely constant, even across a relatively brief time span or for only a few repeated measures. In the strict sense if a level encompasses variability at all, then it has simultaneously aspects both of levels and transition, of plateau and of either decline or ascendancy, in the rate of performance or behavior being measured. By a level we would want only to imply a range of behavior *within* which the behavioral constancy showed less variability than between it and other groups of measurement.

We later employ the term "stage" to refer to a plateau or nodal point of conceptual development, "transition," as the in-between state of conceptual development from a less abstract to a more abstract stage or nodal point, and "regression," of which we make but little and restricted use (see Chapter 9), as a kind of dedifferentiation, or more accurately of deintegration, in which the individual abandons a more abstract level of functioning in favor of a more concrete level. We would like to stress, in accord with the emphasis of Murphy (1947), that under conditions of conceptual progression, regression, or arrestation there is no such thing as a pure or discontinuous level of concreteness-abstractness. Each always has some characteristic of another, adjacent or more remote, level.

Since the primary focus of this book is on the differential aspects of varying levels of concreteness-abstractness, both as "cause" and "effect," let us turn to a fairly detailed characterization of this important conceptual property.

Concreteness-Abstractness

Some General Characteristics

Concreteness-abstractness is assumed to be an attribute of the concepts or *patterning* of stimuli and *not* of the stimuli themselves. It is a quality of the tie or linkage between a subject and an object and does *not* per se refer to the subject or the object. In the words of Goldstein and Scheerer (1941), whose work has been so instrumental in demonstrating the importance of this conceptual dimension, it refers to "A capacity level of the total personality in a specific plane of activity" (p. 2).

Variation in the level of concreteness-abstractness results in differences in "stimulus boundness," the extent to which the receiving and responding individual is restricted to or can go beyond the physical characteristics of the immediately impinging stimuli in organizing his evaluation and experience of a situation. The greater one's abstractness, (1) the greater is his ability to transcend immediacy and to move more into the temporally and spatially remote, (2) and the more capable he is of abstracting relationships from objects of his experience and of organizing them in terms of their interrelatedness. The greater one's concreteness, on the other hand, the greater the degree of stimulus "oughtness" in dictating his response, with concomitants almost opposite to greater abstractness. Furthermore, whereas the more abstractly functioning individual tends toward differentiating his world into many facets and integrating them holistically but interdependently, the more concretistically functioning person is more likely to make only few differentiations of his environment and to leave these cognitive "elements" in a greater state of isolation. Thus although both the more concretely and more abstractly functioning persons might display holistic cognitive structures and responses, the underlying basis of the two would be vastly different, the former resting on an undifferentiated totality whereas the latter is underlaid by a differentiated and integrated holism. As Murphy who, like Spencer, views cognitive activities as developing through the three stages of undifferentiation to differentiation to integration, suggests:

> . . . the statement that the organism reacts "as a whole" has a different meaning at each stage of development. *Diffuse* wholeness at the first level of development is different from the more and more *differentiated* wholeness exhibited at the second level in the maturational phenomena, and differs again from the *integrated* wholeness which appears when the differentiated functions achieve a stable, articulated interdependence (1947, p. 67).

Greater abstractness, according to Goldstein and Scheerer (1941), provides the bases in the individual for the following "conscious" and "volitional" modes of behavior:

1. To detach our ego from the outerworld or from inner experiences.
2. To assume a mental set.
3. To account for acts to oneself; to verbalize the account.
4. To shift reflectively from one aspect of the situation to another.

5. To hold in mind simultaneously various aspects.
6. To grasp the essential of a given whole; to break up a given whole into parts, to isolate and to synthesize them.
7. To abstract common properties reflectively; to form hierarchic concepts.
8. To plan ahead ideationally; to assume an attitude towards the more possible and to think or perform symbolically (Goldstein and Scheerer, 1941, p. 4).

The more concrete behavior, on the other hand, "has not the above mentioned characteristics" (p. 4). In fact, it is the discontinuous opposite to abstract behavior, in the thinking of Goldstein and Scheerer (1941). Having as its "outstanding" characteristic, the closeness of responses or patternings to "immediate reality," suggest these authors, it is demonstrated in such ways as rigid dependence upon the familiar, response to object more in isolation than as member of an abstracted class, greater concern with specific details, and a tendency to evaluate objects in terms of their personal use to the subject rather than being grouped according to a more abstract characteristic (such as form, color, or material) (pp. 87–93).

The Dimension of Concreteness-Abstractness Is Qualitatively Continuous

The difference between the more concrete and the more abstract ways of ordering the world, although marked indeed, are viewed by us as representing variations in magnitude and not quality. This conceptual dimension is thus taken to be continuous rather than discrete.

It should be pointed out that viewing concreteness-abstractness as different ends of a continuum is not in line with the position of Goldstein and Scheerer. These authors maintain:

> . . . There is a pronounced line of demarcation between these two attitudes which does not represent a *gradual* ascent from more simple to more complex mental sets. The greater difficulty connected with the abstract approach is not simply one of greater complexity, measured by the number of separate, subservient functions involved. It demands rather the behavior of the new emergent quality, generically different from the concrete (1941, p. 22).

Within these discontinuous levels, however, these authors point out that gradations exist, of more and less concreteness or abstractness, but still these gradations do not blend so that the lowest level of concreteness would also represent the lowest level of abstraction.

Murphy (1947), on the other hand, who approaches the problem of concreteness-abstractness in other terms—as levels or stages in the developmental sequence from undifferentiation to differentiation to integration—views the behavioral manifestations of these conceptual properties as representing a common continuum.

> Yet with reference to all organismic philosophies which stress totality, [he suggests] emphasis needs to be placed upon the continuum that exists between levels one and two, i.e., between pure undifferentiatedness at the one theoretical extreme and absolute sharpness of differentiation at the other, and likewise on the continuum between the second level, complete differentiation, and the third level, complete integration. These extreme or pure cases are seldom completely realized in fact, but enormous variations exist which can be ranged between the extremes (p. 67). . . . The three stages in development characteristically appear in the order named, but a step back and then forward again is frequently observed. And alongside the differentiated and the integrated, some of the original undifferentiated survives (pp. 67–68).

The question of whether a more abstract level of functioning is only a quantitative extension of a more concrete level, and the two levels are hence continuous, as Murphy suggests, or is so qualitatively different from the more concrete functioning that it is discontinuous from it, as Goldstein and Scheerer maintain, is indeed an old—and yet unresolved—one. It is, among other questions, the problem of reductionism versus holism, or relatedly, of quantity versus quality, issues with which psychology—indeed all of science—has spent much effort. Points of view on this issue, which most clearly separated the "Gestalters" and the "Structuralists," for instance, have not been agreed upon but only bypassed or overlooked in pursuit of a concern with different types of questions.

It seems to us that although ". . . the stream of behavior" may be seen not "to flow smoothly, but to occur in easily perceived bursts and breaks" (Barker, 1957, p. 156), such variation could as well represent a continuity as be expressive of a qualitative break.

Attribution of a discontinuity is probably a function of the aspect of behavior being observed or measured and the method by which the observation is obtained. It frequently results from concern with phenotypic expressions rather than with genotypic function and underlying process. The genotype may be expressed in phenotypic opposites: one person, for example, might show his insecurity by reacting very aggressively whereas another would reticently withdraw from contact with others. Thus one investigator who was more concerned with functions of behavior might from the same behavioral manifestations infer what he considered continuities; another whose observations were of expressions of this function might infer such marked variability that he would attribute it to breaks and discontinuities. In short, before speaking of continuities and discontinuities, due attention must be given to the *what* that is being measured and the dimension of the observation. Very pertinent to this issue is the elaboration of William James on his assertion that objection to viewing the stream of thought or consciousness as continuous is "based partly on a confusion and partly on a superficial introspective view."

> The confusion is between the thoughts themselves, taken as subjective facts, and the things of which they are aware. . . . The things are discrete and discontinuous; they do pass before us in a train or chain, making often explosive appearances and rending each other in twain. But their comings and goings and contrasts no more break the flow of thought that links them than they break the time and the space in which they lie. A silence may be broken by a thunder-clap, and we may be so stunned and confused for a moment by the shock as to give no instant account to ourselves of what has happened. But that very confusion is a mental state, and a state that passes us straight over from the silence to the sound. The transition between the thought of one object and the thought of another is no more a break in the *thought* than a joint in a bamboo is a break in the wood. It is a part of the *consciousness* as much as the joint is a part of the *bamboo* (James, 1890, Vol. I, p. 240).

Examples of Concreteness-Abstractness

We shall leave unresolved the issue of whether concreteness-abstractness is more appropriately viewed as a qualitatively continuous or discontinuous dimension; the following examples, which parallel the criteria of Goldstein and Scheerer, are intended to give the flavor of the difference between more abstract and more concrete functioning:

1. DIFFERENTIATION BETWEEN THE OUTER AND INNER WORLDS IN THE EGO AND EXPERIENCE

In extreme concrete patterning the subject is unable to assume an "as if" attitude or set. He does not distinguish between the external world and his own wishes, dreams, and desires; they are experienced as continuous. Werner shows how this holds true for infrahuman species, for "primitives," for very young children, and for "psychotics." Young children, before a stabilized self is evolved, often have great difficulty in distinguishing between a world of fantasy and the real world. The primitive dreams something and this becomes the world in terms of which he orients his own behavior and expects others to behave, even to the point of giving to him what the dream indicated that he had (Werner, 1957; Levy-Bruhl, 1923).[1]

[1] In our usage of primitive thinking as an example of concrete functioning we are aware of our departure from the usual position of the social scientist. It is

The young child and the primitives have never differentiated their world, whereas a psychotic or brain-damaged person, on the other hand, may have initially differentiated his environment but lost it due to some impairment so that consequently he manifests many of the same characteristics as the children and primitives. The psychotic may organize his conceptual system and behavior in terms of "voices" or "biddings" from a physical, extrapersonal source, while the brain-damaged person may be no less controlled by the physical characteristics of the stimuli. Illustrative of the latter is the behavior of a brain-damaged patient described by Goldstein and Scheerer (1941) when asked to repeat the sentence:

> . . . The snow is black. [First he refused, insisting the snow was white.] . . . The examiner explained to him that such senseless phrases can be repeated even though they are not true, and then urged the patient to repeat the sentence. Now the patient repeated the requested sentence, but mumbled immediately afterwards: "No the snow is white." The same patient could not be induced to repeat the sentence "the sun is shining" on a rainy day (pp. 4–5).

He could not relinquish his fixed and narrow system of ordering to the point of permitting a different, hypothetical, evaluation.

2. ASSUMPTION OF A MENTAL SET WILFULLY AND CONSCIOUSLY

An extreme contrast between concrete and abstract behavior is demonstrative of the difference between a taxic or tropistic response, on the one extreme, and response to a complex problem by insightful solution, on the other. In the former, because of a stimulus oughtness, the subject can (even must) behave in a certain way as long as certain physical stimuli are present; in the latter, this is not so. For example, a brain-damaged patient described by Goldstein and Scheerer was unable to set the hands of a clock to a time suggested by the experimenter but could recognize what time it was when the clock, with hands already set, was presented to him (p. 5). A striking parallel of

important to keep in mind that concreteness-abstractness refers to a structural dimension of conceptual functioning, not to the content or objects of thought. Hence to the extent that any individual, "primitive" or "cosmopolite," manifests (a) lack of differentiation of the self from his environing world or (b) animism (for example, practicing sorcery in an attempt to control an omnipotent environment), he will be considered to be displaying conceptual functioning that meets some of the criteria we have proposed for concreteness. Needless to add, membership in Western or other complex societies does not gurarantee functioning at an abstract level, as can be noted from the prevalence of compartmentalized functioning, stereotypy and other expressions of conceptual closedness.

this at the infrahuman level is reported in a study of the behavior of a spider carried out by Grunbaum and quoted by Werner (1957):

> . . . The spider sits in the funnel and is occupied with an entangled fly. A vibrating wire (48 cycles) is put through the wall of the nest and through the mesh of the web, and then brought into contact with the abdomen of the spider in the region of the spinning wart. As soon as the wire thread touches the body of the spider, she drops her prey, dashes forth from the nest, and fastens onto the wire in the mesh of the web, shrouding it industriously with her spinnerets. Although the wire cannot possibly serve as food, the spider does not cease her attack so long as the wire continues to vibrate (p. 106).

3. ACCOUNTING FOR ONE'S ACTS TO ONESELF OR TO OTHERS AND VERBALIZING THE ACT

This is closely akin to "taking the role of the other," emphasized by G. H. Mead (1934). To do this, however, demands a certain level of differentiation of the parts of the acts and integration of them in a way that interdependence and reciprocity are recognized. The young child, to assume the position of both the respondent and recipient, to carry out "a conversation of attitudes," to use Mead's phrase, must have differentiated the self from others and be able to imagine that "When I do this, he should do that," and vice versa. This recognition of interdependence and reciprocity can occur only extremely rudimentarily, if at all, prior to the advent of language ability.

Goldstein and Scheerer (1941) give as an example of the above the brain-damaged patient who was able to throw balls into boxes of varying distance from him without ever missing. However, when the subject was asked which box was further and which was nearer, he was ". . . unable to give any account or to make a statement concerning his procedure in aiming. Another patient points correctly to the source of a noise, but cannot state the direction from which the noise originated" (p. 5).

4. ABILITY TO SHIFT REFLECTIVELY FROM ONE ASPECT OF THE SITUATION TO ANOTHER

This refers to the extent to which the subject can shift his own behavior or set from one type of task demand to another as the situation becomes altered. The more concrete subject may continue his way of responding even when the situation becomes markedly altered:

> A patient [related Goldstein and Scheerer (1941)] who has just succeeded in reciting the days of the week is now asked to recite the alphabet. He cannot shift to this task, and only after repeated promptings, or better stated, after the examiner has commenced to call out the alphabet, can the patient follow in his recitation (p. 5).

This and other examples of effects of brain damage cited by the above authors is paralleled at the infrahuman level by the nest-building activity of the bee, for example, described by Werner (1957):

> A small solitary-bee uses the house of a certain species of snail as a place to lay her eggs. After the eggs are laid in the snail's shell, the bee makes a hole 6–7 cm. deep in the earth, and places the shell in this hole. When Ferton removed such a shell from the hole into which the bee had just slipped it, the insect continued with its work, filling the hole, smoothing over the earth, and otherwise finishing the task exactly as if everything was normal (p. 109).

5. THE SIMULTANEOUS HOLDING IN MIND OF VARIOUS ASPECTS

Certainly before the variously differentiated parts can be integrated into a more comprehensive and interrelated totality the "elements" must be sufficiently contiguous in the conceptual storage-bin so that they can be put together. The more abstract the functioning of the individual, however, the larger time span that is possible between the events that are related—from almost zero, for some infrahuman species, to marked temporal and spatial separation, for the normally functioning human adult. As Whitehead suggests (1938), ". . . The distinction between men and animals is in one sense only a difference in degree. But the extent of the degree makes all the difference. The Rubicon has been crossed" (p. 38). Some of these differences may be seen from the results of studies on delayed response, on delayed and double alternation, and other tasks involving retention of order of sequence (Munn, 1950).

In one of the earliest studies on the topic, Hunter (1913) found that the maximum time intervals in which different species could respond correctly to a delayed response test was: the rat, up to 10 seconds; the cat, up to 18 seconds; the dog, up to 3 minutes; a two-and-one-half-year-old child, up to 50 seconds; and a five-year-old child up to 20 minutes or more. On a related task, where, for example, the animal is placed in a box with three pedals or platforms, which it has to push a certain number of times and in a certain order to obtain food, clear-cut differences are found in the length of order that can be mastered correctly by animals at varying levels on the phylogenetic scale. The median lengths of correct sequences were: the guinea pig, 1; the rat, 1; the kitten, 3; Rhesus monkey, 5; and Cebus monkey, 9½ (Munn, 1955). On the alternation tasks animals can delay only briefly for correct responses as compared to a human who is functioning at normal level of abstraction.

Almost all of our educational practices are based on the assumption that once something is differentiated and learned, it can be "held in mind" until later training experiences (somewhere in the ideal and remote future) give rise to the differentiation of new parts that will be interrelated with older ones for the formation of a higher level of knowledge. This educational tenet, probably faulty for even the more abstract individual, certainly would be unwarranted for such persons as the patients described by Goldstein and Scheerer (1941):

> A patient is instructed to press the lever in the reaction time apparatus set-up at the appearance of the red light. He does this correctly. If, however, instructed to respond to only one of two colored lights which are given in irregular succession (red, green), the patient responds by pressing the lever whenever any one of the lights appears. A patient is instructed to cross out the letter X in one of the concentration tests. She begins by following the instruction but after having carried out the task correctly through a few lines of the test, she continues to cross out every letter (p. 6).

6. GRASPING THE ESSENTIAL OF A GIVEN WHOLE, BREAKING IT UP INTO PARTS, ISOLATING AND SYNTHESIZING THEM

The more concretely functioning individual tends to make only gross differentiations of simple dimensions, and these he fails to perceive as being interrelated. Hence he tends to keep each differentiated part compartmentalized or isolated from the others, preventing synthesis in the cognitive outcome. Goldstein and Scheerer (1941) illustrated this by showing that:

> If a [brain damaged] patient is confronted with a picture which tells a story (The Terman-Binet Pictures or the Kuhlman, e.g., the Snowball or Blind Man's Bluff), he is able only to enumerate individual items and does not grasp the point. He neither finds the essential relations between the persons acting in the picture, nor can he grasp the gist of the story. Evidently, the patient is unable to synthesize the individual events into a meaningful whole (p. 6).

This is paralleled by the behavior described by Werner (1957) of a four-year-old girl who failed to differentiate the aspects of a drawing made by an older child of a duck sitting on a rock. The drawing consisted of a crude ellipse with an X marked at a point on the lower side and the duck, with his feet within the ellipse and his body out, on the top side.

> The little girl pointed to the place on the drawing marked by a cross, and said: "Duck!" I asked: "But where is the duck?" The child indicated the

> large circle. I repeated the question, saying: "Where is the duck's head?" The child pointed to the duck's breast. Finally I asked: "How big is the duck, then?" The child replied by framing the whole contour of the picture with her hands (pp. 112–113).

Gross differentiations and compartmentalization of the parts also are typically manifested by persons of strong social stereotypes. One consequence of this lack of organizational synthesis is demonstrated in behavior that from the point of logical consistency may appear contradictory. One might editorialize and proselytize for the brotherhood of man and at the same time, incognizant of the logical inconsistency, maintain strongly that Negroes should "be kept in their place."

7. THE REFLECTIVE ABSTRACTION OF COMMON PROPERTIES AND THE FORMATION OF HIERARCHIC CONCEPTS

> A patient can count numbers on his fingers [state Goldstein and Scheerer (1941)] and by various roundabout methods; in this fashion he can even obtain the results which look like subtraction and addition, but he is entirely unable to state whether 7 or 4 is more and has no concept of the value of numbers whatsoever. Patients of this type have no understanding of analogies or metaphors, since in both the abstractions of a common property is necessary. They fail on a simple syllogism or on tests of finding the common denominator of several items (p. 7).

This behavior approaches in appearance and concreteness the "talking" and "counting" of horses and dogs featured in motion pictures, carnivals, and so forth. These animals, with the help of cues from the trainers, can make what seems to the naive observer numerical distinctions, but in reality they have no conception of number as such whatsoever. Also:

> . . . The primitive American Abipone Indians can tell without counting whether one of their dogs is missing from the pack when they leave for the hunt; it is simply not necessary for them to count because they experience the individuality of all domestic animals in a characteristically concrete manner. Even when a group of totally unknown objects or persons is under consideration, the primitive man often tries to conceive it as a manifold of characteristically divergent individuals. Thurnwald reports of the Solomon Islanders: If five newly arrived persons are to be designated, one does not say that five persons have just come, not even if their names are not known. One may say: "A man with a large nose, an old man, a child, a man with a skin disease, and a little fellow are waiting outside" (Werner, 1957, p. 288).

8. PLANNING AHEAD IDEATIONALLY AND THE ASSUMPTION OF THE ATTITUDE OF "THE MERE POSSIBLE"

Individuals performing at the more concrete level could hardly be expected to represent formidable opponents in chess or in any other skill that necessitated a strategy involving a planned course of future action. Conceptualizing the future is markedly limited in such persons, their concern being with the immediate here and now. Goldstein and Scheerer's brain-damaged patients of this sort, for example, could easily find their way in walking from the ward into a room or from the hospital to their home, but they were unable to draw a map of their route or to describe it verbally. Similarly, one of the striking effects of a prefrontal lobotomy is to reduce the subject's concern with the future, apparently resulting from his loss of ability to transcend the immediate present. This is much akin to the behavior of the child who may be heading toward one goal object and suddenly become diverted by another object in his path. Both have only rudimentary concepts of futurity and hence are more distractible by whatever is in the immediate present.

The more concretely functioning subjects furthermore cannot transfer a response from one context to another. For example, some of the patients of Goldstein and Scheerer could write their names on paper but could not make the same writing motions in the air, and other patients could not continue hammering after the nail was removed.

Some Effects of Differences in Concreteness-Abstractness on Reactions to Interpersonal Stimuli

Differentiation May Occur from Direct or Indirect Experience with an Object or Class of Objects

Both the quantity and quality of differentiations and integrations that one makes, hence the level of abstractness attained, may result from direct, face-to-face, experience with a phenomenon. Or the level of abstractness may represent distinctions based not upon direct experience with the object to which they refer but upon social norms and other short-cut dicta, which may have been accepted from the various groups, especially reference groups, with which their holder has had contact. In both cases, of course, experience is involved—as it inevitably must be. But in the latter situation the bases of differentiation are more or less handed to one in ready-made form, the result being that a group-defined mold is indirectly provided to one into which his subsequent discriminations and experience of the object(s) will be cast—even if later direct experience of the object occurs.

The epitome of ready-made and indirectly derived categories for differentiating and integrating one's world are the schemata provided by social stereotypes. Most of the group prejudices come from contact with related stereotypes instead of direct contact with the group toward which the prejudice exists (Horowitz, 1936; Hartley, 1946; Goodman, 1952; Sherif and Sherif, 1953). The acceptance of such social stereotypes is presumably a consequence of the degree of one's positive identification with the group holding the stereotypes. Adoption of these stereotypes necessarily limits the number and kind of differentiations and integrations one will subsequently make of the phenomenon under observation. If the group-provided conceptual mold is rigid enough, the holder of the stereotype will tend, because of a more closed concept, to perceive the objects in a way to reinforce and not to weaken his conceptual schemata.

Effects of Stereotypes and Other Socially Transmitted Categories Are Made Possible by the Advent of Language Ability

Until the child develops the capacity for language, he is restricted for the most part to a very concrete level of functioning and to direct experience with the object in his consequent concepts of it. Once language emerges, however, it provides a basis for the child's moving into a plane of greater abstract ability where he no longer is bounded by the sensory present. Instead he is now capable of getting his concepts and ways of ordering events in ready-made form from cultural sources as these are mediated to him by significant others about him —first by his family and later by his peers and other reference groups. Studies of the development of prejudice in the young child show this clearly (Horowitz, 1936; Horowitz and Horowitz, 1937; Criswell, 1939; Clark and Clark, 1940; Goodman, 1952). The extent to which the initial racial concepts of a child, prior to the level of abstract functioning that makes possible the internalization of social norms, may contrast with his later stereotypes is strikingly demonstrated in a study by Stevenson and Stuart (1958). A group of Mexican, Negro, and white children attending an integrated nursery school reacted with mild bewilderment and simple curiosity when they first discovered the differences in skin color amongst them. Some of the white children, due to their numerical minority, needed to be reassured by their parents that nothing was wrong with them simply because their own skins were lighter than those of most of their schoolmates.

The advent of language ability does not, of course, insure progression of the individual from the more concrete to the more abstract levels of functioning. That is to say, language is necessary for progression but not sufficient. Arrestation may occur at any stage of development or level of abstractness not only because of lack of language ability but also often because of limited "effective intelligence" (Copple, 1957), brought about by restricted cultural alternatives presented to one as stimuli and by experiences connected with social training that dispose one toward insecurity and fear of moving on to the more abstract planes, further away from the more secure ties provided by concreteness (see Chapters 5 and 6). In reality, social stereotypy seems to be related in a curvilinear fashion to language ability and differentiation. Prior to language development only the grossest kinds of differentiations may occur, and these are more on the basis of biogenic needs and direct experience, with the result that social stereotypes cannot be transmitted and learned. With the appearance of language, however, gross differentiations may now be made on a new basis, that of socially transmitted stereotypes. Such stereotypy will tend to prevail until the individual makes finer differentiations, some of which may have elements of socially transmitted bases in them whereas others may be a consequence of direct experience with the object of stereotypy, experiences which may invalidate some aspects of the original blanket stereotype.

Greater Concreteness Tends to be Accompanied by Absolutism and Categorical Thinking

The more concretely functioning individual, possessed of concepts based on minimal dimensions and alternatives, tends to be more categorical and absolutistic in his cognitive processes. He is more likely to conceptualize in bifurcations, in black or white, or at the most in minimum alternatives. Consequently he will be more stereotyped in his responses and more antagonistic to events that deviate from his narrowly circumscribed system of ordering. Simultaneously he will tend ordinarily to be more resistant but actually, under certain conditions, more susceptible to altering his tentative but more inflexible conceptual patterning. Brain-damaged persons often display these characteristics (Goldstein and Scheerer, 1941; Teuber, Battersby, and Bender, 1951; Semmes, Weinstein, and Ghent and Teuber, 1954) as do children who are first beginning to learn social norms and rules of the games. And so do many "primitives" whose development has been arrested by limited cultural alternatives.

The almost ritualistic adherence to rules by the social novitiate for whom the rules are undifferentiated is poignantly sketched by Smith (1957) in a description of childhood absolutism:

> But whatever way you played, that was the way, *that* way the only way to play, and you would have no more of me telling you than I will of you telling me now (p. 10).
>
> I suppose this is just an indication of my advanced years, but I don't know things now like I used to know them. What we knew as kids, what we learned from other kids, was not tentatively true, or extremely probable, or proven by science or polls or surveys. It was so. . . . We were savages, we were in that stage of the world's history when the earth stood still and everything else moved. I wrote on the flyleaf of my schoolbooks, and apparently every other kid in the world did, including James Joyce and Abe Lincoln and I am sure Tito and Fats Waller and Michelangelo, in descending order my name, my street, my town, my county, my state, my country, my continent, my hemisphere, my planet, my solar system. And let nobody dissemble: it started out with me, the universe was the outer circle of a number of concentric rings, and the center point was me, me, me, sixty-two pounds wringing wet with heavy shoes on (pp. 22–23).
>
> . . . If you cut yourself in the web of skin between your thumb and forefinger, you die. That's it. No ifs or buts. Cut. Die. . . . If you eat sugar lumps, you get worms. If you cut a worm in half, he don't [*sic*] feel a thing, and you get two worms. Grasshoppers spit tobacco. Step on a crack, break your mother's back. Walk past a house with a quarantine sign, and don't hold your breath, and you get sick and die. Play with yourself too much, your brain gets soft. Cigarettes stunt your growth. Some people are double jointed, and by that we didn't mean any jazz like very loose tendons or whatever the facts are. This guy had two joints where we had one. A Dodge (if your family happened to own a Dodge) was the best car in the whole world (Smith, 1957, pp. 23–24).

Violation of one rule at this poorly differentiated, shakily integrated, and concrete phase of concept development tends to be met with an absolutistic application of another rule. Piaget's study of the moral development of the child (1932), for example, showed younger children to make no discrimination between the badness of another child's wilful and accidental breakage of an important family possession or, consequently, to vary in the certainty and severity of the punishment they thought was deserved for the act.

Werner's (1957) comparative study of mental development and Levy-Bruhl's classic work on "primitive mentality" (1923) are replete with examples of absolutism among children, "primitives," and schizophrenics. In line with Piaget's finding that it is the act itself and not the intent of the act that is judged by children with poorly differentiated and more concrete conceptual standards, Werner (1957) quotes anthropological works to show the same thing among many "primitives":

> From his varied experience with Indian tribes, Radin decides that ethical traits of personality are not thought of as living principles or potentialities inherent in the individual. He concludes that for a primitive people "ethics is based on behavior. . . . It is not the motive, the hidden intent, but the action itself which determines the evil-doer." "Criminal intent," says Lowie, "does not play nearly the same role in primitive law as in our own jurisprudence." Goddard relates an incident occurring among the Hupas which might serve as a classic example. "A child was accidentally burned to death in a fire that some woman had built outdoors to heat water for washing. Although this woman was in no way reprehensible, the life of her own son was sought in recompense." Even if allowance is made for various exceptions to the rule, "it remains true that the ethical motive of an act is more frequently regarded as irrelevant in the ruder cultures than in our own courts of justice" (p. 426).

Greater Concreteness Is Expressed in Attribution of External Causality and Oughtness to Rules

In the cognitive functioning of an individual, for example, a child, with poorly differentiated and concrete concepts:

> . . . Outer world and inner experience constitute an undivided unity, of such a kind that the events of the surrounding world appear to be intimately linked with the ego and its needs (Werner, 1957, p. 319). [Similarly] Primitive man is certain there is no fundamental difference between the sphere of subjective phenomena and that of (intersubjective) objective phenomena (Werner, 1957, p. 339).

One result of this lack of demarcation between the "outside" and "inside" world is that wish, belief, and other feelings are viewed as being coextensive with the outside world and to be inherent in the external world. As part of "mystic and invisible forces," of which Levy-Bruhl speaks so much (1923), the feelings and inclinations one has are evaluated as coming from outside him in the form of bidding to a kind of action; they do not originate within him. This view of external causality may become so compelling that when one wants something he may legitimately demand it—not because *he* wishes it but because the external and *omnipotent force* wishes him to have it (Levy-Bruhl, 1923). Dreams are also among the vehicles through which the mystical force lets its wishes be known and such a divination is reality for the more undifferentiated and concrete thinker. Illustrative of this point is Levy-Bruhl's (1923) quotation from the Reverend W. B. Grubb:

> . . . This man arrived at my village from a place about a hundred and fifty miles off. He asked me for compensation for some pumpkins which

I had recently stolen from his garden. I was thoroughly surprised, and told him I had not been near his village for a very long time, and so could not possibly have stolen his pumpkins. At first I thought he was joking, but I soon perceived that he was quite serious. It was a novel experience for me to be accused by an Indian of theft. On my expostulating with him, he admitted quite frankly that I had not taken the pumpkins. When he said this I was more bewildered still. I should have lost patience with him, had he not been evidently in real earnest, and I became deeply interested instead. Eventually I discovered that he had dreamed he was out in his garden one night, and saw me, from behind some tall plants, break off and carry away three pumpkins, and it was payment for these that he wanted. "Yes," I said, "but you have just admitted that I had not taken them." He again assented, but replied immediately: "If you had been there you would have taken them" thus showing he regarded the act of my soul, which he supposed had met his in the garden, to be really my will, and what I should actually have done had I been there (pp. 106–107).

Young children also fail to distinguish between their world of fantasy and dreams and the objective world about them. Werner (1957) points out that:

For the child the reality of the dream and of the waking world are relatively undifferentiated. Children have to learn to distinguish between the dream and waking reality. At this stage waking reality often exhibits some of the characteristics peculiar to the dream; the events of the waking world, for example, are often immediately configurable through the emotions of fear or wishfulness. Some illuminating examples of this configurative power of the wish will demonstrate how much less well defined is the transition from the dream to the waking world of fantasy. A 4:2 year-old girl unintentionally throws her slate to the floor. I look at her angrily, and immediately she says in all seriousness: "The cat did it!" In this instance there was no jesting or playfulness. It may be said that the wish to put the blame on someone else realized itself spontaneously (p. 390).

Failure of the individual to differentiate between his own experience and the external world results in his self not being clearly and consistently articulated. Until the self does reach a certain growth, it does not enter as a major referent into the individual's attribution of causality. Instead of perceiving the self as the source of cause of an event, external or internal, the cause is seen to stem from external sources.

In a general way there is no such thing as chance to a mind like this, nor can there be, [asserts Levy-Bruhl]. Not because it is convinced of the rigid determinism of phenomena; on the contrary, [he continues], indeed, since it has not the most remote idea of such determinism, it remains indifferent to the relation of cause and effect, and attributes a mystic origin to every event which makes an impression on it. Since occult forces are always felt to be present, the more accidental an occurrence seems to us, the more significant it will appear to the primitive mind. There is no necessity to explain it; it explains itself, it is a revelaton (pp. 43–44).

With further differentiation of the self from the rest of the world, the individual comes to attribute greater causality to his own acts. This more advanced type of causal reasoning, which has been termed "if . . . then" thinking by Werner (1957, p. 323), can be seen from Piaget's study of the development of the child's understanding of the dream (1929) from which he inferred three different levels of interpretation between the ages of four and eight years:

(1) The dream comes from outside and remains external (p. 91).

[An example of this, in questions and answers.]

Where does a dream come from?—From the night.– . . . Where are the dreams made?–Out there– . . . What sends them?–The clouds (p. 93).
(2) The dream arises in us ourselves but is external to us (p. 106). [This is exemplified by] Where do dreams come from?–When you are asleep, you think someone is beside you. When you see something in the day, you dream of it at night. . . . Where is it made?–In the room (p. 108).
(3) The dream is internal and of internal origin (p. 117): The dream is "when you think of something"–Where is the dream?–In my head.–As if there were pictures in your head? . . . –No, you see a picture of what you've done earlier (p. 119).

The attribution of external causality as a consequence of gross differentiation and concreteness can be seen in cases other than children and "primitives." For example, the history of medicine and "psychiatry" show that the early notions and practices in these areas stemmed from the belief that the sickness was due to the entrance of some foreign agent, often the representative of the devil, into the body. Treatment consisted of removing this alien agent, by bleeding the affected person or by "beating the devil" out of him. Many rural farmers still practice the bleeding of animals that are sick, and some cut the tails off healthy pigs in order to safeguard the pigs' good health. Other "medical" practices in remote spots of America include wearing beads or some piece of metal around the neck to ward off disease. Some people even grease with animal fat the rusty nail on which a barefoot boy so often steps—after, not before—he steps on it.

Among the most invariant and pronounced attribution of external causality is the explanation generally offered by the zealot for the religiosity and righteousness with which he proclaims and pursues his "cause"—irrespective of its content or direction (Hoffer, 1951). The zealot rationalizes that he is but carrying out the will of some master strategist, is but acting in accord with an absolute and irrefutable truth, is but fulfilling his responsibility to some transcendent force "that's bigger than all of us." Thus in his prosecution of Servetus, who had dared assail certain of both Catholic and Protestant doctrines,

". . . Calvin was fortified by the conviction that he was doing the work of God. 'It would be hypocrisy,' he said, 'not to own that the Lord has been pleased to employ me' " (Ergang, 1939, p. 202). Little different is the insistence of the avid segregationist that "Certainly our stand against integration is a good, Christian stand—for after all, He made the different races, didn't He?" (Quoted in the *Denver Post*, April 29, 1960.)

In later chapters we show how the attribution of causality relates to resolution of incongruous information. The more concrete individuals, those who tend more toward attributing the cause of their behavior to some outside force, such as "fate," will, for example, be shown to be authority oriented and hence to be very susceptible to influence attempts by authority sources but to be resistant to evaluations of inferior sources.

Concreteness Disposes toward Catechisms and Word Magic

The fact that an individual does not differentiate between the objective and subjective world has the further result that a name, like a dream, wish, or divination, is synonymous with the external reality. In the psychological world of the "primitive" and young child "a name is in no sense regarded as something imposed wilfully, or as something fortuitous, a mere sign. A thing cannot be grasped until its name is known. The name not only stands in intimate relation to the thing; it is part of the object itself" (Werner, 1957, p. 254). The assignment of a name or label to a phenomenon results in attribution of characteristics to the phenomenon that accord with the name. This holds to a striking degree even among individuals more conceptually differentiated and integrated (Gibson, 1929; Bartlett, 1932; Carmichael, Hogan and Walter, 1932), but is even more true for children and "primitives" who ". . . experience names both as things in themselves and as fused in the object they denote" (Werner, 1957, p. 255). Malinowski reports that the Trobrianders were certain that the pronouncement of the word "spider" resulted in a web-like structure in the tayter vine (Malinowski, 1935, p. 235). Piaget (1929) has demonstrated in the earlier stages of childhood—up to five or six years—the child believes that the name is inside or attached to the thing. ". . . During the first stage (5–6) the child supposes that we come to know the names simply by looking at them. We need only to look at the sun to know it is called 'sun' " (p. 68). In line with this, one six-and-one-half-year-old remarked, " 'If there weren't any words it would be very awkward. You couldn't make anything. How could things have been made' (if there hadn't been names for them)?" (Piaget, 1929, p. 62). Even more illustrative are the responses of another child concerning the name of the Saleve:

> How did it get its name in the beginning?—From a letter.—And where did the letter come from?—The name.—And the name?—From the mountain.—How did the name come from the mountain?—By a letter.—Where did the letter come from?—The mountain.—Clouds are called clouds, aren't they? Where does the name of the clouds come from?—The name? That is the name.—Yes, but where does it come from?—The clouds.—What do you mean when you say it comes from the clouds?—It's the name they've got.—But how did the name happen? How did it begin?—By itself.—Yes, but where did the name come from?—By itself (Piaget, 1929, p. 64).

The belief that names are essential properties of things is the basis of all word magic. All one has to do, in line with this premise, to transform the object into whatever he wishes is but to affix to the object the name that embodies the characteristics sought in the object. Belief in word magic may reach such proportions that little direct aggression is manifested because "putting the curse" on the unfavored object or wishing misfortune to befall it is sufficient "to do it in" (Hallowell, 1949, Levy-Bruhl, 1923; Werner, 1957). Positive effects can be achieved by word magic also, an assumption that underlies the practices of shamen and other religious figures in blessing objects by the application of standardized words.

The conditions of undifferentiation and concreteness that give rise to word magic result also in the catechismic employment of names without appreciation for the full denotative implications of the name. Words may be said and names affixed without an understanding of what the words mean. Such was the case of the three-and-one-half-year-old child who argued adamantly with his father that a man dressed as David Crockett, "the King of the Wild Frontier," was not Davy Crockett at all "because he doesn't have any front ear." Equally illustrative is the description made of his dog by Dennis the Menace to a couple of other neighborhood pests. Explained Dennis to his enraptured audience of two: "He's part Great Dame, part Irish Set-up, and Dad says he's got a lotta puddle in him, too." [1]

Greater Concreteness Tends to Be Accompanied by Negativism and Resistance to Suggestion

It appears that unless suggestion comes from an authority source who is symbolic of power and security the more concrete individuals are resentful of suggestions. Some individuals, whom we later describe

[1] Copyright by the Hall Syndicate, Inc. Reprinted by special permission.

as being at the second stage of concreteness (those who have only a modicum of differentiation-integration), seem to be negativistic toward suggestion from anyone, especially if he represents authority. But even the more negativistic individual, if caught up in a sufficiently unstructured or unanchored situation, one where he has difficulty in orienting himself in time and space, may model his evaluations after those of others about him, even hated others (Bettelheim, 1943). In one study of social influence under varied conditions of environmental structure (Sherif and Harvey, 1952), subjects in the more unstructured condition were more influenced by another's judgment, but at the same time they tended to deny that they had been influenced and to express resentment toward the presence of the other person.

It is our belief that the preceding experiment demonstrates one of the essential conditions of negativism, namely that the more concretistically functioning individual who has structured the situation in terms of only a very few rigid conceptual alternatives tends to protect these unitary and narrowly defined structures through warding off and resisting the evaluations of others, even if these are at only slight variance from his own. The expression of this is an attempt to ward off events that only might render more fragile the unstable orientations in time and space:

> . . . Primitive peoples, as a rule, show themselves hostile to everything coming from without [avers Levy-Bruhl (1923)], at least unless it be from neighbouring tribes like their own, people of the same race, customs and institutions, with whom they could live on friendly terms. From the real "stranger" they neither borrow nor accept anything. Any changes, even if they are undoubted improvements, must be forced upon them (p. 384). [He continues,]
> . . . They form, as it were, sealed systems in which every entrant runs the risk of setting up a process of decomposition. They are like organisms capable of living for a very long time whilst the general environment changes but slightly, but which very rapidly degenerate and die when invaded by new elements (p. 384).
> . . . Hence relations that appear to us perfectly natural and harmless, run the risk of exposing the group to dangers which are ill-defined and therefore all the more to be dreaded. The slightest intercourse with foreigners, the simple fact of receiving food or implements from them, may lead to catastrophe. Who knows how this may affect such-and-such an occult power, and what may be the result? Hence arise those signs of dread and distrust among primitives which the white races often interpret as expressing hostility (p. 385).

Concreteness Disposes Toward Ritualism

When facing a novel and relevant situation one casts about for some sign of familiarity, some psychological landmark or object to which he can relate and from which he can orient himself. [Later we say even to define his self.] One expression of this is the ceremonial behavior often preceding one's departure to a "foreign" or strange place. This behavior is manifested at various age levels and strata of society, but of course, it is most strikingly displayed by persons whose previous contacts with the surrounding world have been extremely limited and to whom accordingly much of the world is a "booming, buzzing confusion." Young children and "primitives," then, are very likely to go through activities aimed at guaranteeing safety to them when they are forced to face the unknown, activities that often take on ritualistic characteristics, with prayerful entreaties or some other gesture aimed at incurring the protective graces of the mystical omnipotent.

Familiar and reassuring objects, whether animate or inanimate, frequently are taken along to ward off the dangers of the unknown. Hence in many tribes it was not uncommon that a warrior's dog, horse, and other implements of his daily existence—sometimes including his spouse—be sacrificed and dispatched to accompany him on his journey to the "Happy Hunting Grounds." And as any reader of "Peanuts" knows, young "Linuses" generally surround themselves with some intimate companion before heading into the unknowns of sleep and night—a blanket, or doll, a toy dog, or some other reassuring object of endearment. Before they set off for the trip through the night, however, many go through repetitive and almost ritualistic activities that, owing to their very repetitiveness, help the child to differentiate his world further and to gain a modicum of structure and security within it.

> . . . These rituals may be so set that any neglect or alternation is felt to be a symbol of disruption, of a state of affairs in which "something is wrong," and, still later, as an injury to the ego proper. . . . A mother writes to Sully about her 2:7 year old boy: "After I have kissed him and given him my hand I must also kiss his doll, which he calls his 'boy,' and which sleeps with him. Then I have to shake the doll's hand, and do the same to the four hoofs of a toy horse which lies at the foot of his bed. When all this has been done he rises in bed and begs, 'Kiss me again and say goodnight just once more.' "
>
> . . . One child clutched the corner of a pillow in his hand while going to sleep. A four-year-old girl held on to a corner of a certain piece of cloth. A boy between the age of three and five slept with a handkerchief under his cheek. A three-year-old girl had to have her handkerchief hanging over the edge of the bed (Werner, 1957, pp. 358–359).

The child's demand for highly consistent and structured activity preceding his going to bed is paralleled by a desire for consistent and stable rules from authoritative adults. As Werner (1957) points out:

> The child's desire to be protected by rules from the dangers of uncertainty at least partially explains his attitude toward the commands of adults, which are often endowed with an absolute significance. Sully remarks with complete justice that children have a tremendous belief in the commands of adults, in the sacredness of rules. "I'm allowed to do this, but not that" is not merely the sign of superficial good conduct, but expresses the child's very need for order and rule (p. 361).

This may be construed as a further sign of lack of differentiation between the self and the external world, a condition that is reflected in an attribution of causality to the external agents, forces toward which effort is aimed at pleasing and winning protection from the threatening world.

The reflection of a striving to establish and maintain ties with the world, the simultaneous resistance to outside influence, and the seeking of objects of familiarity for reassurance is assumed to occur when any relevant situation of sufficient ambiguity is encountered. This is so among "primitives," children, adolescents, older people facing the necessity of role shifts, or any normal adults facing a problem situation that is important to them but one for which their characteristic modes of ordering are inadequate. Not only was resentment of other's suggestions noted in the experiment by Sherif and Harvey (1952), for example, but also subjects were observed to try in other ways to cling to a landmark of familiarity in highly ambiguous environment (a large, totally dark room). Many, in the course of finding, without aid, the places at which they were to sit, came into contact with some physical referent, such as a post placed by the experimenters to complicate the environment further and to render it ambiguous. Upon finding these points some would refuse to leave them until the experimenter made his way to them and guided them toward their chairs. Others would radiate out from these points in systematic directions and distances seeking other objects to aid them in defining the environment. They would place their heels against the stable object, take a counted number of standardized steps out into the unknown in one direction, retrace their steps to the starting point, and then repeat the sequence until they were successful in orienting themselves enough to make their way to the goal or until they gave up in exasperation. As we shall suggest in Chapter 9, behavior very similar to that of the above subjects characterizes the obsessive-compulsive individual who, presumably owing to the threat connected with moving away from his extremely narrow and tenuous beacon of safety, clings tenaciously to his current concept of and response toward a given situation.

It seems to us very probable that the tendencies of the more concretely functioning individual—to think categorically, to adhere rigidly to rules, to use word magic, to attribute external causality, to be simultaneously resentful and susceptible to influence from others, and to be ritualistic—all are expressive of his attempt to hold on to his rather tenuous way of ordering the world until he can, through further interactions with his environment and articulations of it, make available to himself a way of ordering that provides a more secure world into which to move. It may be that before the individual ever willingly abandons any concept or way of relating to the world and unresistingly separates himself from an anchorage of even minimum stability, he must first come to feel that the new or different way affords him a more adequate and secure way of structuring his environment and satisfying his needs. Under conditions devoid of choice, however, where the individual has no alternative but to relinquish or forego his ties to or desire for an object, it is assumed he will try to hold on to those anchorages that will minimize negative affect. In trying to "make the best of a bad situation" this might mean relinquishing a tie (at least for the time being) to a positively valued object, which albeit of importance to him is not as central as the combination of other objects that would have to be foregone were he to choose differently. The basis of this is elaborated in the next chapter.

Generality of the Effects of Variation in Abstractness

Most of the preceding examples of the effects of low levels of abstractness were in reference to children and "primitives." It should be stressed that the examples were just that, and hence the variations in abstractness-concreteness are not restricted to the groups mentioned. They may be seen, to a somewhat lessened extent it may be true, among adults and more "educated" people. In the present view an individual may become arrested at any given stage of concreteness-abstractness, at least in some of their concepts. Hence an academician or "intellectual" might at least in certain of his concepts show clear signs of concrete functioning, such as absolutism, external causality and oughtness, word magic, and ritualism.

The history of the development of major ideas demonstrates that many "scientists" (seemingly little less than gangland members, adolescents, primitives, and young children), often make only the most rudimentary differentiations and as a consequence react with absolutism and hostility even to slight departures from what they consider to be the irrefutable gospel (Ayers, 1955).

Word magic of a sort may also be indulged in by scientists, as is shown by the apparent belief by some that to name or label a phenomenon is equivalent to explaining it. Indeed, a vestige of word magic seems to be almost inherent in the structure of the language, if studies on the effect of labeling are indicative. That the structure of language, the cohesive ingredient of most of man's concepts, acts as an intervening filter through which the world passes on its way to evaluation was recognized almost a century ago by Cassirer (1944), De Laguna (1927), and others. The field work of Franz Boaz and his students suggested that such simple judgments as color discriminations were affected both qualitatively and quantitatively by the color categories existent in a given ethnic language and employed by the judge. Observations akin to this one, which have received fairly recent experimental verification by Brown and Lenneberg (1954), have been stressed by semanticists, such as Korzbyski (1951), and metalinguists, such as the late Whorf (1956). They are currently receiving further empirical and experimental elaboration by anthropologists (Hallowell [1949], and Hoijer [1953]) and by psychologists working in the area of psycholinguistics.

Whether the label has to do with color or more complex dimensions, once it is assigned to an object characteristics are subsequently attributed to the objects that are consonant with the label but which may be in complete violation of the object's veridical attributes. In the same way that one moves one's evaluation or structuring of an unstructured and rumor-ridden environment in the direction of leveling and sharpening (Allport and Postman, 1947), one moves similarly in the direction of rendering his memory and other cognitive reactions toward an object consistent with the label assigned it (Bartlett, 1932; Carmichael, Hogan and Walter, 1932; Gibson, 1929). Thus, for example, an ambiguous drawing that is assigned a particular label (such as "spectacles") upon initial presentation is subsequently reproduced to appear like the object so named should appear, with omissions of the features not fitting the label and additions consonant with one's need to complete it.

Tendencies toward overt approach or avoidance of an object parallel the characteristics imposed upon it by the label. This is so, even though the conceptual premise from which the behavior emanates may be undifferentiated and not in accord with objective reality. But veridical or not, the "real world" to the receiving individual is the world that is filtered through his conceptual matrix. It is this world, as distorted and unreal, as undifferentiated and bifurcated as it may be, that the individual conforms to in his own behavior and demands similar conformity from others. This is true for "civilized" man as well as for the Ojibwa Indians, for example, who take drastic steps to prevent the untrained child from eating or even touching the "kinnebikonin," snakeberries that are erroneously labeled as deadly poisonous among the tribesmen (Hallowell, 1949). Among the Ojibwa, as no doubt it will be among the 1984'ers—the child never has the chance to ascertain the true nature of the berries and to correct the error of the label. When very young he is prevented from making accurate differentiations based on direct experience with the berries, and by the time he is no longer physically restrained he has so internalized the undifferentiated dicta of his culture that he now "knows" the berries are poisonous. He now joins the ranks of the seniors who have as one of their main goals in life the revelation of the "real truth" to the juniors.

Such is the history of superstitions, social stereotypes, and many academic and religious "truths." They are often propagated and enforced as the gospel, without attempt or permission to check their validity. A person who accepts a particular stereotype because of his being an identifying member of the social order is unlikely to question the stereotype. It has become his own and is a basic aspect of his internal standards or schemata so that he perceives confirmations and not refutations. It would appear that under such conditions an assumption such as that of Vernon—". . . the more often a schema is utilized, the more available it will be, the more adequate and veridical will be the perceptions which arise from it, and the more effective the action" (1957, p. 336)—will hardly hold true. Instead, once a concept is formed and a label is attached to it (generally simultaneous if not synonymous activities) one's perceiving, judging, thinking, memory, and other activities may be so channeled along seemingly grooved routes that stereotypy of cognitive functioning results, rendering one unable to make differentiations not encompassed in his limited repertory of verbal categories. Veridicality may occur with such closedness; but it would be more likely not to.

The success of the Chinese Communists in "brainwashing" American Army captives, we believe, represents a dramatic demonstration of the woeful vulnerability of persons dependent on catechismic concepts and stereotyped labels. What were, for many prisoners, very concretistic conceptual systems broke down when they were forced to face events that contradicted these concepts. Belief that America is the best of all possible lands, held by many as an undifferentiated concept that was little more than a stereotype and a catechism, could be maintained only for a limited time in the face of "brainwashing" techniques that confronted the captive with points of view with which his often bifurcated conceptual schemata could not cope. Many of these men who knew only that communism was bad and capitalism was good, with very few notions of the whys and wherefores, tenaciously resisted communism at the outset, but when they began to alter their stand, a shockingly large number broke completely loose from their own inflexible moorings. Having no alternatives of their own to fall back on, they reanchored themselves to the position advocated by their captors. It is probable also that many who were torn from their own stand did not reattach themselves to communist dogma. It may be that from this latter group of individuals, those who were torn asunder from their initial ties but in some way failed to attach themselves to communism, came a large proportion of the 38 per cent of American Army captives of the Chinese who seemed just to have lain down and died.

This possibility seems to be in accord with the experimental finding that the more authoritarian individuals, although very resistant to changing their concepts at lower levels of stress, tend to "go to pieces" when they do shift at higher levels of stress, as manifested in loss of discrimination between positive and neutral stimuli (Harvey, 1958).

3 Conceptual Functioning and Motivation

The preceding chapter was devoted to a general characterization of concepts, especially how these postulated constructs served as the mediating link between the organism and his environing world. It was suggested that concepts, in the form of subject-object relations or ties, operate as kinds of schemata, as a kind of filtering or metering system in terms of which impinging events are differentiated and integrated, indeed through which reality is read by the experiencing agent. The degree of concreteness-abstractness of the linkages between the subject and object was stressed as a determining characteristic of the way events are evaluated and reality is read.

The present chapter is concerned with the problem of how concepts serve as a basis of motivation: through disposing an individual to order the world in a particular way and to react in certain ways, both at the covert and overt levels, when such standardized ways of ordering are either *confirmed* or *refuted.*

Conceptual Confirmation and Refutation Characterized

One of the basic postulated aspects of a concept is a property we term *directionality,* a course or direction of action toward each and every object to which it relates. Such directionality could be expressed in many ways: in terms of attractions-repulsions, in terms of negative-positive valences, in terms of approach-avoidance, or in terms of positive and negative evaluations. Directionality, therefore, implies a preference for an outcome, striving, or predilection toward either approaching or avoiding the object to which the activated concept relates. Whether approach or avoidance tendencies are generated by the conceptually relevant object depends, presumably, on the perceived instrumentality of the object, whether it is evaluated as congruent or incongruent with motive satisfaction or goal attainment (Rosenberg, 1956).

The directionality of a concept, which varies in its definitiveness and strength, provides the basis of both conceptual confirmation and refutation. *Conceptual confirmation* is the state resulting from the perception or evaluation of an impinging event as being compatible with or facilitative of the response directionality associated with the concept(s) operative at the particular time. *Conceptual refutation,* on the other hand, is the condition occurring when an impinging event is evaluated as conflicting with or being incompatible with the behavioral directionality implicit in existing concepts or subject-object relations. The better defined the directionality of a concept and the greater its strength or preference of outcome, the more pronounced are the behavioral and affective consequences of confirmation or refutation.

Special note should be taken of certain aspects of the preceding characterizations. First, confirmation and refutation are viewed as phenomenological constructs, psychological states that are dependent upon the evaluation of the situation by the receiving individual or observer. Thus these terms do not refer directly to physical properties of external stimulus events. It should be stressed, nonetheless, that we do not mean to imply that such physical properties of the stimulus impingements are unrelated to their evaluation as either confirming or refuting. Indeed as we have maintained previously and shall stress subsequently, all cognitive activity, including perception or evaluation, is jointly determined by the dispositional and situational factors operative at the given moment. Our use of these constructs as phenomenological rather than stimulus properties stems from the simple fact that a one-to-one correspondence fails to exist between properties of stimuli and the experience of them.

Note should be taken, secondly, of our use of the term "perception" or "evaluation" in the above definition. By these terms we simply mean to imply that the individual "senses" or at some level of awareness *discriminates* the impinging event as being either similar or dissimilar in varying degrees to his existing mode of interpretation of it. Although a relevant question, we do not attempt to offer criteria aimed at distinguishing between the discrimination processes at the varying levels of awareness, such as conscious-unconscious or subception-perception. We are referring only to the process in which the individual is sensitized toward, differentiates an impinging event, and places it psychologically into some sort of relationship to his existing conceptual standards by evaluating it as being in some degree either compatible or incompatible with them. And such an act of relating can occur at varying levels of articulateness or subject awareness.

The motivational consequences of conceptual confirmation and refutation parallel, in fact are probably synonymous, respectively, with *goal facilitation and impediment* since the directionality of a concept represents a goal orientation of approach or avoidance toward the motive- or concept-relevant object.

At the more concrete level of functioning, such as that of children and infrahuman species, goal blocking and facilitation would more likely relate to some external object, animate or inanimate. At the more abstract level of functioning goal blocking and facilitation, instead of being restricted to the effects of concrete physical objects or features of the environment, could as well, and probably more frequently do, stem from conceptual refutation and confirmation, such as verbal reproof and reward from sources of significance in the eyes of the subject.

Concept confirmation and refutation may occur in relation to either approach or avoidance tendencies. If the direction of the goal orientation of a concept is approach, then confirmation would result from the situation being evaluated as favoring increased proximity to the goal object. If the directionality were avoidant, then confirmation would result from interpreting the situation as contributive toward increasing the distance from the negative object. Refutation, of course, would be the consequence of a contradiction of the directional striving by the situation. For example, consider the concept: Alcoholic beverages should not be used under any circumstance. Confirmation of this concept would occur from interpretation of events as being consonant with avoidance of alcohol. Conceptual refutation, on the other hand, would result from evaluating an event as favoring the use, for any reason, of alcohol.

Some Necessary Conditions for Confirmation and Refutation

Out of the totality of events impinging at a particular point in time, not all of the myriad of possibilities are of behavioral relevance to the individual at that moment. For a stimulus to be relevant it must relate to the operative concepts or other motives of the individual in either an impeding or facilitative way.

Even further, out of the mass of stimuli that have *potential* relevance to the subject so far as their objective properties are concerned, only a small fraction of these probably are so perceived or recognized by the individual. Stimulus relevance often exists only as a potential, its particular fruition or realization hinging upon the presence of the object at the appropriate moment, upon a particular interaction, a particular wedding of it with existant concepts that lie dormant until they are triggered off by a certain stimulus or range of stimuli. This kind of interdependence, to which we alluded in the preceding chapter, is summarized aptly by Cantril and Bumstead (1960):

> These registered effects of the past are in a sense carried with a person all the time—but in *potential* form. It is inconceivable that all of the registered effects of the past should be relevant to a present, concrete transaction. If, for example, a person has, as we say, an anti-class X prejudice, this prejudice is operative only when some member of class X or some symbol of class X exists in awareness for the prejudiced individual. Where is the prejudice when it is not present? It is absent, non-existent but potential. It is not then what we have called an "essential factor," because it apparently does not participate in and therefore makes no difference in the transaction we are studying at the moment. Yet it is available if and when an appropriate occasion is encountered and its potential significance is relevant (Cantril and Bumstead, 1960, p. 104).

For an event to be reacted to as either confirming or refuting, the condition of relevance, at some level of subject awareness, must have been satisfied. And, if we might relate this to an old question of the learning theorist, the mere physical presence of an object and/or the frequency of its proximity are not sufficient. They may be necessary conditions, however, to result in the indispensable interlocking of the particular stimulus with the particular concept(s) or other contingent predispositions operating at the appropriate moment.

The fact that an event objectively is discrepant from a concept on some dimension and in some direction does not mean that such a discrepancy will be taken by the subject as representing either confirmation or refutation of a particular concept. Such lack of correspondence between variations in the stimulus and accompanying effects, overt and covert, may be due to a host of conditions. For example, the discrepancy might be so great between the subject's concept and the impinging stimulus that the event (another's evaluation, say) would be interpreted as irrelevant to the issue at hand. Such conceptual discontinuities have been noted in several studies, where the discrepant events have been both the evaluations of another person (Asch, 1952) and inanimate psychophysical anchors (Rogers, 1941).

An individual, instead of noting the discrepancy and interpreting it as irrelevant to his own concept, may actually fail to note the concept-event incongruity and, at least so far as measured effects reveal, to act as if no discrepancy existed. Such ways of behaving were found to occur in prejudiced subjects who failed to get the point of the Mr. Biggot cartoons (Cooper and Jahoda, 1947), as well as more authoritarian individuals who failed to "receive" the negativity of information to which they were exposed (Harvey and Beverly, 1959). Such "selective inattention" could probably be treated as expressive of the same kind of functioning that underlies "perceptual defense," whatever this process ultimately may prove to be. The many intricacies and complexities relating to this problem, both in terms of measurement and theoretical interpretation, need not, however, detain us on this point.

An individual might perceive an event as being both discrepant from and congruent with his concept and still not manifest the kinds of behavior that we present shortly as tending to result from conceptual confirmation or refutation. Such a person might react by declaring, "You see it one way, and I see it another." Such a response probably would come only from persons functioning at a more abstract level, in terms of ways of ordering that not only allow for but also may even demand that alternate interpretations are possible. Assume that such an individual whose view of reality argues for multiple alternatives is informed that X, as he thought it, was not X at all, but was Y. He could change this concept of the object he had labeled "X" with very little resistance and with little or no affect. He might even feel good because to change could be confirming other of his concepts, such as his view that reality is open to multiple interpretations. This and other possibilities of simultaneous confirmation and refutation of different concepts, or even possibly of the same concept in a case of ambivalence, will be faced again later when we enter the discussion of the multidimensionality of an individual's conceptual system.

Some General Reactions to Confirmation and Refutation

We have characterized confirmation and refutation respectively as the evaluation of a stimulus event as compatible or incompatible with the directionality or volitional aspect of a concept or motive. Let us turn now to a brief consideration of some of the effects of such psychological states. We are not attempting, nor is it our desire, to present a lengthy compendium of specific or more phenotypic responses to confirmation and refutation. The actual frequency of these is as numerous as are the levels of analysis and their representative measures that one chooses to employ in representing the effects. Accordingly, we are restricting our depiction to *more* genotypic outcomes rather than concerning ourselves with an endless listing of more phenotypic possibilities. We underscore *more* genotypic because there is no such thing as a pure or fixed genotype or phenotype. As in Aristotle's form and matter (with which genotypes and phenotypes are respectively synonymous), what is a genotype to the "lower" levels it embodies is in turn a phenotype when its own membership character within a more comprehensive organization of relationships is considered.

The more generic outcomes of confirmation and refutation with which we primarily concern ourselves are (1) *affective arousal* and (2) certain behavioral manifestations, which we term *behavioral resolutions,* ways in which the generated predispositions are expressed. Such outcomes are not assumed to be independent; they are taken to be expressive of a common denominator.

AFFECTIVE AROUSAL

One of the most psychologically significant consequences of confirmation or refutation is the quality and intensity of the affect generated by such an evaluation. It may, in fact, prove to be that the affect generated by the arousal of a concept or a more biogenic motive acts as "the outstanding kernel of the whole experience" (Koffka, 1922) and serves as a kind of spearhead that other of the effects tend to follow or with which they tend to be consonant. It is not necessary, however, to treat affect as "cause" to demonstrate its inextricable relationship to the volitional directionality. Conceptual confirmation tends to generate positive affect whereas refutation or violation of goal directionality tends to be accompanied by negative affect. When the coin is reversed and affect is viewed as cause instead of effect, approach tendencies are noted to occur toward objects related to positive affect while avoidance tends to result toward objects of negative valence.

Let us, at the expense of redundancy, stress a point that is significant to our position, a point which differentiates our theoretical stand from some quite similar to it. The "zero point," "adaptation level" (Helson, 1947), or baseline from which the effects of a discrepant stimulus are to be gauged is the behavioral directionality, including its strength, implicit in a concept or any motivational predisposition. To establish this means, in some cases, no more than ascertaining the extent to which the event was evaluated as deviating from expectancy, "expectancy" being the referent point that some writers (for example, McClelland et al., 1953) consider the appropriate zero point for calculating effects of stimulus discrepancies. It is probable, as other writers have also proposed (Rotter, 1954; Atkinson and Reitman, 1956), that expectancy is an appropriate baseline only if it implies a wish, predilection, or preference toward a particular outcome or a directional striving toward some portending occurrence. If expectancy is so defined as to strip from it the property of directionality and predilection, then its appropriateness as the baseline for gauging effects of stimulus incongruities, in either direction, is rendered nil. This may be illustrated by one of the examples used in the earlier development of their theory by McClelland and his associates who at that time viewed affect to be ". . . the innate result of certain discrepancies between expectations and perception" (1953, pp. 67–68).

> . . . Take flunking out of school, for example. One might argue that if the student half expected it, he should feel pleasure since his expectation is confirmed. Although it is true that he may get some fleeting satisfaction from having predicted correctly, this is more than outweighed by the non-confirmation of other expectations built up over his whole life history such as doing a good job, being a professional man, etc. (1953, p. 66).

Even if the individual in this example expected to the point of certainty that he was going to flunk out of school, no prediction as to the likely effect from confirmation of expectancy alone could be made without considering this in relation to the preference of the student. If he were motivated strongly to stay in school, the greater the error in his prediction the greater would be the positive affect because, although negating his expectancy, it would confirm the volitional directionality of his motive, his desire to stay in school. On the other hand, the less is the error in his prediction that he would flunk out of school, that is, the smaller the expectancy-event discrepancy, the greater would be the negative affect, due to a refutation of the striving to stay in school. Only for those students trying to flunk out of school would a confirmation of a parallel expectancy represent at the same time a confirmation of the directionality of the motive.

Thus the corroboration or negation of an expectancy in whatever degree, unless it is made to include directional striving, is itself a poor predictor of affective arousal. Effects of deviations from expectancies must be viewed against the backdrop of the goal orientation, approach or avoidance, of the individual under scrutiny. Complete violation of expectancy may result in positive affect if such violation were at the same time confirming the directionality of the concept(s) or motive. Verification of an expectancy, on the other hand, even if not to the point of a zero discrepancy between the expectancy and concept, a condition McClelland et al. (1953) postulate as resulting in boredom, will result in negative affect if such corroboration is in contradistinction to a striving or goal orientation of the individual.

If expectancy is endowed with a behavioral predilection or preference of outcome (Rotter, 1954; Atkinson and Reitman, 1956), the effects of its negation or confirmation follow the same principles as confirmation or refutation of other concepts. The particular outcome would have to be analyzed in a kind of cost and credit fashion in relation to the totality of concepts triggered off by an occurrence, some of which could be confirmed whereas others were simultaneously refuted with the attendant consequences of concomitant negative and positive affect.

Let us, as a last example, use the case borrowed by McClelland et al. (1953) from Hebb. These authors tend to feel that if a reader of a detective story, for example, is able to predict with complete accuracy the outcome of a plot, boredom and negative affect should occur since an assumed necessary condition for positive affect and avoidance of boredom is some discrepancy greater than zero but not in excess of some optimal range. The extent to which prediction or expectancy is supported is meaningless per se, we are suggesting, unless something is also known about the directionality of the reader to preference. A person who wanted the story to come out in just one way would feel positive and not negative affect from complete confirmation of expectancy if the expectancy was also consonant with his want. A person who would prefer novelty would probably experience boredom and negative affect from the same degree of expectancy corroboration.

The "butterfly curve" postulated by McClelland et al. (1953), showing that maximum positive affect is achieved by the stimulus discrepancy that is neither too small nor too large, is inapplicable to the present view of affective consequences of conceptual confirmation and refutation. Although consequences of deviations from expectancies may follow a curvilinear function, affective arousal generated by refutation of a volitional directionality should follow a linear function. That is, the more a goal is perceived as being blocked, the greater is the attendant negative affect (up to the ceiling of complete blocking). Departure, if any, from a linear function should be toward an accelerated increase of negative affect with increased refutation. The same principle, with different affect, should obtain for conceptual confirmation or perceived goal facilitation.

One of the main concerns of this book is the extent to which individuals vary in their desire for or seeking after novelty or something other than a complete verification of their expectancy. Individuals who vary on the dimension of *concreteness-abstractness* later will be seen to vary on the extent to which they seek differences versus homogeneity or expectancy corroboration. For example, the more concrete individual, the one who feels that only one concept of reality or a phenomenon can be right, can tolerate almost no discrepancy before his concept is refuted and negative affect is aroused. The more abstract person who, on the other hand, believes that a situation should be interpreted in many, but equally correct, ways would have his concept refuted by the situation or person that argues for lack of alternatives. Thus the same event might be evaluated and experienced in an affectively opposite manner by these two persons. The one who could tolerate only small differences would experience conceptual confirmation and positive affect if the deviation of the stimulus were small, whereas the person who could not tolerate homogeneity would experience negative affect and conceptual refutation. Much of the present book is in one way or another related to this point.

BEHAVIORAL RESOLUTIONS

Not only is a state of affect assumed to be generated by conceptual confirmation and refutation but also, as we suggested earlier, consonant behavioral predilections are assumed to accompany such affect, consequences both triggered off by the same event.

As we sketch in a later part of this chapter and stress in later chapters, *what* is confirming or refuting, hence the cognitive and behavioral outcomes, depends on the particular organizational properties of the constellation or system of concepts involved. These characteristics stem to a great extent from the different conditions surrounding the history of conceptual development (Chapters 4 and 5). Owing to variation in organizational aspects of the underlying concepts, an event that would be confirming of one set or system of concepts could be refuting of another system with a different structural make-up.

Either approach or avoidance tendencies may be expressed at the overt (motor) or covert (symbolic) level. We would define approach as the tendency to *minimize* and avoidance as the tendency to *maximize* the psychological distance between one's concept(s) and a source, the object (person, place, or thing) perceived as the agent of refutation or confirmation.

Both approach and avoidance, it would appear further, may be carried out in either of two ways, ways that elsewhere have been labeled respectively as assimilation and contrast (Harvey and Caldwell, 1959). Approach, the minimization of psychological distance, may occur in a communication situation by the subject's either changing his concept and moving toward the evaluation of the source or by distorting the source's stand so that he renders it more similar to his own. Avoidance, in the same type of situation, could occur by the subject distorting the stand of the source away from his own concept or by changing his concept in the direction opposite to that recommended by the source (boomerang).

There are countless more specific phenotypic means by which the minimization and maximization of psychological distance may be expressed, depending on organizational properties of the system of concepts involved. The various resolutions that we present in Chapter 7 represent one classification of the means by which a given directionality of approach or avoidance can be maintained or enhanced. Given the situation where a good friend, for instance, violates a positive concept of the subject toward some other object, among the many ways such an incompatibility may be resolved is, for example, through the technique we, in Chapter 7, refer to as "neutralization."

Through this vehicle the subject seeks to maintain his approach tendencies toward both the friend and toward the other object by such behaviors as making excuses for the friend, transforming the friend's behavior to the point where no contradiction exists, namely, maintaining that the friend was not serious, that the friend was for some reason not responsible, and so forth. The resolution process of neutralization, as well as many of the others, may also be employed to maintain or enhance the directionality of avoidance. Reverse the above situation by having a disliked person make a positive evaluation of an object toward which a person felt positively. Depending on the strength of the negativity, and so forth, the subject could maintain or maximize his distance from the source by attributing negative characteristics to him, by believing he was insincere, untrustworthy, and the like.

The point is that the mechanisms of resolution can be viewed in terms of approach or avoidance, depending respectively on whether the process is engaged to maintain or increase a psychological closeness or to maintain or increase a psychological farness. It may appear that we are stretching the terms of approach and avoidance to the point of meaninglessness. In so doing, however, we are but trying to focus attention on our basic assumption that the behavioral expression of motive arousal, the way such tendencies are resolved, follows the pattern felt by the subject as furthering or maintaining the directionality of greater strength toward the object of greater relevance to him. In order to lessen redundancy, we shall speak of the various ways of maintaining the approach or avoidant inclinations as *maintenance or resolution processes,* the assumption always being that such behaviors are but more phenotypic representatives of the more generic tendencies of minimization or maximization of psychological distance.

The examples given above of the ways in which response predispositions may be expressed are reflective of a fairly highly abstract or symbolic level of functioning. At the more concrete level, such as that of the young child, for instance, the approach and avoidance tendencies tend to be expressed more overtly, more at the motor level: by walking toward the positive object, having tactual contact with it, putting it in its mouth (if an inanimate object or sometimes even if an animate object) if the tendency is approach; by running away from or attacking it if the tendency is avoidant. The same directional inclinations are expressed more abstractly by attributing positive characteristics to the source, by changing one's concept toward him, and by transforming his behavior in a positive direction, if the source is positive, and by doing the reverse toward the object perceived as the causal agent of negative affect. The implications of this for concept or attitude change and interpersonal relations will be presented in Chapters 7 and 8.

Multiple Concepts Are Generally Involved in Confirmation and Refutation

It is probably rare that a single concept of a single dimension is triggered off by a relevant stimulus impingement, despite the simplicity of our presentation up to this point. More probable is the simultaneous engagement of more than one concept, which gives rise to the possibility of contemporaneous confirmation and refutation concomitantly with both approach and avoidance tendencies and positive and negative affect.

All of the aroused affective and response predispositions may be sufficiently similar so that they conjoin to point to a single course of feeling and action. In such a hypothetical instance no conflict would occur since no competing tendencies were operative at the same time. Where all the concepts engaged did not in their resulting, disposing effects direct toward a common action, however, conflict could be the result. The magnitude of the conflict would, we think, be dependent upon: (1) the number of concepts in competition, (2) the relative strength (which later we term centrality-peripherality) of each, and (3) the degree of incompatibility among them, which could vary from similarity through orthogonality to dissimilarity in their directionalities.

Conflict would be greatest under those conditions where the competing response tendencies were of high and equal strength, a condition that presumably could occur from the simultaneous engagement of several contradictory response tendencies of lower strengths, *or* from the arousal of fewer competing concepts of greater centrality. The assumption here is based on a notion of "pooling," that is, the strength of a predisposition in any direction is a function of the *number* of concepts pointing in that direction and, in some multiplicative manner, by their *respective strengths*. Thus a given strength of a response tendency presumably could be obtained by increasing either the frequency of the concepts involved and/or their centrality.

The occurrence of conflict need not result only from the concurrent arousal of approach and avoidant tendencies. Approach-approach or avoidant-avoidant conflict may also be generated by the arousal of the appropriate sets of concepts.

One way we have found meaningful to view conflict is in terms of the model of a *fulcrum.* As suggested above, intensity of the conflict increases as the weight or strengths on both sides of the fulcrum increase and approach equality or a balance. Conflict is reduced by imbalancing the fulcrum, which can be achieved by either increasing the weight on one side and/or decreasing it on the other. The specific ways in which conflict may be resolved are, of course, numerous. As Kelly points out:

> Different constructs sometime lead to incompatible predictions, as everyone who has experienced personal conflict is painfully aware. Man, therefore, finds it necessary to develop ways of anticipating events which transcend contradictions. Not only do men differ in their constructions of events, but they also differ in the ways they organize their constructions of events. . . . The same man may resolve in one way at one time and in the other way at another. It all depends upon how he backs off to get perspective (Kelly, 1955, p. 56).

It is our assumption that in conflict the individual behaves in a way to maximize positive affect. This would mean in a situation of conflict, to act in the way expected to minimize cost and to enhance credit, a way that if successful would yield the greatest *net* positive affect. Where one were forced to make a choice, this would result in choosing objects of greater positive valence and attempting to maintain the directionality toward them. Given a situation where the conflict was between a concept highly positive toward one object and only moderately so toward the other, the conflict would be resolved in favor of the more positive object (Osgood and Tannenbaum, 1955; Harvey and Caldwell, 1959). If, however, *one* very positive object were pitted against several less positive ones, it could happen that the *total value* of the combined objects would be greater than that of the single object, and the individual would behave in a way to favor the combination. This notion is akin to Bentham's "felicific calculus," the idea that each act is preceded by the culculation of anticipated pain and anticipated pleasure. If the latter is greater than the former, the act will be carried out; otherwise it will not. Although not implying the rationality of the calculation attributed by Bentham, we are coming very close to features of his position by agreeing, in the condition where multiple concepts are operative and conflict ensues, that one behaves in the way aimed at attaining the highest possible net positive affect. This position, in one variety or another, which implies an ascertainment of "costs" and "credits," finds current expression in several writings (for example, McClelland et al., 1953; Thibaut and Kelley, 1959).

The notion that in any resolution of a situation there is some degree of cost and credit implies the simultaneous operation of more than one response or evaluative alternative in some degree of perceived incompatibility with other possibilities. From the vantage point of this book, this means the simultaneous engagement of multiple concepts, some of the consequences of which are considered within a relational or systemic framework we term the *self*.

Concepts and the Self-System

Self Is Synonymous with the Totality of Concepts

The totality of one's concepts, of one's subject-object relationships, in their intertwined interdependencies are viewed as constituting a *system*, a system we label "self."

The simplest concept is one involving two points on a single dimension, and the most complex concept is one embodying an infinity of points on an infinity of dimensions. Thus in one sense the self could be viewed as one very complex, hierarchic, concept into which simpler concepts pour or converge in a stream-like fashion. Or it could be viewed as comprising an open-ended number of less inclusive concepts that, in their myriad of interdependencies and interlinkings, operate as one larger system or as a series of smaller systems or subsystems.

We at this point term the organized totality of one's concepts as a system, and later we treat constellations of more highly interrelated concepts within this more inclusive set of relationships as subsystems (of the self).

There is no necessary reason why the totality of concepts should be termed "self." Such a matrix of relationships could simply be referred to as concepts, or even as X, Y, or Z. Our reason for the label "self" is twofold. First, it is our desire to call attention to the motivational and affective significance of one's way of relating and tying to the world. The treatment of concepts, moreover, has tended historically to be in the fashion of classical conditioning and a progressive linking of smaller and simpler elements into more complex concepts, and we wish not to have our treatment of concepts equated with this atomistic approach. The second reason for the term "self" to encompass the concepts is that this term has been used historically to refer to many of the motivational relevancies that we emphasize (for example, James, 1890; Cooley, 1912; Sherif and Cantril, 1947).

The self, as we employ the term, refers to the network of subject-object relationships that provides the individual with ties to the world and moorings for his orientation in time and space (Sherif and Cantril, 1947; Werner, 1957). It is on the basis of this web of conceptual ties that one's psychological being exists and without which man as uniquely man could hardly be. Indeed it is possible, as we shall try to demonstrate later, that the complete severance of one's subject-object relationships or prevention of their evolvement may drastically impair or even destroy one's being both as a psychological entity and as a living organism.

Some General Properties of the Self-System

INTERDEPENDENCE OF PARTS

Perhaps the most essential, or at least most salient, characteristic of a system—organic or inorganic, from ameba to man—is an interdependence of the operative components. It is because we desire to emphasize the interdependent operation of concepts that we treat the concatenation of subject-object relationships that we have termed the self in a systemic way; it is not because we are interested in systems per se.

If a concept never operates in complete isolation from others, this implies a degree of interrelatedness that gives rise to the potential of one subject-object relationship being affected by its interdependency, direct or indirect, with others. To the extent that concepts are interrelated, to that degree their functioning may be affected by their membership character or embeddedness in the more inclusive system of concepts operative at a particular time. As Murphy, who uses the construct "organization" with the same meaning we are giving to "system" says:

> . . . Organization involves, first of all the transmission of energy from one region to another; second, the simultaneous passage of energies in various directions in an interdependent fashion as described above; third, the consequent adjustment of one part to another, . . . of which homeostasis or the maintenance of constancy is one aspect . . . . organization embraces the entire organism-environment relation, of which the organism is the nodal but not the complete functioning system (1947, pp. 39–40).

It should be kept in mind that the construct "system" is itself a relative one. The whole universe could, in Aristotelian reasoning, be viewed as constituting one vast system since each of its parts is related in either an ascending (matter) or descending (form) way. A human being, according to Aristotle's position, would be form to all its subparts. Yet the same person would be matter when compared to all of mankind since he would now represent only a subfacet of the larger, more comprehensive totality.

Therefore, with the possible exclusion of physical and mechanical systems made by man, a system is not fixed. The most important aspect of a system is a constellation of interrelationships. Thus any phenomenon at any level can be treated in a systemic way as long as it is not viewed as constituted by a fixed entity but as comprised of a matrix of relationships that both embodies and reciprocally is embodied by other sets of relationships. This form and matter view of a system does not imply, of course, that all of the possible relationships within a system contribute an equal weight. Indeed, it is possible that one factor relates so weakly to others that for all practical purposes its contribution could be omitted from consideration.

The extent of interrelationship required in order for the operation of the various factors to be considered a system is, of course, arbitrary. Presumably the investigator could specify any degree of interrelatedness he chose; he could even dictate what specific variables must be interrelated at a criterion level before he would label the relationships as a system. He could postulate criterion levels of the relationship of one concept to others before it is included in the same constellation or subsystem with them. We, however, do not attempt to do this. Instead we leave as an open question such criteria and suggest that perhaps a more relevant question would be the extent to which concepts are interrelated under varying conditions.

CAPACITY TO EVALUATE THE SITUATION

Every system that is not completely closed is in some way and to some degree sensitive to a certain range of events or relevant stimuli. Coupled with this sensitivity as an inseparable activity is the capacity to evaluate the relevant stimuli as either in line with or deviant from the goal directedness or function of the system. The stimuli that have relevance for any system, the objects to which it may become sensitized, are determined by the function and structure of the system. One weapons system whose function it is to destroy certain kinds of missiles might be sensitive only to missiles that give off radio signals, a second only to missiles that give off intense heat, and others only to missiles that give off some other specific cues. Furthermore, the same objects or cues might be reacted to differently by different systems. We later show in detail how variations in the organization and structure of the subsystems of the self give rise to differential detection and evaluation of different and of similar stimuli.

Sensitization of a system is assumed to be the immediate precursor to evaluation of and response to the situation. The selectivity in sensitization presumably reflects a lower threshold to the reception or detection of the presence of a particular stimulus object or class of objects. This heightened sensitivity and lowered threshold may be manifested in either or all of three ways: (1) a detection of a particular stimulus object at a lower level of stimulus intensity; or (2) a greater or more intense arousal of the conceptual system at a constant level of stimulus intensity; and (3) a greater determination of a response by one dimension rather than another when competing stimulus dimensions are presented. In all of them, the relationship between the response "output" to the magnitude of the stimulus "input" is higher for the more sensitized than the less sensitized system. In any case, the receiving organism becomes attuned toward particular stimuli on which his attention is more focused and which stand out more saliently, or as *figure,* against the background of other less relevant stimuli impinging at that time.

Stimulus figure or salience may result from either of two general conditions: from a greater intensity of one relevant stimulus in relation to other stimuli; or from increased motivational arousal with stimulus intensity constant. Sensitization and threshold thus are characteristics of a receiving system and not of the impinging stimuli. At the same time, it is only from responses to controlled stimuli that sensitization can be inferred.

CAPACITY TO MAKE RESPONSE CONSONANT WITH EVALUATION

A third characteristic of a successfully operating system is the ability to respond "appropriately" to the situation following evaluation of it. If an individual detects and evaluates a situation as being dangerous, for example, it is of little avail if he does not also have some capacity to respond consonantly, either by flight or fight for instance, to such a situation.

We assume that the individual's reaction to a situation is in keeping with his calculation of the best route to maximum avoidance of negative affect or to facilitation of positive affect. In a situation where conflicting concepts within the self-system are simultaneously triggered off, positive affect is maximized, "the best is made of the situation," by responding in a way that favors the concept(s) of greater importance or centrality in the self-system.

How such "felicific calculus" is expressed under varied conditions is treated further following a consideration of the function and structure of the conceptual systems. All three of the preceding systemic characteristics, interdependence, sensitization, and response, are largely determined by the *function* and *structure* of the subject-object relationships. Let us turn now to a sketching of the function of a conceptual system and its effects.

Function of the Conceptual System

Evolvement and Maintenance of Self

We have already expressed the assumption that one's web of concepts supplies him with linkages to the environing world, ties through which reality is read and through which one defines one's being in space and time. In the sense that concepts provide one with such ties, the totality of which we termed the self, it could be said that one function of concepts is the evolvement and maintenance of the self.

Care must be exercised in attributing a function or an aim to a system of concepts lest we become guilty of a circularity as unbeatable as that of Voltaire's Master Pangloss:

> Master Pangloss . . . could prove to admiration that there is no effect without a cause, and in this best of all possible worlds the baron's castle was the most magnificent of all castles, and my lady the best of all possible baronesses.
>
> "It is demonstrable," said he, "that things cannot be otherwise than they are; for as all things have been created for some end, they must necessarily be created for the best end. Observe, for instance, the nose is formed for spectacles; therefore we wear spectacles. The legs are visibly designed for stockings; accordingly we wear stockings. Stones were made to be hewn and to construct castles; therefore my lord has a magnificent castle; for the greatest baron in the province ought to be the best lodged. Swine were intended to be eaten; therefore we eat pork all the year round. And they who assert that everything is right, do not express themselves correctly; they should say that everything is *best*" (Voltaire, 1759, p. 2).

By function we mean a state or end product toward which an existent set of factors or contingencies conduce. This condition would be altered if the underlying relationships that served as its foundation were modified too markedly. The function of a family is served by marriage in interaction with the other necessary supportive activities. Note that we are implying neither fixity nor oughtness to such a function as a family, nor to functions of concepts. In the fashion suggested by the relationship of form to matter, or genotype to phenotype, the family itself may be viewed as matter, as an underlying facet or subpart of a larger set of relationships or of a more inclusive end product, say of a society.

Function then represents a kind of genotype, a superordinate state based upon its inclusion of interdependent subparts or phenotypes. For example, a river represents such an outgrowth. So one could say in this sense that one function served by a tributary is to feed the river, a function served by a river is to feed the more inclusive body of water, and so forth, up the ladder of making each level part of a more comprehensive level. There are various *levels* of function, therefore, function being the state (form) toward which other subfacets (matter) are seen as converging or contributing.

Hence there are any number of functions that we could attribute to conceptual systems. The one we are concerned with primarily, however, is that of *evolvement and maintenance of the self* with self defined as the intertwined totality of one's concepts or subject-object relations. Hence some kind of differentiation and relating to one's environing world is necessary for the self to come into existence. Every concept and every differentiation and consequent patterning in one's life history enters into the total matrix constituting his self. The self at any given time is represented by the concepts existent at that time, irrespective of their complexity or object referents. Not all concepts contribute equally to the definition and operation of the self-system; their relative contribution depends on such organizational properties as centrality and others that we describe shortly.

This notion of the self implies, of course, the necessity of differentiating and integrating one's environing world in such a fashion that a more or less consistent evaluation of it can be made in a way allowing the individual to cope with his world. Without the capacity to break the world down into relevant parts and to relate or pattern these differentiations in a way consistent with organismic needs, survival of the individual himself, or any organism for that matter, would, we assume, be impossible.

In this sense then, concepts serve as the vehicle or the function for evolving a self and maintaining the organism. The particular way such function is carried out varies from person to person, however. One person may differentiate and integrate his world in one way whereas another person may function in quite a different way. These variations in the outcome of differentiation and integration result in structural differences in conceptual organization, differences that are reflected in differential detection, evaluation, and reaction to a class of stimulus events, effects to which most of the later chapters in this book, in one way or another, are devoted.

The matrix of concepts embraced within the self serve as kinds of channels through which the environing world is evaluated. Yet properties of the external situation reciprocally influence the conceptual standards. Thus concepts affect the formation of subsequent concepts, and one reacts to the environment in a way that will maintain the concepts as unaltered as possible. And in a situation of conceptual refutation and conflict, where the modification of some one or more existing concepts becomes inescapable, the individual resolves this in a way calculated to give him maximum net positive affect, as we discussed earlier.

Because confirmation of the more central concepts tends to give rise to positive affect, it becomes synonymous with the maximization of positive affect so that this maximization and maintenance of the self, especially the more central aspects, go hand in hand. Thus in this sense, affect could be viewed as furthering the function of self maintenance: with negative affect, which is experienced in the face of situations portending threat to subject-object relations, serving as a kind of warning signal; and positive affect, the result of perceived situational consonance with the volitional directionality of the concepts, serving as an indication of self support. The experienced affect, at varying levels of articulateness, seems to depend on sensitization. In fact, its quality may be viewed as representing experiential cues to possible confirmation or refutation of more central concepts. In contrast to William James, we are not implying a necessary connection between affect and cues to potential threat or reinforcement but simply that they tend to go together.

If one chose, one could forego the assignment of the label "function" to the above behaviors and instead postulate that it is a tendency of any system, including a conceptual or self-system, to act in a way to maintain itself or to resist "intrusion" from the outside (to borrow a phrase from Campbell, 1958). Herbart (1834) and Kohler (1929), to select two historical examples, have as an essential aspect of their theories the assumption that any psychological or experiential structure possesses as an inherent feature the energy disposing it toward maintenance of its integrity. Herbart applied the notion of self-preservation to his treatment of ideas, their competition and conjoining; whereas Kohler viewed the law of pregnanz, the "maintenance of good form," as a general law of nature expressed in all structures, physical or psychological.

Examples of Essentialness of Subject-Object Relations to Self-Survival

BRAINWASHING

Brainwashing provides one of many such examples. The entire procedure of the Chinese was to sever or render inoperative the existing subject-object relations of their captives, especially the Americans (Schein et al., 1957; Segal, 1957). Separation from their unit, breakdown of the military structure to which they had been accustomed, severance of previous friendships with military buddies, and cutting of the relationships to the folks back home were combined with other aspects of the "brainwashing" treatment to demolish the most basic ties of the captives. More telling for our point than the acceptance of communist doctrine by a relatively small number was the large prevalence of "give-up-itis" and high incidence of death among the American Army captives from the apparent loss of the will to live, resulting from refutation of their more basic ways of ordering and relating to their world.

MARGINALITY

Marginality in its many expressions could also be used to illustrate the result of severance or severe refutation of conceptual linkages to the environment, both at the human and infrahuman level. Conditions typifying such severe refutation are adolescence, old age, and such minority group status as that of the mulatto second-generation American. These, and others, are all conditions conducing toward an undifferentiated environment through either the ambiguity of the roles or through rendering inoperative the existing roles or standardized ways of responding to the environment. Effects of marginality have also been noted to occur among animals, for example, among adolescent moose and elk (Altmann, 1960). These animals, when forced from their mother, kept from the adults, and permitted to belong to no group, often acted in a way analogous to the "give-up-itis" of the many American captives in Korea with loss of the motivational vitality underlying the will to live. They failed to clean themselves, their coats became unkempt and ragged, they became susceptible to disease, and they were more likely to fall victim to preying wolves and other pitfalls in their environment.

SENSORY DEPRIVATION

Sensory deprivation, which occurs when an individual is placed in an environment where his contacts with and ties to physical aspects of his environment are impaired (Sherif and Harvey, 1952; Bexton et al., 1954; Goldberg and Holt, 1958; Miller and Ludwigh, 1958; Vernon and Hoffman, 1956), has certain characteristics that are common to both brainwashing and marginality. The individual in all these cases is faced with a highly unstructured situation, one that he has not differentiated and hence for him lacks stable points of reference by which he can successfully orient himself in time and space.

The findings of Harlow on the "need for contact" (1958) as well as the suggestive results obtained by Spitz (1949) might be illustrative of both the need to differentiate and to integrate the environment and of some of the necessary antecedent conditions for the success of these processes.

ANOMIE AND ALIENATION

Anomie and alienation, the assumed consequences of a state of normlessness at the social and personality levels respectively, probably are expressive of the same common denominator as underlies marginality, brainwashing, and sensory deprivation, namely the impairment or severance of certain of the individual's ties or linkages to important aspects of his environment. Among these examples the main difference in strain upon subject-object relatedness lies more in the nature of the object to which aspects of the self are anchored than in the nature or function of the linkage itself. Regardless of whether the object of relatedness is a physical feature in a person's environment, a social norm, or another person, all of these referents comprise anchorages to which the self in varying degrees is moored and defined. Individuals vary, of course, in the degree of centrality of or dependence of the self on the ties to the different classes of objects—to other persons, to social norms, to physical referents. Hence persons vary in their reactions to confirmation and refutation of their self ties to the different objects. The greater the centrality of the ties to any object or class of objects, the more pronounced are the consequences of confirmation and refutation. Thus the individual whose self is dependent primarily on stable linkages to other persons is maximally threatened by disapproval, or any other responses from others that portend severance of the relationship. The person who is tied more to concrete, physical aspects of his world presumably would suffer more from sensory deprivation or cut of the environmental ties. And the individual whose self is defined largely in terms of social norms and roles will suffer more severe consequences when the linkages to these object-referents are cut or threatened. The result of the severance of the status or role-linked ties is described graphically in the account of a man's self-disintegration in the novel, *Appointment in Samarra,* by John O'Hara.

Suicide is viewed by many sociologists as an outcome of anomie or impaired function of social norms (Durkheim, 1897; Powell, 1958). Particularly consistent with the present point of view is the position of Powell (1958), enunciated in conjunction with his study of occupation, status, and suicide. Viewing the self as a conceptual system embodying social norms, especially those norms surrounding status based on a successful occupation, Powell depicts suicide as being more likely in our society when failure linked to status and occupation occurs.

> When the ends of action become contradictory, unaccessible or insignificant, a condition of anomie arises. Characterized by a general loss of orientation and accompanied by feelings of "emptiness" and apathy, anomie can be simply conceived as meaninglessness. Meaning, however, is not given in the conceptual scheme as such; it emerges in action. The self creates meaning by its active encounter with the world. When dissociated from a conceptual framework, communication breaks down and the self cannot validate its existence as a "me" (Powell, 1958, p. 132).

Severance of status related self-ties such as often occurs at retirement and job failure is not the sole cause of anomie and attendant suicide. The same negative consequences may occur, Powell postulates, from "envelopment," a condition that results when the status and role referents to which the self is anchored are so numerous that none of them exercise a salient or guiding effect. At this extreme, holds Powell:

> . . . if totally enveloped by the norms of the culture, the self cannot act as an "I," but, instead, mechanically reacts to a rigidly structured "me." In both cases [envelopment and severance] the self is rendered impotent—unable to act—which engenders the meaninglessness of anomie (Powell, 1958, p. 132).

Powell's position on the conditions of anomie lead us to a closing and somewhat parenthetical comment on sensory deprivation. It is possible that effects very similar to those obtained by "depriving" an individual could be obtained by "overstimulating" him, by exposing him to an environing field of light and sound of homogeneous and high intensities. In both cases, the individual would be surrounded by an undifferentiated field where nothing stood out sufficiently saliently to serve as anchorage for the self and a guide to action.

Structure of the Conceptual or Self-System

Structural Differences Represent Variations in Quality

By structure, which in one sense represents the reciprocal of function, we mean the extent to and way in which the component concepts are individuated and interrelated within the framework of the totality of concepts. The interrelatedness among concepts comprising the self can be conceived in terms of innumerable depictions: Hebb's cell-assembly model (1949), the interpersonal linkages and interdependencies inherent in a group as represented by a sociogram, as well as by other representations of the interlocking nature of the parts of a more inclusive set of relationships. Yet it is apparent that any such depiction fails to capture and convey the entire significance of interdependencies, that of the potentially limitless variation in the *qualities* that may result from combination of the different parts and from the different combinations of the same parts. Chemistry illustrates this problem, a problem that is even more complex at the level at which we are concerned because of the greater openness of the conceptual system and the presumably larger variation in which aspects of concepts may become interrelated both in the nature of their differentiation as well as in the way they are related and hooked to others. Theoretically any kind of differentiation could occur and these conceptual "elements" could then be linked together in an infinity of possible ways: each part to every other part, reciprocally or unilaterally, or one part or series of parts to no or few others.

By structural variations in the self-system we do *not* mean differences in the referents of the subject-object relationships, although important variations in these object referents may be considered. We wish instead to stress the differences in the *nature of the linkage between the subject and the object,* the way a person has related that object to others of his relevant conceptual standards. Individuals may have concepts toward the same object, concepts which at first glance might even appear similar, such as the common response from a learned psychologist and a layman, "All psychology is psychology." From a structural standpoint, however, these two superficially similar concepts may be markedly different. The concept of the psychologist—presumably—would be based upon an abstraction derived from the integration of a large variety of individuated parts, whereas the concept of the layman would be of a different quality due to its lack of differentiation and necessary difference in the way it was integrated.

Structural Variation Is the Outcome of Differentiation-Integration

Concepts in all their variations, both intra- and inter-conceptually, represent the end product of *how* the individual has broken his world into parts and has tied these parts together. It is through differentiation and integration that the component parts of a conceptual matrix are provided, both in terms of their quality and quantity. Without this process, little or no variation could occur in the interrelatedness of concepts because, at the most, only a very global, diffuse, and unarticulated breakdown of the environment could occur.

The absence of the individuation of parts is one of the pronounced characteristics of the behavior of the human infant as well as of other undifferentiated organisms and systems. Until a certain level of differentiation is attained, stimulation of any budding part tends to result in an involuntary response of the total organism, a holistic response very different, as Murphy has stressed (1947), from the activation of a total system whose parts are well articulated and incorporated into a pattern of interrelated functioning. As the system comes to be more differentiated and its parts interdependently integrated, the engagement of single or multiple components of the system comes more under voluntary or volitional control, a condition that Goldstein and Scheerer (1941) included among their criteria of abstractness.

Unlike the undifferentiated infant who responds in a diffuse, overgeneralized way, the more highly developed person may respond by engaging one or all parts of the system at once. Such ability, although representing a landmark of more abstract activity, would at the same time indicate a condition in which wide structural variation was possible. If a physical analogy might be employed, this ability could be well illustrated by a symphony orchestra. This is a system built upon highly articulated and individuated components that are interlinked in a high state of interdependence. Yet any one instrument may be engaged in a solo, with all others inactive or serving as background. Or any or all parts can, if desired, be simultaneously activated in a synchronous way.

The conceptual counterpart of such synchronous orchestration would approach the "best of all possible worlds," to borrow from Master Pangloss, so far as the attainment of abstract functioning is concerned. The ability to engage any or all aspects of the system simultaneously as situational exigencies dictate bespeaks a high level of adaptive efficiency and psychological parsimony. Individuals vary in the extent to which they approach this quality of conceptual activity, probably with no one achieving the highest of all possible levels since the continual openness at this highest level must necessarily be an always retreating end.

Let us consider now four somewhat more specific structural properties that affect the level of abstractness attained, the quality of the self that evolves and hence the way the function of self-maintenance is reflected in differential detection, evaluation, and response, affective and overt. We first shall briefly characterize these properties and then in the final section of the chapter give examples of their effects. The properties we shall consider include: (1) *clarity-ambiguity,* (2) *compartmentalization-interrelatedness,* (3) *centrality-peripherality,* and (4) *openness-closedness,* all of which, along with other properties we are not treating, represent outgrowths of the way the environing world is differentiated and integrated. These structural properties in their infinite concatenation serve as the prism through which the world is filtered and cognitively partialed into the many aspects of reality. As individuals vary in their conceptual structures, so must they vary in their yardsticks for reading the world.

We are assuming that structural or organizational dimensions of a conceptual or self-system are continuous, varying from zero to infinity. In making this assumption, we are trying to escape some of the pitfalls of positing discontinuities, especially the insurmountable difficulty of having to specify the number of units required of a particular dimension for it to be called X, and how many units it must have before it becomes Y or Z or . . . N. Thus we avoid the problem of how central a concept must be, how much its potential affect, before it is to be called an "attitude" or some more neutral sounding term, for example. Instead of trying to specify such numerical criteria for an "attitude," we would say, for example, that concepts vary in their centrality-peripherality. A person can choose whatever gradation on this dimension he wishes and call it whatever he chooses, "attitude," "belief," or "opinion." We are not interested in what a range or point on a dimension is called. A more relevant question, it would seem to us, would be: How does a particular magnitude or dimension affect the outcome?

As persons who deal with "attitude," "value," and so forth, tend to reserve these terms for concepts of "greater" centrality, although how much greater they never say, so those dealing with "self" or "self-concept" have tended to reserve these terms for more central concepts. But they too have never faced the question of just how central a concept must be before it is considered as part of "self" or how peripheral before it is to fall in the other discontinuous category of "not-self." We would say that self is the totality of one's concepts, which vary on numerous dimensions, including centrality-peripherality, and that it is both pointless and artificial to attempt to draw discontinuous boundaries between the self and the not-self, between attitudes and other concepts. We would put the question this way: What are the effects of certain magnitudes of certain dimensions on the phenomenon under consideration?

Characterization of Structural Properties

The following organizational or systemic characteristics are assumed to be equally applicable to a single concept, to a matrix of concepts within the larger system, or to the totality of concepts constituting the self, all of which may be viewed as representing a system, albeit a miniature one in the case of a single, simple concept.

CLARITY-AMBIGUITY

Clarity-ambiguity refers to the distinctness with which the component aspects of the system, smaller or larger, are differentiated or articulated. The greater the articulateness of a concept(s), the greater is its clarity; the less the articulation or individuation, the greater is the ambiguity or the more vague are the interconceptual boundaries. Each member or instrument of a symphony orchestra would have high clarity, in that each component part is well defined within the larger organization. The status positions in a formal or otherwise well-defined group would similarly be representative of high clarity. An informal group or a set of concepts in its budding stages might be possessed of high ambiguity, of a lack of definitiveness, or of individuation of the constituent parts. The very young infant who involuntarily responds all over when stimulated is also representative of ambiguity.

COMPARTMENTALIZATION-INTERRELATEDNESS

Compartmentalization-interrelatedness refers to the extent to which concepts within a system are interconnected. A concept may remain fairly isolated from others, or it may come to be hooked to any or all of them. A necessary condition for the emergence of a group, an effective orchestra, or an abstract conceptual activity, is that the articulated concepts must become integrated into a larger framework, so that if the situation demands, a high intercommunication or interfacilitation among them can "voluntarily" be called into play.

CENTRALITY-PERIPHERALITY

Centrality-peripherality refers to the degree of essentialness of a concept to the larger constellation of concepts, the total self-system or a subsystem of the self, which might or might not be the same. There are numerous ways in which centrality may be reflected. A conceptual linkage or subject-object relationship could be completely destroyed or severed, and its effects on other concepts and the larger system noted. With the exception of concentration camps, brainwashing, death of a loved one, and similar situations, most environmental manipulations are not sufficiently severe or compelling to do this. Other manifestations of greater centrality that may be elicited by less severe refutation (or confirmation) include: higher affective arousal, either negative or positive; a more intense feeling of threat and anxiety in conditions portending violation of the directionality of the concept(s); heightened sensitivity and openness or receptivity to those stimuli perceived as confirmatory; and increased closedness to negatively relevant objects.

The place of a concept on the centrality-peripherality dimension would determine its place on what some might call the hierarchy of values or of motives.

OPENNESS-CLOSEDNESS

Openness-closedness refers to the receptivity of the system to external events or to varied interpretations of the situation. Assumed to be a function of the degree of centrality, this dimension may ultimately prove to be no more than one operation or index for centrality. It may also turn out to be synonymous with the intensity function of an attitude or other concept, being expressed in the degree of certainty and commitment one feels and hence in the number of alternative interpretations one is willing to pursue.

One operation by which openness-closedness, as we conceive of it, could be demonstrated would be the ratio of one's "latitude of acceptance," to one's "latitude of rejection," as these ranges are defined by Hovland, Harvey, and Sherif (1957). The greater the departure of this ratio from unity, in either direction, the more closed the underlying conceptual schemata would be assumed to be in one direction and the more open it would be in the other direction.

Conceptual Structure and Concreteness-Abstractness

Thus far we have not expressed explicitly the relationship that we assume to exist between concreteness-abstractness and variation in the structure of conceptual systems. The relationship, we believe, is a direct one, with any level of concreteness-abstractness reducible to the structural properties of the concepts at the particular time. To use once again the analogy to Aristotle's theory of form and matter, concreteness-abstractness may be viewed as form that encompasses the less generic structural features that may be treated as matter.

Other structural dimensions in addition to the four outlined above are no doubt necessary to account for the maximum variation in concreteness-abstractness. Yet we assume that variation in the structural properties we have described will result in variation in the level of concreteness or abstractness at which the conceptual system operates. Like any highly articulated and synchronized system—a symphony orchestra or a highly developed biological being—more abstract functioning is assumed to be rendered possible by a system of relationships comprising a multiplicity of well-defined and highly interrelated parts. More concrete functioning, on the other hand, is assumed to result from poorly differentiated concepts, which, as a consequence, are less numerous and unlikely to be interrelated. Owing to the greater frequency and interrelatedness of his conceptual parts, the more abstractly functioning person is capable of entertaining more alternatives (is more open) than is the more concretely functioning individual. Furthermore, because of the multiplicity of parts, the interrelatedness amongst them, and the attendant capacity to entertain more alternatives, no single self-referent or subject-object linkage is as central to the person with a more abstract system as it is to the individual whose conceptual system is more concrete. The greater the abstractness, the less are the definition and maintenance of the self dependent upon a single or specific self-referent or subject-object relationship. Contrarily, the greater the concreteness of a system, the greater is the likelihood of the placement of all of a person's "eggs" into a single psychological basket. A consequence of the latter state is a more brittle self-structure, one that may be more resistant to change at low levels of stress but one that, when it does yield, is more likely to break or fall to pieces. Again, the reactions of many American captives to brainwashing attempts of the Chinese seem to accord with this possibility.

Interconceptual Variation on Structural Dimensions

A point to be stressed is that not all of an individual's concepts fall at the same point on any of the above dimensions. In some of his concepts one may be very open, for example, while very closed in others. One might feel many interpretations are possible in the area of science but that there is only one religion. One set of one's concepts might be very isolated from others although other subsystems are highly interrelated. Thus a very prejudiced person might proclaim man to be his brother's keeper and also feel that Negroes are something other than human.

Because of such interconceptual variations individuals can be simultaneously more abstract on one subsystem of concepts and more concrete on others. Thus one could speak of an individual's score or place on the various dimensions for each of the subsystems separately or for the total self, that is, for all subsystems combined. It should be kept in mind that later when we speak of open-closedness, and so forth, we shall be referring to the place of an individual's *more central* set of concepts or subsystem on this dimension and *not* about his total self. Ultimately the latter problem must be faced, along with the question of the extent to which closedness, for example, in one area of concepts tends to be general across other areas.

Effects of Structural Variations on Confirmation and Refutation

The first section of this chapter was concerned with a definition of conceptual confirmation and refutation and an explication of the general conditions and effects of each. The second part of the chapter was aimed at outlining some of the more important structural or organizational dimensions of conceptual systems, variations that result in differential sensitization, evaluation, and response to the impinging events, even with the event objectively held constant. In this last section we attempt to tie together the two earlier sections by indicating briefly how variation in the systemic properties of conceptual clarity, interrelatedness, centrality, and openness may affect evaluation and response to common events.

Effect of Clarity-Ambiguity

This factor, in conjunction especially with the degree of interrelatedness of the involved concepts, operates to determine the specificity or diffuseness of the aroused affect and response inclinations. In conditions of high conceptual clarity and low interrelatedness, that is, when the concepts involved are well-defined but are more isolated from or minimally associated with others in the self-system, more specific objects are relevant. Because of the greater specificity of subject-object linkages, the resulting affect, positive or negative, and the response predilections, approach or avoidance, tend to be toward a more specific or less generalized class of objects.

In yet another case, where the involved concepts may be interrelated or connected either because they were never clearly differentiated in the first place or they were linked together following a prior differentiation, a wider range of stimuli is capable of generating affective arousal and behavioral predispositions. Critical differences exist, however, between the effects from engagement of subsystems of concepts that are interrelated in these two different ways. The activity resulting from the first instance, where the concepts involved were interrelated through their having been clearly differentiated and hooked together because of the abstraction of a common underlying dimension, could be more abstract. The individual with such a conceptual system could be more creative, could change set more easily, and could more or less voluntarily engage all or fewer of the system of concepts as the situation "demanded." On the other hand, the individual whose concepts are ill-defined and are interlinked because they have never been clearly differentiated will behave more concretely. Stimuli will have a greater "oughtness" for him because of his greater lack of differentiation, much in the fashion of the infant prior to a clear development of individuated parts. The latter individual will be more stereotyped in his responses than the former due to his greater inability to call into play in an orchestrated way his concepts singly or in totality.

If one chose, he could restrict the term "interrelatedness" to mean an interlinking or association of concepts *following* differentiation instead of applying it also to conceptual interdependencies resulting from lack of differentiation. The terming is not important as long as cognizance is taken of the basic differences between these two phenotypically similar structural states. Let us suggest how such differences may be reflected in two problem areas of psychology, anxiety and what is generally termed stimulus generalization.

Anxiety is generally defined as a fear which is ill-defined or not specific to a particular stimulus object. Such pervasiveness of affect would more likely result from real or expected refutation of concepts that were interrelated due to lack of clear differentiation. Such lack of differentiation could result either (1) from the concepts never having been differentiated, or (2) through a loss of differentiation due to some threatening or otherwise unpleasant experience, which resulted in a kind of conceptual "regression" or "dedifferentiation." Anxiety, the prerequisite of which is threat to subject-object relations, should be greater in the latter than in the former instance, especially if the concepts involved are high on the hierarchy of centrality.

Similar responses to different (but not too different) stimuli are generally referred to as stimulus generalization. We would like to suggest, following the points above, that what is called generalization may just as well occur from lack of differentiation or lack of discrimination among stimuli. Perhaps it would be more appropriate, more in keeping with the attributed relevance of stimulus generalization, if this term were reserved for behavior stemming from differentiated (clear) concepts that have been interrelated. Those phenotypically similar responses, which stem from undifferentiated (ambiguous) but interrelated concepts, might more aptly be referred to simply as lack of differentiation.

Such a distinction has several implications. Take the example, used earlier, of a learned psychologist and a layman who maintained "all psychology is psychology" and made this response across situations. The psychologist's behavior would stem from differentiated and interrelated concepts, and accordingly would be an example of stimulus generalization; but he could also make distinctions. The behavior of the layman, on the other hand, would represent the expressing of ambiguous but interrelated concepts, and hence would more nearly qualify for the label of undifferentiation.

Because it is more abstract, generalization based on differentiation and interrelatedness is more likely to lead to creative, adaptive responses. It is not unlikely that the American soldier who held that "America is the best of all possible lands" due to differentiation and integration behaved very differently toward brainwashing attempts than did the soldier who knew this response only as a kind of catechism, without differentiation.

Effects of Interrelatedness-Compartmentalization

The apparent lack of consistency of an individual's behavior across several situations, a problem that has especially plagued researchers concerned with generality of attitudes and personality, can perhaps be better understood when considered in relation to the degree of conceptual compartmentalization that characterizes the concepts of a particular person. The greater the compartmentalization, the more easily a person can vary his response without any knowledge of contradiction or feeling of conflict. In terms of avoiding conflict, compartmentalization is very effective. It is also parsimonious in terms of energy expenditure because a person never faces the problem of reconciling contradictory concepts or tendencies. Such need for reconciliation only occurs if the boundaries between the simultaneously operating concepts are not too impermeable, only if the concepts are somewhat interrelated through prior differentiation and interlinking of them.

Concepts characterized by a high degree of clarity and compartmentalization dispose one toward both specific and stereotyped evaluation of and response to the situation, specific because of the definitiveness of the concepts and stereotyped as a consequence of isolation from the influence of other concepts.

Greater compartmentalization of concepts could result from at least two reasons: (1) from failure ever to have linked the concept(s) to other concepts; or (2) from having relinquished such linkage through a kind of "deintegration," employed as a defensive maneuver to avoid the conflict or punishment experienced from interrelating or associating the particular concepts. For example, the child who learns that one is his brother's keeper and proceeds to apply this concept to a Negro may meet with unfavorable consequences that result in his severing the ill-defined connection between the two concepts. Compartmentalization due to the latter conditions probably would be more difficult to overcome than that stemming from the former circumstances.

Effects of Centrality-Peripherality

This is the dimension more often recognized as crucial to attitude functioning and change. The more central a concept the more resistant the individual is to changing it, the greater the negative affect when it is refuted and the higher the positive affect when it is confirmed. Similarly the stronger are the behavioral tendencies of approach or avoidance as centrality is increased. When the operative concepts are rendered in conflict, such as generally occurs in an attitude change situation where concepts toward the "source" and target "issue" are rendered incompatible, one seems to behave in the way that favors the more central concept(s). A central concept coming into loggerheads with a peripheral concept results in little conflict and little negative affect because the change easily occurs in the weaker concept with the more central one left largely unaltered.

It is assumed that the total degree of centrality, at least in terms of the strength of response potential and affective arousal, as we proposed earlier, is some multiplicative function of centrality and the number of concepts involved. Thus although one would behave in a way to favor A, a more central concept, when it is pitted singly against either B or C, which in relation to A are less central concepts, when B and C are combined against A the pattern of choice and behavioral resolution would now favor the combination of B and C if their pooled centrality were greater than A's. Clearly such conceptual mechanics are yet to be worked out, although the early work on conflict (Underwood, 1949) seems to be in line with this possibility.

Because of variations in the training conditions underlying conceptual differentiation and integration (Chapters 5 and 6) any of one's concepts or subsystems of concepts can come to be of greatest centrality to him. The subsystems to which much of this book is later devoted are assumed to represent constellations of concepts of greatest centrality to different persons. It should be kept in mind, however, that when we treat the subsystems of concepts taken to be most central to that particular individual that we are not assuming we are characterizing the conceptual functioning of that individual across all of his concepts. To the extent that the other concepts were similar in degree of centrality, compartmentalization, and the like, the greater, we imagine, would be the likelihood of such a possibility. We would like to suggest that the old question of generality of attitudes, personality, values, and so forth, all of which represent concepts for us, might prove more meaningful and potentially solvable if these structural properties are taken into consideration.

Effects of Openness-Closedness

Complete closedness would mean the inaccessibility to external impingements; if one's concepts were completely closed they would be impossible to refute. No effect, therefore, affective or otherwise, would result. Extreme racists often manifest such a degree of closedness that it is virtually impossible to get "information" into their system. Closedness, which seems to stem largely from greater centrality, gives rise to the tendency to ward off potentially refuting stimuli.

But what is refutive varies with the particular structure and level of abstractness attained by a set of concepts. One can presumably be closed at any level of concreteness-abstractness, but because of structural variations the closedness would be reflected quite differently. For example, at the more concrete level, where one's concepts tend to be more bifurcated, absolutistic, and black-white, one tends to be closed to events that imply multiple and alternate evaluations of the situation. At a more abstract level of functioning, where one's concepts include multiple alternatives and relativistic premises, closedness would be to absolutism, categoricalness, the very things to which the more concrete individual would be open.

A further, perhaps even more basic, difference between the closedness of a more abstract and a more concrete system lies in the length of the time interval in which conceptual closedness is maintained. For the more abstractly functioning system closedness would be more temporary and is more likely to occur only during the time that the environmental "input" is being differentiated and integrated with existing parts. For the more concretely functioning system, on the other hand, closedness is of longer and more invariant duration, with less likelihood of even short-termed opening of the system to admit in new "inputs." The more abstractly functioning individual might deliberately "close his mind" to new impingements while he was maximally "squeezing" information out of prior "inputs." The more concretely functioning person might actively ward off the new impingements, not so much to facilitate articulation, as to avoid threat to his more brittle conceptual structure in which only a minimal number of distinctions of any impingement are possible.

Stimuli can become so threatening and can portend such degrees of conceptual refutation and negative affect that they are almost exclusively warded off. Such extreme closedness, representative of certain psychotics, will be illustrated in more detail in Chapter 9.

Some evidence from real-life, non-laboratory cases seem to suggest that the individual strives more toward maintenance of a particular level of concreteness-abstractness, reflected in variations in the structural properties we have described than of a particular content or directionality of a concept. For example, Whittaker Chambers, an avid Communist one day, was an equally avid anti-Communist the next. Or an avid and closed religious zealot may become a vehement atheist. In such instances, which could be multiplied ad infinitum, the directionality of the concept is reversed but such structural aspects as centrality and closedness are kept more intact.

These examples in which conceptual direction is reversed but structure is maintained, reflected dramatically in the shift from love to hate, as described by Freud, follow the notions of saccadic functioning (described in Chapter 2), which is more likely to occur at the more concrete levels of functioning due to poverty of conceptual alternatives. Given an either-or view of the world, when an event does not fit a person, it is automatically placed in the opposite category.

The same tendency to change the directionality of a concept more readily than to alter its organizational characteristics under conditions of greater concreteness such as high centrality, high compartmentalization, and high closedness, is often seen in reactions to psychotherapy, examples of which will be presented in Chapter 10.

Let us call attention to one implication of the above for behavior theory, to difference in interpretation that may result from focusing attention on the more phenotypic versus the more genotypic aspects of behavior. In terms of the more phenotypic, such directional "flip-floppers" as those described above would be viewed as behavioral opposites. Yet if the yardstick for gauging were conceptual organization, then such phenotypic reversal would be seen as opposite expressions of the same thing.

There is no question but that the consequences of such directional changes are significant, especially if the effects on other persons are considered. At the same time, we must not assume that because behavioral expression may take opposite forms that the underlying structure has also undergone a parallel inversion. One possible implication of this for attitude scaling is that a neutrality point should not be placed between the positive and negative poles, but instead the negative and positive poles should be more adjacent to coincide with their greater structural similarities. This point is also relevant for those few remaining psychologists who think of themselves as classical Behaviorists.

The importance of structural variations in a person's system of concepts becomes more apparent when they are considered in relation to different levels of development on stages of concreteness-abstractness, the major concern of the next chapter.

4 Stages of Conceptual Development

How do concepts develop? We view concepts as jointly determined by the internal state of the organism and conditions of the relevant environment. Out of this interdependent totality of dispositional and situational determinants our emphasis shall be on those internal states represented by the stage of development of the individual at the particular time and on those external factors embodied in the training conditions to which the individual is exposed. The present chapter deals specifically with the stages of development; the next chapter considers the specific training conditions that affect the course of development through these stages. In the present chapter we consider these training conditions only very generally, in terms of their either favoring or restricting progression in development at a particular stage. Once the stages of development have been set forth in this chapter, then the specific effects of training described in the next chapter may be seen more clearly.

The Process of Development

Development was described earlier as a saccadic process, occurring as a series of "bursts" or "leaps." In saccadic movement there is an initial placing of end points, boundaries, or brackets around a concept, providing the basis for making finer discriminations between the antithetical poles. When training conditions permit these developmental leaps to occur, it is as if the organism were experiencing two readings or perceptions of the same event or object. The process of development is thus viewed as consisting of generating and integrating discrepant feedback or differentiations from the environment. Saccadic development is identical to the general notions underlying the term "plateau" in learning and to what Bartlett (1958) has called "closing the gap" in thinking.

An essential assumption in the present approach is the importance of antithetical poles or opposites in development. Ilg and Ames have remarked, "Nature seems to have this awkward way of going to opposite extremes as the child develops" (Ilg and Ames, 1955, p. 31). If considered from the viewpoint of progressive development, the process may not be entirely awkward, as the following points illustrate:

1. The discrimination of extreme opposites can be made more easily than the discrimination between less different stimuli. Once these opposite poles have been discriminated, the person is in a position to make finer and more difficult discriminations. The reference points placed around the extreme limits of a given conceptual system (that is, the two poles) therefore serve as anchorages for making finer discriminations within the "gap."

2. Interpretations based on opposite poles are more easily integrated than differentiations based on concepts that have no necessary relationship to each other. That is, black and white are opposites, but they are also both colors. Therefore the very opposition of the two poles on the same dimension facilitates integration whereas the integration of differentiations based on unrelated anchors would be more difficult.

3. If the person can differentiate such opposing poles and integrate them, such a process represents the "optimal" developmental leap because the emerging conceptual system would have the characteristics of maximal abstractness relative to the poles of the original concept on which it was based.

The facilitating effects of "opposites" upon progression may be viewed in another way. Progression is facilitated under conditions of clarity of the initial concept, openness of the developing concept to discrepant (particularly opposing) events, and the successful integration of these two systems of mapping into a new conceptual schema.[1]

This view of the process of development is one of emerging concepts. When training conditions favor the generation of discrepant conceptual orderings (opposing poles) a new synthesis can emerge if the opposing or discrepant differentiations can be integrated. The new synthesis

[1] Differentiation and integration were described earlier as the vehicles through which various levels of abstractness emerged. In ageement with Murphy's (1947) view of development, in three phases extending from a stage of greater diffuse wholeness to integration, we view each stage of development in the same way. However, we view the process of progression *from any stage to the next most abstract stage* as including three related and perhaps simultaneous phases: (1) the base or initial stage, which is more concrete, more diffuse, and non-conflicting; (2) the emergence of discrepant or conflicting differentiations; and (3) the integration of the new and old differentiations into an emergent, more abstract conceptual schema. We deal with the above three aspects as *phases* of progression from one stage of development to the next most abstract stage, *not as stages* as Murphy's language implies.

contains modified aspects of the two initially discrepant poles. When a new synthesis emerges, it in turn serves as a baseline for the possible generation of new discrepant differentiations and the development of new syntheses.

For the most part, the present chapter is concerned with a description of certain syntheses that serve as nodal points or plateaus in development as it progresses from more concrete to more abstract linkages for dealing with a given range of stimuli. Although there are innumerable facets of conceptual development, we emphasize four syntheses or nodal stages representing four levels along the concrete-abstract dimension. The more concrete stages emerge from the synthesis or integration of simpler, more bifurcated poles, whereas the more abstract stages emerge from the integration of poles characterized by a more complex conceptual structure.

The Order or Course of Development

From the present viewpoint we assume that the most general effect of developmental conditions is the extent to which these conditions induce openness or closedness of the concepts to discrepant differentiations (developmental leaps), required for the emergence of more abstract concepts for coping with a given range of stimuli. Furthermore, viewing development in terms of progressive stages implies that certain more concrete systems of ordering must be mastered or articulated before more abstract levels can emerge. *Assuming that environmental conditions facilitate openness to the discrepant conceptual orderings or differentiations required for progression, we maintain that the development of more abstract conceptual structures follows a given course.*

In this chapter we assume training conditions that permit progressive development and outline (a) the discrepant poles and (b) the nature of the syntheses or integrations that emerge at various levels along the concrete-abstract dimension. These are presented in Table 1.

Table 1 will be elaborated and clarified in this chapter and to some extent in Chapter 5 since the course of development cannot be fully described in the absence of the specification of the training conditions. However, Table 1 presents the conceptual poles that generate discrepant or conflicting differentiations of relevant stimuli in the proposed order, at each level of abstractness. The table also indicates the nature of the emergent, more abstract concept, following the synthesis of the two more concrete poles at each level.

It is apparent that the developmental leap at each stage involves the integration of one form of "dependence" and one form of "independ-

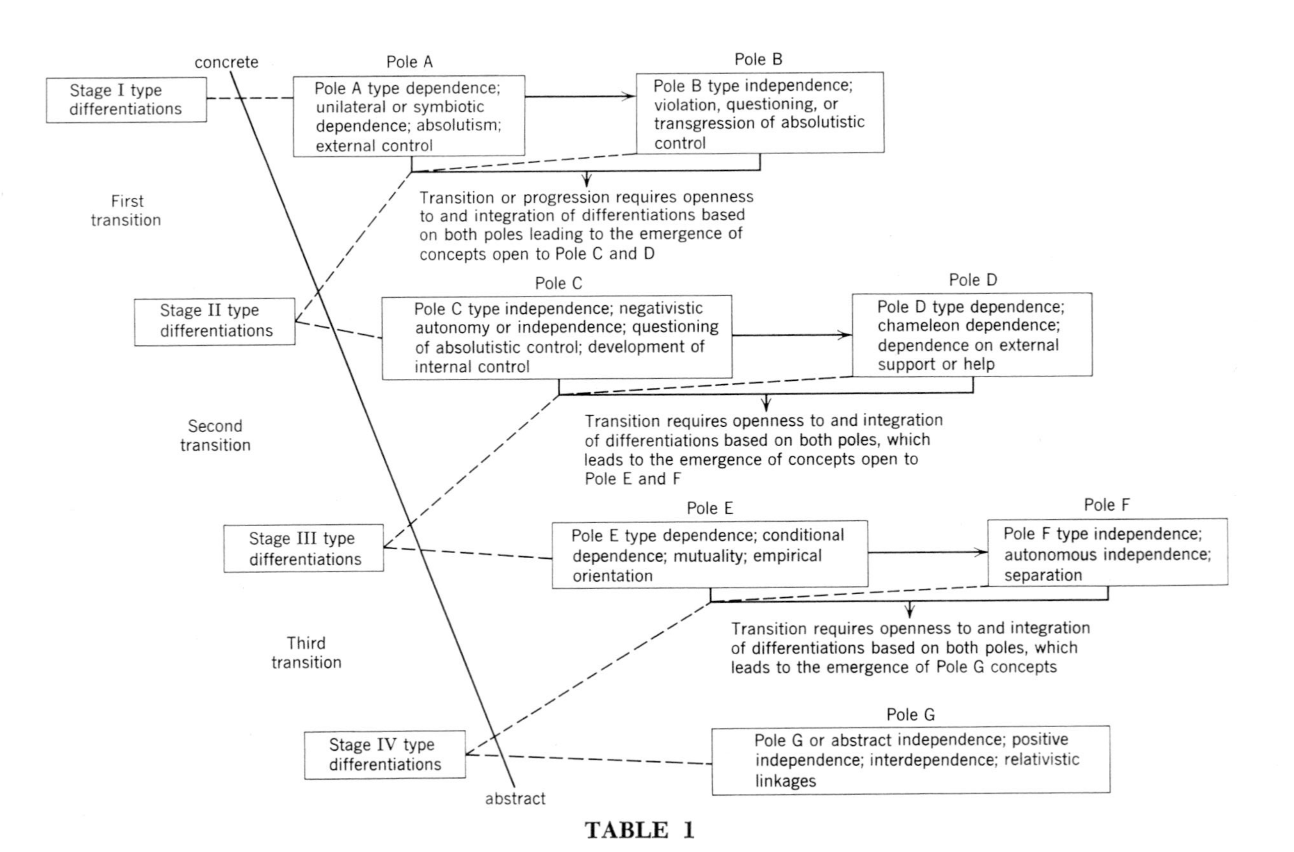

TABLE 1

Stages of Progressive Development

ence." In its most general form, then, progressive development involves the emergence of more abstract conceptual schemata for mediating these two basic orientations. The "independent" pole of a concept at one level (for example, pole B) is somewhat similar to the "independent" pole of the emergent concept at the next level (for example, pole C). The same is true of successive "dependent" poles.

Although not immediately apparent in Table 1, the "independent" poles at differing levels of abstractness differ in terms of their embeddedness in a different concept. For example, pole B (opposition) at the first level is embedded in a system of ordering extending to unilateral dependence on absolutistic standards, whereas pole C (second stage independence) is embedded in a system of ordering extending to dependence upon a *differentiated* source or object of support. Independence at the second stage (pole C) is described within a different system of ordering than at the first stage.

The Results of Development: Progression and Arrestation

1. PROGRESSIVE DEVELOPMENT

Progressive development at every stage involves training conditions that induce openness of the conceptual system to differentiations (or evaluations) based on both opposing poles of the most central concept, and the integration of these conflicting differentiations into a new conceptual system. As described in Table 1, progression therefore refers to the emergence of concepts that are open to differentiations based on both poles. This permits positive, or approach tendencies, to both poles as well as the potential occurrence of the conflicting differentiations required for progression. Four stages representing the four conceptual systems or syntheses shown in Table 1 are discussed as the first, second, third, and fourth stages in the development of more abstract forms of subject-object linkages.

Before proceeding to a more detailed consideration of the process of development and the stages involved, an initial "common sense" overview of these nodal stages may help provide a general orientation for this chapter. We begin our study of the developmental process at the point where an individual is placed in a new or novel situation.[1]

[1] In beginning with this stage, we assume that development has progressed beyond a stage of omnipotence (Ausubel, 1952; Sullivan, 1953). That is, what we refer to as "the first stage" assumes that the subject has already developed the potential for learning in response to the methods outlined in the next chapter and that he has developed a relationship to the source. Failure to do so is illustrated by early infantile autism (Kanner, 1943).

To the extent that the situation is novel, the individual finds himself in an unstructured situation in which there is a minimum of development of concepts or programs for transforming stimuli into response systems. As such, the concepts are maximally undifferentiated, and the subject will be maximally sensitized to external control. Functioning at this relatively undifferentiated level is more bifurcated and is aimed toward establishing structure and the avoidance of ambiguity. This stage, characterized by more absolutistic or concretistic concepts, is referred to as the first stage. In child development this level of functioning represents greater dependence on the field and *less* articulateness of his world.

The second stage in development of more abstract concepts is described as typifying a gross differentiation of the self from the external field. It represents the emergence of internal control. If an individual is to develop to more abstract levels of functioning in a given area, then he must develop the potential to utilize conceptual orderings as tools since otherwise he will remain a slave to the more externally derived, fixed concepts of the first stage. Progression beyond the initial stage represents the emergence of the potential to free oneself, in Fromm's (1941) terms, from absolutism and to manipulate or reorganize a given ordering system in the absence of external control. Second stage functioning is characterized by the questioning of control, oppositional tendencies, the testing of limits, and an avoidance of dependence.

After an individual's conceptual orientations are differentiated from external control, the possibility of *dependence* emerges since the successful differentiation of the self from the external field does not automatically imply an independence from field forces. Indeed, it is only after such a differentiation that the individual can begin to articulate the external world and his unique relationship to it. Further progression therefore involves the "testing out" of alternate conceptual orderings. At this third stage the individual reorganizes his own concepts (internal causation) in order to experience the consequences of these different orderings. Third stage functioning, involving a high degree of sensitization to the reactions of others, will be characterized by mutuality, conditional dependence, and an "empirical" attitude. During the third stage the individual is still relatively dependent upon the reactions of other people in testing the consequences of given conceptual orderings. Further progression to the most abstract stage considered involves the development of internal and informationally-based concepts that act as a referent for evaluating feedback from the environment, including the reactions of other people.

Functioning at the fourth stage is maximally abstract, involving the availability of a variety of conceptual orderings along which stimuli can be differentially evaluated. As a result such functioning may involve the integration of differentiated concepts into abstract internal referents. At this stage the person is not only clearly differentiated from the field but also he has developed the capacity to reorder and resynthesize articulated concepts. Therefore, functioning at this stage is described in terms of the individual's maintaining an interdependent relationship with the environment around him.

2. ARRESTATION AT A GIVEN STAGE

If environmental pressures are out of synchrony with the conceptual structures required for the emergence of a more abstract synthesis, fixation or arrestation of development occurs. Viewed conceptually, such asynchrony produces one positive pole and one negative pole at a given level, an effect which prevents progression. In terms of the first stage described in Table 1, if environmental pressures inducing openness to unilateral dependence and closedness to opposition to absolutistic control are experienced, then pole A (unilateral dependence) becomes positive and pole B (internal control) becomes negative, and the net effect is arrestation at the first stage.

Asynchrony in relation to the first stage might also take the form of environmental pressure inducing openness to opposition (approach tendencies to pole B) while inducing closedness to unilateral dependence (withdrawal tendencies to pole A). The net effect in this circumstance is also arrestation, but at the second stage. The more specific details of such arrestation will be treated in Chapter 5.

3. TRANSITIONAL ARRESTATION

If environmental pressures are out of synchrony with the conceptual structure in such a way that each of the two poles becomes both positive and negative, transitional arrestation, or arrestation between two stages, results. Such environmental pressure simultaneously induces both positive and negative evaluations of each pole, thus retarding integration and the evolvement of more abstract systems of ordering for transforming impinging stimuli into responses.

General Introductory Remarks

RELATED CONCEPTIONS

In positing a particular order of progressive development, which interacts with environmental conditions, we are in agreement with a number of earlier writers. In using the concept "transitoriness of instincts," William James (1890) contended that the instinct would not materialize unless it was triggered off by particular environmental stimuli at a given time. Later Tinbergen (1955) demonstrated a similar effect experimentally by his work on imprinting. He showed that ducklings could be taught to follow a given object (rather than their mother) if exposed to that object at a given stage in development, but not at other ages. Moreover, once learned at a critical period, such a response tended to persist. Many studies on maturation indicate that the mastery of a skill proceeds at a much faster rate during certain stages of development. Training before this stage has little effect, but if the training is delayed too far beyond this critical stage, a permanent deficit may result (Shepard and Breed, 1913; Bird, 1925; Carmichael, 1926; Gesell and Thompson, 1929).

Freud (1938) posited stages in personality development that are ordered in terms of the nature of psychosexual attachments. He further postulated that fixation or arrestation of development could occur at any level as a result of "excessive" frustration or "excessive" gratification of the psychosexual attachments at that level. Presumably, in progression there is an absence of such excesses. The traditional psychoanalytic approach, which has been integrated into a more generic framework by such writers as Fromm (1941), Sullivan (1953), Horney (1937), and Erikson (1950), postulated opposite training effects as antecedent conditions for fixation. Whiting and Child (1953) point out that excessive gratification and excessive frustration should produce different effects. However, it is also possible that both extremes could produce different forms of arrestation or fixation at the same level of progressive development, a possibility that we later explore in detail. In addition, other recent investigators (for example, Hess, 1959) assume that (1) development is characterized by progressive stages and (2) that training interacts with these stages of development.

RANGE OF RELEVANCE

We assume that the principles of development described apply to a fairly broad range of developmental phenomena: child development, development of groups, concept development, development of complex skills in education, and the like. Thus, although we emphasize child development and speak of the developing organism, we assume that the principles are fairly generic. As such, the work of Piaget (1932, 1954), Gesell (1940, 1948, 1956), Erikson (1950), Ausubel (1958), Sullivan (1953), Sullivan, Grant, and Grant (1957) in child development; Bennis and Shepard (1956), Martin and Hill (1957) in the development of small groups; Kennedy (1960) in the development of simulated groups; Parsons (1955) in the development of cultures; and Freud (1938), Rotter (1954), and Rogers (1958) in the development of therapeutic relationships are relevant to the present view. In short, the present treatment is seen as relevant to all forms of *psychological* development, viewed structurally.

Throughout this chapter, as in this book generally, we are dealing with the structure rather than the content of experience. In considering development we are not concerned with growth curves or the increasing magnitude of any particular response. Whatever the subject is learning (attitudes toward parents or group members, attitudes toward religion or mathematics) our emphasis is upon developmental changes in the concepts that mediate between stimuli on the one hand and responses on the other. This approach to development says nothing about *what is being learned;* it is relevant only to the stages of development of concepts that generate the learned responses.

One qualifying assumption may be noted here. In contending that development occurs through a series of progressive stages, we are assuming that the development in question begins in a novel situation. If a person is placed in a novel situation, or if a situation becomes sufficiently novel, then we would expect conceptual development to proceed according to the stages described. We return to this point later, but mention it here for emphasis because if the situation is not novel, or if the person has experienced developmental progression in related areas that generalize to the new area, then the progressive nature of development, especially in its earlier stages, becomes more difficult to observe since these earlier stages become "collapsed" in time, as it were.

MOST EVIDENCE RELEVANT TO STAGES OF DEVELOPMENT IS OBSERVATIONAL

The notions underlying progressive development are central to the later dimensionalization of functioning and training methods. However, these assumptions regarding development are presented in the sense of general guide lines, rather than as empirical facts. In utilizing these assumptions the reader will discover that much of the evidence presented in this chapter is anecdotal and observational. Although we are aware of the difficulties in using such evidence, there is no apparent alternative available. Therefore, we evaluate our view toward development against these observations in terms of their consistency. We hope that these assumptions regarding development will lead to useful formulations. However, the present explication of assumptions also brings them into the potential domain of empirical investigation in their own right.

Having presented a brief overview of our approach to development, a more detailed consideration of each stage is now undertaken. The relevant observations and materials related to those stages are presented.

First Stage: Unilateral Dependence

Conceptual systems in the first stage are characterized by external control, by the acceptance of externally derived concepts or schemata not built up through experience with the actual stimuli, and by the absolutistic nature of such concepts. In a new or relatively unstructured situation, a person's functioning is maximally anchored in external control and is therefore characterized by seeking external criteria for evaluating his behavior. The term unilateral is intended to convey the fact that functioning in this stage is adjusted to match absolutistic, ready-made conceptual criteria. Unilateral dependence implies a lack of differentiation between a rule and its purpose; between authority and one's own experience; between one's thoughts about authority and oneself. First stage functioning is assumed to have the following characteristics: things are endowed with power as in magical thought; answers to questions are accepted more in the sense of absolutes (Werner, 1957); thinking is more concrete ("this is the way it is because it is"); behavior associated with this stage is characterized by a greater immediacy, by greater sensitivity to limits, to what is right and wrong, to what is tolerated and not tolerated, and by greater submissiveness to external control.

According to Bennis and Shepard (1956) the first stage in the development of a group involves a preoccupation with authority and submission, or in their words, ". . . the characteristic expectations of group members are that the trainer will establish rules of the game and distribute rewards. He is presumed to know what the goals are or ought to be" (p. 420). At this stage these authors view the group's behavior as a plea for the leader to tell them what to do. In problem solving the beginning stage of conceptual functioning is characterized by rigidity and all-or-none shifting. In the initial stage of psychotherapy, patients begin by seeking a direct solution (Rogers, 1951), or as Rotter (1954) observed, they hope that ". . . the therapist will . . . either in some magical way provide him with a better personality or in some way or other remove the frustrations from his external circumstances" (p. 355).

In the study of the moral development of the child, Piaget (1932) refers to this stage as moral realism. According to Piaget, this stage possesses three features:

> . . . In the first place, duty, as viewed by moral realism, is essentially heteronomous. Any act that shows obedience to a rule or even to an adult, regardless of what he may command, is good; any act that does not conform to rules is bad. A rule is therefore not in any way something elaborated, or even judged or interpreted by the mind; it is given as such, readymade and external to the mind. It is also conceived of as revealed by the adult and imposed by him. The good, therefore, is rigidly defined by obedience.
>
> In the second place, moral realism demands that the letter rather than the spirit of the law shall be observed. This feature derives from the first. . . .
>
> In the third place, moral realism induces an objective conception of responsibility. We can even use this as a criterion of realism, for such an attitude toward responsibility is easier to detect than the two that precede it. For since he takes rules literally and thinks of good only in terms of obedience, the child will at first evaluate acts not in accordance with the motive that has prompted them, but in terms of their exact conformity with established rules (pp. 106–107).

According to the normative observations made by the staff at the Gesell Institute of Child Development (Ilg and Ames, 1955), characteristics of conceptual functioning similar to those in the first stage are first observed at about the age of two. The normative two-year-old ". . . can occasionally put another person's wishes above his own. . . . though he cannot as yet share with other children. . . ." (p. 25). As the authors point out, however, early child development is characterized by rapid and violent swings from one extreme of functioning to another. The stages are close together so that the normative two-and-a-half-year-old child is stubborn and domineering.

It appears from the observational data that a child encountering a relatively new environmental demand is likely to begin an entirely new developmental cycle. Thus behavior typical of this first stage of functioning was reported to be characteristic of children of two, five, ten, and sixteen years of age. (See Table 2.) The relationship of first stage functioning to new environmental demands may be seen when we note that these ages approximate the normative years when children (1) begin to talk, (2) begin school, group play, (3) begin to look to peers as opposed to the family as a model, and (4) begin to take on the adult role, respectively. For example, the normative five-year-old is described as ". . . a good age. . . . His mother is the center of his world. . . . He likes to do things with her and for her, likes to obey her commands. He likes to be instructed and get permission" (p. 33). And the normative ten-year-old, after passing through all ranges of behavior, as ". . . his parents' word is so utterly law . . . He not only obeys easily

TABLE 2

Cyclical and Saccadic Nature of Progressive Social Development *

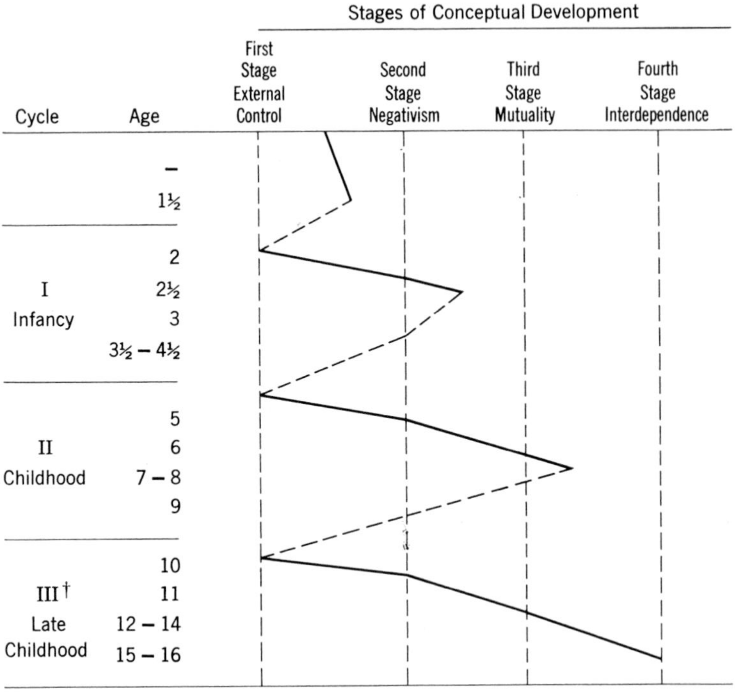

Cycle	Age	Stages of Conceptual Development: First Stage External Control	Second Stage Negativism	Third Stage Mutuality	Fourth Stage Interdependence
	–				
	1½				
I Infancy	2				
	2½				
	3				
	3½ – 4½				
II Childhood	5				
	6				
	7 – 8				
	9				
III† Late Childhood	10				
	11				
	12 – 14				
	15 – 16				

* Based on an interpretation of the normative observations taken at the Gesell Institute (Ilg and Ames, 1955).
† This part of the graph is hypothetical to show the expected progression to more abstract functioning in the third cycle.

and naturally, but he seems to expect to obey and gains status in his own eyes by his obedience" (Ilg and Ames, p. 40). Naturally first stage behavior at five is different from first stage behavior at ten, particularly if progression through more abstract levels has occurred between these ages. Less difference between first stage functioning at different ages would be expected if arrestation occurred at an early age (see Chapters 5 and 6). Developmental norms representing a return to an earlier stage of organization after progression to varying levels of abstractness would be required for diagnosis or a statistical description of development.

Since first stage functioning may be quite desirable from the source's standpoint (for example, the parents' wishes) he may attempt to prevent the subject's progression beyond this stage. Procedures that prevent progression beyond the first stage may be implicitly justified by conceiving of first stage functioning as highly desirable and valued. For example, in education, absolutistic functioning is often confused with development; in dogma it can be viewed as faith; in totalitarian states as being a good citizen; and in personal development as being "good," obedient, or trustworthy. Although this early level of functioning represents some degree of all these "positive" characteristics and may be advantageous in certain situations, the nature of relatedness in the first stage is nonetheless concrete, unilateral, and absolutistic.

Transition to the Second Stage (First Transition)

In order for development to progress beyond this unilateral level of functioning, new differentiations must evolve and become integrated with old differentiations. From pole A of first stage concepts, the opposite pole of the conceptual system, which represents the simplest and next most abstract differentiation, is resistance to external control (pole B). Training that induces sufficient openness to such oppositional tendencies, and simultaneously sufficient openness to and trust in external control, maximizes the potential for integrating these opposing motivational tendencies and for developmental progression to the second stage. In common language, parents whose behavior both promotes trust and gives permission and encouragement to develop assertiveness, opposition, and age-appropriate independence provide the necessary basis for developmental progress to what we refer to as the second stage.

Through the integration of differentiations based on unilateral absolutistic control and opposition to external control, the subject is able (1) to free himself from the constraints of symbiotic dependence, (2) to differentiate between external and internal control, and (3) to manipulate the criterion applied to his own behavior through the potential of generating different systems of ordering outside the framework of external control. Under conditions of progression, first stage tendencies are less absolutistic and second stage tendencies are less negativistic, compared to functioning that is arrested at these stages.

The emergence of second stage concepts involves the differentiation of the subject from the source, thus opening the possibility of dependency at a different level of abstraction. The difference between dependency in the form of evaluating others as supportive and dependency in the form of viewing others in terms of absolutistic control is similar to the difference between imitation and symbiotic relatedness. Dependency in the form of mutuality cannot be experienced until the self and the source have been differentiated.

Second Stage: Negative Independence

Negative independence represents functioning that is negatively related to external constraints. Since such functioning represents a lessening of the importance of external control and the initial budding of internal control, we use the term, negative independence; the term does not imply any necessary hostility or aggression. Hostile reactions represent the extreme manifestations of closed second stage relatedness, which denotes the arrestation of development at this stage. For progression to occur beyond the first stage, the subject must test the limits of absolute solutions and rules in order to avoid complete reliance on externally given conceptual systems; otherwise he will remain dependent upon external control. A person working in a problem-solving situation, for example, would never attempt an alternative solution unless he resisted or questioned the initial solution. Such questioning cannot occur if the person feels that the original solution is absolute and under the control of the source.

Second stage concepts represent a differentiation from external forces, but such concepts are not highly articulated. However, they are the foundations on which informational and interdependent standards can develop and represent the initial form of internal control. Put in the language of the present conception of development, the person must successfully progress through second stage concepts in order to move on to the third and fourth stages.

This stage has been referred to as "freedom from" authoritarian control and contrasted with positive freedom, independence, or "freedom to" (Fromm, 1941). Coffey (1954) refers to an early stage of "resistance" in group psychotherapy, and Bennis and Shepard (1956) report that group development proceeds from a preoccupation with submission to a preoccupation with rebellion. Functioning at this stage is characterized by such clichés as "I'll do it myself"; by the emergence of "self will."

A comprehensive study of the emergence of a period of resistance in infants and young children has been carried out by Levy (1955). He gives many examples, such as "the battle of the spoon" and "clash of wills" and includes certain forms of "shyness" in this class. According to Levy:

> Whatever the measure of non-compliance,—the intelligence test, the physical examination, observations of spontaneous behavior, experiments, the clinical case record or ordinary inquiry—all studies confirm the existence of a period in the early childhood of most children in which

negativism is more frequent than in the period preceding or following. . . . There was a clear rise in frequency as the age of 18 months was reached, and a decided fall in frequency when the age of two years was past. The findings were also consistent with the mother's accounts of the child's behavior at home (p. 210). [And later in considering the common features of oppositional behavior he states] A number of them appear to have a common function of resistance to external influence. This influence would determine when an act is to begin, . . . and when it is to end. . . . (p. 213).

Observations at the Gesell Institute (Ilg and Ames, 1955) indicate a period of negativism directly following the "obedient" stages outlined under the first stage (see Table 2). The first onset of second stage functioning was observed at about eighteen months and again at two and one-half, six, and presumably again, at about eleven. At two and one-half behavior was described as:

He wants exactly what he wants when he wants it. . . . Everything has to be done just so. Everything has to be right in the place he considers its proper place. . . . With no ability to choose between alternatives . . . the child at this age shuttles back and forth endlessly between any two extremes, seeming to be trying to include both in his decision. "I will—I won't." . . . He wants to go on and on with whatever he is doing (pp. 25–26).

This behavior, characterized by conflict between compliance and opposition and rituals and stubbornness is an excellent example of the transition between first and second stage functioning, which is described in detail in the chapters to follow.

At two and one-half the conflicting first and second stage tendencies do not appear to be well integrated, as shown by the continued vacillation between "will-ing" and "won't-ing" as well as by ritualistic behavior. In the next cycle of development from five to ten (second swing of the pendulum in Table 2) children demonstrate the characteristics of a more successful transition to second stage conceptual functioning. At six years of age, typical behavior is much closer to our description of negative independence, internal control, and the avoidance of dependency. Normative functioning is described as:

. . . *he* wants to be the center of his world, even though he hasn't yet developed a secure sense of himself [negative independence]. . . . Whatever is wrong, Mother gets the blame [externalization of blame]. . . . he tends to be extremely negative in his response to others. That he has been asked to do something is in his eyes sufficient reason for refusing to do it [internal control and avoidance of dependency] (Ilg and Ames, 1955, pp. 34–35).

The progression to second stage functioning is perhaps the most critical point in child development, education, and group development.

As Levy states, "Without this resistant character the organism's response would be determined entirely by external stimuli. . . . The capacity to resist external influence thus enables the organism to use and develop inner controls" (p. 213). Levy also quotes a study by Hetzer (1929) who compared two groups of seven-year-old children divided on the presence or absence of a "stubborn period" in development. Children who had not gone through the "stubborn period" were significantly more dependent on the teacher's help than others.

The value, therefore, of second stage functioning lies primarily in its providing the essential basis for the development of mutuality, dependence, and later interdependence. In order to appreciate this value, the observer must view this stage in developmental perspective. The immediate quality of second stage functioning may strike the observer as disagreeable. In contrast to first stage functioning which may be viewed as desirable by certain sources, the oppositional quality of second stage functioning may be strongly resisted by power-oriented, absolutistic sources or by sources who are insecure regarding their own status and competence. The immature quality of second stage functioning may also prove threatening since it is likely to be less predictable or dependable. Despite these immediate, potentially disagreeable qualities, second stage functioning is an essential stage in development. The overthrow of feudalism, authoritarian control, or the divine right of kings is analagous to the transition to second stage functioning. As Fromm (1941) has so eloquently described, however, such revolutions do not magically lead to true independence or interdependence. In nations, as in individuals, development is assumed to proceed through stages, but national development is slower because the controlling authority of nations is generally very effective in prohibiting oppositional behavior. Indeed, first stage functioning, on the part of the masses, is usually enforced and held up as a model of citizenship. In this sense many revolutions, regardless of the change in creed, do not represent what we mean by progression; they are power battles within the first stage in which the outcome merely changes the external authority.

Transition to the Third Stage (*Second Transition*)

The extreme pole of second stage concepts would allow for such differentiations as evaluating others as interfering with negative independence on the one hand and as models or supportive agents on the other. Progression to third stage represents approach tendencies toward, openness to, and the successful integration of differentiations based on these opposite poles of the second stage. Only those training conditions that simultaneously generate differentiations based on opposition to external control and dependency on others lead to the emergence of third stage concepts; such concepts are open to differentiations based on both mutuality and autonomy and allow further progression of the second stage conceptual system to dependency ties. The integration of the two opposing motivational tendencies in level II transition represents the emergence of a new conceptual system in which the form of relatedness to objects involves conditional dependence and mutuality. As development progresses through these stages the form of relatedness becomes progressively less stimulus bound, more relativistic, and less unilateral. Although the third stage represents a swing toward dependency, this form of dependency is markedly different from that described in the first stage.

Third Stage: Conditional Dependence and Mutuality

This stage may be characterized by conditional or "as if" functioning, in that it involves learning about one's relationship to the environment in a more objective way. The progression is from externally derived structure (first stage) through resistance to external control (second stage) and, if this can be achieved, to a more empirical approach in the third stage. The history of science appears to follow a similar developmental course, beginning first with primitive forms of dogma, then going through a stage of questioning, and then adopting empiricism. In experimental work on problem solving the questioning or oppositional second stage may be momentary because of the peripheral relationship of the subject to the problem. However, in science, in the development of groups, and in child development, the second stage may be the most critical.

In social behavior the transition is from a stage of opposition to other people's attitudes or intentions (an exaggerated bifurcation of self and external forces) to a stage in which other people's intentions and wishes are taken into account. As third stage concepts emerge, a more objective view of the social environment becomes possible. The person in the third stage views other people less subjectively (that is, less in terms of his own motives and less in terms of absolute standards) and more in terms of other's standards and past experience. His understanding of other points of view, rather than resisting or submitting to them, makes mutual relationships possible. Third stage functioning also involves holding alternative views of the self, of events, and of others simultaneously with a minimum of concern for ambiguity.

Piaget's study of the development of moral concepts in children is illustrative:

> There is no doubt that by adopting a certain technique with their children, parents can succeed in making them attach more importance to intentions than to rules conceived as a system of ritual interdictions. . . . It is when the child is accustomed to act from the point of view of those around him, when he tries to please rather than to obey, that he will judge in terms of intentions. So that taking intentions into account presupposes cooperation and mutual respect. . . . In order to remove all traces of moral realism, one must place oneself on the child's own level, and give him a feeling of equality by laying stress on one's own obligations and one's own deficiencies . . . thus creating an atmosphere of mutual help and understanding. In this way the child will find himself in the presence, not of a system of commands requiring ritualistic and external obedience, but of a system of social relations such that everyone does his best to obey the same obligations, and does so out of mutual respect. The passage from obedience to cooperation thus marks a progression analogous to that of which we saw the effects in the evolution of the game of marbles: only in the final stage does the morality of intention triumph over the morality of objective responsibility (Piaget, 1932, pp. 133–134).

In this passage Piaget is emphasizing a form of relatedness between the subject and the rule rather than changes in behavior toward a rule. The two forms of relatedness he describes are very similar to the present first and third stages. In describing moral realism, Piaget points out that justice is defined in terms of adult authority or an external criterion that is absolute and does not change with situational changes. This stage is equivalent to our first stage functioning and, according to Piaget, is typical of children below seven or eight years of age; [1] on the other hand, the functioning described by Piaget above, which is similar to the third stage, is more typical of children between the ages of eight and eleven. Studies indicate that reciprocity, defined as "eye for an eye" and representing aspects of the first and second stages in our sense, descreases with age (Durkin, 1959a, 1959b) whereas empathic behavior or mutuality increases (Piaget, 1932). Also, younger children are more absolutistic, whereas older children (eighth graders) show overt concern for possible mitigating factors in the interpersonal situation being judged (Durkin, 1959b).

Group functioning in the third stage is characterized by cooperation instead of submission and by competition rather than dominance and opposition. Although third stage functioning is essential for the occur-

[1] It should be noted that the age at which children pass through these stages will vary across different content areas. Here Piaget is speaking of the development of the abstractness of moral concepts. Earlier we were speaking of the abstractness of a child's level of functioning in relationship to his parents.

rence of cooperation, many individuals use the words cooperation and competition for functioning that is clearly at the unilateral or oppositional level and, as Bennis and Shepard (1956) observe, it is just such individuals who tend to retard group development. These authors observe that at this third stage:

> The power problem is resolved by being defined in terms of member responsibilities, . . . [and,] at least within the life of the group, later activity is rarely perceived in terms of submission and rebellion (Bennis and Shepard, 1956, p. 424), [and further that] any slight increase in tension is instantly dissipated by joking and laughter. The fighting of Phase I [the second stage] is still fresh in the memory of the group, and the group's efforts are devoted to patching up differences, healing wounds, and maintaining a harmonious atmosphere (Bennis and Shepard, 1956, p. 429).

One of the most significant aspects of the transition from the second to the third stage is the change in the conception of causality. Although the foundation for this change is established by earlier stages, at the third stage the individual's behavior becomes the independent rather than the dependent variable. In attempting to integrate counterpersonal and mutual evaluations the person functioning at this stage is more likely to think in terms of the locus of causality residing primarily in his own behavior.

> The rule of constraint, which is bound up with unilateral respect, is regarded as sacred and produces in the child's mind feelings that are analogous to those which characterize the compulsory conformity of primitive communities [first stage]. But this rule of constraint remains external to the child's spirit and does not lead to as effective an obedience as the adult would wish. Rules due to mutual agreement and cooperation, on the contrary, take root inside the child's mind and result in an effective observance in the measure in which they are incorporated in an autonomous will [third stage] (Piaget, 1932, p. 365).

In social behavior the third stage represents an empirical phase, similar to the data-gathering phase in science. The person reacts in alternative ways toward others in order to experience their reactions. By observing the reactions of others to his own reactions and finding out more about their standards, he is better able to control the consequences of his own behavior and learn about his own characteristics and limitations. It is as if he were using the environment, or other people's standards, as a mirror to develop a more abstract criterion of his own behavior. Cooley (1912) refers to this procedure as the "looking-glass self." During this stage mutuality, obtaining satisfaction from pleasing others, and empathy replace unilateral functioning and concern with dominance and power. A new basis for relating to people is established.

Taking on the roles of other persons can be viewed in terms of the subject's setting up hypotheses and carrying out experiments on the effects of his own social behavior. An excellent account of this process, referred to as "conversation of gestures," has been given by G. H. Mead (1934) and more recently by Sarbin (1954). The net effect is the emergence of a more objective understanding of the relationships between the subject and his environment. Make-believe play in childhood and the intensive role-taking behavior of adolescents are characteristic of third stage functioning. On this basis, we would expect that the absence of make-believe play and role taking would be associated with arrestation of progressive development at some more concrete level. The significance of third stage functioning for social development is impressively demonstrated by Kelly (1955) who utilizes the technique of role-therapy to induce modifications in conceptual organization.

In child development functioning more typical of the transition from the second to the third stage and of the third stage is modal at ages three, seven and eight, and again perhaps at fourteen and fifteen. Observations indicate that each phase or cycle of third stage functioning is preceded by a stage of opposition, "out of bounds behavior" or negative independence (Ilg and Ames, 1955). For the infant at age three typical functioning is described as:

> Quiet. . . . seems to love to conform. . . . uses the word "Yes" quite as easily as he formerly used the word "No" . . . likes to give as well as take . . . "We" is another word he uses frequently. It expresses his co-operative, easy-going attitude towards life in general. . . . He no longer seems to need the protection of rituals [that is, he has progressed beyond level II transitional functioning]. . . . The child is no longer rigid, inflexible, domineering. . . . He likes to make friends and will often willingly give up a toy or privilege in order to stay in the good graces of some other person. . . . (p. 27).

No doubt the advent of language has much to do with this initial progression to third stage functioning in infancy, and we would expect an association between speech problems and increasing difficulties in developmental transition to the third stage.

As we found in second stage functioning in the first infant cycle (age two to four and one-half), the first cycle of third stage functioning does not represent a complete transition. When this stage is reached in early childhood it is less differentiated from the first stage and does not represent the level of empathy and "subjective responsibility" described above. In the second cycle in Table 2, the occurrence of third stage functioning at around seven or eight years of age, the effect of the conflicting differentiations (based on the counter personal and dependent poles of the concepts) and representing transition to the third stage, is more clearly apparent.

At age seven the modal behaviors observed (Ilg and Ames, 1955) are typically transitional (between second and third stages) as illustrated by the following descriptions:

> Seven . . . has calmed down [from earlier oppositional tendencies]. . . . But he is more likely to complain [seek support]. . . . More apt to retreat from the scene muttering than to stay and demand his own [more covert oppositional tendencies. Opposition has been tempered by conflicting dependency evaluations]. . . . He often demands too much of himself [over-striving represents self-assertion and insures that he will be cared for]. . . . tends to feel that people are against him, that they don't like him [*emergence of sensitization to rejection by others due to his oppositional tendencies*] (Ilg and Ames, 1955, p. 36).

As we indicate in later chapters, these characteristics, along with the tendency to dramatize everything, are typical of the transition from the second to the third stage and characterize the functioning of individuals when progressive development is arrested at this transitional level (Chapter 6).

Following the difficult transition period at seven, modal behavior at eight is described as less conflicting and, in some respects, more characteristic of third stage functioning:

> . . . he is constantly busy and active . . . enjoying new experiences . . . trying out new things, making new friends [the empirical attitude]. . . . with his newly increased powers of evaluation, he may recognize his all-too-frequent failures. Then, tears and self-disparagement! [the emergence of internal causation and self-blame]. . . . He needs protection both from trying to do too much and from too excessive self-criticism when he meets with failure [behavior leading to support and protection from others and the emergence of depressive feelings]. . . . Now he is interested, not just in how people treat him, but in his *relationships* with others. He is ready for, and wants, a good two-way relationship [mutuality]. Furthermore, it is not just what people do which concerns him, but also what they think [sensitization to relationships and learning about the effect of his own reactions on others] (Ilg and Ames, 1955, pp. 37–38).

Transition to the Fourth Stage: (Third Transition)

Since the evaluations and judgments at the third stage are based largely on the effect that one's reactions have on others, we have used such terms as conditional dependence, empiricism, and "the looking-glass self." Just as empiricism is tied to data, so the third stage evaluations are dependent upon the standards of others. The subject is dependent upon external conditions or upon observations of the effect of his own behavior.

The extreme pole of this conceptual system would represent evaluations based on autonomous standards. Transition to the fourth stage requires openness to differentiations based on autonomy and represents the integration of differentiations based on mutuality and autonomy.

In order for a person to experience autonomy as positive and not conflicting with mutuality, he must view both poles of the third stage as positive. If the training conditions have produced such structure, then the way is open for the integration of mutuality and autonomy, which leads to the emergence of a fourth stage conceptual system involving interdependence of informational standards. Interdependent evaluations represent what we assume to be the most abstract level of conceptual development.

Fourth Stage: Interdependence

In the fourth stage mutuality and autonomy are integrated so that neither interferes with the other and yet both are important. We refer to this integration as positive interdependence. The nature of subject-object linkages at this level is abstract, interdependent, and informational. The abstractness and lack of subjectivity are exemplified by the characteristics of group functioning that Bennis and Shepard (1956), following Sullivan (1953), call "consensual validation," which was observed to follow the more compulsively cooperative phase.

> Its chief characteristic is the willingness and ability of group members to validate their self-concepts with other members. The fear of rejection fades when tested against reality. The tensions that developed as a result of these fears diminish in the light of actual discussion of member roles. . . . what ensues is a serious attempt by each group member to verbalize his private conceptual scheme for understanding human behavior—his own and that of others. Bringing these assumptions into explicit communication is the main work of subphase 6. This activity demands a high level of work and of communicative skill. Some of the values that appear to underlie the group's work during this subphase are as follows: 1. Members can accept one another's differences without associating "good" and "bad" with the differences. 2. Conflict exists but is over substantive issues rather than emotional issues. 3. Consensus is reached as a result of rational discussion rather than through a compulsive attempt at unanimity. 4. Members are aware of their own involvement, and of other aspects of group process, without being overwhelmed or alarmed. 5. Through the evaluation process, members take on greater personal meaning to each other. This facilitates communication and creates a deeper understanding of how the other person thinks, feels, behaves; it creates a series of personal expectations, as

distinguished from the previous, more stereotyped, role expectations (Bennis and Shepard, 1956, p. 433).

In the field of personality Fromm (1941) and Erikson (1950) describe higher levels of development as involving the interdependence of mutuality (love) and autonomous informational standards against which instrumental activity (work) is judged. Such interdependence frees relationships from constrictions due to power, resistance to control, or fears of rejection, thus permitting a more abstract and objective form of understanding and participation with others. On the basis of the development of autonomous informational standards the individual can experience rewards, as a result of instrumental activity or work, in terms of his own past experience rather than being dependent on some external source. Erikson (1950) portrays the significance of this level of development as follows:

> I know no better word for it than ego integrity. Lacking a clear definition, I shall point to a few constituents of this state of mind. . . . It is a post-narcissistic love of the human ego—not of the self—as an experience which conveys some world order and spiritual sense, no matter how dearly paid for. It is the acceptance of one's one and only life cycle as something that had to be and that, by necessity, permitted of no substitutions: it thus means a new, and different love of one's parents. . . . Although aware of the relativity of all the various life styles which have given meaning to human striving, the possessor of integrity is ready to defend the dignity of his own life style against all physical and economic threats. For he knows that an individual life is the accidental coincidence of but one life cycle with but one segment of history; and that for him all human integrity stands or falls with the one style of integrity of which he partakes (Erikson, 1950, pp. 231–232).

In child development the earliest observations of behavior typical of the transition to fourth stage functioning are reported around nine years old, that is, in the second cycle of development shown in Table 2. In the first cycle of development in infancy the modal child appears to show tendencies toward the development of third stage concepts but this development is an insufficient base for progression to any form of interdependence. Instead, the child's growing confidence in his abilities leads to a negative form of independence between the ages of three and one-half and four and one-half. But with the new social conditions and problems that arise around five the pendulum swings back to a greater reliance on external control. During this cycle (cycle II) conceptual development approaches or reaches the fourth stage for some children as illustrated by the following descriptions of modal behavior for nine-year-old children:

> He lives more within himself, is surer in his contacts with the outside world, is more self-contained and self-sufficient . . . often insists on being extremely independent [conflict over autonomy] . . . though [he] may be interested in adults . . . he is much less interested than he was earlier in the relationship itself [less sensitivity to maintaining relationships and rejections]. . . . He wants and needs to have his maturity, his independence and his separateness [autonomy] respected. . . . if treated as the mature creature he considers himself to be, the 9-year-old usually gets along pretty well and does display a remarkable amount of self-reliance and capability. . . . However, there is a disquieting side . . . He does tend to worry . . . and . . . can be extremely anxious. . . . (Ilg and Ames, 1955, pp. 38–39).

It will be noted that these descriptive statements are quite different from functioning at the earlier three stages. The functioning of typical nine-year-olds represents a transition to the fourth stage rather than progression to full interdependence. Progression to interdependent functioning of the fourth stage is more likely in the adolescent cycle of development. The increasing reliance upon internal causation in the fourth stage is characterized by a strengthened capacity to face problems and to tolerate anxiety. The initial transition to the fourth stage may produce anxiety and worry, as observed above, but once the conceptual system becomes stabilized, such reactions are much less likely. Therefore, the subject not only develops autonomous skills and informational standards for problem solution but also a high degree of tolerance of anxiety and resistance to stress. The implication is that future adaptation to threat involves progressive development, as opposed to the warding off or defensive tendencies that lead to increasingly closed conceptual functioning.

The most general characteristic of such abstract functioning is resistance to stress. As more abstract forms of subject-object linkages develop there is greater self-awareness. It is this greater self-awareness or attribution of internal causation that is critical for stress tolerance as will become increasingly clear in later chapters. More abstract functioning is based on a conceptual system that has been open to a variety of conflicting forms of subject-object relatedness that have been progressively integrated during development. Consequently there is a greater reservoir of resources to overcome and withstand stress of various forms—failure, control, rejection, or isolation. An individual approaching a problem in a concrete way, with a single fixed solution, will continue to use the same solution in spite of situational changes. However, when he eventually fails, he will develop avoidance and other defensive orientations including the blind acceptance of some other externally anchored solution because of his undifferentiated conceptual structure and his lack of self-awareness. Concrete functioning may be characterized by more decisiveness, but it breaks down more rapidly under stress. Abstract functioning is less categorical, but it has a greater potential to mobilize under the impact of stress.

In problem solving as in science we would associate this level of development with that of theory, if the term "theory" is used in the sense of a systematic body of abstract informational standards that develop over time. Like any other area, however, scientific theory or problem solution can be taught to produce arrestation at any stage, for example, so that the subject would accept theoretical tenets concretistically in terms of the first stage, as fixed and beyond his control.

Fourth stage functioning is characterized by abstract standards developed through the exploration of alternative solutions against a variety of criteria. These standards are systematically related to the informational consequences of exploration and as such are "tools," not masters, since they are subject to change under changing conditions. Abstract functioning is characterized both by the availability of alternate conceptual schemata as a basis for relating and by the ability to hold a strong view or attitude that does not distort incoming information.

Some General Considerations

We began this chapter with assumptions organized in terms of the course, process, and results of development. Having considered the four stages in some detail we conclude this chapter with comments organized around the same three areas.

Progressive Development Implies Increasing Abstractness

In this chapter we have emphasized stages involved in the development of increasing abstractness of subject-object linkages. We have also emphasized the more central ties in the self-system, stressing personality characteristics and social functioning. Because of this emphasis on the process of development, however, we should not overlook the importance of studies that have demonstrated that in general children do relate to their world in a more concretistic, less differentiated way, when compared to adults (Lazarus, Baker, Broverman, and Mayer, 1957; Werner, 1957; Piaget, 1954). These studies have emphasized the abstractness of a subject's relatedness to tasks or the abstractness of perception. Older children are more abstract than younger children, in the sense that functioning or perception is less diffuse, less absolutistic, less all-or-none, less stimulus-bound, and more differentiated. Older children can generally break a stimulus field down into its parts and integrate these into new wholes more effectively than younger children.

If concreteness-abstractness refers to the nature of the linkage to objects, for example, to mathematics or religion and not to the content or magnitude of such attitudes, then there is no need for the artificial division between a psychology of abilities on the one hand and a psychology of personality on the other. Concreteness and abstractness are equally relevant to functioning directed toward problems or tasks and functioning directed toward politics, religion, or other people. In all of these, progressive development can be described in directional terms, as proceeding from the concrete to the abstract. It should be noted, however, that there is a great need for more research to shed light on this concrete-abstract dimension. Such research has two requirements: first that the investigator does not impose environmental pressures that would retard the course of progression and second that each individual be studied as an individual and not in terms of normative measures at given points in time (that is, the measurement of progressive development should be made in terms of individuals, not the average of individuals). Both requirements are absent in much psychological research due to the highly controlled and artificial nature of training sequences (restricting progression) and the normative treatment of data based on groups of individuals, as opposed to the assessment of the course of progression in each unit being studied.

Interrelations of Saccadic and Cyclical Development

The assumed course of development charted in Table 2 includes both saccadic and cyclical movement. The most important rule determining such movement is: if the situation changes markedly (as occurs during certain periods of child development), then a cyclical movement occurs in which functioning reverts to a more concretistic level. The basis for this cyclical reversion to first stage functioning when faced by highly novel circumstances is that of the greater reliance upon absolutistic or external control relative to earlier functioning in more familiar circumstances. Following this reversion to first stage functioning, development once again proceeds in a saccadic fashion.

It follows from this analysis that any rapid change (whether experimentally or naturalistically induced) that produces a cyclical reversion to first stage functioning thereby precludes progressive development beyond a certain level of abstractness. The relationship between cyclical and saccadic movement therefore determines the maximum rate of change at which any form of change, whether experimental, cultural, or social, can occur without leading to a decrease in the potential abstractness of further saccadic movements.

Determining the most appropriate synchronization of saccadic and cyclical development would appear to be a major problem in numerous areas: determining the stage at which a child should enter school or be placed in a more complex situation, determining the effects of social mobility in the broad sense, and so forth. Such decisions would presumably be based upon the person's reaching the maximum level of abstractness through saccadic movement within a particular cycle of development before introducing the novel circumstances. The introduction of novel situations prior to reaching a level of maximum abstractness may not appear to affect his behavior adversely immediately (for example, in entering kindergarten) because the change involves a cyclical swing back toward the first stage, which is essentially independent of the earlier level reached. However, such reversion would affect the rate of progression beyond the stage of abstractness reached in the original cycle.

The Generality of Developmental Stages

As we have indicated briefly, a person need not reach the same level of abstractness of subject-object ties in all areas of development. Individuals vary considerably in terms of the generality of their stage of functioning. Some persons may reach the fourth stage in many areas of development whereas other persons may function at the fourth stage in some areas, but at the second stage in other areas. It is not difficult to find someone, for example, who functions at a very abstract level at work, such as in physics, but functions at a very concrete level in other areas. The problem of the generality-specificity of conceptual functioning is one of the most important areas for subsequent research. Although there is very little evidence available we will summarize a few tentative views regarding generality:

1. Areas of development that engage the same conceptual system are more closely related functionally for the individual because of the similarity of the underlying motivational orientation (Rotter, 1954).
2. The more that significant areas activate the same level of conceptual functioning, the more integrated is the self system.
3. Reaching an abstract level of development in one area enhances the likelihood of reaching that same level in other areas of development.

4. The more closely related the areas in terms of stimulus similarity, the greater is the likelihood of generality.

5. The more similar the training in the two areas, the greater is the likelihood of generality.

Following the third assumption, we would expect that the level of development at one age level would be statistically indicative of the potential level of development at some future time.

Concluding Remarks

We have argued that progressive development to more abstract levels of functioning rests on the occurrence and integration of particular kinds of differentiations. From our assumptions, for example, it follows that the initial absence of externally derived supports, control, or structure as in an ambiguous situation (that is, absence of external structure) leads to the retardation or arrestation of progressive development at some point in the developmental ladder. This follows because we assume that one of the foundations for further progressive development is the integration of differentiations based on externally derived structure and internal opposition to it. Training conditions that restrict the emergence of the concepts proposed would be expected to result in the arrestation of progressive development at some point below the fourth stage. We turn now to a direct consideration of the interaction between stages and training methods.

5 Training Conditions Influencing Conceptual Development

How do training conditions affect the course of development? Throughout this book all cognitive outcomes are viewed as being conjointly determined by situational and dispositional factors operating at a particular time. That is, conceptual development progresses as environmental pressures (training conditions) interact with a particular conceptual state of an organism. In the last chapter we dealt with some of these nodal conceptual states as "stages," and in this chapter we deal with the interactive effect of various environmental "presses" on these conceptual structures.

That we described stages before training conditions does not imply that the "push" in stages is assumed to be more important than the "pull" of environmental training conditions. In describing conceptual development we could have begun by describing the training conditions before the stages. In following this order we would first have dimensionalized the training conditions and then used these conditions as a basis for deriving the stages. The derivation would rest on logic as follows: "Given these various forms of training, what kinds of adaptive orientations (stages) would emerge as the object of training (the person) attempted to cope with this condition?"

However, we are proceeding by describing first the stages through which conceptual development is assumed to occur and then presenting the training conditions. Therefore, the logic underlying the present dimensionalization of training conditions involves the following: "Given these conceptual stages, what forms of training would be likely to produce progression or arrestation at each of these various stages?" It should be noted that, regardless of order, the central principle is the hand-in-glove interdependence between stage and training condition, which rests on the assumption that the organism is continuously adapting to whatever environmental conditions are encountered. Once we have set forth both sets of factors, then we may view their joint consequences as we do later in this chapter.

Principles of Progression and Arrestation

In the last chapter, three principles related to the degree of synchrony between training condition and articulation at a particular stage were set forth. The application of these principles to the four stages of development summarized in Table 3 will serve as a starting point for dimensionalizing training. However, in order to understand Table 3 it is important to distinguish between two forms of arrestation: *nodal arrestation* (or what was referred to in the last chapter as "arrestation at a given stage") and *transitional arrestation*. By *nodal arrestation* we mean the arrestation of progressive development at any stage in progressing to fourth stage functioning, that is, at the first, second, or third stage. Nodal, in the Oxford dictionary, is defined as "a line or point of absolute or comparative rest in a vibrating body or surface . . . a stopping or starting point." We use it in this sense in order to differentiate it from *transitional arrestation*, which implies the arrestation of progressive development at some point between any two nodal stages.

Nodal Arrestation

In the last chapter we noted that if the training conditions (environmental pressures) are out of synchrony with the degree of conceptual articulation in such a way that one pole is positive and the other pole is negative, *nodal arrestation* will occur. Put in more specific terms, nodal arrestation is induced by training conditions that maximize openness of the conceptual system to one pole of the central structure while maximizing closedness [1] to differentiations based on the opposite pole (see Table 1 on p. 88, and the left-hand column in Table 3). Under these conditions no developmental "leap" occurs, and therefore integration required for the emergence of a new conceptual schema and

[1] Closedness and arrestation may have identical meanings under some circumstances. However, the two terms should be clearly differentiated. Arrestation is more specific in that it refers to closedness to particular kinds of differentiations–those differentiations that would be required for the development of more abstract syntheses. Closedness is used to refer to the avoidance or neutralization of any set of conditions. That is, arrestation implies closedness to differentiations required for more abstract development; closedness could also refer to differentiations utilized at more concretistic levels as well.

progression does not occur. As Table 3 indicates, arrestation may occur at any stage of development. For example, if training induces closedness to differentiations based on independence from external field forces or control during first stage functioning, second stage concepts cannot emerge. On a similar basis, training that maximized closedness of the conceptual system to differentiations based on dependency and support after second stage concepts have fully emerged and on autonomy after the emergence of fourth stage concepts would be expected to be associated with nodal arrestation at stages II and IV, respectively.

The arrestation of development at the first stage is not meant to imply that the subject will remain exactly like a child or that the arrestation of development of an attitude at the first stage would mean that the functioning in relation to the attitude object would remain exactly the same over time. Rather, arrestation refers to the concrete-abstract dimension. After arrestation, development continues within the conceptual limits of the stage reached. There are other components of functioning, more phenotypical than the concrete-abstract dimension, which vary, to some degree, within a given level or stage of functioning. Some of these characteristics are discussed in Chapter 6.

Transitional Arrestation

In Chapter 4 we noted that if the training condition is out of synchrony with the conceptual articulation in such a way that each of the two poles becomes both positive and negative, *transitional arrestation* will occur. Put more specifically, transitional arrestation is due to training conditions that induce some degree of openness of the conceptual system to the conflicting differentiations based on both poles of the central concepts but minimizes the conditions for their integration. Partial openness or partial closedness, involving simultaneous approach and avoidant evaluations of each conceptual pole, would be expected to produce such an effect. Transitional arrestation may occur between stages I and II, between II and III, and between III and IV, representing three levels of abstractness of conflicting systems of subject-object relatedness. The three levels will be referred to as level I, level II, and level III transitional arrestation, respectively.

Progressive Development

As we maintained in the last chapter, if the training conditions (environmental pressures) are synchronized with the degree of conceptual articulation, *progression* will occur. More specifically, progression at any stage of development requires training characteristics that (1) induce openness of the conceptual system to developmental leaps

TABLE 3

General Conditions Determining Arrestation and Progression

Stage	Poles of Conceptual System at Each Stage	Training Leading to Nodal Arrestation Involves	Training Leading to Transitional Arrestation Involves	Training Leading to Progression Involves
I	A. External control B. Opposition to external control	Conditions maximizing openness to differentiations based on pole A and maximizing closedness of differentiations based on pole B. Arrestation at stage I. (pole A, +, pole B, −)	Conditions producing partial openness (approach and avoidance) to differentiations based on both poles (A and B), minimizing the degree of integration between them. Arrestation at level I transition. (pole A, + −, pole B, + −)	Conditions producing openness to and integration of differentiations based on both poles: Emergence of a new conceptual system. Progression to stage II. (pole A, +, pole B, +)
II	C. Negative independence D. Dependency on others	Conditions maximizing openness to differentiations based on pole C and maximizing closedness to differentiations based on pole D. Arrestation at stage II. (pole C, +, pole D, −)	Conditions producing partial openness (approach and avoidance) to differentiations based on both poles (C and D), minimizing the degree of integration between them. Arrestation at level II transition. (pole C, + −, pole D, + −)	Conditions producing openness to and integration of differentiations based on both poles: Emergence of a new conceptual system. Progression to stage III. (pole C, +, pole D, +)

III	E. Mutuality F. Autonomy	Conditions maximizing openness to differentiations based on pole E and maximizing closedness to differentiations based on pole F. Arrestation at stage III. (pole E, +, pole F, –)	Conditions producing partial openness (approach and avoidance) to differentiations based on both poles (E and F), minimizing the degree of integration between them. Arrestation at level III transition. (pole E, + –, pole F, + –)	Conditions producing openness to and integration of differentiations based on both poles: Emergence of a new conceptual system. Progression to stage IV. (pole E, +, pole F, +)
IV	Interdependence			

required for progression, or to put this another way, openness to evaluations or differentiations based on both poles of a particular conceptual system, and (2) favor the integration of these two extreme sets of differentiations.

Distinction between Functioning Characterized by Arrestation or Progression at Each Level

The conceptual structure of systems representing nodal arrestation, transitional arrestation, and progression at each stage is illustrated in Table 3. It is important to distinguish between these three related structures at each stage of development.

Nodal arrestation at any stage implies closedness to one pole and a lack of conflict in the subject-object ties; *transitional arrestation* at any level implies partial closedness or approach and avoidant tendencies to both poles and highly conflicting subject-object ties; whereas *progression* implies a maximum degree of openness to differentiations or interpretations based on both poles. *The distinction between functioning that is relatively arrested at a given stage and functioning at the same stage that represents a "passing through" or progression is a highly important distinction in personality measurement and diagnosis.* Assessing the extent to which a system is in progression involves determining the degree of closedness and conflict in relation to each pole at each stage.

When considered in relation to training methods, the notion of stages of development unfortunately becomes much more complex than the descriptions contained in the last chapter.

Functioning at a given stage is assumed to vary as a consequence of training method. The difference between arrested functioning and progressive functioning within a given stage illustrates the limits of this variation. However, as we indicate in this chapter, there are finer discriminations between these two extremes, which rest on intermediate training methods and which are more difficult to assess. That is, different training methods generate different conceptual linkages and different levels of functioning immediately, at the first stage, and at each successive stage reached beyond this stage. However, the degree of progression to more abstract levels is still viewed in terms of the extent to which the environmental pressures (training conditions) permit the appropriate differentiations and integrations in the order proposed in the last chapter. Therefore, *training conditions affect the nature and rate at which development progresses.*

Dimensions of Training Conditions

The most general question to which we now turn is, "What training conditions are associated with closedness or openness to poles at each stage?" We derive two primary dimensions along which training methods can be ordered: (1) The unilateral-interdependent dimension, which is the most generic form of ordering, and (2) a more specific dimension referring to the imposition of control within each pole of the more general dimension. This more specific dimension considers (a) the reliable-unreliable dimension assumed to be relevant to the imposition of unilateral training methods and (b) the protective-informational dimension assumed to be relevant to the imposition of interdependent training methods. A further, more specific training dimension, which refers primarily to the inhibition of system specific tendencies, is discussed in Chapter 6.

It is appropriate at this point to re-emphasize that our concern is in the dimensionalization of training conditions, not in the content or goal of training. From our point of view the goal of training or its content may have little relationship to what the subject *really* learns as he copes with the environmental pressures. Since the present focus is upon the nature of the relatedness formed, or the nature of the concepts established, we are concerned with a systematic dimensionalization of these environmental pressures or *methods* of training.

Unilateral-Interdependent Dimension

In discussing the development of mediating concepts, training conditions are described as varying along a dimension from unilateral to interdependent methods. This generic dimension along which training

TABLE 4

Unilateral-Interdependent Training Dimension

	Unilateral	Accelerated Autonomy	Interdependent
Consequences	Subject learns to look externally for criteria of matching; to fit stimuli into absolutistic schemata. External causation.		Subject learns to view own behavior as causal in concept formation; to utilize hypothetical concepts for informational appraisal. Internal causation.

conditions can be scaled extends (1) from a point at which the training agent presents the schemata of mapping or a ready-made concept to the subject (2) to a point at which the training agent does not provide an externally derived concept for mediating between situational effects and resolutions. If we assume that both training agents have the same goal in mind, regardless of the method employed, it is apparent that these two extreme classes of training present a very different set of environmental pressures with which the subject must cope. In adapting to the latter situation the subject must learn an appropriate conceptual orientation autonomously.

In coping with unilateral training in which the training situation provides ready-made concepts, the subject learns to fit responses or evaluations to stimuli or situational conditions so that they match the function expressed by the concept. Having established the concept, the training agent's role is also channeled along the lines of rewarding matchings that fit the stated concept and punishing matchings that fail to fit. As a consequence the subjects' responses are viewed primarily in terms of being right or wrong, good or bad. Put another way, the subject is extrinsically valued (Ausubel, 1958).

In coping with interdependent training on the other hand, the subject has no preestablished inflexible concept to learn. Since the concept is not implicitly or explicitly provided, the training agent desiring that the subject learn to function effectively in reference to some goal must control the environment in some systematic way so that the desired concept will emerge. In the extreme case, the environment would be arranged so that the subject would experience informational consequences about exploratory matchings, which would lead him to develop certain concepts in the situation. Here the role of the training agent is to manipulate the environment and to encourage exploratory activity. In the hypothetical pure case of interdependent training, the subject's reactions are determined by the *informational* consequences of action, and the subject is intrinsically valued for instrumental or exploratory maneuvers in their own right as opposed to achievement in reference to a fixed concept (Ausubel, 1952).

From a point in the center of this dimension (Table 4), which we will refer to as "permissive" or accelerated autonomy training, to the left training becomes increasingly unilateral and to the right it becomes increasingly interdependent. Each major training method is now discussed.

UNILATERAL TRAINING

Operations for unilateral training. Operations for unilateral training are (1) external source determination of absolute criterion for behavior, (2) rewards and punishment directed toward these ends, and (3) extrinsic evaluation (Ausubel, 1952, 1958) of the subject.

The distinction between unilateral and interdependent training is not simply a matter of the goal of the training agent since we assume that almost all training involves a goal of some kind. The distinction is based rather on the extent to which the goal involves an end that is absolute and externally fixed. Unilateral training is characterized by a greater rigidity, immediacy, and explicitness in the way by which the source reacts to the end product of the subject's behavior. The criterion is explicitly and directly determined by the source. Source-determined goals can be expressed to the subject either directly or indirectly. Direct expression involves orders, directions, and explicit statements regarding final response requirements, whereas indirect expression involves the source's implicit use of a predetermined criterion. In either case the source's administration of rewards or punishments is determined by the degree to which the subject's behavior is in accord with the standard held by the source.

The distinction between unilateral and interdependent training, therefore, cannot be based on the occurrence of rewards and punishment but is rather a matter of the focus of rewards and punishment. Unilateral training is characterized by the source's judging the subject's behavior in terms of how well responses match some external criterion, and it is on this basis that we use the term, extrinsic evaluation (Ausubel, 1958). The subject is valued in terms of his achievement relative to some external criterion held by the source rather than for himself. The three operations for unilateral training—source-determined criteria, reward and punishment focused on ends of behavior, and extrinsic evaluation—should prove to be highly interrelated. However, in practice, a single operation may not provide a sufficient basis for the classification of training conditions. Training could be considered unilateral without direct source expression of the criterion (indirect expression), but such uncertainty in classifying could be clarified by noting the focus of rewards and punishments. Furthermore, if an investigator were unable to observe the training conditions directly, it might be possible to infer unilateral training on the basis of the source's expression of attitudes congruent with the extrinsic evaluation of the subject.

The occurrence of exploratory activity or activity that is tangential to the externally derived criteria is likely to be either ignored or punished under unilateral training conditions. Unilateral training is characterized by a maximum of behavioral manipulation of the subject and a minimum of environmental manipulation by the source. The subject's achievement or end product of his behavior is central in training. The judgment of this end product is made against an external criterion in a black-white fashion, that is, right or wrong, good or bad. It was in this categorical, controlling sense that this training condition was described as behavior-control training (Schroder and Hunt, 1959).

Examples of unilateral training. One of the best examples of unilateral training is the autocratic atmosphere created by Lewin, Lippitt, and White (1939) in their classic group experiment. Autocratic atmosphere involved the following: all policy determination was in the hands of the leader, all steps were dictated, and the leader was clearly the source of control.

Many terms have been used to describe child-rearing practices similar to unilateral training: domineering, authoritarian, and so forth. Several of the Fels' behavior-rating scales (Baldwin, Kalhorn, and Breese, 1949) have been constructed to assess the extent to which the parent was the source of the control. Although the scales do not specifically refer to the focus of control, it seems clear that a similar distinction to our unilateral-interdependent training is implied (cf. also Baldwin, 1955). Scales describing parental behavior related to unilateral training are: restrictiveness of regulations, quantity of suggestion, and coerciveness of suggestion (Baldwin et al., 1949).

In attitude-change studies, the presentation of only one side of an issue, either in an irrational fashion or with an absence of participation or mutuality, would exemplify this form of training. Attitude change relying on direct external suggestion, power, and control (Kelman, 1958) or using an absolute rather than a gradual approach (Harvey and Rutherford, 1958) would also be relevant.

ACCELERATED AUTONOMY TRAINING

Operations for accelerated autonomy or permissive training. The middle point on this generic training dimension (see Table 4) represents training in which the directionality of control is least apparent. Accelerated autonomy training does not mean an absence of all control because, as we note later, extreme permissiveness or indifference have controlling effects on behavior.

Operations for accelerated autonomy training are: (1) a lack of source determination of criterion or standards, (2) a lack of environmental manipulation aimed at presenting progressive barriers to instrumental behavior, and (3) an absence of a specific referent for defining rewards or punishments. In clarifying this third operation, we may note that the source's evaluation of the subject is non-specific and undifferentiated rather than being based on particular achievements or instrumental effort, and the role of the source is permissively accepting, to a point, in extreme cases, often termed "indulgent."

Examples of accelerated autonomy training. Such training is rarely used to produce specific effects, for example, in attitude-change studies or in learning studies, but it has been investigated in various group situations. The laissez faire atmosphere used by Lewin and others (1939) is relevant. The atmosphere is described in terms of "no control," "complete freedom for the group and the individual in decision making," and a "lack of participation by the leader." Such training represents a lack of direction of control by an indifferent source. Certain education practices described as extremely permissive and child-training practices described as underdominating and indulgent also exemplify this form of training. Since these training characteristics are relevant to the way in which control is imposed, they are discussed more fully in the next section of this chapter.

INTERDEPENDENT TRAINING

Operations for interdependent training. Three major operations for interdependent training are: (1) reality or relative determination of criterion, (2) rewards directed primarily toward means and exploratory acts, and (3) intrinsic evaluation, that is, the source places a value on the subject "intrinsically," as a person, somewhat apart from the evaluation of his achievement measured against the source's criterion.

The nature of interdependent training may be conveyed by describing briefly a few techniques that have the effect of inducing interdependence between the source and the subject or of differentiating the role of the source from the criterion or from authoritative control.

(1) The extent to which the environment is controlled prior to training. Environmental control may be achieved by devising a graded series of experiences that the subject will almost certainly follow because of the way the environment is programmed. A simple example in child training is the extent to which a parent removes valuable, breakable, or dangerous objects before allowing the child to explore a situation. The unilateral alternative is to control or direct the child's behavior away from such objects during exploration. ("No, no. Don't touch.") The use of environmental programming is becoming increasingly important as a major psychological tool for gaining control of behavior, for example, in group functioning (Kennedy, 1960), therapy (Jones, 1953), teaching (Skinner, 1953; Anderson and Moore, 1959).

(2) The extent to which rules are imposed in an impersonal way. For example, parents can induce children to go to bed by saying, "When the bell rings (which is, of course, under the control of the parent), it is bedtime" (impersonal). Or by saying, "Go to bed now" (authoritative). Baldwin (1955) used an example of the way some nursery school teachers convey rules in an impersonal way. Instead of saying, "Don't throw the sand," the teacher may say, "The sand stays down." Although subtle, such differences in training have important implications for the developing conceptual framework of the person being trained. Under conditions of impersonal imposition, the source acts as an interpreter of reality rather than as the source of an order. Therefore, the subject learns to look to the consequences of his own behavior as a basis for the evolvement of concepts.

(3) The extent to which the source explains reality to the subject: a symbolic means of manipulating the environment. Obviously, this technique cannot be used unless the subject can understand the "explanation" given by the source. Partly because of this fact the advent of language has important general implications for the distinction between unilateral and interdependent training. The availability of language permits the source utilizing unilateral training to make the rules more explicit and permits the source utilizing interdependent training to provide informational explanations about the nature of reality.

Interdependent training is characterized by rewards directed toward autonomous instrumental activity rather than toward the achievement of external criteria. Exploratory behavior, effort, the discovery of alternate solutions become the focus of unilateral training and are encouraged and rewarded.

Such rewarding of exploratory behavior is related to the third operation, the intrinsic evaluation of the subject (Ausubel, 1958). By intrinsic evaluation, we mean that the subject is valued for himself, for what he is, rather than for what he can accomplish in relation to some external criterion. Evaluation is divorced from achievement. In general, the absence of externally administered punishment represents an overall operation for interdependent training. The basis for using such a referent lies in the fact that in interdependent training the discrepancies between the source's standards and the subject's behavior are handled by further environmental control in order to achieve eventual behavioral modification rather than through more direct forms of behavioral control such as punishment.

Examples of interdependent training. Interdependent training is generally similar to what Lewin et al. (1939), Baldwin, Kalhorn, and Breese (1945), and Baldwin (1955) have referred to as democratic training and to what has been referred to earlier as environmental control training (Schroder and Hunt, 1959). Lewin et al. have described democratic atmosphere as involving the leader's acting as an interpreter of reality for the group and exerting a moderate amount of control. Although these authors did not distinguish between interdependent and unilateral control, it would appear that the democratic situation involved less unilateral control. Baldwin et al. (1949) described democratic training in such terms as justification of policy, democracy of policy, non-coerciveness of suggestion, readiness of explanation, direction of criticism toward approval, clarity of policy, and understanding and non-restrictiveness of regulations.

In contrast with permissiveness, interdependent training involves the following: (1) rational and mutual determination of relativistic criteria, (2) selective rewards for instrumental behavior, and (3) environmental manipulation. Examples of interdependent training in attitude-change procedures are the utilization of two-sided presentations (Hovland, 1957), of mutual discussion and participation (Hovland, Janis, and Kelly, 1953), and of a gradual procedure utilizing a graded series of steps leading to the desired end (Harvey and Rutherford, 1958).

GENERIC CONSEQUENCES OF UNILATERAL AND INTERDEPENDENT TRAINING

Before proceeding to the more specific forms of training we may note the very general effects of training variations on the unilateral-interdependent dimension. Unilateral training results in the subject's developing a conceptual orientation based on external causation. In unilateral training, the subject experiences the criteria of his behavior as absolute and fixed and the source of rewards as external. Rewards are transformed as absolute events over which he has no control. Means are inevitable consequences of the ends.

The results of interdependent training are that the subject develops an orientation by which ends or the criteria of behavior are not experienced as fixed or absolute. Since the end product of a response sequence is not specifically tied to or rewarded by an external source under interdependent training, the criterion of behavior develops over time as being differentiated from external control. The "end response" has functional significance largely as information for structuring further exploratory behavior by the subject. The criterion for behavior is more relative in the sense that it is experienced as being functionally related to the exploratory manipulation of reality factors, over which manipulation the organism has some control. The more specific behavioral implications of these antecedents are discussed under the imposition dimension below.

One major implication that follows from the distinction which we have drawn between fixed and relative criteria is that fixed criteria imply less differentiation between the subject and the source; that is, under unilateral training, there is less differentiation between the internal and the external. The criteria for thoughts, wishes, and actions of the subject are defined by the source and are in this sense largely synonomous. Being frustrated by reality is experienced as being frustrated by the source. Under unilateral training, therefore, environmental frustration is more likely to lead to resentment of the source. The subject experiencing such resentment is more likely to become sensitive toward the source's evaluations and feelings and to view the source as a power or as an external force. In a similar way, the experience of positive environmental events is also attributed to the source (Baldwin, 1955).

We assume that it is the training method rather than the content of the responses being trained that determines the nature of conceptual development. Therefore, we expect that the same type of conceptual consequences will occur following the teaching of any cultural content providing the methods of training were similar.

Dimensions of Imposition

The unilateral-interdependent dimension provides an ordering of training methods that generally determine the development of forms of relatedness varying on the concrete-abstract dimension. The more specific problem is to specify the precise form of unilateral or interdependent training that leads to the progression or to the arrestation of development at a given stage. In this section we propose a more specific training dimension: the manner in which both unilateral and interdependent training are *imposed*. We view unilateral training as varying from reliable to unreliable imposition of control, whereas interdependent training is viewed as varying from a protective to an informational form of source imposition (see Table 5). As Table 5 illustrates, we are assuming that as the training methods become more interdependent, the nature of the relevant dimension of imposition also changes. Although necessarily similar in some respects to the training operations described earlier for unilateral and interdependent training, these four forms of training are more specific descriptions of training conditions, specifically with regard to imposition.

TABLE 5

Variations in Imposition on the Unilateral-Interdependent Dimension

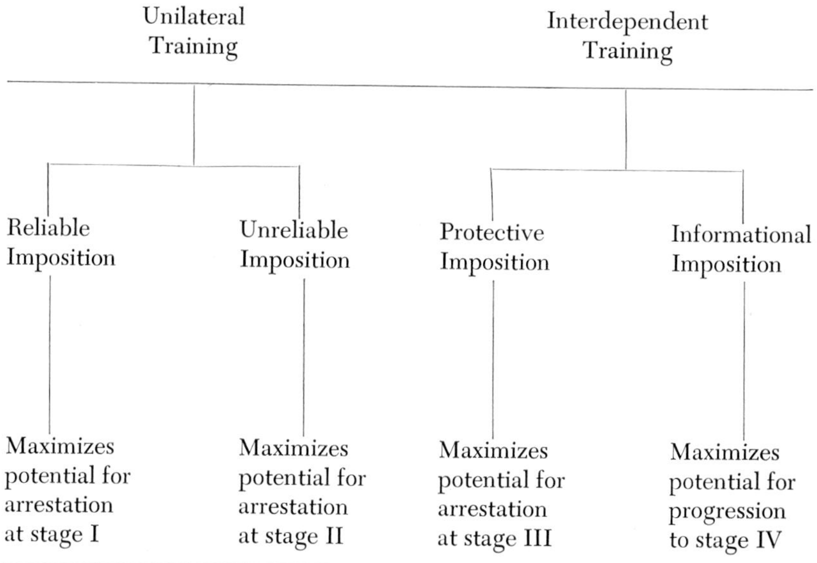

RELIABLE UNILATERAL TRAINING

This training consists of the imposition of reliable and consistent criteria so that the subject can learn to behave in accordance with these external standards. Rewards and punishment are administered in a reliable manner. Classes of behavior that are outside the range of acceptance of the source are consistently punished, and behavior inside the range of acceptance is consistently rewarded. Alternative interpretations or evaluations of the external criteria are masked out (Lidz, Cornelison, Terry, and Fleck, 1958), ignored, or punished. Reliable unilateral training is here described as being within the ability limits of the subject so that he can learn to interiorize the external absolute criteria and behave according to these standards.[1]

Reliable unilateral training may be regarded as "protective" in a particular sense, which may be illustrated by a study by Levy (1943). In studying the effects of maternal overprotection, he found that such training could be dimensionalized along a dominance-indulgence dimension. On the dominant side, which corresponds fairly closely to the present reliable unilateral training, the mother's controlling and

[1] Unilateral training that is not within the subject's ability limits is described later in this chapter under unreliability and acceleration.

highly directing behavior led to more docility and submissiveness in the children. Although such training is extremely controlling, it is also consistent. The training has also been described as overdomination (Ausubel, 1952). Autocratic training, certain types of formal education, and attitude-change techniques using irrational, absolute, and power-oriented suggestion would also be relevant to reliable unilateral training conditions.

UNRELIABLE UNILATERAL TRAINING

The unreliability referred to in this condition is defined from the viewpoint of the subject rather than the source. On the assumption that the subject would experience them as unreliable, the following conditions illustrate this training: (1) inconsistency of control, (2) absolute source expectations that are beyond the limits of the subject, and (3) a lack of affectionate, benevolent, or rewarding components in the training.

By inconsistent imposition we refer to erratic or shifting source expectations of the subject, which lead to inconsistent patterns of rewards or punishments. Training that is beyond the subject's ability level bears a generic similarity to inconsistency since both create an unreliable training environment from the subject's viewpoint (Coffin, 1941). In the extreme cases, the environment is too complex for the subject to learn to make meaningful discriminations on the basis of the external consequences. From a conceptual point of view, the subject is in a consistent situation of failure, but, as we indicate below, failure comes to be experienced differently under these conditions. The ability of the subject must be considered because the lower the ability level, the greater the likelihood that unilateral training will be experienced as unreliable. Research (Schroder and Hunt, 1959) has consistently shown that the consequences that we expect to follow unreliable unilateral training occur more frequently in the lower ability groups.

In the first two conditions (inconsistency and excessively high expectations) the subject does not experience reliable patterns of reward. Similar generic consequences are expected from the third condition—lack of approval—since the source's failure to provide approval, even when the subject's behavior conformed to the external criteria, would be experienced as unreliability by the subject. Such conditions are generally associated with rejecting or neglectful parental attitudes, for example. Although we assume that indifference and neglect on the part of the training agent produce effects similar to inconsistency and excessively high expectation, these conditions (that is, indifference and neglect) may be conceived as being more closely related to the center of our major dimension (Table 3) than to the unilateral training pole.

Many examples of such training have been reported in studies of child development and are referred to in later chapters. Although such training would not likely be used to produce attitude change, it is frequently used to counteract propaganda by inducing the notion in the subject that the behavior of the opposing source is characterized by the operations outlined. One of the most common forms of unreliable unilateral training is illustrated by the driving parent who aims to obtain the subject's dependency by arbitrary and irregular control, resulting in a distrustful relationship. Under these conditions the environment is indirectly hostile, whereas indifference and particularly neglect reflect a more directly hostile environment.

PROTECTIVE INTERDEPENDENT TRAINING

Under protective interdependent training the subject is rewarded for instrumental behavior. The ends are no longer the central feature of the training method. Variation on the protective-informational dimension is related to the way in which the source enters into the subject's autonomous instrumental behavior. Protective imposition utilizes support both as a reward and as a means of guiding instrumental behavior along certain channels. The source helps the subject and provides an example or a model for his behavior in new situations. The most significant aspect of protective interdependent training, however, is that the source is likely to anticipate the subject's potential failure and then enter into his instrumental activity as a helpful, supporting figure before the occurrence of failure.

In a very general sense both reliable unilateral and protective interdependent training could be described as "protective" (Levy, 1943). However, in reliable unilateral training, which involves the source's establishing absolute criteria for behavior, protection takes the form of control in the service of these external ends. In reliable unilateral training it is the ends, or the source-determined criteria, that are central; failure is equivalent to transgression. In protective interdependent training, on the other hand, the source anticipates failure relative to the subject's instrumental behavior, rather than defining it in terms of an absolute criterion. In protective interdependent training, protection is a form of intrinsic evaluation embedded in the relationship between source and subject; therefore, failure is equivalent to rejection or a lack of support. In protective interdependent training the subject is induced to take a more active, mutual, give-and-take role (Heathers,

1955), and there is less "masking out" (Lidz et al., 1958) of subject-defined criterion, that is, of internal control. The degree to which protective interdependent training is overdominant, inhibitive, or overcontrolling is separate from the unilateral-interdependent distinction and is taken up as a third more specific dimension of training in Chapter 6.

INFORMATIONAL INTERDEPENDENT TRAINING

When control is achieved through informational imposition, the source controls the subject's environment so that exploratory activity leads to meaningful progression of skills within the subject's ability limits. One of the major characteristics of this method is that learning occurs through the subject's independent exploration of progressive barriers. Because this condition does not involve evaluating behavior on the basis of a particular solution or external criterion, informational interdependent training maximizes the subject's discovery of alternate solutions. The source in this form of training is not, however, non-directional or neutral; rather he explicitly directs his approval toward instrumental accomplishments. Approval in this condition is neither personal nor extrinsic but refers to what may be called informational participation. If the control of the environment is coordinated with the ability of the subject, protection is unnecessary. Therefore, failure as well as success can be treated in an informational context with a minimum of evaluation or absolutistic control.

Through instrumental activity, the subject learns from experiencing the consequences of his own actions. In informational interdependent training he is not only unprotected (free to experience the consequences, including failure) but also the consequences have meaning to him in terms of reality based on his own past experience. When behavioral consequences are evaluated against an externally given criterion (reliable unilateral training), reality testing necessarily involves the manipulation of behavior in reference to a fixed criterion. In informational interdependent training, the source enters as a reflecting agent clarifying the information consequences of the subject's behavior in terms of the subject's reality world (Cantril, 1950).

In discussing a method of child training similar to informational imposition, Benedict (1938) states:

> The essential point of such child training is that the child is from infancy continuously conditioned to responsible social participation while at the same time the tasks that are expected of it are adapted to its capacity. The contrast with our society is very great. A child does not make any labor contribution to our industrial society except as it competes with an adult; its

work is not measured against its own strength and skill but against high-geared industrial requirements. Even when we praise a child's achievement in the home we are outraged if such praise is interpreted as being of the same order as praise of adults. The child is praised because the parent feels well disposed, regardless of whether the task is well done by adult standards, and the child acquires no sensible standard by which to measure its achievement. The gravity of a Cheyenne Indian family ceremoniously making a feast out of the little boy's first snowbird is at the furthest remove from our behavior (Benedict, 1938, p. 163).

In a complex society such as our present one, it is not surprising that frequently the training takes the form of being unilateral, permissive, or protective simply because of the sheer amount of content that must be taught. In such circumstances the use of informational imposition or more direct reality experience is difficult.[1] However, effective environmental control utilizing simulated situations might be introduced that would partially overcome this problem in education, training, and development in general.

One of the best illustrations of informational interdependent training is described in the interesting framework being developed by Anderson and Moore (1959) as an "autotelic" situation. In order for teaching to produce autotelic activities three conditions are necessary:

(1) [The teaching devices] must be "cut off," in some suitable sense, from the more serious aspects of the society's activity—those aspects connected with immediate problems of survival and well-being. If a child is learning the intricacies of interaction by experience, the activity in which he is experiencing or practicing interaction *must* allow him to make many mistakes without endangering the lives or futures of those around him. Similarly, such rewards as he receives from the activity must not be too expensive to those around him—or again the activity may have just those serious consequences which the teaching devices must avoid.

(2) But in spite of the fact that the teaching device must avoid these serious consequences, some motivation must be built into the activity, else the learner may lose interest. If we rely on the distinction between activities that are *intrinsically* rewarding, and those that are rewarding only as a means, or *extrinsically* rewarding, we may say that the rewards in the learner's activities must be intrinsic, or inherent in the activity itself. Such activities we call *autotelic:* they contain their own goals, and sources of motivation.

(3) And finally, they must help a child to learn the relevant techniques (Anderson and Moore, 1959, p. 5).

By utilizing such a method of training, Moore (1960) has demonstrated most of the consequences we would expect from such informational interdependent training, particularly in regard to the rate at

[1] Mothers in child guidance clinics often admit to dressing and feeding young children though feeling that the child is ready to begin learning these tasks himself.

which the child's conceptual schema develop. In Anderson and Moore's words (1959):

> If we are correct in supposing that autotelic cultural products help us learn about our environment, then it would seem reasonable to try to fabricate autotelic teaching devices. If, for example, one should wish to teach a child some complicated cultural product such as English orthography, the following procedure would be suggested. After making a detailed analysis of the task to be learned, one should put the child in an environment which is thoroughly autotelic, and in which the task is presented. Our heuristic considerations would lead us to expect order of magnitude differences in rate of learning. And experimental studies have fulfilled this expectation. Using autotelic contexts suggested by these heuristic considerations, Moore brought some pre-school children to the point where they were reading and writing first grade stories, and typing on an electric typewriter with correct fingering—and all in a matter of weeks (Anderson and Moore, 1959, p. 12).

Before proceeding to a consideration of the interactive effects of these training conditions with stages of development it may be helpful to recapitulate the four generic forms of training as they are summarized in Table 6.

Interactive Effects of Training Conditions upon Stages of Development

We assume that the nature of the training condition not only determines whether progression or arrestation occurs but, in addition, that functioning at a particular stage of development differs according to the training conditions that are being experienced. This variation is summarized in Table 7.

Interaction between Reliable Unilateral Training and Stages of Development

Reliable unilateral training would be expected to maximize openness to differentiations based on external control and to maximize closedness to differentiations based on pole B of first stage concepts, namely opposition to external control. Therefore, we propose that such training is antecedent to the eventual arrestation of development at the first stage (cf. left-hand column in Table 7).

In order for progression from the first to the second stage to occur, the person must be open to both pole A and B in the first stage. Such openness requires training methods that include at least one of the following characteristics: (1) permission of more subject autonomy, (2) inducement of an internal conception of causality, (3) encouragement of

TABLE 6

Definitions and Examples of Training Conditions

	Condition			
	Reliable Unilateral	Unreliable Unilateral	Protective Interdependent	Informational Interdependent
Definition:	Arbitrary, but consistent, imposition of source-defined standards or absolute criterion.	Inconsistent control. Excessively high goals. Indifference and neglect.	Encourages subjects to explore environment, but guides exploration. Source anticipates failure.	Encourages subject to explore environment. Reflects informational consequences to subject. Subject reacts to consequences of own behavior.
Examples:	Overdomination; autocratic training; bureaucratic role training (Merton, 1940).	Parental rejection; parental neglect. Overly high demands based on impulsive or changing standards.	Some forms of maternal overprotection; training that emphasizes "getting along with others" and avoiding failure.	Intrinsic evaluation (Ausubel, 1952). Some forms of democratic training. Autotelic activities (Anderson and Moore, 1959).

TABLE 7

Interaction between Training Conditions and Stages of Development

Stage or Level	Training Conditions: Reliable Unilateral	Unreliable Unilateral	Protective Interdependent	Informational Interdependent
First stage	Openness to pole A and closedness to pole B. Arrestation at stage I.	Openness to pole B and increasing closedness to pole A.	Openness to pole A and pole B. Plus stage III tendencies in pole A.	Openness to pole A and pole B. Plus stage IV tendencies.
Level I Transition		Openness to pole B and closedness to pole A increasing.	Integration of modified pole A and pole B.	Integration of pole A and pole B.
Second stage		Failure to integrate pole A and pole B. Closedness to pole A and to pole D. Arrestation at stage II.	Emergence of stage II concepts. Increasing relative openness to pole D.	Emergence of stage II concepts. Openness to pole C and D. Stage IV tendencies.
Level II Transition			Openness to pole D and closedness to pole C increasing.	Integration of pole C and pole D.
Third stage			Failure to integrate pole C and pole D. Closedness to pole C and pole F. Arrestation at stage III.	Emergence of stage III concepts. Openness to pole E and pole F.
Level III Transition				Integration of pole E and pole F.
Fourth stage				Emergence of stage IV concepts.

alternative solutions to problems, (4) involvement of an interdependent relationship between the subject and the source, and (5) involvement of intrinsic evaluation or reward for instrumental behavior, leading to feelings of self-worth and confidence in independently coping with the environment. Reliable unilateral training satisfies none of the above requirements. In addition, the fact that it maximally favors the adoption of pole A, stage I, differentiations (see Table 3 on pp. 116–117), favors arrestation of progressive development at stage I (see Table 7).

Under this training the utilization of differentiations based on absolutistic control and unilateral or symbiotic dependence (Fromm, 1941) become ends in themselves, rather than the means or a step in the progression to more abstract levels. First stage functioning under completely reliable unilateral training is expected to be maximally closed to overt oppositional tendencies; therefore, further integration is impossible and progressive development is arrested. Further development proceeds within the conceptual limits of the arrested form of a stage I system of relatedness. Development within relatively closed systems at various levels of abstractness are discussed in Chapter 6.

Interaction between Unreliable Unilateral Training and Stages of Development

Unreliable unilateral training would be expected to maximize openness to differentiations based upon opposition to external control and to maximize closedness to differentiations based on any form of dependency upon others for support or help. Therefore, we assume that such training will lead to arrestation of development at the second stage (see Table 7).

In order for progression from the second to the third stage to occur, the person must be open to both poles C and D in the second stage. Such openness requires training methods that include at least one of the following characteristics: (1) maintenance of positive relationships between the subject and source in order that opposition on the part of the subject represents budding internal control rather than hostility; (2) fostering of the subject's viewing his own behavior as affecting the criterion by which it is evaluated, and (3) involvement of intrinsic evaluation. None of these requirements is met by unreliable unilateral training so that arrestation at the second stage occurs.

Unreliable unilateral training results in tenuous, distrustful subject-source relationships that produce closedness to pole D. In second stage functioning, oppositional tendencies originate initially as means or early tendencies toward internal control. However, under unreliable unilateral training, these oppositional tendencies become ends in themselves. Such transformation of opposition into hostility and aggression is accompanied by a transformation of dependency (pole D) as dangerous and threatening, since it is perceived as a form of control.

In order to understand the interaction of this training condition with stages, we need to consider the effect of unreliable unilateral training at every stage. As indicated in Table 7, the effect of this training upon first stage functioning is to produce exaggerated pole B differentiations. A major effect of this training upon functioning at the first stage is to produce closedness and avoidance toward pole A differentiations involving external control. Therefore, the net effect would be toward an increasing positiveness of pole B: opposition to external control and the avoidance of compliance and control. Under these conditions transition does not represent an integration of external support or control with oppositional interpretations. The emerging conceptual system, therefore, does not permit generating new differentiations required for progression beyond stage II.

Unreliable unilateral training retards or restricts the emergence of third stage concepts that are open to pole D interpretations (viewing others as models, or as being supportive). When oppositional tendencies become ends in themselves, involving closedness to pole A and openness to pole B during the first stage, we speak of the outcome as arrestation at the second stage of functioning. In this sense, such arrestation at the second stage involves the arrestation of development at the very outset of the second stage.

It will be recalled that we are assuming that an individual has progressed beyond an omnipotent stage before reaching what we describe as the first stage. The child must experience *some* concretistic dependence on the parent, even though short-lived, in order to reach the second stage. Impersonal, neglectful training which prohibits entirely the emergence of first stage orientations will not therefore lead to second stage functioning, but rather to some form of autistic functioning, more concrete than the level at which we enter the developmental ladder. Unreliable unilateral training, as used here, necessarily permits the development of first stage orientations to a sufficient degree that oppositional tendencies (to external control of the first stage) may develop.

The introduction of unreliable unilateral training very early in the course of the developmental sequence produces both a strong negative "weighting" of the source and a decreased tendency toward what Ausubel has referred to as ego-devaluation and subsequent satellization (Ausubel, 1952). Therefore, the foundation for progression to the third stage, namely mutuality and cooperative behavior, is almost entirely absent.

If unreliable unilateral training is imposed somewhat later (when the subject begins to function at the second stage), then such constriction is likely to be perceived as frustrating and unreliable by the subject since oppositional behavior in the framework of progression is not directed against the source. However, such restriction results in greater closedness both to pole A and to pole D differentiations. Punishment for aggression as well as oppositional tendencies does not decrease the aggressive tendencies but merely changes the form of their expression (Sears, Maccoby, and Levin, 1957).

Interaction between Protective Interdependent Training and Stages of Development

Protective interdependent training is expected to maximize openness to differentiations based upon support, dependency, and imitation while maximizing closedness to differentiations based upon autonomy. The effect of this training condition, therefore, is to produce a particular form of progression through the first two stages and to the eventual arrestation of development at the third stage of functioning.

In order for progression from the third to the fourth stage to occur, the person must be open to both poles E and F at the third stage. Such openness requires training conditions that facilitate both mutuality and autonomy. Since this requirement is not met by protective interdependent training, arrestation at the third stage is expected.

Protective training induces a sensitization to other people's reactions to one's own behavior and thereby increases the tendency to rely on the support of others in unstructured situations. As a result of such training, the subject adopts alternate attitudes or solutions that will insure continuing support other than for informational purposes. The aim, therefore, is not only to avoid the withdrawal of support but also to avoid autonomy and to maintain positive relationships by pleasing others. Training that sensitizes the subject to viewing others as the anticipators of success and failure increases the closedness of third stage concepts to differentiations based on autonomous informational standards.

Table 7 illustrates a point touched on earlier: that protective interdependent training interacts with functioning at the first stage to lead to functioning modified by the intrusion of third stage tendencies such as greater sensitization to rejection, approval, separation, and mutuality. When protective interdependent training occurs in relation to first stage functioning we would also expect that the differentiations based on pole B would involve more "attention getting" characteristics when the subject was frustrated or confronted by an ambiguous situation. Under this training condition, oppositional tendencies would likely enlist the support, attention, and interest of others. Protective interdependent training therefore provides partial openness to pole C at the second stage and the accompanying differentiation between subject and source requisite for one type of progression to the third stage. However, the fact that second stage functioning under this training is not characterized by sufficiently complete openness to pole C is a primary determinant of the later arrestation at the third stage; the "independent" activities are in the service of dependency goals.

The initiation of internal control or oppositional tendencies is in conflict with the learned tendencies to look to others as supporters and as anticipators of potential dangers. The venture into negative independence is too closely tied to attention-gaining devices (for example, tantrums) and is accompanied by increasing and excessive openness to pole D differentiations (that is, dependency interpretations). The possibility of the emergence of a conceptual system capable of generating differentiations based on mutuality and autonomy, which are both required for progression beyond the third stage, is reduced, leading to the arrestation of progressive development at the third stage.

Interaction between Informational Interdependent Training and Stages of Development

Informational interdependent training is assumed to maximize openness to differentiations at every stage based on both conceptual poles, including both mutuality and autonomy in the third stage functioning. Such training permits the most rapid and the most successful integration of each of these opposing differentiations, leading to the eventual emergence of fourth stage conceptual functioning.

This training condition is optimal for producing the most abstract form of functioning. In this connection we may note that when we assumed in Chapter 4 that the training conditions were optimal, we were simply assuming that informational interdependent training was present. Given this circumstance, development proceeds through the three stages described in the last chapter to the fourth stage of functioning.

This training does not consist of a constant set of conditional procedures applied by the source throughout the training sequence. In this sense, we would agree with Ausubel's (1952) notion of intrinsic evaluation that changes in relation to the developing child. However, the principles underlying informational interdependent training remain constant, whether the subject is functioning at the first, second, or third stage. In this training the behavior of the source is highly interdependent in regard to the subject's behavior. In other forms of training described, either the source dominates the subject or the subject dominates the source. Neither circumstance provides for a developmental sequence in which the critical integrations required for abstract forms of relatedness may occur (see unilateral training above and permissive training below). It is this interdependent flow of information between the subject and the training situation that provides both a truly open-loop feedback situation between the subject and the source and the maximum openness of the conceptual system to more abstract differentiations at each stage. These two characteristic effects of informational interdependent training are basic to the resulting progression to more abstract levels of functioning.

When it occurs in relation to first stage functioning (see Table 7), informational interdependent training involves controlling the environment in order to provide structure and external supports (pole A). This training reinforces attempts at internal control regardless of the excellence of the outcome judged against an external criterion. The reward pattern is ipsative and hence favors openness to pole B. Since the source and subject are in an interdependent open-loop situation, environmental pressures and stages of development remain in maximum synchrony. The developing approach tendencies to pole A and pole B facilitate integration and the emergence of second stage concepts open to both pole C (internal control, negative independence) and pole D (dependency on informational supports). Later, since the conceptual system is equally open to both interpretations, further development involves the emergence of a new conceptual system open to poles E and F (mutuality and autonomy), and informational interdependent training provides an environment in which these differentiations become integrated so that neither interferes with the other.

A study by Baldwin (1946) is particularly relevant to the change in training condition relative to the developing organism. He demonstrated that the correlation between children's adjustment and parental warmth was .64 for three-year-olds and .16 for nine-year-olds, and between adjustment and parental interference it was —.09 for three-year-olds and —.50 for nine-year-olds. These results suggest that different components of training have different effects at different stages of development. We assume that informational interdependent training maintains maximum synchrony between the developmental stage and the environmental pressures and, therefore, maximally facilitates progression.

Short-Term Effects of Training Conditions

In this section we consider the short-term effects of the four "pure" training conditions on conceptual functioning. Training conditions interact with stages of development in the complex way that we have attempted to portray in Table 7. The nature of functioning at any stage is influenced both by (1) training conditions through the early stages of development and (2) by the training condition at a particular later stage of development. For example, protective-interdependent training presumably exercises its optimal effect on functioning after the emergence of oppositional tendencies at the beginning of the third stage. However, as Table 7 indicates, different training conditions would be expected to produce specific differences in functioning in the early stages of learning, for example, in the first stage.

In this section we consider evidence bearing on the short-term effects of the four polar training conditions as it may support the expected effects. These expectations are presented at the generic level along the top row of Table 7. The studies we describe are somewhat limited in that they do not take account of dispositional characteristics of the subject. That is, a particular subject may be so highly predisposed to activate third stage functioning that the short-term effects of a training condition may have little effect on him. In Chapter 8 we discuss the interdependent effects of situational and dispositional factors. For present purposes, however, let us assume that studies utilizing different training methods would be expected to show immediate gross differences in functioning in the direction specified. Many different forms of evidence are presented in the chapters to follow, particularly in Chapter 8 where the discussion of the contemporaneous effects of situational variables represents a more thorough treatment of this problem.

Short-Term Effects of Reliable Unilateral Training

Coping with reliable unilateral training leads to the development of a conceptual system characterized by poor discrimination (by the subject) between self and source. Concepts are more absolute and more compartmentalized. In this training, the source determines directly the associations that the subject adopts toward events. Accordingly, the source is perceived as omniscient and powerful. Once such undifferentiated subject-object relationships are formed, the associations are like absolute rules that permit no alternatives. In addition, such associations are rigid, externally anchored, and experienced as outside the range of the subject's influence. The effect of such training induces maximal openness to change induced by an external source, but the change in behavior or solution that occurs is categorical, all or none, or black-white. This black-whiteness is a product of the external determination of ready-made concepts described in Chapter 2.

Merton's (1940) account of the effect of standardized bureaucratic role experiences (bureaucratic training) on personality is relevant. In his words:

(1) An effective bureaucracy demands reliability of response and strict devotion to regulations. (2) Such devotion to the rules leads to their transformation into absolutes; they are no longer conceived as relative to a given set of purposes. (3) This interferes with ready adaptation under special conditions not clearly envisaged by those who drew up the general rules. (4) Thus, the very elements which conduce toward efficiency in general produce inefficiency in specific instances. Full realization of the inadequacy is seldom attained by members of the group who have not divorced themselves from the "meanings" which the rules have for them. These rules in time become symbolic in cast, rather than strictly utilitarian (Merton, 1940, p. 564).

If the subjects are pretrained to use a particular solution by reliable unilateral type training, then progressive changes in the problem to be solved, which would generally produce an alternate solution, have less effect on the nature of the solution than the same task changes have for subjects trained by other methods (Schroder and Rotter, 1952). Furthermore, when the task was changed sufficiently to produce a change in the solution for persons trained under reliable unilateral conditions, the solution change was more categorical. In this experiment the categorical nature of attempted solutions was indicated by a relative absence of "looking for alternative solutions." When adopted, new solutions were absolute and persisted more rigidly under conditions that called for further modification in solution.

This study indicates the concreteness of the learned associations produced by reliable unilateral training. If rigidity is defined in terms of the nature of change (brittle, or categorical), then we expect reliable unilateral training to maximize rigidity. However, the relationship between rigidity and resistance to change is very complex in that we assume the interrelationship is determined by both the level of reliable unilateral training and the means of attempting to induce change. Let us consider two levels of training—short-term and long-term—and two means of inducing change—direct external influence by a powerful source versus task or environmental change induction (as in the study referred to above). Under short-term conditions we would expect, in addition to rigidity, that the subject would be resistant to change induced by environmental factors but would not resist change induced by powerful sources. (It should be noted, however, as we have implied earlier that even though resistance to change may be slight, when change occurs under these conditions, it is of a categorical nature.) However, if the training conditions are long-term, involving child training practices over a long period of time, we would expect the subject to be resistant to both forms of change. These latter effects are dealt with in greater detail in later chapters.

Short-Term Effects of Unreliable Unilateral Training

Unreliable imposition of unilateral control produces a conceptual system in which subject and source are differentiated, but in a very tenuous fashion. The subject attaches a very low "weight" to the source, since he distrusts him. This form of training produces subject-source relationships that are directionally opposite to those described in the first-stage systems. Responses learned under this training are also relatively resistant to change, but this resistance is not accompanied by such rigidity as occurs as a consequence of reliable unilateral training. Resistance to change following unreliable unilateral training is due to a lack of informational value of feedback, rather than to an excessive reliance on an absolute fixed criterion.

One important characteristic of this training is assumed to be that social rewards and punishments are relatively ineffective. The main features of this training can be exemplified by the partial reinforcement paradigm. When associations are established on the basis of unreliable rewards, these associations are more tenuous (less strong) and more tenacious (Schroder, 1956). Viewed in terms of experimental studies, this particular outcome of training has become almost synonymous with resistance to extinction. However, many other related training conditions consistent with the operations outlined above would be expected to produce the same effects. Phares (1957) instructed one group that success on a problem was a matter of skill and another group that the task was so difficult that success would be largely a matter of chance (unreliable). He found that the latter group changed least (change measured in terms of level of aspiration) as a consequence of the occurrence of success or failure. The tenacious maintenance of a high level of aspiration in the face of failure by rejected children who perceive themselves as extrinsically valued by parents (Ausubel, Balthazar, Rosenthal, Blackman, Schpront, and Welkowitz, 1954) also exemplifies the effects of unreliable unilateral training.

Short-Term Effects of Protective Interdependent Training

As a result of protective interdependent training, the subject learns to view other relevant persons as supportive, and/or as supplying the criterion for behavior in the absence of internal informational standards. Because the source is associated with the successful solution of problems in this condition, positive and supportive subject-source relations come to be the primary concern. Therefore, uncertainty regarding this subject-source relation comes to be associated with the expectancy of failure and a general decrease in confidence.

Change in behavior developed under protective interdependent training should be maximally effective if through source induction. Since source-induced change is also at times effective in first stage systems, it is important to distinguish between the two conditions. Three major distinctions may be noted. First, protective training leads to more effective discrimination between subject and source than unilateral training, so that concepts are less absolutistic. Second, protective training is linked to persons as sources of support (interpersonal relationships) whereas unilateral training is linked to persons as sources of external criteria and rules (power). Third, there is a difference in the nature of resistance to change produced by these two conditions. Whereas reliable unilateral training leads to considerable resistance to change, protective training occurring in relation to a problem-solving situation would not produce fixed, compartmentalized concepts. That is, there is no reason to expect resistance to change in an impersonal problem-solving situation in which the social relationships are not salient in reference to the solutions.

Subject-object associations in this condition are not experienced in the form of absolute rules as being right or wrong in terms of some external power over which the subject has no control. Rather, the associations produced by protective interdependent training are conditional in that they can be changed at any time in the service of their effects on relationships. As a result of this training, the self becomes the agent of causality much more than in functioning based on conceptual systems reflecting less differentiation of the subject from external conditions.

Many experimental procedures exemplify certain components of this training. Training methods that induce normative sets (Deutsch and Gerard, 1955) or a group set (Thibaut and Strickland, 1956) produce judgments and behavior that are highly dependent upon the judgments of other people. In these conditions and other learning sequences involving verbal approval or agreement by the source as the criterion of behavior, such behavior tends to persist despite the changes in the situational stimuli so long as verbal approval or relationships remain salient (Kelman, 1958).

A major effect of protective training is to increase the subject's sensitivity to isolation, which in turn increases approval-seeking and socially accommodating responses aimed to avoid rejection. In inducing greater relative social deprivation or isolation, protective training would be expected to be associated with the same consequent effects as experimentally induced deprivation or isolation. Levin and Baldwin (1959) have recently shown that children were more likely to want to exhibit their work after a condition in which success followed a previous failure (after an increase in sensitivity to failure or rejection) than after a condition in which success was not preceded by failure. Of even more direct relevance is a study by Gewirtz and Baer (1958) who have shown that 20 minutes of social isolation had the effect of increasing the effectiveness of verbal rewards.

Short-Term Effects of Informational Interdependent Training

Under informational interdependent training the subject learns to view autonomous exploratory behavior as a means of solving problems. He does not learn to rely on the support of others or on ready-made concepts as a means of relating to objects. Failure or difficulty in instrumental activity does not become associated with feelings of worthlessness, negativism, or rejection, but, instead, difficulty is transformed into informational feedback on which the subject learns to depend. He learns to relate to objects in terms of internal standards developed through experiencing the consequences of his own exploratory action. This training maximizes the subject's sensitivity to situational change because subject-object associations are anchored in informational standards that are maximally under the control of, and relevant to, the subject's exploratory behavior.

Subject-object relations in this system are flexible and open to change as required by changes in the situation. In a problem-solving situation, such training would be expected to lead to early solution change as the nature of the problem progressively changed. Such change in solution would be characterized as flexible rather than rigid, so that at all times the subject would be open to or sensitized to alternative solutions (Schroder and Rotter, 1952). Such functioning is more inefficient in situations that demand obedient, fixed, or automatic behavior. The effect of such training can be summarized by the description "abstract closedness." One of the main characteristics of abstract functioning is that the person can take on the "closed" state in order to explore the consequences of a given system of ordering, but he can also open his conceptual system to discrepant views or systems of ordering. That is, although informational training leads to strong standards or attitudes, these standards are not absolute. In contrast to the subjective projection of first stage functioning, the more abstract concept does not "shut out" alternate observations or evaluations. *Incoming information is not distorted by fitting it onto an absolutistic conceptual schema.*

Up to this point we have described the nature of four generic training conditions and the effect of these conditions upon development. These four extreme training methods provide what we assume to be the "ideal" conditions antecedent to the eventual arrestation of the first, second, and third stage and for progression to the fourth stage. Before concluding this chapter we shall consider the interaction between training conditions and stages of development in regard to the transition between stages.

The Effect of Training Conditions upon Transitional Arrestation

Transitional arrestation is associated with training that induces premature or accelerated developmental "leaps." When environmental pressures are out of synchrony with the stage of development, the result is the development of both approach and avoidant tendencies toward both poles of a conceptual system. If environmental pressures pull or induce conflicting differentiations before the subject reaches sufficient clarity of differentiations based on the earlier pole, such pressures result in the simultaneous arousal of positive and negative tendencies to each pole. Acceleration produces a lack of clarity of one form of relatedness before experiencing the next. As a consequence, not only does the subject develop partial openness (positive and negative evaluations) to each pole of a concept but also he fails to discriminate sufficiently between the two poles.

Environmental pressures or training conditions that are in synchrony with developmental stages induce new and conflicting differentiations sequentially. Before experiencing a new conflicting basis for functioning (that is, a conflicting pole) the subject should gain some facility in functioning on the basis of the earlier set of differentiations. The development of some confidence in functioning based on unilateral dependence (pole A, first stage) is required before the development of oppositional tendencies (pole B). In a similar way, conditional dependence should follow differentiations based on internal control in order to satisfy the requirements of synchrony and to enhance progression.

We propose that accelerated forms of training at any stage increase the simultaneity of development of conflicting differentiations. By acceleration we mean that the environmental pressures are ahead of the developmental rate, that is, premature in relation to level of clarity of earlier differentiations. As a result of such premature conflict each set of differentiations develops positive and negative attitudes, which retard or restrict the possibility of integration and progression.

That is, by accelerated training we mean training that is imposed before the subject is ready. Such premature training constitutes pressures that demand the emergence of differentiations based on a given pole, for example, pole B, before the subject has reached sufficient articulation of pole A or before he has achieved sufficient structure and trust as a background for oppositional tendencies to be integrated. Acceleration has generally referred to early independence training (Whiting and Child, 1953). However, we propose that *any* training method can be accelerated and that the object of the training, whether it be toilet training, language, or other forms of achievement, is of less importance than the training condition through which acceleration is mediated.

In this section three forms of acceleration are described. These methods parallel the training dimensions already discussed and are referred to as (1) accelerated unilateral training, (2) accelerated autonomous training (in the center of the unilateral-interdependent training dimension on Table 4), and (3) accelerated interdependent training. These three forms of accelerated training represent the antecedent conditions for the arrestation of progressive development at transitional points between the four stages: between (1) the first and second stages, (2) the second and third stages, and (3) the third and fourth stages. These three transitional points will be referred to as levels I, II, and III, respectively (see Table 8). Between the extremes of progression and transitional arrestation (involving, to some degree, conflicting or compartmentalized subject-object linkages) there are many degrees of integrative difficulty, which may retard progression at a particular transitional level and may result in a potential developmental flaw at that point. Such flaws may then recur in future related cycles of development. The relationships between training and arrestation (including transitional arrestation) are presented in Tables 8 and 9, which are elaborations of Tables 5 and 7.

In Table 8 the two training dimensions, noted earlier, are collapsed into a single dimension, which permits expressing their combined complex effects on overall development conceived as progressing from concrete to abstract systems of conceptual functioning. When viewed in relation to the level of concreteness, this generic training dimension is unidimensional though quite complex. When viewed more phenotypically or more specifically, this dimension becomes multidimensional. Our approach to development permits investigation at either the general or specific level and provides a set of theoretical propositions for integrating dimensions, which at one level of analysis are more specific and unrelated, into a single dimension at the next most general level. The nature of these various dimensions will be fully developed at the beginning of Chapter 6.

TABLE 8

Consequences and Forms of Arrestation Produced by Various Training Conditions

	Unilateral Training		Autonomous Training		Interdependent Training		
Training Dimensions	Reliable Imposition	Accelerated Unilateral	Unreliable Imposition	Accelerated Autonomous	Protective Imposition	Accelerated Interdependent	Informational Imposition
Major consequences	Maximizes pole A diff., minimizes pole B.	Maximizes conflict between pole A and B diff.	Maximizes pole B diff., minimizes conflict.	Maximizes conflict between pole C and D diff.	Maximizes pole D diff., minimizes conflict.	Maximizes conflict between pole E and F diff.	Maximizes stage IV diff., minimizes conflict.
Arrestation of progressive development	Stage I nodal arrestation	Level I transitional arrestation	Stage II nodal arrestation	Level II transitional arrestation	Stage III nodal arrestation	Level III transitional arrestation	Progression to stage IV
Generic dimension	Concrete Conceptual Systems						Abstract Conceptual Systems

diff. = differentiations

TABLE 9

Interactive Effects of Generic and Arrested Training Conditions upon Stages of Development

Stage or level	Training Conditions						
	Reliable Unilateral	Accelerated Unilateral	Unreliable Unilateral	Accelerated Autonomous	Protective Interdependent	Accelerated Interdependent	Informational Interdependent
First stage	Openness to pole A and closedness to pole B. Arrestation at stage I	Increasing conflict between pole A and B	Openness to pole B and increasing closedness to pole A	Openness to pole A and B increasing openness to pole B	Openness to pole A and B plus stage III tendencies in pole A	Openness to pole A and B differentiation	Openness to pole A and B; plus stage IV tendencies
Level I		Conflict between pole A and B. Positive and negative evaluations of both poles. Arrestation at level I	Openness to pole B and closedness to pole A	Integration involving an exaggeration of pole B	Integration of pole A and B	Integration of pole A and B	Integration of pole A and B
Second stage			Failure to integrate pole A and B closedness to pole A and D. Arrestation at stage II	Increasing conflict between pole C and D	Emergence of stage II concepts. Increasing relative openness to pole D	Emergence of stage II concepts. Openness to pole C and D. Stage IV tendencies	Emergence of stage II concepts. Openness to pole C and D. Stage IV tendencies

Level II	Conflict between pole C and D. Positive and negative evaluations of both poles. Arrestation at level II	Openness to pole D and closedness to pole C	Integration of pole C and D	Integration of pole C and D
Third stage		Failure to integrate pole C and D closedness to pole C and hence to pole F. Arrestation at stage III	Increasing conflict between pole E and F	Emergence of stage III concepts. Openness to pole E and F
Level III			Conflict between pole E and F. Positive and negative evaluations of both poles. Arrestation at level III	Integration of pole E and F
Fourth stage				Emergence of stage IV concepts

Accelerated Unilateral Training and Level I Transitional Arrestation

Accelerated unilateral training is characterized by imposition that is consistent and controlling as well as pushing and demanding. It involves (1) training that is not so far beyond the ability of the subject that the subject does not achieve an occasional reward, (2) a high degree of extrinsic reward for achieving these ends, and punishment, including the withdrawal of love, for failure to do so.

Such accelerated training differs from unreliable unilateral training only in degree. Accelerated unilateral training does not imply such great irregularity or arbitrariness; therefore, it produces less distrust and more interiorization of absolutistic criteria. In contrast to unreliable unilateral training, accelerated training involves excessive (as opposed to unreliable) achievement demands whereas unreliable unilateral training involves inconsistency and changing standards.

Relevant to these operations are the child training practices underlying what Brown (1953) refers to as the rigid, anxious, authoritarian personality. He states:

> Suppose two indulgent, child-centered parents have feelings of social and economic marginality. . . . Such parents will encourage behavior that safeguards or enhances their status and will punish and suppress those inclinations in their offspring which threaten that status. . . . As a result he will have many bitter experiences of failure and will learn to anticipate this unpleasant outcome of achievement-related tasks. But because his occasional successes have been so well rewarded he will want very much to succeed and will keep trying (Brown, 1953, pp. 474–475).

Under these conditions we would expect the development of partial openness to both poles (a double approach-avoidant conflict) and transitional arrestation at level I (see Table 9).

On the one hand, the conceptual orientation is directed toward the achievement of rigid, externally-defined goals (pole A differentiations) and, on the other hand, it is toward the tendency to reject such goals and negatively "weight" the source (pole B differentiations). Such subject-object relatedness involves a conflict of tendencies to achieve the external goals and view the source as omnipotent versus tendencies to fear the consequences of failure and to reject external control. We would expect such training to induce a maximum of compulsivity and concern about achievement. By this we do not necessarily imply a higher level of achievement but rather that achievements should be more concrete (Lazarus, Baker, Broverman, and Mayer, 1957). Such persons should accordingly show greater concern about achievement or sensitivity to it, measured as a threshold, for example, through the use of a projective technique (McClelland et al., 1953).

Accelerated Autonomous Training and Level II Transitional Arrestation

Accelerated autonomous training is characterized by: (1) a lack of directionality of control and (2) indiscriminate approval. This training is very similar to what Ausubel (1952) describes as underdomination or permissiveness. We agree with Ausubel in distinguishing between this training and what he describes as overprotection (or what we refer to as protective-interdependent training). Under accelerated autonomous training the role of the source is "submissive," and the subject becomes omnipotent. In contrast to protective interdependent training, the source in accelerated autonomous training does not enter into the subject's instrumental behavior either when the subject begins to fail or when the subject is on the threshold of experiencing negative or dangerous consequences. This training condition presents a minimum of barriers or restraints; the likelihood that the subject will seek barriers is made even less by the application of indiscriminate rewards regardless of the quality of the outcome of the subject's behavior.

Therefore, we would expect such training to induce conflicting systems of subject-object relatedness. The resulting conceptual orientation toward objects involves a conflict between, on the one hand, the tendency to be independent of the source and to maintain a position of omnipotence or self-assertion in relation to the source (modified by second stage pole C differentiations) as opposed, on the other hand, to the tendency to seek or depend upon the approval and support of the source (second stage pole D differentiations). Although such conflicting subject-object associations may not be so apparent in this training situation as in accelerated unilateral training, the conflict becomes very apparent when the source is changed. An underdominated child may experience little conflict in the home situation interacting with the overpermissive parents, but when this child is interacting with more demanding persons, for example, peers, the conflict becomes more intense. In a peer-group situation, the child's quest for independence and omnipotence is more likely to produce ostracism and rejection than the indiscriminate approval that he customarily expects. Accelerated autonomous training not only fails to develop frustration tolerance but also fails to produce the instrumental skills necessary for resolving conflict or becoming independent in a positive or interdependent sense.

As was true earlier for the four generic training conditions the effect of accelerated training differs according to the stage of development in the person experiencing such a condition (see Table 9). However, the critical effects of accelerated autonomous training do not become apparent until the subject reaches the second stage of development. The resulting arrestation at level II is characterized primarily by an inability to cope with internal control and negative independence.

Accelerated Interdependent Training and Level III Arrestation

Accelerated interdependent training is characterized by (1) non-controlling source expectation of premature, autonomous (but not extrinsically valued) responsibility, (2) an environment that is somewhat beyond the ability level of the subject, and perhaps may be somewhat unpredictable, and (3) a relative absence of the highly supportive components of training described as operations for protective interdependent training. The major effect of such training is to arouse simultaneously the opposing motivational tendencies of third stage pole E and pole F differentiations. Under these conditions the conflict lies between tendencies to behave in a way that would be congruent with informational standards (or independent exploratory behavior), as opposed to tendencies to behave in a way that would be congruent with other people's standards and thus avoid the possible negative consequences experienced earlier in relying on premature informational standards.

General Considerations

TRAINING CONDITIONS AND POWER RELATIONSHIPS

In any training situation each member (the source and the subject) can effect each other's outcomes to some degree, however slight it might be for the subject under some circumstances. In this sense each has some power over the other.[1] Thibaut and Kelley (1959) define two types of power as follows: "If, by varying his behavior, A can effect B's outcomes *regardless of what B does,* A has *fate control* over B (p. 102). . . . If, by varying his behavior, A can make it desirable for B to vary his behavior too, then A has behavior control over B" (p. 103).

[1] A current story in psychological circles illustrates this point. A somewhat bored psychologist (Mr. A.) at a small meeting passed away his time by "shaping up" one of his colleague's behavior. Every time his colleague (Mr. B.) pounded his fist on the table to emphasize a point, Mr. A. would reward him by such social techniques as subtly agreeing with him and so on. As expected, Mr. B.'s fist-pounding increased considerably. The next day Mr. B. was overheard to say "Mr. A. is a peculiar person; you can make him agree with your viewpoint by slamming your fist on the table."

The relationship between power formulations and training conditions will concern us more when we deal with attitude change in Chapter 8. Here we will merely raise the possibility of what appear to be some interesting connections between Thibaut and Kelley's terms and our training dimensions.

Reliable unilateral training maximizes the possibility that in the early stages of the training the source has fate control over the subject because the source establishes the criterion. As learning proceeds, providing S can adjust his behavior to match the source criterion, the situation becomes one of behavior control. Under these conditions the subject learns to adjust his behavior to absolutistic rules. The less the subject can learn to adjust to the source's rules (unreliable unilateral training), the more the situation remains one of fate control, and the subject minimally learns to adjust his behavior to the source. In the initial stages, under protective interdependent training, the situation contains many elements of fate control of a distinctive nature. The source anticipates and controls the consequence of the subject's behavior (in a protective sense) regardless of what the subject does. Under this training the subject learns a "behavior control" orientation. He learns to anticipate the behavior of others and adjust his own behavior to these anticipations so that he can maintain a supportive relationship to others. This is similar to Thibaut and Kelley's notion of a conversion from fate control to behavior control. Informational interdependent training minimally involves fate control and achieves behavior control primarily through appropriate *environmental* manipulations.

Training Conditions and Maternal Behavior Concepts

The dimensionalization of training one employs should not and perhaps cannot be independent of the more general theoretical orientation one utilizes. In this sense the training dimensions currently proposed are based upon and represent an interrelated aspect of a general theory of development, personality organization, and functioning.

A recent investigation by Schaefer (1959) suggests that descriptions of maternal behavior, as conceived in a number of studies, may be ordered within a two-dimensional space as reproduced in Table 10. Although our developmental theory would be likely to produce a somewhat different dimensional space, the interrelationships between the various descriptions of maternal behavior presented by Schaefer in Table 10 are in general agreement with our analysis. One set of descriptions involving primarily authoritarian control is similar to the present reliable unilateral training. The opposite cluster, referred to as

TABLE 10

A Hypothetical Circumplex of Maternal Behavior Concepts *

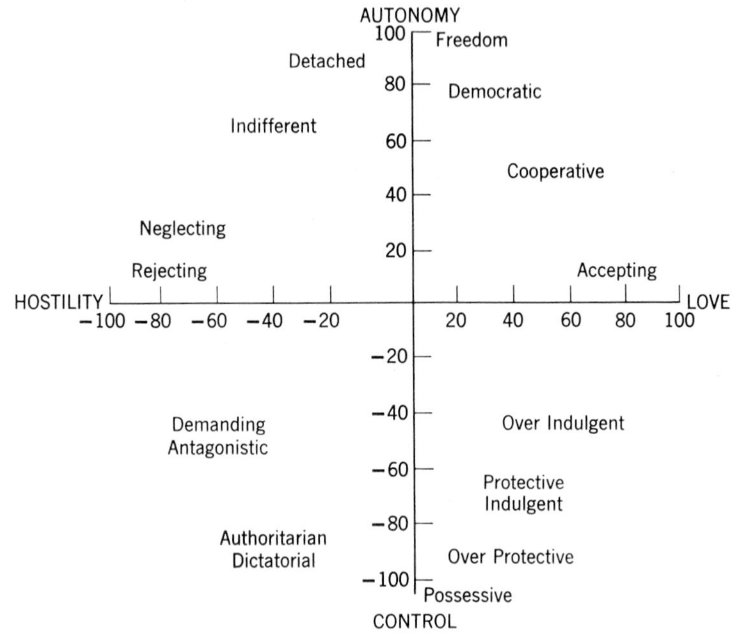

* Reproduced from E. S. Schaefer, A circumplex model for maternal behavior, *J. abnorm. soc. Psychol.*, 1959, 59, p. 232.

democratic and cooperative practices, bears a general similarity to the present interdependent training, which we also view as being opposite to unilateral training. Another cluster of descriptions exemplified by neglect and indifference is similar to the present unreliable unilateral training, whereas in the other quadrant protective and indulgent practices are interrelated as we have suggested in describing protective interdependent training.

The Problem of Variation in Training Conditions

In outlining a schema for development we have assumed that training conditions remain essentially constant. In most present training situations sources do not apply systematic principles of learning in an explicit manner. Consequently the training condition represents an implicit theory of learning (Loevinger, 1959) that is not differentiated from the subjective past experiences of the source. Although a parent may often be unaware of how the child will construe a given training procedure, the psychologist must attempt to understand the child's mode of experiencing the training in order to discover systematic regularities between training conditions and their consequences.

If the training condition is implicit, we expect that it would remain relatively constant. Although the content of the training may vary widely, the method or the condition antecedent to the development of conceptual systems is more probably very difficult to change.

In discussing the difficulties involved in modifying parents' attitudes, Ausubel (1952) comments:

> Anyone who has worked with emotionally disturbed children realizes both the difficulty and the importance of changing parent attitudes. . . . Why this is so should not be difficult to understand. . . . In every case they relate to potent needs which are current in the economy of the parent's personality organization (p. 295). . . . Another factor making for difficulty in changing parent attitudes is the complexity of the relationship between these attitudes and the formal philosophy of child-rearing to which a parent subscribes (Ausubel, 1952, p. 296).

However, if training methods are understood more objectively, specific changes can be introduced when indicated. Such objective understanding provides a basis for assessment and modification.

Training conditions that assume a passive static organism are more likely to result in the arrestation of development at some level. Conversely, training conditions that involve interdependence in which the subject's reactions affect the training agent and vice versa should foster progression.

Training conditions are also influenced by the broader social environment. For example, the personality characteristics of group members presumably interact with the method of training and produce significant effects on group development. Bennis and Shepard (1956) refer to the presence of these effects, but the systematic investigation of their nature is a problem for future research. Such research is of crucial importance for training and modification because of its implications for the explicit selection of group members on the basis of specific characteristics that would induce particular developmental effects. Presumably the effects of a given training method could be magnified by such specific selection.

In child development, the influence of the social environment upon the training condition is illustrated by the interaction between parental practices and sibling characteristics. Studies investigating the effects of sibling order on development have shown that first children are more adult-oriented, sensitive, good, and studious and that second children are more peer-directed, easy-going, and friendly (McArthur, 1956). In a very general sense, this difference would be expected if second children are (1) more likely to develop to the level of stage III functioning in social behavior and (2) if there is also a greater tendency for progressive development to be arrested at this stage. The second child has more opportunity to utilize mutuality and reciprocity and to lean on the standards of the older sibling in interacting with others. Evidence from another study (Schroder and Janicki, 1959a) indicated that adolescents selected as predisposed toward third stage concepts tended to have more older siblings. On a probability basis we would expect that persons with slightly older siblings of the same sex would be less likely to undergo developmental arrestation at the first stage, owing to the greater opportunity to experience participation and mutuality in early training. However, this is a complex question for future research. A thorough analysis of these conditional effects would involve not only birth order but also (1) the effect of birth order under different training methods, since training variation would produce different interaction effects, and (2) a more specific analysis of the details of order, for example, the sex of the siblings and the discrepancy between the developmental level of the siblings.

The Interrelationship between Training Conditions and Stages of Development

In our view, one of the more important criteria for a theory of development is its potential to systematize the complex interrelationships between training conditions and stages of development so as to account for the effects of both short- and long-term training conditions. Table 9 is an attempt to illustrate our analysis in summary form. It should be emphasized again that stages of development interact with specific training conditions so that (1) functioning at one stage differs from functioning at another stage regardless of the training and (2) functioning at a given stage of development differs according to the nature of the training method. We have maintained earlier the importance of distinguishing between the arrestation of progressive development at a given stage and various forms of progression through that stage. This means specifically that it is necessary to distinguish between each one of the cells in Table 9.

Such distinctions have implications for both assessment and modification procedures: (1) To estimate the nature (progression or arrestation) and level of conceptual development measures may be taken at any point, with assessment of these measures based both on the antecedent and the consequent conditions. (2) Assessment is systematically related to and has direct implications for future training or remedial work (see Chapter 10). (3) The diagonal squares represent the basic consequences of various kinds of long-term training. *They outline our present dimensionalization of conceptual systems in terms of personality organization.* These dimensions are of central importance for the understanding of the effect of refutation (Chapter 7), the interrelationship between dispositional and situational factors (Chapter 8), and the manner of coping with the effects of threat (Chapter 9).

In the next chapter we deal with the more arrested or closed forms of the conceptual systems that are implicit in the ordering of the diagonal squares in Table 9.

6 Structure of Conceptual Systems: Dimensions of Personality

What are the relatively stable conceptual systems that emerge from the interactive effects of the training conditions and stages of development? We assume that the result of these training conditions and stages of development described in the last two chapters is to produce particular forms of conceptual structure that we consider in the present chapter. The aim is to derive the dimensional variation of conceptual structure or organization from principles stated earlier. It should be noted that the present dimensionalization of personality organization is theoretically based and does not depend upon the relative presence or absence of these patterns in particular cultures. Rather than beginning with the occurrence of actual functioning characteristics in a given culture, we have chosen to use a developmental schema for ordering training methods and from these principles derive the resulting dimensional structure. Therefore, to the extent that a particular culture does not utilize certain training practices it would not be expected to produce certain patterns of conceptual structure.

It is important to stress that in this chapter we are dealing with systems that are relatively closed to progression or systems that are developmentally arrested at points along the concrete-abstract dimension. Up to this point our emphasis has been upon a description of the stages when the conceptual systems are open to progression. In Chapter 5 we outlined some of the major training conditions hypothesized to be antecedent to the arrestation of development at various levels. At this point, then, the focus is shifted to relatively stable systems of personality organization typifying some degree of closedness to further progression. The term system is substituted for stage and level for transitional stage to imply the relative arrestation of development at a given point (for example, system I, system II, system III, and level I, level II, and level III).

An alternate way to express this change of focus in the present chapter is to emphasize the transition from a between-systems to a within-systems analysis. The introductory section of this chapter is devoted to a general analysis of some of the main "within-system" dimensions. The main body of the chapter is concerned with a description of various systems of personality organization falling along the concrete-abstract continuum.

General Dimensions of Personality

Variation between Systems: The Concrete-Abstract Dimension

The most general dimension along which we order conceptual systems is the concrete-abstract dimension. As indicated in Table 11, this dimension may be viewed in terms of four nodal stages or systems of

TABLE 11

Summary of Major Forms of Arrested Conceptual Structure

Stage	Pole	Openness Closedness	Consequences	Terminology
I	Pole A	+	Nodal arrestation	System I or
	Pole B	–	stage I	stage I systems
	Pole A	+ –	Transitional arresta-	Level I systems
	Pole B	+ –	tion at level I	
II	Pole C	–	Nodal arrestation	System II or
	Pole D	+	at stage II	stage II systems
	Pole C	+ –	Transitional arresta-	Level II systems
	Pole D	+ –	tion at level II	
III	Pole E	–	Nodal arrestation	System III or
	Pole F	+	at stage III	stage III systems
	Pole E	+ –	Transitional arresta-	Level III systems
	Pole F	+ –	tion at level III	
IV	Pole E	+	Progression to nodal	System IV or
	Pole F	+	stage IV	stage IV systems

\+ refers to openness to or approach tendencies toward that pole
– refers to closedness to or avoidance tendencies toward that pole

TABLE 12

Hypothetical Dimension between Two Systems at Any Level of Abstractness

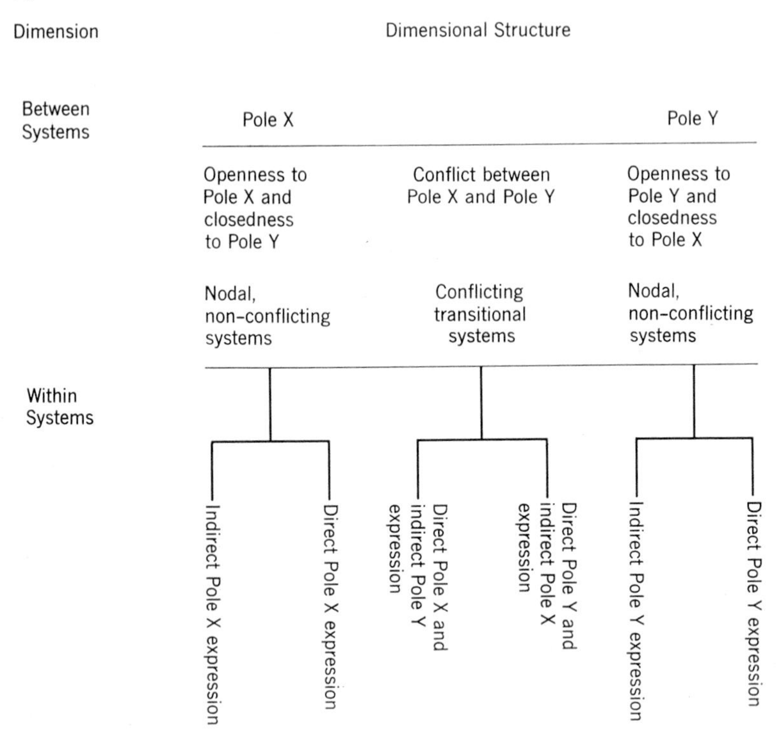

functioning that represent three phases of developmental transition: from stage I to stage II, from stage II to stage III, and from stage III to stage IV. For purposes of establishing more specific dimensions we may regard each of these three transitional phases as generically similar, but varying in terms of the level of abstractness as expressed in Table 12.

Each of these three subdimensions may be viewed in Table 12 as extending from a system that is open to one conceptual pole (X) and closed to the other (Y) through systems that are partially open and partially closed to both poles to the other extreme in which the system is open to only one conceptual pole (Y) and closed to the other (X). (Poles X and Y represent hypothetical poles at any level of abstraction.)

If the subdimension between stage I and stage II were viewed in the light of Table 12 the following would result: on the left-hand side of Table 12 is system I, which is open to pole A (absolutistic control) and closed to pole B (opposition to external control), while on the right-hand side is system II, which is open to pole B (opposition to external control) and closed to pole A (absolutistic control). Midway between these two systems are systems with varying degrees of conflict between pole A and pole B. This hypothetical dimension in Table 12 when applied in relation to the concrete-abstract dimension serves as the basis for deriving the two dimensions of within-system variation: indirectness-directness of nodal system expression and the indirectness-directness of transitional system expression. Taken together directness and indirectness are synonymous with clarity-ambiguity discussed in Chapter 3.

Variation within Systems

Before considering the two within-system dimensions separately, it may be noted that what we refer to as the indirectness of nodal expression and the indirectness of transitional expression are similar in that both represent some form of conflict, and in this sense they can be considered as forms of covert expression. Although we recognize this similarity, for expositional purposes we wish to differentiate between variation in expression within nodal systems and the more transitional systems because the antecedents underlying these expressive differences are somewhat independent. Indirectness of expression in nodal systems represents conflict between opposed expressions of the same pole (for example, pole A) whereas indirect expression in transitional systems represents conflict between the expression of opposing poles or conflicting differentiations (for example, pole A and pole B).

THE DIRECT-INDIRECT DIMENSION WITHIN NODAL SYSTEMS

In nodal systems the indirect or direct expression is primarily a function of system-specific inhibition or facilitation, respectively. In this section we consider the general nature of this dimension within any one of the four nodal stages, and later in the chapter we describe the specific nature of this variation at each nodal stage. The relevant terms for dealing with this problem are presented in Tables 11 and 12.

Before continuing, two points already discussed should be emphasized:

(1) Table 11 is an oversimplification of the range of differentiations to which each system is open and closed. System II might be considered positive toward or open to pole C and negative toward or closed to pole D while system III might be considered positive toward pole E and negative toward pole F. It should be remembered that although adjacent "independent" poles (for example, B and C) and "dependent" poles (for example, D and F) are similar, they differ in their embeddedness

in a more concrete or abstract system of ordering. For example, pole C differs from pole B because of its embeddedness in mutuality, but arrestation of progressive development at the second stage implies closedness to mutuality or to pole D and relative openness to oppositional or negativistic tendencies represented by pole B or pole C.

(2) Although expressive variations may occur at every level of abstractness, we assume that such variation decreases as the level of abstractness increases. The basis for this assumption is that the more interdependent the system of relatedness, the less is the necessity for warding off certain stimuli, which is the underlying function in indirectness. More specifically we propose that when training is not strictly interdependent (that is, if it is reliable unilateral, unreliable unilateral, or protective interdependent) the subject learns two modes of expression simultaneously, expressions that are systemically similar *but expressively opposite.* Therefore, the more unilateral the training (or the less informationally open the training loop), the greater is the potential variation in expression. Later in this chapter we contend that in system I submission implies dominance; that in system II fear implies hostility; and that in system III seeking support implies the fear of rejection.

We assume that indirectness of expression results from inhibition. Although inhibition or punishment may decrease the occurrence of a particular behavioral orientation in the specific inhibiting situation, the tendency for the same behaviors to occur in other situations may not be affected or may increase as a result (Dollard, Doob, Miller, Mowrer, and Sears, 1939). R. Sears, Whiting, Nowlis, and P. Sears (1953) summarize this effect as follows:

> Behavior directed toward the gratification of these drives [aggression and dependency] can be elicited by any instigator that has commonly been associated with reinforcement during the acquisition and activation of the drives. . . . By stimulus generalization, the instigator quality would spread to other people and other frustrations . . . punishment establishes an avoidance response to these instigators which elicit the punished action. In other words, on future occasions the instigators produce a conflict between "approach" and "avoidance" actions. This becomes important in connection with the influence of stimulus generalization. Miller has shown that avoidance responses have a steeper excitation gradient than approach responses. As a result, a punished child tends not to respond overtly (e.g., with aggression or dependency) to the instigators (e.g., mother) to which his responses were originally established, but to respond instead to other instigators that lie farther out on the similarity dimension (Sears et al., 1953, pp. 181–182).

The occurrence of such displacement requires an already existing motivational orientation toward the inhibited behavior. In our terms the effect of inhibition on a given behavioral orientation will vary according to whether or not the inhibition is system specific. The effect of inhibition upon non-system specific behaviors, based on less central concepts, will tend more toward total extinction. However, the effect of inhibition upon system-specific behaviors that are central to the subject's relatedness to his world of objects is quite different; here, the conceptual orientation or the relatedness remains unchanged, but the way the behavior is expressed, changes. *That is, the effects of inhibition will be understood in relation to centrality.* One of the most important operations defining a system-specific response would be the extent to which its inhibition leads to a more indirect form of expression rather than to extinction. In this section we deal exclusively with the effect of the inhibition of responses generated via central concepts.

Regardless of the conceptual system, we propose that inhibition produces the following effects: (1) more indirect or distorted expression in the inhibition situation, expression displaced to other tangential situations and exhibited in fantasy; (2) less exploration and less active utilization of such orientations; and (3) more dependence of the subject on his environment, or more passivity in relationship to his environment, that is, the lower his expectation that he can maximize system-specific rewards by manipulating his own behavior. In addition to representing directness-indirectness, this dimension may be regarded as a variation in independence-dependence.

Although the above principles apply to each of the three relevant systems (I, II, and III) the particular direct expressions that are inhibited and the nature of the inhibition differ between systems. In system I, dominant expressions are inhibited by increasing external control; in system II, aggressive, independent expressions are inhibited by the fear of others; and in system III active socially accommodating expressions are inhibited by increasing overprotection.

However, regardless of the system-specific components, indirect functioning as compared to direct functioning within any system is characterized by a lower expectancy that environmental change can be wrought by the manipulation of the subject's own behavior; thus the subject becomes more dependent on some aspects of his environment. The system-specific aspects of this dimension are dealt with under each nodal system at various points in this chapter. It is noted that indirect and direct poles of arrested systems of functioning bear a considerable similarity to Freud's general notion of positive and negative fixation.

System-specific indirectness bears a complex relationship to the degree of concreteness. The more generalized the indirectness (that is, the more situations that elicit indirect expression) the greater is the relative closedness to more abstract differentiations. Indirectness of expression is associated with greater impulsivity and concreteness within the conceptual range of abstraction in each system.

THE INDIRECT-DIRECT DIMENSION WITHIN TRANSITIONAL SYSTEMS

The indirect-direct dimension involves a variation in the expression of the underlying transitionally-arrested system, which is assumed to be a function of the degree of conflict toward opposing poles. In considering the indirect type of expression it is helpful to visualize the hypothetical dimension in Table 12, which represents any one of the three transitional levels along which variation on the directness dimension may occur. We assume that accelerated training practices lead to the simultaneous emergence of conflicting forms of subject-object relatedness and that this emergence prohibits integration and progression. We assume that the individual experiencing such conflict will attempt to resolve it by some form of expression, and that subsequent functioning can be understood as maintaining the particular adaptation level reached. We assume further that if the conflict involves two central pressures, the result is not an extinction of the weaker pressure but is rather an increasing indirectness of expression of both tendencies, although the weaker tendency becomes more indirect.

When two conflicting forms of relatedness are central, as is the case in transitional arrestation, two related classes of resolution can occur:

(1) *Compartmentalization.* The two opposing polar expressions, for example pole X and pole Y in Table 12, may become highly compartmentalized and function independently. If such compartmentalization occurs, the boundaries between the conflicting systems become highly impermeable, and the different modes of functioning alternate from one situation to another. The more concrete the transitional system the more compartmentalized it can become, but some degree of compartmentalization can occur at more abstract transitional levels. In a more phenotypical context compartmentalization could be exemplified by an individual holding inconsistent attitudes. Abelson and Rosenberg (1958) have recently proposed a method for discovering such imbalance in attitude structure. Presumably some degree of compartmentalization would be present if a subject were positive to the following three statements: (1) I am for having coeds at Yale. (2) I want good grades. (3) Having coeds at Yale would undoubtedly interfere with having good grades (Abelson and Rosenberg, 1958, p. 6).

As the conflicting concepts become more central, the reduction of imbalance becomes progressively more difficult. An extreme and central form of compartmentalization would be exemplified by behavioral alternation between two opposed functioning systems as is found in cases of multiple personality and dissociated states (see Chapter 9).

(2) *Conflict.* Under most circumstances, however, the degree of compartmentalization between the two poles of functioning is not so extreme. In place of functioning characterized by alternation between one extreme and the other, behavior is characterized by conflict and the combined influence of both sets of pressures. Although the boundaries between the two systems are somewhat permeable in this condition, the systems remain essentially unintegrated. It has been shown that conflict between opposing tendencies does not generally lead to behavioral alternation between the two tendencies (Festinger, 1957). Research on conflict indicates that once a choice between two alternatives has been made, behavior is characterized by increased consistency and is accompanied by an increased sensitization and openness to information that is congruent with the alternative chosen. There is also an avoidance of or an increasing closedness to information relative to the rejected alternative (Festinger, 1957).

This compensatory tendency illustrates the basic motivational principles relating to the maintenance of positive affect outlined in Chapter 3. The paradigm used by Festinger refers to the conflict that results when a subject is forced to choose between two equally preferred objects. After the choice has been made, the subject becomes selectively sensitized. In present terms, if the two conflicting tendencies are central forms of relatedness, the rejected alternative still exerts an influence on behavior so that the resolution represents the combined effects of both tendencies in which one system of relatedness becomes more direct and central than the other.

We propose that the more central (strong, important, high in valence) the conflicting alternatives and the more equal the strength of the two alternatives, the stronger will be the tendency toward the more extreme form of compartmentalization. However, when conditions favor the choice of one alternative over the other, even though the weaker is still relatively central, functioning is characterized by the more direct expression of one alternative and the more indirect expression of the weaker alternative.

Systems on the pole X side in Table 12 are characterized by (1) stronger and more central pole X expression, (2) pole X expression that is modified by the weaker, less central, and conflicting pole Y tendencies, (3) the greater relative indirectness of modified pole Y expression as opposed to the more direct forms of pole Y expression. Systems in the center of the dimension in Table 12 are characterized by extreme degrees of compartmentalization and alternating tendencies.

The systems on the pole Y side are characterized by the opposite tendencies listed for the pole X side of the dimension.

An important difference between systems characterizing the two expressive poles of any transitional dimension is that when the more abstract pole (pole Y) is relatively more direct, the *general* type of system expression would be expected to be more indirect. The basis lies in the point that indirectness of expression of systems on the pole Y side is facilitated not only by conflicting differentiations based on the opposite pole, but also by the relative lack of clarity of differentiations based on the more abstract pole, compared to the more concrete pole (pole X). If environmental pressures induce conflict between pole X and pole Y at a given stage, from the very beginning, pole Y differentiations, representing a later and more abstract development, would be less well articulated and more indirect.

We now consider the main characteristics of both sides of the dimension in each transitional system. For communicative convenience systems falling along the two areas of the transitional dimension are differentially labeled by inserting the relative directness of expression of the two conflicting poles after identifying the particular transitional level. For example, level I (A > B) transitional systems (pole A more direct), level I (B > A) transitional systems (pole B more direct), and so on (see Table 13).

In conflicting or compartmentalized systems the resolution process is based on the principles of the maximization of positive affect (which is system specific in each case). This involves:

1. The *avoidance* or neutralization of situations that might increase the potential for the occurrence of expressions based on the less central pole. For example, functioning based on level I (B > A) transitional systems is expected to be characterized by the avoidance of any environmental pressures that would enhance pole A evaluations such as absolutistic control. In the Festinger paradigm (1957) this would be exemplified by the tendency to avoid contact with supportive or positive evidence regarding the rejected alternative after making a choice between two objects that were originally equally preferable.

2. The *overdriven* pursuit of, or bolstering of, situations that may enhance the more central pole and the overcompensatory expression of resolutions based on the more central pole. In level I (B > A) transitional systems the result would be overdriven and overcompensatory reactions favoring the indirect negation of any form of external control. In a situation involving the choice of one alternative between two objects that were originally equal in preference, such overcompensatory reso-

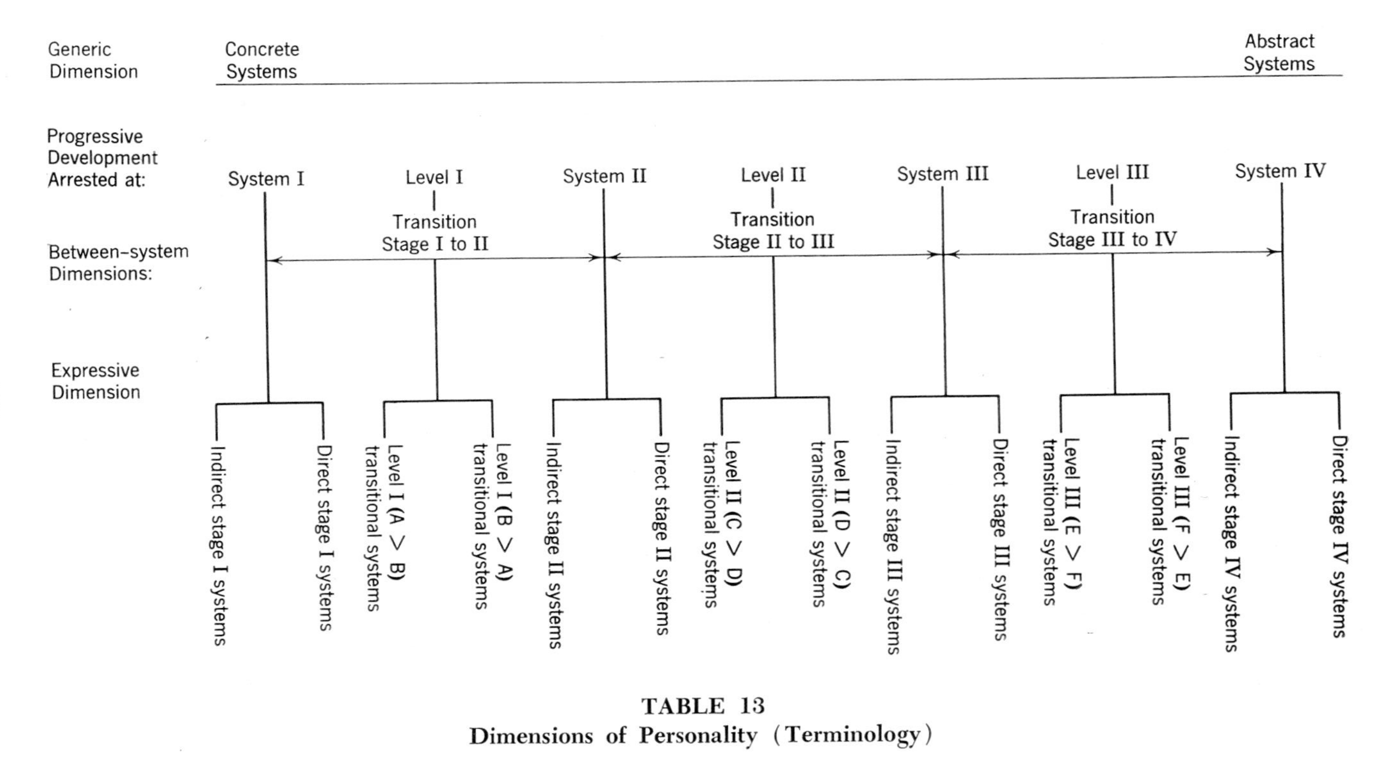

TABLE 13
Dimensions of Personality (Terminology)

lutions would take the form of an increased sensitization to information that might support the accepted alternative.

The combined effects of these developmental and training conditions are summarized in Table 13. This table presents the major conceptual systems and the dimensions of personality. The most generic concrete-abstract dimension is first broken into three generically similar dimensions, differing in degrees of abstractness. This produces four nonconflicted classes of systems (systems I, II, III, and IV) and three conflicting or transitional systems (levels I, II, and III). These seven systems serve as the focal points for organizing the remainder of this chapter. The discussion of each system includes an analysis of the more specific, within-system, differences, in terms of the indirect-direct dimension of expression. The nodal and transitional systems of stable or arrested personality organization are identified and described in terms of (1) the most central conceptual poles, (2) pressures to which each system is maximally open or closed, and (3) the relationship between general functioning characteristics and developmental conditions.

Dimensional Limits

Since these dimensions can be expressed more or less generically, the representation of a dimension depends upon the purpose of the investigator. Earlier in this chapter we described three basic transitional dimensions, which extend from one stage to the next most abstract stage through varying degrees of transitional conflict (Table 13). When these dimensional cut-off points are used we emphasize the similarities and differences between (1) the sequential stages, for example, system I versus system II, and (2) within the conflicting or transitional systems, for example, between level I (A > B) and level I (B > A) systems. When focusing upon development, these dimensional limits seem to be more appropriate and therefore this focus is used in this chapter.

However, for other purposes it may be convenient to think of the dimensional limits in terms of the overtness or centrality of system characteristics or expression (Tables 13 and 14). When construed in this way, the most concrete dimension would include indirect and direct system I expression and level I (A > B) transitional systems. In all cases pole A expression is more overt. The next dimension would extend from level I (B > A) transitional systems through indirect and direct system II expression to level II (C > D) transitional systems. Since pole C of stage II concepts is similar to pole B expression of stage I concepts, these three systems can be grouped together on the basis of similarity of overt expression. Two other dimensions involving the

TABLE 14

The Dimensional Limits of Systems Generating Similar Expressions

General Expressive Classification	Transitional Systems In Which More Abstract Pole Is More Central (Poles B, D, and F)	Nodal System	Transitional Systems In Which More Concrete Pole Is More Central (Poles A, C, and E)
System I		Indirect and direct stage I systems. Pole A more central, closed to pole B, that is, to opposition.	Level I (A > B) transitional systems. Pole A tendencies more overt and central.
System II	Level I (B > A) transitional systems. Pole B tendencies (negativism) more overt and central.	Indirect and direct stage II systems. Poles B or C more central, closed to absolute control and dependency (poles A and D).	Level II (C > D) transitional systems. Pole C tendencies (assertiveness) more overt and central.
System III	Level II (D > C) transitional systems. Pole D tendencies (dependency) more overt and central.	Indirect and direct stage III systems Pole D (accommodation) more central. Closed to opposition and autonomy (poles B and F).	Level III (E > F) transitional systems. Pole E tendencies (mutuality) more overt and central.
System IV	Level III (F > E) transitional systems. Pole F tendencies (autonomy) more overt and central.	Indirect and direct stage IV systems. Integration of pole A and pole B of stage III. Interdependence.	

greater centrality of, and overtness of, systems III and IV tendencies are also illustrated in Table 14.

These dimensional limits combine systems that are similar in terms of the nature of the most central concepts and the nature of overt expression. For example, stage II related systems include level I (B > A) transitional systems, stage II systems, and level II (C > D) transitional systems. All these involve varying degrees of the greater overtness of oppositional or negativistic tendencies. But from another point of view these three stage II related classes of systems are relatively more heterogeneous, for example, in regard to the nature of the underlying conflict. Consequently, when dealing with personality organization we emphasize the three basic transitional or between-system dimensions, but when our focus moves to a study of conflict resolution in Chapter 7, we utilize the cut-off points described in Table 14.

Generalization of System Functioning

The relative closedness of a conceptual system to the next most abstract form of differentiation required for development constitutes the degree of arrestation. The more closed the system to differentiations required for progression, (1) the more progressive development will be retarded, (2) the more difficult is the instigation of re-educative or modification procedures, and in the more extreme cases, (3) the more generalized is the level of arrestation across different areas of the life space. These factors are of particular importance in considering the total personality.

When we speak of a particular system as being engaged, we refer to a particular area of development, for example, to interpersonal relationships to parents, to mathematics, to religion, to politics. In Chapters 4, 5, 6, 7, and 8, we are not particularly concerned with the total personality, but rather are dealing with the characteristics of various systems of functioning regardless of the class of object or the degree of generalization. The same reasoning could be applied to any concept, attitude, or solution in any area of development or even to the total personality provided that the personality was characterized by a given level or stage of functioning in most areas of the life space. The advantage of dealing with single concepts or attitudes in research work, as we show in Chapters 7 and 8, is that the problem of generality is reduced. When dealing with the total self-system or personality, however, we must take cognizance of the level of conceptual structure in a sampling of areas in the life space. Some individuals may be relatively homogeneous in that the same conceptual system is engaged over most relevant areas; others may be very heterogeneous, utilizing system I concepts in some areas (for example, religious attitudes) and system IV concepts in other areas (for example, social relationships).

In the next few chapters we are chiefly concerned with the characteristics of system structure and functioning regardless of the area. In the remainder of this chapter the focus is upon systems that are relatively closed to differentiations required for progressive development. In Chapters 9 and 10, however, the focus also includes the increasing generality of conceptual structures involved across different areas of development for a given person.

Stage I Conceptual Systems

We have proposed that reliable unilateral training increases the closedness of stage I concepts to progressive development. Under these conditions development proceeds within the conceptual limits of stage I functioning. Investigations indicate that unilateral reliable training is associated with greater submissiveness (Symonds, 1939; Baldwin, 1955), suggesting that the subject initially learns submission to source demands as a means of obtaining system-specific reward. However, as development within this system continues the subject learns to anticipate the consequences of his behavior, which means that, under conditions of reliable unilateral training, he learns the role of the source upon whom the subject's behavior is externally determined. In a sense, in system I *submission implies the acquisition of the dominant role,* implying an acceptance and internalization of external dominance. Such an acquisition is illustrated by children's scolding themselves, for example, children may say, "No, no" as they reach for a forbidden object, or say, "Naughty" as they engage in a prohibited activity. We propose that reliable unilateral training maximizes the simultaneous acquisition of dominance and submission, which are closely related to the phenomenon of "identification with the aggressor" (Anna Freud, 1950). As Hoffer (1951) expresses it:

> The disorder, bloodshed and destruction which mark the trial of a rising mass movement lead us to think of the followers of the movement as being by nature rowdy and lawless. . . . [Actually,] The true believer, no matter how rowdy and violent his acts, is basically an obedient and submissive person. The Christian converts who staged razzias against the University of Alexandria and lynched professors suspected of unorthodoxy were submissive members of a compact church. The Communist rioter is a servile member of a party. Both the Japanese and Nazi rowdies were the most disciplined people the world has seen (Hoffer, 1951, p. 115).

A similar view has been proposed by Maccoby (1959) as follows:

If most things that an individual wants are not under his control but under the control of others, then presumably much of the vicarious trial-and-error that he engages in must involve his trying out various approaches to getting the help or avoiding the censure of others, and imagining the probable responses to these approaches. . . . Our position says that a child should covertly rehearse both the rewarding and the punishing actions characteristic of his parents, for both are highly relevant to him in guiding his plans about future actions (Maccoby, 1959, p. 246).

Developing Orientations in System I

Subsequent development in this system is characterized by the categorical or black-white nature of judgment and the emergence of depersonalized criteria and roles, which are now discussed.

THE CATEGORICAL NATURE OF JUDGMENT AND THOUGHT

The subject attempts to cope with reliable unilateral training methods by making rigid discriminations between those behaviors that are tolerated and those behaviors that are not tolerated by the source. The subject therefore becomes sensitized to relatively inflexible dichotomies such as right or wrong and true or false. To be unsure about the external criterion is catastrophic for the person because external criteria represent the most central anchor for making judgments about the consequences of his behavior. Ambiguity of criteria is threatening and is avoided primarily through the adoption of categorical rules, which provide ready-made, concrete structures against which decisions can be made (Adorno et al., 1950).

Another significant orientation which emerges, concerns the manner in which self-evaluations function in relation to externally given criteria. The more a person bases his self-evaluation on externally anchored judgments the less likely he will be to experience rewards following improvment or progress judged against his own past experience. The person functioning in terms of system I tends to evaluate his behavior in terms of the perceived discrepancy between the "real" and the more absolute "ideal." This orientation is consistent with the development of a strong "conscience" or "superego," which would be expected as a result of this training (Peck, 1958). The following verbal response is illustrative of the external and categorical nature of self-evaluative judgments in this system. The subject was first asked to place people known to him, five years ago, at regular intervals along a scale extending from most negative to most positive. Then he was asked, "Where would you place yourself?"

I probably have myself on the scale twice; to put it in other terms I have a double scale. Now, the basic assumption of this scale, I guess, in my mind is that the values I assign to people, the box in which I label them, is really not a strict invention of my own but that, let's say, most other people would have. If I had put, let's say, some people at a given point, that these people would pretty much see themselves on the scale at the place where I put them. Yes, I think this is the basic assumption; otherwise, the scale is not valid. . . . What I mean by a double scale or two points on the scale, which is basically the same thing, is that there is one point where I wanted to see myself and where I wanted others to see me, and a point where I really think I am. I guess this is pretty clear what I mean by that sort of a point for an ideal "I" which included all of my ideals and the type of person I wanted to be which equaled the person I wanted others to think me to be, and then let's say my honest judgment of myself which shows how far off I am, let's say, from the ideal.

ABSOLUTE OR IMPERSONALIZED CRITERIA AND ROLES

Up to this point we have been speaking of the source as providing or embodying the direct criterion of the subject's behavior. As development proceeds within system I the criterion for behavior continues to be external (because of closedness to opposition that limits the development of internal control), but the personal authority of the source is replaced by absolutistic and *impersonalized* rules. This change is regarded as a within-system change since the associations remain unilateral and absolutistic. The shift in locus of criterion from the source's personal authority to generalized rules occurs in part through experience with a variety of authorities. Once such rules take on importance, they cease to depend upon other people and come to represent absolute, categorical, impersonalized rules, which are beyond the influence of people and rest instead on extrapersonal power or "natural" law.

Another developmental consequence of reliable unilateral training is that when the subject resists source control at some point such resistance is expressed indirectly because the system is maximally closed to opposition to external control. One orientation that "minimizes" the effect of source control *without opposing it* openly is the curtailment of the expression of positive or negative affect. Passive resistance serves the function of active opposition. As one subject reported, "I remember being mad at my mother but didn't express it . . . I suppressed my pleasure too . . . I didn't want people to know what went on in me. . . . If other people can affect me, they can control me . . . I would try to keep it so that others would find difficulty in knowing what I was thinking." Passive resistance is one of the most common modes of reacting to an authority who utilizes power to restrict oppositional tendencies, and it is often deliberately used as a weapon against such authority, as exemplified by Mahatma Ghandi (Fischer, 1950). By "deliberate use" we mean the utilization of passive resistance by a person who is not necessarily functioning in terms of system I, but rather is merely using a system I technique when he finds himself in a situation much like that of a person arrested at stage I functioning. In this case the choice of technique might consist of a more abstract process.

Development within system I involves the emergence of depersonalized roles and the categorical labeling of roles that are enacted in the presence of certain stimuli regardless of the context. Authoritative sources, being associated with external criteria, are labeled omnipotent and therefore induce submission; neutral sources induce an ambivalent tendency to submit and dominate; whereas non-authoritative sources are viewed as inferior and therefore either disregarded or rejected. The submissive role, whether enacted by the self or another person (for example, minority groups), comes to be viewed as weak and inferior and the dominant role as superior.

Other people are assigned absolute status positions, and the subject develops different roles, which he adopts toward people depending upon their status position. The definition of these absolute roles and rules is generally determined by the value orientations of the power figures in the subject's membership group, thus avoiding ambiguity of criteria. In this sense the personality organization would be more tradition oriented (Riesman, 1950). Again we illustrate the categorical nature of roles by a subject's response. First the subject was asked to order people known to him five years ago along the scale from most negative to most positive. His response, when asked to describe the basis of ordering, was:

> On the right I put the people I respected for some reason or other because of knowledge or achievement, people who went into the group of authority, people who I felt obliged to because of some favor. Then sort of the equals, in the middle, and to the left the people I didn't like because they were stupid, useless, or boring, and those whom I out-and-out hated. . . . Now if you put all of those people on a scale . . . I think you can hardly find a situation, but that I mean my reaction to people or my attitudes towards them, which was not completely influenced by where they were on the scale, and, therefore, I don't think that there was hardly any situation in which I was purely 100 percent natural myself. I would say that everything to the right of the middle point, or to the right of the equal, first of all, gave me a feeling of uneasiness, either because I felt obliged for a favor they rendered me or I didn't want to make a mistake because I faced the person in authority. . . . Now, if we go to the middle, this group of people should really be the people who should have given me the most pleasure and ease or what have you. These are the people to whom I felt I belonged and I had the wish of belonging, and my whole attitude in this

case was a kind of hunting for clues or "do I really belong" or "am I accepted?" So again, even in this group I don't think my behavior was unstudied or, for the lack of a better word, "natural." . . . It was in this group that I really pushed and tried to get ahead of them. I wanted to lead, I certainly had impulses in this direction with these people. I think these two kinds of descriptions already make the third one quite obvious, that is, with the people to the left of the middle. I think that I was somehow so strictly trained and had enough of what you call social graces that I was never rude to these people, but I certainly tried to avoid them, tried to avoid their company, tried to avoid conversation with them because I felt it was a waste of time. I could learn nothing from them, any discussion with them would be fruitless. I said that I was probably never rude, but I certainly was often very curt, and certainly, if I could not avoid contact and discussion, I probably spoke down to them. When I look all through this, what I just said, one thing which strikes me as relevant, besides the way I look at people, is that if we should want to connect all of this up that the only situation in which I am natural when I don't play a role, where I don't condition my behavior after something I want, is when I am unpleasant and am sort of nasty to those people to the left.

STAGE I SYSTEMS, ACHIEVEMENT, AND AUTHORITARIANISM

The importance of an external criterion to both the subject and source for judging personal achievement in system I is associated with a greater concern about achievement. However, as we stated earlier (Chapter 5), this concern does not necessarily mean that these individuals will perform at a higher level of achievement. Rather, we would expect achievement efforts in system I to be characterized by concreteness, literal adherence to instructions, with a minimum of elaboration or creativity. Supporting this expectation is the finding that child-training practices similar to reliable unilateral training apparently suppress curiosity in children (Baldwin et al., 1949).

The tendency to bifurcate events in terms of black-white categories would also be expected in this system. There should be a greater tendency to view persons who are different from oneself (non-membership groups and those who follow a different criterion) as inferior. Such a form of relatedness has been described as authoritarianism (Adorno et al., 1950) and ego-defensiveness (Katz, Sarnoff, and McClintock, 1954; McClintock, 1958). Therefore, to the degree that the California F scale assesses stereotypic thinking, authoritarianism, and the external attribution of causality, this scale could be an operation for arrested forms of system I functioning. However, the F scale would also appear to measure system II (Extrapunitive) tendencies and system III (Other-directed) tendencies (cf. McClintock, 1958) to some extent, and owing to item content would not be expected to pick out the authoritarian "liberal."

If system I is viewed as similar to authoritarianism, the material from interviews with parents of high F subjects described by Adorno et al., supports our contentions that (1) discipline was administered primarily for the violation of absolutistic or moralistic rules, (2) discipline was presented as a force outside the child to which he must submit, and (3) the values imposed by the parent were entirely the values of adult society, beyond the comprehension of the child (Adorno et al., 1950). Using the same approach Hart (1957) found a significant tendency for the parents of high F subjects to utilize "non-love oriented" techniques of punishment, described by Whiting and Child (1953) as involving physical punishment, threats of physical punishment, and punishment by ridicule.

The original work of the California group (Adorno et al., 1950) identified the authoritarian personality with (1) rigidity, the intolerance of ambiguity, and the dogmatism of attitude, (2) a greater tendency toward anti-introceptive orientations as opposed to reflective insight, (3) the anti-scientific attitudes based on a relative inability to question rules, dogma, or principles, and (4) an anti-democratic ideology.

From our point of view this system I form of relatedness lacks the mutuality, interdependence, and autonomy required for democratic functioning. However, it should be noted that there is no *necessary* relationship between the form of relatedness and the content of any particular attitude, for example, between authoritarian relatedness and anti-Semitism. Although the nature of relatedness and content may be empirically related in a given subgroup or culture, the two aspects are independent—for example, in another culture authoritarian relatedness (or system I relatedness) may be associated with anti-Americanism. The cross-cultural comparison of correlations between the form of relatedness and its content would shed light on the training practices used by cultures in reference to particular content areas.

Indirect-Direct Variation within System I

Since reliable unilateral training involves the simultaneous emergence of submission and dominance, the source's inhibition of dominant behavior produces greater indirectness and passivity of system I functioning. Levy's (1943) study of the effects of "dominant" overprotection and Ausubel's (1952) observations of the effects of parental overdomination are similar to inhibitive unilateral training. These investigators found this training to be antecedent to the development of such traits as docility, obedience, politeness, submission, timidity, disinterestedness, and passive quarrelsomeness. In indirect expression, the subject depends more upon the source and his behavior is characterized by submissiveness. In direct expression, on the other hand, in which the dominant role is not inhibited, the subject is more likely to utilize an impersonalized criterion and to be more reality-oriented, tradition-directed, and his behavior may appear to be "independent" or active.

Since dominance and submission are different expressions of the same general conceptual system, we would expect to find an association between these two tendencies. Such an association has been commonly observed in clinical practice. In Fromm's (1941) words:

> It seems that this tendency to make oneself the absolute master over another person is the opposite of the masochistic tendency, and it is puzzling that these two tendencies should be so closely knitted together. No doubt with regard to its practical consequences the wish to be dependent or to suffer is the opposite of the wish to dominate and to make others suffer. Psychologically, however, both tendencies are the outcomes of one basic need, springing from the inability to bear the isolation and the weakness of one's own self. I suggest calling the aim which is at the basis of both sadism and masochism: *symbiosis*. Symbiosis, in this psychological sense, means the union of one individual self with another self (or any other power outside of the own self) in such a way as to make each lose the integrity of its own self and to make them completely dependent on each other. The sadistic person needs his object just as much as the masochistic needs his. Only instead of seeking security by being swallowed, he gains it by swallowing somebody else. In both cases the integrity of the individual self is lost. In one case I dissolve myself in an outside power; I lose myself. In the other case I enlarge myself by making another being part of myself and thereby I gain the strength I lack as an independent self. It is always the inability to stand the aloneness of one's individual self that leads to the drive to enter into a symbiotic relationship with someone else. It is evident from this why masochistic and sadistic tendencies are always blended with each other. Although on the surface they seem contradictions, they are essentially rooted in the same basic need. People are not sadistic or masochistic, but there is a constant oscillation between the active and the passive side of the symbiotic complex, so that it is often difficult to determine which side of it is operating at a given moment. In both cases individuality and freedom are lost (Fromm, 1941, pp. 157–159).

In more indirect system I functioning there are fewer situations or a narrower range of situations that elicit dominant behaviors. Also the expectation that the criterion of a person's behavior can be mediated through his own behavior will be lower for indirect than direct system I functioning. For example, in the extreme case of indirectness the expression of dominance might be restricted to situations involving a powerless and weak individual or minority group.

Stage II Conceptual Systems

Arrestation of progressive development at the very beginning of stage II, leading to system II conceptual functioning, has been described as a consequence of unreliable unilateral training. What begins as an early, perhaps immature, attempt to behave independently of external control transforms, under unreliable unilateral training, into a negative attitude toward the external source. This developing counterpersonal system of relatedness hastens the abandonment of the absoluteness of, or trust in, external criteria (closedness to pole A). The subject learns to view the source as unreliable, to look upon control with suspicion, and to externalize blame. Accordingly, he views attempts at control by the source as interfering or malevolent. The aim of behavior is to avoid any form of dependency on authority or control because of the negative consequences associated with such controlling attempts.

The underlying motivational orientation involves two expressions, which develop simultaneously: (1) the avoidance of control, stemming from the fear of others, which may be associated with "flight," and (2) the destruction of the source of control. Related to this second form of expression is the perception of any situation that places the subject in a dependent relationship or under any form of control, as an attack that comes to be associated with aggression. Utilizing Miller's (1937) analysis of displacement, Whiting and Child (1953) conclude that "hypotheses that trace fear of others to the projection and displacement of aggression are much the most consistent with the whole range of findings we have been able to present" (Whiting and Child, 1953, p. 303–304).

From our point of view, the punishment or inhibition of aggression should result in (1) fear of others, both in terms of being controlled or becoming dependent, (2) indirect expression of aggression, (3) displacement of more active or direct forms of aggression,[1] and (4) a greater tendency toward passivity or toward behavior calculated to avoid retaliation in the training situation. The less aggression is inhibited (for example, due to neglect or indifference) the more direct is its expression and the less is the fear of others.

[1] It has been shown, for example, that cultures having fewer nurturant agents protect the infant less, show him less affection, are more inconsistent, take less care of his needs and are more punitive (inhibitive unreliable unilateral training) exhibit more aggressive beliefs about supernaturals (that is, displace the more active forms of aggression) (Lambert, Triandis, and Wolf, 1959).

Developing Orientations in System II

Confronted by unreliable unilateral training, the subject does not learn to adopt the role of the source. Since the training conditions necessary for the emergence of conscience or empathy are both lacking in this condition, interpersonal relations are very tenuous. Other people are "negatively" weighted, particularly in situations in which they demand some form of dependency. Negative weighting may be inferred from such referents as (1) source deprecation following a controlling or negative communication, (2) lack of effectiveness of social rewards and punishments (see Chapter 7), and (3) the inability to form lasting reciprocal relationships with others (see Chapter 9). In this sense functioning described as anti-social, "psychopathic," or "delinquent" would exemplify development arrested at stage II, but as we show in later chapters not all functioning commonly described as anti-social is stage II in origin.

One apparently puzzling feature of this argument is the common observation that "delinquent" groups are very cohesive (Whyte, 1943). Two points may be noted in relation to this apparent contradiction. First, not all delinquent gang members are functioning within stage II systems. Second, the system of subject-object relatedness of group members does not necessarily determine the degree of cohesiveness in group functioning, but only the *nature* of cohesiveness. The cohesiveness of system II–disposed group members would be expected to rest upon the extent to which the norms protected them from both dependence on each other and from interpersonal interference. The rigid differentiation between member roles and the explicit formulation of role expectations of each member would serve this purpose, and it is just such characteristics that have been observed in delinquent gangs. This is not to deny that such groups are also characterized by hierarchical structures.

One of the general orientations that emerges as a result of development within closed stage II systems is the tendency to maintain self-evaluations in the face of negative evaluative information. In order to maintain self-evaluation under such circumstances, reactions such as deprecating the source or externalizing blame may be utilized. These defensive reactions prevent the modification of behavior as a consequence of informational feedback. It has been shown that children, who perceived themselves either as extrinsically valued by parents or as rejected, are likely to hold omnipotent conceptions of their own capacities and to maintain tenaciously high levels of aspirations in the face of failure (Ausubel et al., 1954). Ausubel (1952) viewed the development of this orientation as one aspect of the child's failure to "satellize," which in turn results from parental rejection or extrinsic evaluation. For Ausubel, satellization consists of the child's obtaining a derived source of status and intrinsic feelings of adequacy through some form of dependency on the parent. Training that involves extrinsic evaluation and also fails to provide the necessary conditions for satellization should closely parallel what we have described as unreliable unilateral training. Referring to the consequences of such training, Ausubel states:

> Hence the shift to a derived source of status and intrinsic feelings of adequacy is blocked. As before, ego aspiration level continues to be determined in reference to the child's *own* power to influence and control his environment: His status remains a creature of his own strivings and capacities. He does not aspire to a position where he shares vicariously in the prestige of others by virtue of a dependent relationship to them (Ausubel, 1952, p. 116).

A related orientation that develops is the avoidance of commitment. Such avoidance is a relatively indirect expression of system II functioning. If an individual cannot anticipate or trust another's reaction he may learn to avoid commitment to other people. The effect of non-commitment is that he cannot be proven wrong and thus can maintain high self-evaluations while avoiding dependency. Like other developing orientations within this conceptual system, non-commitment serves to avoid the dependent relationship on another person that has been associated with negative consequences in the past. In addition, however, non-commitment also reduces the occurrence of approval and may increase the difficulties encountered in relating to others and interfere with subsequent development to more abstract levels.

Indirect-Direct Variation within System II

Arrestation of development at stage II may be a result of two specific forms of unreliable unilateral training: (1) unreliable control or (2) neglect and indifference. Unreliable control leads to indirectness of system II expression. By unreliable control we mean training pressures that attempt to control or force the child to be dependent on the parent without providing the basis for a trusting relationship beween parent and child. Trust is a necessary condition for the child to attach positive weighting to the parent. In more theoretical terms such training leads to closedness to pole A of stage I, a minimum of interiorization of external criterion, and a minimum of conflict between pole A and pole B. The subject simultaneously learns a fear of others, based on a projection of his own inhibited aggressive tendencies toward them. Therefore, indirect system II expression is assumed to be a function of unreliable control.

On the other hand, direct system II expression stems from neglect or indifference. The more indirect form of system II functioning is based on the fear of a distrusted source and accompanied by behaviors calculated to avoid hostility from and dependence upon such sources or other persons. The direct tendencies are aimed more at validating the subject's ability to oppose dependence on authority or control. In both forms of expression, since the source is essentially negative, the subject fails to interiorize external criteria as absolutes (conscience or superego). In this sense there is a minimum of systemic conflict between pole A and B tendencies. However, this lack of conflict stems not from an integration of the two poles, as it would in progression, but from closedness to or a rejection of pole A and other forms of dependence.

Accelerated unilateral training induces relatively less distrust and greater openness to pole A. As pole A thereby becomes more central, there is an increase in the degree of conflict within the system (that is, between pole A and pole B). We now turn to this transitional dimension, falling between the reference points of pole A and pole B.

Level I Transitional Arrestation

We have proposed that accelerated unilateral training is one of the major conditions underlying the level I transitional dimension. Such training is expected to result in the simultaneous development of two compartmentalized systems of relatedness, which involve conflicting motivational orientations: (1) dependency upon absolutistic criteria (achievement) against which self-esteem is judged and (2) the avoidance of dependency on external criteria against which self-evaluation is judged. The dimensions shown in Table 15 are an ordering of conflicting conceptual systems at one extreme at which pole A differentiations are most central and are expressed most directly whereas pole B differentiations are less central—that is, level I (A > B) transitional systems—at the other extreme at the right hand pole at which pole B differentiations are more central than the conflicting pole A differentiations—that is, level I (B > A) transitional systems.

The point of arrestation on the dimension in Table 15 is determined by how extreme the severity of acceleration of unilateral training is, extreme acceleration presumably permitting the subject to achieve only occasional rewards (Brown, 1953; Grosslight and Child, 1947). The

TABLE 15

Arrestation at Various Points along the Level I Transitional Dimension

Stage I	Pole A				Pole B	Stage II
	Reliable Unilateral Training		Accelerated Unilateral Training		Unreliable Unilateral Training	
		→		←		
		Increasing conflict between pole A and pole B	Maximum Conflict	Increasing conflict between pole A and pole B		
		Greater openness to and overtness of pole A tendencies. Level I (A > B) transitional systems		Greater openness to and overtness of pole B tendencies. Level I (B > A) transitional systems		
	Differentiations minimally involve opposition to external control	Avoidance of conditions producing evaluations based on opposition to external control		Avoidance of conditions producing evaluations based on external control	Differentiations minimally involve external control	
	Concern about achievement	Overdriven concretistic achievement		Overdriven indirect negativistic tendencies toward absolute criteria	Minimal concern about achievement	

degree of severity or acceleration must be judged relative to the subject's potentialities and developmental readiness-to-achieve at the demanded level.

When pole A is more central, we expect (1) an avoidance of opposition to external control and (2) overcompensatory pole A tendencies, in the form of concretistic striving in "safe" areas, for example, areas having a high degree of structure such as achievement in the more traditional professions and occupations, or achievement in science characterized by the lack of creativity or questioning of basic principles. Such overcompensatory achievement reduces conflict in two ways. First, by cautiously conforming to the accelerated demands, opposition to authority is avoided. Secondly, the achievements may lead to broader rewards and permit a less direct dependence on the source thus also reducing the likelihood that resentment of accelerated demands will be expressed. Achievement and fear of dependency are closely related in level I (A > B) systems, the fear of dependency being more indirectly expressed.

At the right-hand extreme of the dimension in Table 15, the level I (B > A) transitional systems, we would expect the following: (1) the avoidance of situations involving external control and (2) overdriven tendencies toward the indirect expression of negativism toward control. Both involve a decrease in overt achievement tendencies, which is generally more typical of stage II related systems involving the greater centrality of poles B or C.

In studying the relationships between training practices and adolescent personality structure, Peck (1958) found that consistency of training induces greater superego strength, or, in our terms, greater dependence on an interiorized absolute criterion (system I relatedness). However, as the severity of training increases (or becomes accelerated, in present terms) the effect is that of a "hostility-guilt complex" (which resembles the transitional conflict between system I and system II). It has also been shown experimentally that unreasonable demands by a source (probably indicating an increase in acceleration or unreliability) result in a low level of persistence or concern about achievement in children (Wolf, 1938). This is what we would expect in level I (B > A) transitional systems.

We expect that conflict in the area of achievement, which most generally characterizes the level I (A > B) transitional systems, will be expressed in projective or fantasy behavior. McClelland et al. (1953) used a modification of the Thematic Apperception Test to measure the degree of concern (and presumably conflict) about achievement through fantasy expressions. Evidence based on the use of this measure appears to support our expectations about the main features of personality organization developing within level I transitional systems.

Accelerated unilateral training should lead to conflict in the areas of achievement and dependency. One index of this conflict is the occurrence of achievement themes in fantasy productions. McClelland and Friedman (1952) found a relationship between dependency and a concern about achievement. They suggest, as do Brown (1953) and Child (1954), that such a relationship could be due to severe independence training by parents who exert greater pressures toward achievement. In a study of college males a positive correlation was found between the severity of child-training practices and achievement themes in fantasy productions (McClelland et al., 1953).

Similarly, Winterbottom (1953) found that the expression of achievement themes by boys between eight and ten years of age was significantly related to the following early training practices: (1) earlier demands for independent achievement and the imposition of certain restrictions at an earlier age (accelerated unilateral training) and (2) reward for fulfilling parental demands and reward for the acceptance of restrictions (training accelerated, but not unreliable). In addition, these results indicated a significant negative relationship between achievement themes and the total number of restrictions in training. To the extent that a high degree of restrictiveness is associated with greater acceleration of unilateral training or with the development of stage II relatedness, this latter result supports the present contention.

Although the level I (A > B) transitional systems are characterized by conflict and concern about achievement, it does not necessarily mean that such training produces higher levels of overt achievement. The complexity of the interrelationship is indicated by Winterbottom's (1953) findings that fantasy measures (conflict about achievement) were generally positively related to actual levels of achievement and, on the other hand, Sanford's (1943) findings that these two measures were *negatively* related. We discuss the complex relationship between the abstractness of conceptual systems and achievement at the conclusion of this chapter, but at this point we may note that such a relationship depends in part upon the measure of overt achievement. For example, we would expect level I (A > B) transitional functioning to be positively correlated with the quantity of output, the detail of output, and so on. If these measures of performance were valued by the source, then the correlation would be positive. However, if achievement involved less structured tasks that demand more abstractness and greater creativity and questioning of principles, we would expect negative correlations owing to the concreteness of functioning at level I.

Lazarus et al. (1957) measured the tendency for subjects to express a concern about achievement using a modification of the Thematic Apperception Test (McClelland et al., 1953). Subjects were asked to reproduce, in writing, a passage they had heard on a tape recorder. (While listening, the subjects were permitted to start and stop the playback as often as they pleased.) Reproductions were scored in terms of their concreteness, defined as a literal, word-for-word reproduction, listening to small sections and reproducing them more or less verbatim, and so forth. In keeping with our expectations, subjects showing greater concern about achievement behaved more concretistically and literally in the experimental task.

Stage III Conceptual Systems

We have proposed that system III functioning, being closed to negative independence (pole C), to autonomy (pole D), and to further progressive development, is induced through protective interdependent training. If the training method protects the subject from experiencing the consequences of his own actions, he will experience uncertainty in situations that are unstructured or in which the supporting source is absent. The subject learns to rely on other people as anticipators of his success and failure, thereby avoiding negative consequences.

It is important to distinguish system III from system I forms of relatedness, since both involve a form of dependency. While system I involves absolute criteria, system III involves criteria relevant to situational conditions. While system I involves dominance or submission, system III involves seeking protection and actively seeking positive relationships with other relevant people. System III behavior is anchored in the maintenance of positive relationships by "pleasing" rather than by submitting to or dominating others. System III functioning is characterized by less diffuseness and a greater differentiation of the self from the world; it is closed to autonomy rather than opposition and open to mutuality rather than unilateral dependence or external control.

Some of the major orientations that emerge following the arrestation of progressive development at the onset of stage III are: (1) the equivalence of failure and rejection, (2) fear of rejection and the premium placed upon maintaining positive relationships, (3) internal causation and self-blame, and (4) jealousy. Within-system expression in system III varies from helplessness and other indirect demands for protection to socially more direct accommodating reactions such as outgoing attempts to please others and the denial of rejection.

Developing Orientations in System III

The resolution of uncertainty or avoidance of failure comes to be associated with the reception of support from a valued person. As development proceeds within system III, the subject becomes more likely to experience "aloneness" as equivalent to failure. Since rejection and the expectation of failure are poorly differentiated, they may be transformed as experientially equivalent: rejection increases the expectancy of failure, whereas failure indicates a lack of support or love from others.

An individual so predisposed is therefore subject to continual "separation" fears. Protective training increases the sensitization to rejection. Experiments have shown that the physical separation of a young child from its mother for short periods of time leads to a "grief" reaction and sensitizes the child to a fear of aloneness, separation, or rejection (Spitz, 1946). Because protective interdependent training effects and physical separation are interrelated, we would expect separation to produce a stronger effect on children so trained than on children trained by other methods. Similarly, experiences related to other forms of separation, for example the severance of relationship ties due to social mobility, divorce, going to college, death of parents, and so forth, would be expected to be more threatening to individuals engaging system III concepts.

Development within this system is characterized by the emergence of orientations in which interpersonal relationships are highly salient. The subject strives for approval and to avoid disapproval or rejection from valued persons. Such individuals are in a state of continual competition with others in order to win approval from relevant people. In interpersonal relationships this approximates what is more generally referred to as "jealousy." Developmental studies indicate that protective and overprotective child-training practices are antecedent to jealous behavior (Radke, 1946). Such a predisposition to interpret other people's behavior along the dimension of acceptance-rejection and to fear rejection produces reactions varying in their activity of expression. A child may behave in a way that indicates his need for the support and affection of the other person (passive expression), or he may compete with others to obtain greater acceptance from a particular person, for example, by adopting his values, pleasing him, and so forth (active expression). If these resolutions should fail, so that the subject perceives himself as being unable to enlist the support of others, rage may be directed against the other person for "withholding" his support (Chapter 9); or the rage may be displaced onto a real or fantasied rival. The latter occurs especially when a particular source is too "valuable" to risk losing by anger expressed directly and overtly.

These reactions illustrate one of the distinguishing characteristics of system III relatedness as opposed to system I and system II relatedness, namely, the tendency for the subject to perceive his own behavior as being causal or as affecting the criterion. Since blame for rejection is initially turned inward and the subject accepts the responsibility for the consequences of his own behavior, he is likely to change his behavior (generally in a more socially accommodating way) so as to enlist the support, help, or affection of other people.

In their study of attitudes, Smith, Bruner, and White (1956) suggest that structure (or the form of relatedness) and the content (or object) of attitudes may be independent. They presented three functional determinants of attitudes: (1) realistic, (2) social, and (3) projective components. Their description of attitudes that engage the "social" process is similar to what we have described as system III functioning. System III relatedness is also similar to what Witkin and his colleagues (1954) described as "field dependent." In these studies, field dependence represented the utilization of external anchors for behavior. However, it would appear that both system I and system III forms of relatedness are included in Witkin's concept. In discussing their results on the Thematic Apperception Test, Witkin et al. noted two orientations within the field dependent group that appear to parallel our distinction between systems I and III.

> In many stories by [high-index] subjects, . . . the principal character was crushed by circumstances; there was nothing that he could do about them [system I]. In other stories, the principal character abrogated his own needs in order to receive protection from others [system III] (Witkin et al., 1954, p. 259).

Although systems I and III are similar at a high level of generality, because both represent external anchors for behavior, it is important for future research to distinguish between them. As we indicate in Chapters 7 and 8 this distinction is not new in the personality and social field. Katz et al. (1954) and McClintock (1958) differentiate between ego-defensiveness and other-directedness. Ego-defensive attitudes toward minority groups are likely to be maintained because they provide an avenue for the indirect expression of hostility. In our terms this represents system I concepts, reflecting the more direct expression of dominance and control toward a weaker, less authoritative stimulus. The other-directed organization is described as a personality ". . . weak in inner authority, i.e., super-ego. . . . In order to ensure acceptance by the relevant group or groups, he acts upon his perceived expectations as to what they demand of him. He characteristically holds those attitudes which he feels that others significant to him maintain" (McClintock, 1958, p. 480). This description is not only similar to system III but also to Riesman's description of other-directedness (1950) and to social accommodation as used by Schroder and Hunt (1959).

The distinction between what we refer to as stage I and stage III systems of relatedness has often been made on the basis of the strength of the "superego" or "conscience." However, Peck (1958) in studying the effects of child-training practices on adolescent personality makes a similar distinction in terms of *different kinds* of "superego." These are: ". . . (a) a strong rigid compartmentalized superego created by sternly autocratic rearing; and (b) a strong superego which was closely knit with ego functions, open to rational appraisal, and created by consistent, democratic, nonsevere rearing in a trustful, approving family" (Peck, 1958, p. 350). The former is related to the training and consequences that are involved in system I, and the latter is closely related to the training and consequences involved in system III functioning. Although these distinctions are limited by the vagueness of such concepts as superego, they indicate the importance of a general schema for handling more specific forms of subject-object relatedness. Fromm (1941) has also drawn a similar distinction between authoritarianism (system I) and conformity (system III).

Indirect-Direct Variation within System III

The more protective the interdependent training, the more indirect and passive is the expression within system III. High degrees of protection are characterized by such factors as excessive instrumental aid, excessive source anticipation of potential danger, less reward for independent instrumental behavior, and protection from entering new situations. In contrast, a more direct orientation is produced by rewards for behavior that gains the support and acceptance of the source and that "earns" the support of other groups in new situations through socially accommodating behavior.

Ausubel (1952) presents a description of overprotective child-training practices that would exemplify the indirect pole.

> The parent makes an effort to provide for his child an environment which is free of any type of hurt, disappointment, frustration or painful contact with the harsher realities of life. This goal is achieved by isolating him from all experiences which could possibly result in such consequences, preventing contact with persons who do not share his benevolent attitude to the same degree, providing a host of precautions and protective devices (including

an excessive amount of personal contact and supervision), and refusing to allow him to plan or do things for himself for fear that injury or failure might result. Calculated risks that most parents regard as necessary for normal development are compulsively avoided (Ausubel, 1952, p. 210).

Compared to direct expression, indirect expression of system III functioning is less well articulated and more immature. It is associated with more immature means of gaining attention and is characterized by increased fantasy productions with themes of independence, recognition, and acceptance. The direct orientation involves active anticipation of the standards of others. It thereby permits the manipulation of one's behavior so as to maximize rewards through the maintenance of positive relationships. Again in contrast, the more passive expression is characterized by helpless, attention-gaining behavior, or the utilization of the "I can't" reaction as a means of avoiding rejection and demanding protection and support (Levy, 1943).

Level II Transitional Arrestation

Accelerated autonomous (permissive) training has been proposed as one of the major antecedent conditions leading to level II transitional concepts. Systems on this dimension are characterized by a conflict between oppositional independence versus the need to be cared for and supported. However, the expression of these system II and system III tendencies are modified in terms of the conflicting forces as illustrated in Table 16.

Many studies have been carried out on the developmental consequences of training methods variously described as permissive (Symonds, 1939), overprotective (Levy, 1943), or underdominative and permissive training (Ausubel, 1952; Baldwin, 1955). For example, Symonds (1939) describes permissive parents as:

. . . those who permit the child a great deal of freedom, allow themselves to be dominated by the child and accede to the child's demands and wishes, who indulge the child and cannot refuse his requests or, on the other hand, who desert him or neglect the child, who do not give him proper training and leave him too much to his own resources (Symonds, 1939, p. 105, 108).

As Mussen and Conger (1956) indicate, this description covers a wide variety of training, or in present terms, from unreliable unilateral to protective interdependent training. The developmental consequences of such training are equally varied. According to Symonds, children so trained were rated more disobedient, careless, irresponsible, rebellious to authority, antagonistic, independent, but self-confident and spontaneous in forming friendships outside the family. These character-

TABLE 16

Arrestation at Various Points along the Level II Transitional Dimension

Stage II						Stage III
	Pole C Negative Independence				Pole D Conditional Dependence	
	Unreliable Unilateral Training		Accelerated Autonomy Training (permissive; indulgent)		Protective Interdependent Training	
		⟶ Increasing conflict between pole C and pole D	Maximum Conflict	⟵ Increasing conflict between pole C and pole D		
		Greater openness to and overtness of pole C tendencies. Level II (C >D) transitional systems		Greater openness to and overtness of pole D tendencies. Level II (D > C) transitional systems		
	Differentiations minimally involve dependency	Pole C and D differentiations: the avoidance of conditions producing evaluations indicative of inadequacy		Pole C and D differentiations: the avoidance of conditions producing evaluations indicating the absence of care and support	Differentiations maximally involve seeking support and dependency	
	Fear of dependency	Overdriven or bolstered assertiveness and the avoidance or neutralization of the exhibition of inadequacy		Overdriven or bolstered indirect tendencies to ensure the availability of care and support, neutralization of rejection	Fear of rejection	

istics extend from counterpersonal or stage II relatedness to stage III relatedness, as we would expect on the basis of the range of antecedent training conditions. The developmental characteristics presented by Levy (1943) and Baldwin (1955) are generally similar to those reported by Symonds.

Development within level II transitional systems leads to the emergence of conflict between assertiveness and the maintenance of interpersonal relationships. Training conditions antecedent to level II transitional conflict are characterized by a lack of emphasis on status difference betwen the subject and the source and by a relative absence of limits or obstacles, including the experience of failure. Furthermore, the source provides intrinsic but indiscriminate positive evaluation. The subject learns to be independent, self-directed, and assertive in the training environment but does not learn to cope with failure or to relate to others on the basis of either absolute criteria, mutuality, or informational standards. The resulting tendency is to react in terms of system II orientation tempered by the effects of intrinsic evaluations. We refer to this reaction pattern as "assertiveness." However, outside the training situation such assertiveness, often characterized by bullying and aggressiveness, meets with resistance (Ausubel, 1952; Levy, 1943). Development does not provide a foundation for positive independence or interdependence, but it does lead to the emergence of independent (system II) tendencies. Intrinsic evaluation by the source sharply decreases counterdependent tendencies and increases the expectation of acceptance due to the privileged nature of the training.

When assertive behavior is unsuccessful (and this is particularly likely to occur outside the home), the conflicting nature of subject-object linkages (between pole C and pole D differentiations) is clearly apparent. As Ausubel (1952) remarks:

> The great paradox accounting for maturational failure in under-dominated children is a super-abundance of the self-assertive aspects of volitional independence combined with a virtual absence of the personality traits that make implementation of this independence possible (Ausubel, 1952, p. 220).

The more indifferent the source and the more indiscriminate the rewards in permissive training, the more we would expect development to result in a greater centrality of pole C concepts. In a similar way, the more protective the permissive training the greater is the centrality of pole D (Table 16).

As stage II–related systems become more central, the occurrence of persistence following failure decreases. Grosslight and Child (1947) demonstrated that training in which success followed a series of failures produces increased persistence. Permissive training characterized by undifferentiated rewards should lead to low persistence, which would particularly characterize level II (C > D) systems. When the inevitable "meeting of failure" outside the training situation occurs, there emerge tendencies to avoid failure and at the same time reduce dependency pressures. These tendencies include a lack of persistence (Schroder and Hunt, 1957), the denial or repression of failure experiences (Rosenzweig and Sarason, 1942), role diffuseness, bullying and assertive behavior (Cameron, 1947; Levy, 1943), and extroversion (Eysenck, 1948, 1953).

These level II (C > D) system tendencies represent modified expressions of pole C, or system II functioning, since they tend to avoid failure and dependency. As Ausubel (1952) observes

> When forced to set an aspirational level in an area outside the home—where he enjoys no special privilege and consideration—he tends nevertheless to transfer to expectations derived from the parent-child relationship despite their unreality. And instead of appropriately modifying these aspirations in line with recent experience—as would be natural for an individual with a more typical history of volitional development—he finds the frustration intolerable and abandons the goal completely (Ausubel, 1952, p. 222).

A similar orientation develops in the social context. Conflicts between pole C and pole D lead to maximum role diffuseness in the absence of absolute or informational standards. Ausubel (1952) states that, ". . . it becomes practically impossible for the underdominated child to abstract any consistent general rule that would indicate when a given ethical precept applies to his own conduct" (p. 225). This level of functioning represents the most concrete form of conditional or mutual relatedness. Since it is the first step beyond oppositional functioning, it also represents the most primitive form of interdependent relatedness. System III relatedness involves differentiated accommodating reactions calculated to influence the source toward adopting a more positive accepting and supporting attitude toward the subject. In contrast level II (C > D) transitional relatedness involves "all or none" accommodating reactions. Role development has been so diffuse and approval so undifferentiated that failure or stress comes to be resolved by the adoption of an alternate diffuse role that functions to avoid failure and maintain an "apparent" assertiveness. Development within this transitional level may occasionally lead to extreme compartmentalization so that the subject utilizes almost unrelated roles according to the situation he is in (cf. the case of Joseph Kidd in White, 1956).

As system II tendencies (stage II–related systems) become more overt and dominant, the characteristic reaction to stress is repressive.

Therefore we would expect measures of concern about achievement (McClelland et al., 1953) and perseverance for achievement or achievement striving (Caron and Wallach, 1959) to relate negatively to the denial of inadequacies, that is, repression after failure. This expectation is congruent with the findings of Atkinson (1953). Caron and Wallach report:

> We have seen that one of our personality factors—Perseverance for Achievement—bears a strong relationship to defensive orientations, Lows [low achievers] reacting to stress repressively and Highs [high achievers] reacting vigilantly [p. 242]. . . . persons low in achievement concern and in achievement striving tend to repress the memory of failure experiences. . . . (Caron and Wallach, 1959, p. 243).

As system III concepts become more central (level II [D > C] systems), the assertiveness and the avoidance of failure take on different characteristics. These represent highly indirect forms of system III functioning, due to the simultaneous pressures of compartmentalized and conflicting pole C and pole D tendencies (Table 16). The resulting avoidance and overdriven tendencies, however indirect, are expected to take on characteristics of pole D relatedness, such as increasing social acceptability and an increasing tendency to seek support. Owing to the weaker, conflicting, pole C tendencies, we propose that level II (D > C) systems are characterized by overdriven and assertive achievement serving the purpose of insuring care and support (indirect pole D expression) and at the same time reducing reliance on relationships (indirect pole C expression). Overdriven assertive achievement would be less rigid and compulsive than achievement based on level I (A > B) systems, and characterized by the indirect seeking of care and protection rather than the avoidance of dependency on external control. The "protection seeking" is expressed very indirectly in these systems, as assertiveness, which appears to be the opposite of such needs.

Achievement and interest based on level II (D > C) transitional systems would be more socially oriented. Since the person functioning at this transitional level has not integrated negative independence and conditional dependence, his perception of relationships and the evaluation of interaction will differ from such perceptions based on progressive stage III and IV functioning. In level II (D > C) transitional systems, mutuality is not well developed, and relationships are viewed more in terms of a market analogy in which dependency and care are "purchased."

In summary, we may note that in stage II systems self-esteem is defensively maintained by non-commitment, source deprecation, and the avoidance of dependency in any form. As we move toward stage III systems of relatedness and conflict between pole C and pole D, there is an increasing tendency to avoid failure without the accompanying counterpersonal or system II tendencies. This dimension runs from the avoidance of dependency and source deprecation (system II orientations) through bullying and assertive behavior, denial, forgetting, and the avoidance of failure (level II [C > D] transitional systems) through overdriven assertive achievement, in order to insure protection and care (level II [D > C] transitional systems) to the avoidance of failure by seeking support from others (system III).

In Chapter 9, various forms of hysteria are considered in the framework of level II transitional systems. We also discuss the relationship between level II transitional functioning and what has been described as "extraversion" (Eysenck, 1948).

Stage IV Conceptual Systems

Stage IV systems involve the integration of the major forms of subject-object relatedness so that behavior is no longer primarily determined by either an external criterion, by opposition, or by some type of dependent relationship. The criterion for behavior is maximally abstract, emerging as informational standards. Behavior is neither dependent on external rules or other people, nor counterdependent upon these anchors—it is maximally interdependent. Learning to anticipate the consequences of behavior is not equivalent to learning the role of the source, as in system I development, but rather involves the development of informational standards through experiencing the consequences of one's own actions.

The subject learns to generate alternative systems of ordering of the same stimuli. Development within this system involves (1) reliance on independent exploratory behavior, (2) a more veridical perception of other persons' standards, and (3) informational standards that are interdependent on, and open to, a variety of influences.

Developing Orientations in System IV

One of the most fundamental characteristics of stage IV systems is what we refer to as "abstract closedness." The more abstract levels of functioning are characterized by the ability to hold strong beliefs and to be ego-involved, while remaining open to alternate evaluations and differentiations, that is, to hold strong beliefs but to be unprejudiced. Such functioning permits ego-involvement without the usual accompanying disadvantages of bias, subjectivity, and distortion. At this abstract level of functioning, presumably, only neurological factors limit effective intellectual functioning.

Under informational imposition the subject learns to depend on his own exploratory behavior as a means of solving problems or overcoming barriers. The training frees him from reliance on other people or absolute criteria as a means of relating. In summarizing some of the major consequences of logical training in which the child is given responsibility, Baldwin (1955) lists such characteristics as self-reliance, cooperation, responsibility, and security. Peck (1958) reported that autonomy was associated with parent-training practices such as stability, warmth, mutual trust, and approval between the parent and the child. It has also been shown that intrinsically valued children, who are task-oriented and have little need for ego aggrandizement, exhibit more emotional control and make fewer demands on adults than children experiencing other parental practices (Gruber, 1954). According to our view, informational imposition involves intrinsic evaluation as well as a task or information orientation.

Development in system IV is characterized by the absence of a positive or negative dependence on other people. Standards are not likely to be anchored in other people's beliefs, although the system is not closed to the consideration of such beliefs. The subject learns to react to other people's behavior independently of his own; he is more able to view others' behavior in terms of their own past experience, as he views his own, and is able to develop greater insight into the motives behind the behavior of other people. The veridicality of this view of others depends no doubt on other factors, including the range of his own experiences and the level of intelligence, but in general we would expect this development to be associated with greater veridicality in person perception. The ability to view others' behavior in terms of their own past experience, not only increases the veridicality of "as if" behavior or putting oneself into another's frame of reference, but also enhances the development of veridical informational standards as anchors for future experience.

This attitude or form of relatedness toward other people extends to other objects, including rules. In stage IV systems, development involves neither a positive nor a negative dependence on rules, on absolute solutions or answers that are externally given. In system IV, rules are understood in terms of their genesis and function, not simply on the basis of their personal effect on the subject. In this more abstract form of relatedness, rules are accepted on the basis of their general function rather than being obeyed in the concrete sense. However, if a change in the situation makes the rule functionally less effective, the person functioning in terms of system IV may attempt to change the rule, just as he might change his solution in a problem-solving situation. The primary concern is upon the development of informational standards continuously attuned to the environment. We expect this functioning to be associated with a strong informational orientation regardless of the salience of other situational components, for example, source, power, attractiveness, and so forth.

This personality organization is similar to what has been described as inner-directedness (Riesman, 1950), "freedom to" (Fromm, 1941), object appraisal (Smith et al., 1956), and independent orientation (Witkin et al., 1954). The term "independence" as used in attitude-change studies and many clinical descriptions often covers what we have referred to as both negative independence or oppositional and positive independence or autonomy. Witkin suggests that his "independents" (subjects whose judgments about "uprightness" were based on the position of their own body rather than on the characteristics of the field) include two different classes of personality organization, one being described more in system II terms and the other more in system IV terms. We distinguish between stage II and stage IV functioning and refer to stage IV functioning as interdependent rather than as independent.

Indirect-Direct Variation within System IV

As indicated earlier in this chapter, the more informational or interdependent the training, the less is the variation in expressive differences within a system. (We obviously do not imply for system IV a narrow, rigid reliance on a few types of behavior.) The more that training involves a dependent or independent situation (control, permissiveness, protection, neglect, and so forth, as contrasted to a highly interdependent situation, the more the subject is exposed to two behavioral orientations, that of the source and that of the subject's role, which is rewarded by the source. When this difference is large, as in stage I systems, the degree of system-specific inhibition determines the expressive outcome. However, as training becomes more interdependent and informational, the dichotomy between the role of the source and the role of the subject, which is rewarded by the source, decreases so that system IV functioning is expected to be much less subject to conflicting expressive modes.

However, despite this integration of expression, we would expect relative differences along the indirect-direct dimension in stage IV functioning. Presumably, environmental poverty, which restricted the degree to which the consequences of informational standards were tested, will tend to induce less environmental manipulation in behavior and more indirect forms of expression.

Level III Transitional Arrestation

According to our view, level III arrestation results from accelerated interdependent training. It will be recalled that accelerated *unilateral* training involves a lack of differentiation between the criteria of behavior and the expectations of the source; it also involves an equivalence between anticipating the consequences of experience and learning the role of the source. In contrast, accelerated *interdependent* training does not represent a conflict between dependency on versus opposition to absolute or external control. There is instead a conflict between "pleasing" others, enlisting their mutual support (regardless of the criterion) versus functioning autonomously on the basis of informational standards (not in opposition to other people's standards). Table 17 indicates the range of level III transitional systems.

These transitional systems are characterized by a lack of integration between mutuality (pole E) and autonomy (pole F) so that judgment or functioning based on one semicompartmentalized system interferes or conflicts with the other. As a result of accelerated interdependent training, the subject learns to rely on his own informational standards in unstructured situations but is unsure of the adequacy of these standards in coping with such situations. Since the subject is capable of attributing causal responsibility to himself, he is likely to experience more severe feelings of inadequacy following autonomous decisions.

As was true for the direct-indirect dimension in more abstract nodal systems, the expressive differences between systems along the level III transitional dimension are smaller than in the more concrete transitional systems. At one extreme of the dimension are systems involving differentiation based more exclusively on mutuality and relationships (system III). Next follow conflicting systems in which socially accommodating reactions (pole E) are modified (by pole F tendencies) in the direction of greater apparent autonomy (level III [E > F] transitional systems). Engaging in large projects in which cooperative activity is demanded would illustrate such functioning. Next are conflicting systems in which autonomy is more central than relationships (level III [F > E] transitional systems). The tendency to avoid unrealistic striving or goals that would require help and support from others would be an example of such functioning. At the other extreme

TABLE 17

Arrestation at Various Points along the Level III Transitional Dimension

Stage III	Pole E Mutuality				Pole F Autonomy	Stage IV
	Protective Interdependent Training		Accelerated Interdependent Training		Informational Interdependent Training	
		⟶ Increasing conflict between pole E and pole F	Maximum Conflict	⟵ Increasing conflict between pole E and pole F		
		Pole E more central and overt than pole F. Level III (E > F) transitional systems		Pole F more central than pole E. Level III (F > E) transitional systems		
	Differentiations maximally involve mutuality and mainenance of relationship (pole E)	Pole E and F differentiations: avoidance of conditions indicating a potential lack of support		Pole E and F differentiations: avoidance of conditions producing evaluations indicating the need for dependent relationship	Differentiations maximally involve interdependence (pole F)	
	Fear of rejection	Overdriven tendencies to maintain the support of others, through autonomous action		Overdriven tendencies to be independent and autonomous, to keep within autonomous ability limits	Interdependent functioning	

are stage IV systems in which mutuality and autonomy are integrated so that one does not interfere with the other.

At the developmental level we are unaware of any studies sufficiently specific either in terms of antecedents or consequents to check these assumptions. However, in Chapter 9 we report some general support for these expectations in the area of psychopathology.

General Considerations

Generic Similarities between Conceptual Systems

As indicated in Chapter 4, developmental stages can be viewed in terms of two phases (Bennis and Shepard, 1956): the first phase including stages I and II and the second phase including stages III and IV. One implication of this "recapitulation" is that arrestation at stages I and III and stages II and IV have generic similarities. Differences do exist in the abstractness of subject-object relatedness in system I and system III (particularly in respect to external and internal causation), but these systems are generically similar in that, for both, judgments and behavior are anchored to external objects, such as rules, power, and relationships. In a non-systemic sense the two forms of relatedness combine to describe behavior that, from an operational viewpoint, is more "dependent." If behavior is externally anchored, it should be subject to more violent swings and oscillations than behavior that is internally anchored; it is subject to greater disturbance partly as a result of ambiguity in the external world. Evidence is presented later to indicate that in conformity studies (Chapter 7) and reactions to stress (Chapter 9) greater response variation occurs as a result of environmental ambiguity when systems I and III are engaged. In these systems small changes in the external situation produce large changes in response varying, for example, from conformity to compulsive maintenance of a standard (Hoffman, 1957).

Generic Similarities between Transitional Systems

At a very general level, the three transitional systems may be described as "conflict about dependence" or "conflict about independence," since progression proceeds through the emergence of more abstract forms of dependence following independence at a more concrete or diffuse level. Three levels of conflict result: (1) unilateral dependence on external control versus opposition to external control, (2) avoidance of dependence versus the maintenance of relationships, and (3) mutuality versus autonomy. Each could be referred to as conflict between dependence and independence. However, we have stressed the importance of dimensionalizing within these general descriptive terms and have emphasized that the context of the generic dependence-independence conflict differs at each level.

Conceptual Systems and Achievement

As we have suggested earlier in this chapter, the relationship between level of abstractness and achievement is quite complex. These relationships are little understood but are, perhaps, of crucial importance for selecting the "criterion" for achievement or intelligence tests, for defining "areas" of achievement, and for selection and guidance purposes. The crucial problem in test construction is obviously the criteria against which tests are validated. The criteria that test constructors use therefore partially determines, among other things, the kind of education a child will receive, the kind of occupation he will work in, or at a more general level the distribution and utilization of human resources. We believe this to be one of the most important areas of psychological research because the present emphasis of testing programs is almost exclusively on the content of experience, ignoring the nature or abstractness of relatedness. In this sense, test construction has not advanced appreciably since Binet, although there has been considerable advance in the sophistication of the statistical techniques used to analyze the data gathered on the basis of such tests.

When achievement is measured against externally given criteria, system I relatedness should be likely to lead to high levels of achievement. The following educational practices should, however, lead to arrestation of academic development at stage I: (1) presenting materials and facts in an absolute way; (2) requiring that the subject learn what is correct or desired by the source; and (3) requiring the absolute reproduction of what the source says is correct in an examination (if a high level of "achievement" is desired). Furthermore, if this form of "achievement" becomes a criterion against which tests are validated for selection purposes, the students who will enter higher education are likely to be functioning at a more concrete level. One symptom of this trend may be the apparently increasing tendency for college students to prefer structure over complexity, facts over arguments, methods over ideas, and absolute and externally defined answers over relative or abstract knowledge.

System II relatedness should be associated with the lowest form of "achievement" when achievement is measured against externally given or absolute criteria. However, this form of relatedness can produce new ideas in science and other fields of activity if the subject can carry on his work independently. Such ideas may be more discontinuous with the current mainstream of social traditions and more rebellious in social fields.

We do not expect system IV functioning to be associated with higher achievement (defined in the above sense) for similar reasons. It is highly probable that training emphasizing informational interdependence would lead to slightly lower "achievement" levels compared to training emphasizing unilateral techniques. The person who has developed more abstract concepts may use broader and different achievement criteria than those used or applied by a particular source and may therefore be "graded down." System IV functioning involves the integration of alternate interpretations and ideas and greater creativity. Such training should therefore result in informational resources capable of handling a broader range of problems, particularly new problems. We believe this result should be a basic purpose of education (cf. Chapter 10).

As described in this chapter, we expect level I (A > B) transitional systems to be associated with overdriven concretistic achievement, motivated by a fear of dependency, and level II (D > C) transitional systems to be associated with overdriven assertive achievement, motivated by a need to be cared for and supported.

Affective Components of Conceptual Systems

Although the various affective states such as shame and anger probably have their bases in biological characteristics of the organism, we propose that systems of relatedness are associated with particular emotional experiences, much as McDougall (1908) indicated in his famous definition of instinct. We present the broad emotional qualities that we believe to accompany threat to each system of relatedness; however, since we cannot provide independent operations for the various emotions, we recognize that such relationships are purely hypothetical at this time. Since the systems are conceptualized in terms of the differing conditions that produce positive or negative affect, it seems plausible that the quality of this affective experience may differ between the systems as well.

Specifically we contend that the experience of guilt or self-castigation is associated with system I. Guilt represents self-punishment for the transgression of interiorized rules over which the subject has no control. According to Levin and Baldwin (1959) "Guilt . . . is a kind of internalized social control mechanism in which the wrong behavior is avoided for its own sake . . ." (p. 171).

We suggest that stage II systems are associated with the emotional expression of aggression when independence is threatened, whereas stage III systems experience negative affect primarily as shame following a weakening of relationship ties. Shame represents a violation of the trusting relationship between subject and source. In this sense shame differs from guilt in that it is not one's behavior that is intrinsically "bad" in an absolute sense; it is that the subject feels he has "let another person down" and is therefore worthless because his own behavior has failed to maintain the support and continuing acceptance of the source. The experience of shame is closely associated with sensitization to relationships. Benedict (1946) and Leighton and Kluckhohn (1947) propose both guilt and shame as external sanctions in mediating compliance or conformity to cultural standards and contend that cultures can be differentiated in terms of their sensitivity to guilt and shame. Levin and Baldwin (1959) characterize shame as "the anticipation of revelation of unfavorable attributes" (p. 150).

We would associate the emotional experience of self-devaluation with threat to stage IV functioning. Since such relatedness is interdependent of absolute rules, and therefore not counterdependent, we would expect a relative absence of guilt, shame, and aggression in system IV. Self-devaluation refers to the experience of failure defined in terms of the inadequacy of informational standards to cope with the consequences of experience. It refers to the tendency to tolerate as opposed to ward off anxiety. The consequences of self-devaluation include an immediate shifting to new alternative conceptual schemata that are goal-directed and a continuing adoption of other alternatives if failure continues. Experimental evidence suggests that subjects selected on the basis of a predisposition to engage system IV concepts do lower their self-evaluation more, following persistent failure (Schroder and Hunt, 1957). As a generalization we would expect a positive correlation between the experience of self-devaluation and the openness of concepts to change under changing environmental conditions.

Dimensions of Personality

Most work in the area of dimensions of personality has been based on factorial studies. The dimensions that emerge, under these conditions, are necessarily limited by the test items used. Nevertheless, these studies consistently support the earlier intuitive observations of Jung (1923) in demonstrating the existence of a general dimension referred to as "extroversion-introversion" (Eysenck, 1953).

The "extrovert" pole (variously described by such traits as carefree, insensitive, free from inhibitions, ascendant, changeable, non-persistent) appears to approximate what we have referred to as stage II related systems (see Table 14). The "introvert" pole (variously described by traits such as sensitive, personal, intellectual, deep, persistent, obsessional, submissive) appears to include the remainder of our dimensions combining stage I, III, and IV systems. Although it is plausible that behavior ratings of system I functioning may show higher correlations with system III than system II functioning (as we have indicated above), test items can be selected to differentiate between these systems (see Chapters 7 and 8).

Concluding Comments

In the past three chapters we have focused upon the central question of "What develops?" All development depends upon the establishment of systems of conceptual linkages. The object of the linkages refers to the content or the "what" of learning, the relatedness or schema refers to the nature or structure of the associations formed, regardless of the content. We have outlined the various systems of functioning, the conditions underlying their development, progressive stages in the development of more abstract systems, and development within the conceptual limits of each system following the arrestation of progressive development. The nature of conceptual systems has been dimensionalized at the most generic level, along a concrete-abstract dimension. More specific dimensions were utilized in deriving the dimensions of training and functioning. The next chapter is concerned in more detail with how these systems function.

7 Functioning of Conceptual System

How do conceptual systems operate? In the present chapter we pursue this question by considering the nature of system-specific functioning—sensitization, interpretation, and resolution—in a *contemporaneous* setting. The problem is to derive the role of specific systems in determining what elements of the *present* situation are most relevant, and what interpretive and behavioral reactions will occur.

As we noted earlier, any system may be viewed as both a cause and an effect. In the present chapter we consider systems as the immediate antecedents of cognitive and behavioral outcomes. It should be emphasized that to consider systems as determinants is simply a device for describing the nature of system functioning, and is not intended to imply that systems are static, inflexible determinants. Every system presumably changes to some degree, as a result of each new experience. But this change occurring as a result of feedback from each experience is a matter of degree, and, for purposes of the present chapter, we intentionally disregard this change in order to convey the flavor of system functioning.

A central assumption in the present viewpoint is that in order to understand a person's behavior in a situation we need to know what conceptual system is operating. The difference in how various people react in the same situation reflects the operation of different conceptual systems. In a similar way, intraindividual difference or similarity in reaction to different situations is also viewed in terms of the underlying functioning of conceptual systems. Since systems exert such a crucial role in determining reactions, an intensive consideration of the nature of this role seems appropriate.

The functioning of conceptual systems determines what aspects of a situation will be relevant and what conditions will produce confirmation and refutation, as well as what reactions will occur as a result of such confirmation or refutation. As we noted in Chapter 3, these functioning characteristics are applicable to systems at every level of generality—from the total self-system to the most specific concept. However, in a particular case, one must always specify what system is being considered in order to derive the particular pattern of system-specific functioning. Therefore, in the interest of simplicity we only deal here with four generic classes of systems although assuming that the present treatment will apply to any system.

Systems To Be Considered

Systems may be viewed as varying along a number of dimensions, as we noted in Chapter 6: degree of abstractness, degree of arrestation (closedness), nature of transitional conflict, and directness of expression. If systems are viewed in terms of these interrelated dimensions, a large variety of systems may be derived, a specification that may be very valuable for certain purposes. However, the present analysis deals with systems at a more generic level in order that the functioning characteristics may be presented in a relatively uncomplicated fashion. The important point is the interrelatedness of structure and function in any system. If we know the structure, we can determine the function. Thus, the present method of deriving functioning characteristics is applicable to any one of the more specific systems in Table 13 on p. 167.

Since the present interest lies in contemporaneous functioning, we deal with four generic classes of systems that are similar *expressively*. Thus, we combine those systems referred to earlier as direct and indirect nodal stage I systems as well as the transitional level I (A > B) system under the single heading of system I, primarily on the basis of their expressive similarity. For purposes of the present chapter we are dealing with arrested systems, or systems that are at least partially closed.

In order to develop principles of system-specific functioning for each of the systems we may begin by reviewing the dimensional limits of each system and by asking what is central in each system. Table 18 indicates the dimension by specifying the positive pole (that is, openness) and the negative pole (closedness) for each system.

These system-specific dimensions serve as the initial point of departure for deriving the characteristics of system-specific functioning. However, in order to accomplish such a derivation it will be helpful to review those motivational principles described in Chapter 3 upon which this derivation will rest.

TABLE 18

Structure of Generic Systems

System	Positive Pole, System Open To	Negative Pole, System Closed To
I	Agreement with generalized external standards	Violation of generalized external standards, including ambiguous situation
II	Freedom from external control	Imposition of control; dependence upon others
III	Mutuality; dependence upon others	Non-mutuality; rejection; aloneness
IV	Expression of autonomy and/or multiple alternatives	Restriction of multiple alternatives

Resumé of Relevant Motivational Principles

For each of the four systems we propose to derive the areas of sensitization, the conditions producing confirmation and refutation, interpretive maneuvers when confronted by potential refutation, and reactions to confirmation and refutation. Therefore, the principles, italicized below, are presented in relation to the particular aspect of system functioning to which they are most relevant.

Sensitization

The structure of a system determines how reality will be experienced, what will be attended to, and what will be ignored. This principle sets forth the basic system characteristic of openness-closedness, or sensitization. One of the manifestations of openness is a *lowered threshold* or heightened alertness to system-relevant events. By system-relevant events we mean simply events occurring along the dimension bracketed by the positive and negative poles in Table 18. These positive and negative points represent the extremes on a dimension that have been differentiated in the past and have now become central. Since lowered threshold to certain events varies between systems, different individuals confronted by the same complex environmental situation will react differently to various situational elements as determined by the salience of the element to the system of functioning in that individual.

Refutation and Confirmation

Events evaluated as disparate from this central dimension are experienced as refuting whereas events evaluated as congruent with the central dimension are experienced as confirming. Refutation occurs therefore when an event is experienced at the negative pole. As described earlier, the negative pole of a particular system is represented by pressure toward functioning at the next higher stage as well as toward functioning at the next lower stage from which the system has progressed. Therefore, in relatively closed systems, the negative pole is identified with avoidance. In similar terms, confirmation involves agreement with the positive pole; more specifically, confirmation occurs in relation to system-specific directional striving and the perception of goal facilitation. Given knowledge of the system structure (Table 18) and of the event experienced, we are in a position to predict the likelihood of confirmation or refutation. The degree of refutation or potential refutation is directly determined by the disparity between the event and the structure of the system. Therefore, refutation or potential refutation may result from either strongly negative events or highly closed systems.

Interpretive Maneuvers

Systems function to minimize refutation (and thus enhance positive affect) by interpretive maneuvers directed at events of potential refutation. System-specific events of potential refutation are indicated by the negative pole in Table 18. If the potentially refuting event can be transformed through some cognitive maneuver, the occurrence of negative affect and blocking of directional striving may be successfully avoided. Two general maneuvers are available: (1) *neutralizing* the potentially negative event (avoidance) and (2) *bolstering* the system of organization (overcompensation). Bolstering minimizes potential refutation in an indirect fashion through reaffirming the positive elements of the system, while neutralizing achieves the same aim through a more direct restructuring of the potentially refuting event. Because the nature of relatedness determining the experience of potential confirmation or refutation varies between systems, the interpretive maneuvers will also vary between systems.

Behavioral Expression

Systems also function to minimize refutation by responses aimed toward eliminating or reducing the experience of negative affect associated with refuting events and to maximize experience of positive affect associated with confirming events. Behavioral expressions, like interpretive maneuvers, have the aim of minimizing refutation. Behavioral expressions, however, are more likely to occur later in a sequence than interpretive maneuvers and, as the name implies, to involve a behavioral, rather than a cognitive, response. Although the distinction may at times be difficult to maintain, it is essentially similar to Heider's distinction between the resolutions of changing sentiment relations and changing unit relations, respectively (Heider, 1958). In its aim to reduce experienced incongruence, behavioral expression may take the form of either attempting to remove the potentially refuting event in some way or changing the system organization slightly so that the event will not be refuting. Such change of system organization may be similar to the reorganization that occurs when progression takes place. As was true for other characteristics, these behavioral expressions will also vary between systems.

Other Conceptions of Interpretive Maneuvers and Resolutions

Before proceeding to an application of these principles it may be helpful to note the relationship of the present derivations of interpretive maneuvers and resolutions to those of some other investigators. These resolutions appear to be related to what Heider (1958) calls "changes in unit relation," and to what Abelson (1959) calls "modes of resolution of belief dilemmas." In describing the various means by which a person reacts to a situation of "imbalance," Heider describes two general resolutions. Before considering these resolutions we may note that an imbalanced situation for the subject is exemplified by a situation consisting of a "positive" person (that is, someone the subject likes) performing a "negative" action (that is, something that the subject regards as disagreeable). Without considering Heider's theoretical model in detail, it is relevant to consider the two general means by which the tension resulting from such imbalance may be reduced: "The situation can be made harmonious either by a change in the sentiment relations or in the unit relations" (Heider, 1958, p. 207). For present purposes the "change in sentiment relationship" may be considered a behavioral resolution, whereas the "change in unit relations" appears to be directly relevant to interpretive maneuvers as the following quotation illustrates:

> Change in unit relations
> a. *p* [the person observing] can begin to feel that *o* [the liked person] is not really responsible for *x* [the undesirable action]. In this way *x* cannot be attributed to *o* and the unit between *o* and *x* is destroyed (Heider, 1958, p. 208).

Such a change appears to be similar to what we are calling *neutralization*. Also in a balance model framework, Abelson (1959) has described a very similar maneuver which he calls denial:

Denial refers to a direct attack upon one or both of the cognitive elements or the relation between them. The value felt toward the object, whether positive or negative, is denied, or the opposite is asserted; or the sign of the relation between the elements is explained away, or the opposite is asserted (Abelson, 1959, p. 344).

Abelson has also described a *bolstering* maneuver which he defines as:

. . . relating one or the other of the two cognitive objects in a balanced way to other valued objects . . . thereby minimizing the relative imbalance in the structure (Abelson, 1959, p. 345).

In order for any of these maneuvers to occur, the person must experience a situation that creates imbalance, or in our terms, potential refutation in subject-object relations. Potential refutation may be reinterpreted either by bolstering or by neutralization in any one of the four systems: however, *what* is reinterpreted will be specific to the system.

Derivation of System-Specific Functioning

For each of the four generic classes of systems we set forth the following functioning characteristics: (1) area of sensitization, (2) conditions producing refutation and confirmation, (3) system-specific interpretive maneuvers (neutralization and bolstering) to refutation, (4) system-specific behavioral resolutions, and (5) system-specific reactions to confirmation. Table 18 indicates the areas of sensitization and defines what constitutes confirmation or refutation for each system. From this information we can derive what the system-specific neutralizing and bolstering maneuvers will be, as well as the behavior resolutions associated with each system. For example, if we are considering system III, the area of sensitization is mutuality-nonmutuality or dependence-rejection. Therefore, to the extent that events are experienced toward the negative pole, that is, as rejecting, they will be experienced as system-specific refutation. Conversely, events connoting the positive pole, or mutuality, will be experienced as confirmation. Faced by potential refutation, the person functioning in terms of system III will deal with the impending event by bolstering the positive pole (mutuality) or by neutralizing the negative (non-mutuality). In more specific terms, these maneuvers will involve reaffirming friendship ties in the former case and denying rejection in the latter instance. Behavior resolutions will involve responses aimed to restore mutuality, for example, seeking reassurance, becoming more dependent, and so forth. Before proceeding to the system-specific derivation of resolutions we

TABLE 19

General Nature of System-Specific Interpretive Maneuvers

System	Bolstering	Neutralization
I	Reaffirmation of external standard	Denial of violation of external standard
II	Reaffirmation of negative independence	Denial of dependence upon others
III	Reaffirmation of mutuality and friendship	Denial of rejection
IV	Reaffirmation of interdependence	Denial of relevance of standards

shall consider the interpretive maneuvers associated with the four generic classes of systems, as in the following table (Table 19).

In the following sections we use Tables 18 and 19 to derive system-specific maneuvers and resolutions. Along with the theoretically derived characteristics of system functioning we describe related experimental findings and related conceptual notions, as well as examples of individual cases. We reserve for later (Chapter 8) a discussion of how system functioning is activated through (1) dispositional tendencies in the individual and (2) situational factors in the environment. For present purposes, therefore, the description of system-specific functioning assumes activation of a particular system and proceeds to view the nature of such functioning in greater detail. We do not intend here to review the entire literature, weighing the evidence to note whether it confirms or rejects the present viewpoint. Rather, we wish simply to convey a fuller understanding of what we mean by system-specific functioning. In this connection we might mention that we see no logical basis for regarding evidence from highly controlled experiments as more important for giving direction to a theory than observations about an individual case (cf. Lewin, 1951, p. 83). Therefore, the reader may wish to judge the current view regarding the nature of system functioning by his own knowledge both of research findings and of what people are like as they function in interpersonal situations.

System I Functioning

Because of the structure noted in Table 18, system I will be sensitized to the dimension of agreement or disagreement with external standards. Therefore, refutation in system I functioning will be associated with events involving disagreement from external standards; confirmation will be associated with events involving agreement with an external standard. Interpretive maneuvers therefore will involve the avoidance of situations violating these external standards. Such avoidance may be accomplished either by bolstering or by neutralization. If bolstering, the avoidance takes the form of reaffirming the nature of the external rules; if neutralization, the avoidance consists of denying the violation of external rules. Behavioral resolutions for situations of system I–specific refutation involve responses aimed toward restoring the relation between the subject and the external rules.

System I Sensitization

On the basis of Table 18 it follows that the operation of system I will be associated with sensitivity to cues concerned with external rules, norms, and cultural prescriptions, with a minimum of alertness to other variations between people. On the basis of the personality organization underlying the authoritarian personality we assume that persons high on the F scale (Adorno et al., 1950) are strongly disposed toward system I functioning. Note that the assumed equivalence rests on *structural* similarity and not upon conservative political content of the F scale, since in our view attitudes involving liberal content may also be held in a system I structure. Sensitization similar to that expected in system I has been observed in persons high on the F scale as may be noted in the following summary of studies described by Bruner and Taguiri (1954):

> Whereas Thibaut and Riecken (1953) report the heightened sensitivity of the high authoritarians to variation in the military rank (or *institutionally derived power*) of the stimulus person, Jones finds that high authoritarians are relatively insensitive when presented with variations in *personal* power (forcefulness) as compared with the low authoritarians. A more general finding on the social perception of the ethnically prejudiced is provided by a study of Scodel and Mussen (1953). They found that people with high ethnic prejudice are less able to judge other people's social attitudes and traits correctly than are people with low ethnic prejudice (Bruner and Taguiri, 1954, p. 648).

System I functioning operates within a framework of external causality. Put in terms of the findings above, other people are not seen as powerful because of themselves (closedness to personal power) but rather as being powerful because they occupy roles that have culturally attributed power.

The system I propensity to read reality primarily in terms of culturally derived power bears a close resemblance to what David Riesman has called the "tradition-directed" type, as indicated in the following:

> A *definition of tradition-direction.* . . . The conformity of the individual tends to be dictated to a very large degree by power relations among the various age and sex groups, the clans, castes, professions, and so forth—relations which have endured for centuries and are modified but slightly, if at all, by successive generations. The culture controls behavior minutely, and, while the rules are not so complicated that the young cannot learn them during the period of intensive socialization, careful and rigid etiquette governs the fundamentally influential sphere of kin relationships (Riesman, 1950, p. 11).

Further evidence of the heightened sensitivity to institutionally derived power may be noted in a study by Roberts and Jessor (1958). They found that when compared with Ss low on the F scale, high authoritarians were less likely to be personally hostile (as indicated by written response to a modification of the Rosenzweig Picture-Frustration method) toward *high status* sources of frustration, but more personally hostile to *low status* sources of frustration.

Situations Producing Refutation and Confirmation in System I

The negative pole in system I functioning is that of opposition to external control or violation of the generalized standard. Therefore, refutation should occur especially in situations involving violation of generalized standards, or those events interpreted in this way. Thus refutation might be produced to a slight degree by novel situations and to a considerable degree by ambiguous situations. Partly because system I functioning is highly concrete and partly because the ambiguous *might* represents a violation of standards, ambiguity produces potential refutation in system I. The intolerance for ambiguity observed in authoritarian Ss is, we believe, clearly related to this expected system-specific refutation. Certain forms of ambiguity should evoke more difficulty than others, with ambiguity involving cultural ground rules ranking high in its threat potential. Getzels and Guba (1955) have studied such ambiguity under the heading of role conflict, which they define as follows:

> The critical characteristic of a role-conflict situation for the role incumbent is that it is in some measure *ambiguous, frustrating,* and, since negative sanctions are attached to non-conformity, *threatening* (Getzels and Guba, 1955, p. 75).

The above definition of role conflict represents a situation very likely to produce refutation in system I. In line with our theoretical expectation, these authors found that persons high in role conflict (as indicated by a "susceptibility to role conflict" measure) were significantly more authoritarian (as measured by the F scale) than were persons low in role conflict.

Also, persons functioning in terms of system I will experience refutation if the prestigeful source who mediates the generalized standard is questioned. Thus, exposure of the "feet of clay" of a leader or the death of a leader will constitute strong refutation in system I.

If ambiguity, role conflict, and potential opposition to control represent refutation for system I, what situations would be expected to represent confirmation? Any highly structured situation in which the cultural prescription is clearly available with no confusing competing alternatives.

Individuals functioning in terms of system I in interpersonal situations will therefore be attracted to other persons who are very conventional and behave according to the rules while they will likely reject or avoid other persons who are unconventional, spontaneous, or individualistic.

Interpretive Maneuvers Associated with System I

In order to consider interpretations specific to system I functioning we must first assume that the person is confronted by a situation of potential refutation. Given this condition we may then derive those system-specific maneuvers that should occur in an attempt to avoid or minimize such refutation.

NEUTRALIZATION

On the basis of Table 19 we note that the generic form of neutralization in system I consists of the denial of events that might involve transgression of rules. We consider several varieties of such system-specific neutralizing maneuvers: failure to perceive, distortion, dissociation, and categorical judgments.

Failure to perceive. In some cases system I functioning consists of a total "blocking out" of potentially refuting events. We would expect a non-susceptibility to attempts to modify attitudes under certain conditions. For example, Harvey and Beverly (1959) found that persons disposed toward system I (High F scale) were less likely to be aware of a communication that was contradictory to their own position than were other persons. A similar process has been reported by Cooper and Jahoda (1947) in their observation that prejudiced persons failed to "see the point" of a communication involving "Mr. Biggot," which was intended to modify prejudiced attitudes.

Failure to perceive a potentially refuting event can occur only in a poorly differentiated or concrete system, and therefore should occur most frequently in system I. A finding by Harvey (1958) illustrates the failure to perceive a potentially refuting event in the form of negative evaluations directed toward the self. He found that, following such negative evaluations made by particular sources, authoritarians not only showed less change in their postevaluation ratings of themselves than non-authoritarians, but also showed less general change in their ratings of the source. It was as if they were denying entirely the occurrence of the refuting stimulus. The system I maneuver of ignoring events in order to maintain the status quo is also clearly illustrated in a study by Janicki (1959). He found that persons disposed toward system I functioning (as defined by a situational interpretation measure) [1] reacted to both praise and criticism in a manner aimed to maintain whatever status relations existed between the source and the recipient prior to the evaluation. The person's postevaluation rating was therefore more likely to be aimed at maintaining the evaluation of one's self in relation to the source than was true for persons functioning in the other three systems.

Distortion and dissociation. Closely related to denial are those interpretive tactics that deal with the refuting event, but recategorize it in less threatening terms. Two such techniques are (1) distortion, or the recall of the negative evaluation as being less negative, and (2) dissociation, or diluting the effect of the negative evaluation by disengaging the source from the communication in some way (for example, questioning that the source actually made the evaluation). Harvey (1958) reported in a study that replicated and extended earlier findings (Harvey, Kelley, and Shapiro, 1957) that persons disposed toward system I (High F scale) were more likely to utilize one or both of these maneuvers following a negative self-evaluation than persons low on the F scale. These tactics are activated by the devaluation by a positive source, a circumstance that is potentially refuting for this system.

Categorical judgments. The concrete, poorly differentiated structure of system I promotes the use of categorical, "either-or" judgments. Support for this association comes from a study by Schroder and McCarter (1959) who found that in making attitudinal judgments about various religions and political parties that the persons functioning at system I (according to a situational interpretation measure) made more extreme judgments than did others. Such persons were more likely to be either very favorable or very unfavorable toward the object being judged with little gradation between these extreme judgments. This finding is similar to that reported earlier by Sherif and Hovland (1953), who found that persons who held negative attitudes toward minority groups,

[1] A forced-choice instrument developed for research purposes, cf. pp. 261–262.

as would be expected in system I, made more categorical, "black-white" judgments.

BOLSTERING

Bolstering maneuvers in system I consist of operations aimed at the reaffirmation of external or culturally prescribed rules and standards. These maneuvers may take the specific forms of reaffirmation of one's duty or obligation, impersonalization, or an increased valuation of criticized aspects.

Reaffirmation of duty. Refutation may be dealt with in system I by reaffirming belief in the "system," literally speaking. Thus, Schroder and Hunt (1959) found that system I interpretations of criticism were more likely to involve statements such as "It is my duty to obey him" and "He has a right to do that."

Such a transformation seems similar to what Heider has described as the "ought" force, as seen in the following:

> As a first approach, the content of "I (or *o*) ought to do *x*" may be said to be fashioned after the idea "somebody wants or commands that I (or *o*) do *x*." In the case of ought, however, it is not a particular somebody that is felt to want or command people to do *x*, but some suprapersonal objective order. It may also be experienced as a supernatural being who personified this objective . . . (Heider, 1958, p. 219).

Impersonalization. Another means by which bolstering may occur is that of impersonalization, or de-emphasizing the personal aspects by focusing upon one's role obligations. Merton has described a maneuver similar to this technique in connection with bureaucratic functioning: "Another feature of the bureaucratic structure, the stress on *depersonalization of relationships* plays its part in the bureaucrat's trained incapacity. The personality pattern of the bureaucrat is nucleated about this norm of impersonality" (Merton, 1940, p. 565). (Italics ours.) To reinterpret one's own actions or those of another as being determined by these externally given "ought" forces serves the dual function of reaffirming the absolute standard, and removing any personal intent that might otherwise be threatening. Heider's comments are appropriate:

> . . . oughts are impersonal. They refer to standards of what ought to be done or experienced, standards independent of the individual's wishes (Heider, 1958, p. 219).
>
> They [oughts] refer to invariant standards, to "laws of conduct" which hold in spite of many variations in incidental or momentary factors (p. 220).
>
> Not only should ought disregard personal desires, not only does ought in principle appear unchanged in spite of incidental situational factors, but it is also universal and should look alike to everybody (p. 222).

Increased valuation of criticized aspects. A very specific example of system I bolstering was noted by Wright (1958) who investigated the reaction of high F scale subjects to non-specific criticism from an authority figure; that is, a classroom instructor disparaged the performance of all persons in the class. Following this, the high F scale subjects did not change their earlier positive evaluation of the instructor, but they did increase their evaluation of other members in the class who had also been criticized, a very clear example of bolstering in which the criticism is diluted by becoming more positive. Note that the bolstering consists of a simultaneous maintenance of respect for authority and a denial of the validity of the criticism. One can think of a very young child who is called a "bad boy" by his father and who can do nothing but insist that he is a "good boy."

Behavioral Reactions to Refutation in System I

When refutation is experienced in system I functioning, the behavioral resolutions are likely to be rapid, inflexible, and/or overgeneralized. Thus, we would expect resolutions of the following forms: (1) forming standards quickly, (2) adopting a rigid pattern of response, or (3) submitting to the wishes of an authority figure in an overgeneralized fashion.

RAPID FORMATION OF STANDARDS

When system I is operating in relation to ambiguous situations, behavior aimed to reduce such normative uncertainty should occur very quickly. Evidence for this expectation is noted in the finding that authoritarians establish a norm more quickly than non-authoritarians in the relative ambiguity of the autokinetic situation (Block and Block, 1951; Harvey, 1959).

BEHAVIORAL RIGIDITY

Another mode of behavioral expression associated with system I is that described as rigidity, or a failure to consider alternative solutions. For example, Brown (1953) found that authoritarians were more rigid in attempting to solve an einstellung problem than were non-authoritarians. Results of this study indicated that such rigidity was associated with system I functioning only under ego-involving instructions; in terms of the present viewpoint, ego-involving instructions contain the implication of the potential refutation that would activate the system-specific behavioral expression of rigidity. Zelen (1955) has reported similar results in the area of level of aspiration. He found that rigidity in setting goals was associated with system I functioning (High

F scale) only under conditions of ambiguity (specifically, the condition involved trials that were of differing lengths of time). The results of both investigations emphasize that potential refutation to the system leads to system-specific resolutions. An implication of this is that more precise description and manipulation of the potentially refuting condition will lead to more accurate prediction of system-specific resolutions.

OVERGENERALIZED SUBMISSION TO AUTHORITY

Closely related to the interpretation of events in terms of "ought" forces is the behavioral expression of submission associated with system I functioning. For example, Block and Block (1952) found that authoritarians are more likely to continue work at the dull, boring task of packing spools into a box when the experimenter gives very slight indication that they should continue, by comments such as "Don't you want to do some more." This pattern of response illustrates the "authoritarian submission" presumed to be one facet of the authoritarian personality (Adorno et al., 1950).

Investigations of the effect of social influence have reported significant correlations between degree of system I functioning (score on the F scale) and conformity to social influence (Crutchfield, 1955; Harvey, 1958). In order for this relationship to occur, two conditions must be met: first, that the interpersonal disagreement represented in the social influence emanate from sources who are clearly powerful, important figures, and second, that the social pressure be unambiguous.[1] As we consider in Chapter 8, the source of influence is of vital importance when the response to such influence is viewed from a system-specific vantage point.

Also relevant is the finding that although system I functioning may lead to yielding under special situational conditions, the person does not differentiate the influenced response from other responses not subjected to influence (Harvey, 1958). The results of this investigation indicated that system I Ss (as measured by F scale) manifested response change in both the influenced and uninfluenced responses. Consonant with the concrete level of functioning assumed to characterize system I, results of this study indicated that when change occurred the modified response was overgeneralized to other response systems.

[1] That system I yielding to social pressure occurs only under unambiguous conditions is illustrated in a finding of Janicki (1960) that system I Ss are inflexibly unsusceptible to influence when the influence is more ambiguous, that is, comes from only one person.

Reactions to Confirmation in System I

System-specific confirmation should facilitate performance as well as produce positive affect. In system I functioning, situations that provide a high degree of structure with clearly prescribed rules of behavior should produce such response facilitation. For example, investigations have found (French and Ernest, 1955; Crockett, 1958) that persons who are disposed toward system I (High F scale) are more accepting of military ideology and authoritarian leadership. One is reminded of an incidental finding from the classic Lewin, Lippitt, and White (1939) study that the only boy who was pleased with the autocratic treatment was a youngster whose father was a colonel in the Army. At a cultural level, Murphy (1953) has noted that Indian students prefer directive, autocratic leadership presumably because they are more accustomed to highly structured direction.

System II Functioning

On the basis of the structure noted in Table 18, system II functioning should be associated with a heightened sensitivity to the dimension of control, ranging from imposition of control to freedom from imposition. Therefore, events experienced as involving imposition of control or dependence upon others will constitute refutation whereas events experienced as providing freedom from external control will constitute confirmation. The avoidance of system-specific refutation by bolstering will take the form of reaffirming one's independence and freedom from external control. Neutralization will presumably involve a minimization or denial of any necessity for dependence or being controlled. Behavioral resolutions to system-specific refutation will involve a general "moving away" or counteracting the experienced imposition.

System II Sensitization

From Table 18 it may be noted that system II functioning is closely attuned to the degree of potential control imposed by events. When system II is operating, reality is therefore "read" in terms of potential restriction—whether actual, or implied by any form of dependence upon the other person—or freedom from such restriction. Thus, functioning in system II is characterized by a tendency to view the actions of others directed toward oneself as potentially threatening. Supporting this expectation is the finding that persons disposed toward system II (situational interpretation measure) are more likely to categorize other people in terms of interpersonal threat (that is, "a person you feel comfortable with" versus "a person who makes you uneasy") than in terms of other personal dimensions such as competence or attractiveness (Hunt and Schroder, 1959).

The sensitization characteristics of this system may be illustrated by noting examples of the conceptual dimensions employed by a boy strongly disposed toward system II functioning, as they were obtained by a modified form of the Role Concept Repertory Test (Kelly, 1955). In describing some of his teachers he used the following conceptual descriptions:

"Miserable . . . always mad . . . sneering . . . try to make you feel little," [and later,] "Wouldn't get along with 'em . . . wouldn't give you half a chance . . . they'd just jump down your neck." [In describing his peers he used the following:] "Always bothering you . . . give you a hard time" . . . Big shots . . . better than everybody . . . show off . . . bragging . . . shoving everyone around" [and later,] "Acts like a friend at times but you know he isn't."

These examples also illustrate many of the maneuvers to be described in relation to this system. However, they capture the flavor of the underlying distrust and orientation away from close interpersonal relationships. Or, as another boy put it in a sentence completion response, "People . . . can be nice to talk to if you like them. Otherwise I don't notice them."

Conditions Producing Refutation and Confirmation in System II

One of the major methods by which people interact, and thus become dependent upon one another, is through evaluating each other, either implicitly or explicitly. However, in system II functioning, the evaluation by others is interpreted as potential control or restriction and thus produces refutation. Because the system functioning is aimed toward defining oneself as being different from others, almost any form of evaluation from another is potentially refuting. Although the experience of refutation will be greater in negative evaluation than in positive, either form will produce refutation. The following sentence completion responses from a boy disposed toward system II functioning exemplify this:

If someone says I am doing poorly . . . I figure I could be doing much worse and I'm probably doing better than someone else, so I don't pay any attention. If someone says I am doing well . . . that's quite all right with me, but as far as I'm concerned it's worthless to me because I figure I could be doing even better.

In contrast, situations involving no evaluation will represent confirmation in this system. For example the same boy gave this response:

I do my best work . . . when I work all alone. This is the only way I can concentrate. If the work is not interesting to me even this wouldn't help.

An even more important form of confirmation here consists in successful opposition to authority. For example, the rebellious teenager who defies parental behavioral and achievement demands will experience confirmation through the defeat of authority rather than in any specific achievement content (though there may be "achievements" in areas disapproved by authority, for example, sexual conquests, car stealing). When the person functioning in terms of system II forms a positive interpersonal relationship, the basis is therefore likely to be mutual opposition to authority.

Interpretive Maneuvers Associated with System II

If the person functioning in terms of system II is confronted by potential refutation what are the system-specific maneuvers that he may employ?

NEUTRALIZATION

The following general patterns of neutralization are associated with this system: (1) *failure to perceive,* (2) *non-commitment or denial of interest,* (3) *denial of responsibility,* and (4) *imputation of malevolence.*

Failure to perceive. System II functioning is associated with a minimization or lack of attention to variations in information. For example, McDavid and Schroder (1957) found that delinquent boys (whose orientation seems appropriately described as system II functioning, cf. Chapter 9) displayed an incapacity to differentiate between events of approval and disapproval. Regardless of the content of the evaluation they were insensitive to the information contained in the evaluation. In another study, Janicki (1959) found that persons disposed toward system II (situational interpretation measure) were less likely to change their self-evaluations following either praise or criticism than were persons disposed toward other systems. These studies illustrate one of the major difficulties in functioning that is arrested at system II: the incapacity to utilize information from others to clarify one's self-definition or other judgments.

Non-commitment. This maneuver consists of erecting the defense of "indifference" in advance against potential control or dependence. From the logic of system II it involves an anticipatory ploy that "beats the other to the punch." For example, Heider's comments on the dynamics underlying the "sour grapes" mechanism are illuminating. He points out that a successful outcome is a function of, among other things, "can" (or ability) and "try" (or intention). The following quotation considers the role of these factors more specifically:

> Sometimes the data make it very clear in the absence or failure of action, whether it is the "can" or the "try" that is the missing condition. But sometimes the data are sufficiently ambiguous so that the person's own needs or wishes determine the attribution.
>
> An example of such egocentric attribution is the sour grapes fable. The fox pretends, or perhaps is even convinced, that he does not want the grapes rather than that he cannot get them. He attributes the failure to the "not want" (and the "not intend" and the "not try") instead of the "not can," since in this case the former is neutral as far as his self-esteem is concerned, and the latter is damaging (Heider, 1958, p. 118).

The "sour grapes" denial of interest thus provides a technique of avoiding, softening, or diluting the consequences of action in advance. Such denial of involvement or non-commitment wards off the likelihood of negative evaluation. An excerpt from an interview with the same boy whose sentence completion responses were presented earlier illustrates this maneuver. The question, "Do you ever work on your car?" was asked. He replied:

> No, I'm not very mechanically minded . . . it's another non-interest of mine . . . I don't have time anyway so I don't try to or bother to learn.

What may be considered as a subtle variation in non-commitment is that of "unpredictable or variable" commitment, or giving off diffuse cues in which either the person's verbal statement or his performance is so inconsistent as to make evaluation difficult. Radiating diffuse or contradictory interpersonal cues in this way serves the purpose of system II in that the subject is always in a position of eluding the observer's interpretation (and/or evaluation). Obviously also, such a maneuver serves effectively to avoid interpersonal involvement and any form of dependence upon others.

Denial of responsibility. Another means of disengaging oneself from any necessity to depend upon others is through denying one's own responsibility. In order for a person to experience success or failure he must first ascribe the performance to himself (Escalona, 1948). Denying responsibility may circumvent negative evaluation, but it also prevents experiences of accomplishment; we have noted earlier the way in which this mode of operation interferes with providing system-specific "reward." This resolution is similar to the impunitive tendency described by Rosenzweig as ". . . [an] attempt to avoid blame altogether, whether of others or of oneself, and to gloss over the frustrating situation as though with a conciliatory objective" (Rosenzweig, 1944,

p. 383). Such a maneuver is specifically characteristic of what we term indirect functioning in system II and as such may be related to so-called psychopathic behavior (see Chapter 9).

Related to this maneuver are findings of Rotter and his colleagues (Rotter, Seeman, and Liverant, 1958; James and Rotter, 1958) who have shown the importance of a variable that they refer to as "internal vs. external control of reinforcement." For example, in one study Ss were preselected by means of a questionnaire measuring the tendency to perceive events as externally or internally controlled and were then confronted with tasks presented as either skill (internal control) or chance (external control). When success in a task was presented (and presumably perceived) as caused by chance (external control), Ss' expectations generalized less and extinguished more rapidly than when success was perceived as due to skill.

In setting forth what they refer to as "techniques of neutralization" by which delinquents rationalize their violation of norms, Sykes and Matza (1957) have described how the delinquent denies responsibility for the act and attributes its cause to forces outside his control, for example, unloving parents, bad companions.

Although the person functioning in terms of system II will deny responsibility for failure or other negative outcomes, he may nevertheless claim credit for positive outcomes. For example, the delinquent who gets away with a theft may express his feeling that this proves his prowess, but when apprehended he may disclaim responsibility by neutralization noted above. This combination of blame avoidance and credit claiming is, in a sense, a "having it both ways" maneuver.

Imputation of malevolence. If a person interprets a situation as occurring because of the malevolent intentions of the source, such an attribution at once serves the protective function of preventing dependence upon the other, as well as establishing justification for retaliation against the source if necessary. Therefore, this maneuver should be associated with system II functioning. For example, in the same interview from which the earlier excerpt was drawn, the following response occurred to a question regarding repairing his car.

> Well, no, some of them could have done it for me . . . I didn't have time to do it, but I don't trust them anyway . . . even if I know they want to go out with me I still trust myself more than them.

This maneuver is similar to the extrapunitive tendencies, defined as "those in which the individual aggressively attributes the frustration to external persons or things" (Rosenzweig, 1944, p. 383). Such tendencies are characteristic of direct system II functioning, which, as we contend in Chapter 9, is basic to antisocial delinquent patterns. Extrapuntive tendencies apparently increase after experimentally induced frustration (Lindzey, 1950), which would also be consonant with system II functioning. Harvey (1958) found that subjects who imputed malevolence ("He was angry at me") to the source of an unfavorable evaluation showed less change in self-evaluation following the criticism. This resistance to external pressure toward self-change indicates the maintenance function served.

Analysis of interpretive responses made by persons disposed toward system II functioning in accounting for a hypothetical situation of criticism indicate that this interpretation of negative intent may take a variety of forms: projected envy ("He just wishes that he was good as I was"), projected egotism ("He thinks he's better than I am"), as well as more straightforward malicious intention ("He's just trying to give me a hard time") (Hunt, 1957).

From the present viewpoint the two tendencies described by Rosenzweig—impunitive and extrapunitive—are genotypically similar in their relatedness to system II functioning. However, we would view impunitive reactions (or denial of self-responsibility) as associated with indirect functioning whereas extrapunitive reactions (or malevolent imputation) are seen as associated with direct functioning.

BOLSTERING

Circumstances may not always permit evasion through non-commitment. What happens when the person functioning in terms of system II is forced to take a stand or set a goal? Since to admit weakness implies dependence on others, the person will be likely to set goals that are excessively high in relation to his past performance. He will try to assert an attitude of hyperadequacy. Support for this contention comes from results indicating that persons disposed toward system II (situational interpretation measure) react to minimal failure by stating excessively high goals and "leaving the field" (Schroder and Hunt, 1957). Such reaffirmation of competence is seen as a "whistling in the dark" techique aimed at minimizing potential refutation through the verbal assertion of high goal statement.

This bolstering tendency in system II is also illustrated by the frequent finding of a curvilinear relationship between goal-setting and self-acceptance or personal adequacy (P. S. Sears, 1940; Rotter, 1943; Cohen, 1954). These studies indicate that persons who are poorly adjusted or low in self-acceptance state either excessively low or excessively high goals. From the present conceptual viewpoint we would argue that the divergence into two extremes of goal-setting represents the operation of different systems: excessively high goals being associated with system II bolstering and excessively low goals associated with the behavioral expression of submission and worthlessness in indirect system I functioning. In both cases the distorted expectation serves to maintain system-specific equilibrium.

Rotter, Seeman, and Liverant (1958) have also reported a relationship between the tendency to displace responsibility to external events (denial of self-responsibility) and setting excessively high goals, a relationship that would be viewed in the present framework as stemming from system II functioning.

Behavioral Reactions to Refutation in System II

Three patterns of behavioral reaction are considered as specifically associated with this system: (1) *source devaluation,* (2) *behavioral avoidance,* and (3) *"boomerang" response.*

SOURCE DEVALUATION

This response is closely related to the antecedent interpretation of malevolent imputation, in terms of the "eye for an eye and a tooth for a tooth" logic prevalent in system II. Put in oversimplified terms, "If he's trying to give me a hard time I have a perfect right to aggress against him," or as a distorted golden rule, "Do unto others before others can do unto you." In studying reactions to unfavorable evaluations of the self, Harvey, Kelley, and Shapiro (1957) found that source devaluation increased as a function of unfavorableness of the rating, and more recently Harvey (1958) has replicated this finding.

In a conformity experiment, Steiner and Peters (1958) found that devaluation of the influencing source varied inversely with the frequency of yielding to social influence. These results directly support the role of source devaluation in avoiding dependence upon others. In addition, Schroder (1957) has shown that persons disposed toward system II are more likely to devalue the source of criticism when reacting to verbal criticism in a role-playing situation.

BEHAVIORAL AVOIDANCE

Another mode for coping with refutation in system II is to "leave the field." It was briefly noted earlier that persons disposed toward system II functioning are more likely to "leave the field," that is, elect to stop working on the problem in a problem-solving situation at the early signs of failure (Schroder and Hunt, 1957). It may be useful to view non-commitment, reaffirmation of competence (excessively high goal setting), and behavioral avoidance as differing system II modes of coping over a period of time and under varying conditions. Initially the person attempts to avoid commitment; forced to state a goal, he states it excessively high; falling short of his goal, he "leaves the field" at the earliest opportunity.

"BOOMERANG" RESPONSE

When a subject in a social-influence experiment hears a majority report that differs from his own judgment, one of several alternative responses is to respond differently in a direction *away from* the majority report, that is, to recoil from the influence. We have borrowed the term "boomerang" from attitude-change literature to describe such a response. This response is clearly functionally related to the source devaluation, which Steiner and Peters found to be inversely related to yielding to social influence. That the "boomerang" response is associated with system II functioning is nicely illustrated in a study by Schroder and Janicki (1959b). In the experiment system II Ss were preselected by a situational interpretation measure and were then enabled to form a judgmental standard (judging distance between two points of light). "Influence" was then applied by exposing a partner to different distances (either shorter or longer) in a constant direction that the partner judged while the system II S was present. The original standard was then presented again to the subject. It was found that persons disposed toward system II reacted by moving *away from* their own earlier standard of judgment in a direction that was opposite to that of the judgment made by the partner, a response pattern that may be considered a "boomerang." Similar support comes from a report by Linton and Graham (1959) that "negative changers" in an attitude change experiment—that is, persons whose attitudes moved in a direction opposed to the communication—showed personality characteristics that would presumably be associated with system II functioning: "Feel physically inadequate, Rebellious toward authority and convention, Expressions of hostility" (Linton and Graham, 1959, p. 94).

Reactions to Confirmation in System II

From the viewpoint of facilitation of performance, persons disposed toward system II would likely function best in a "control group" that is, no experimental manipulation whatsoever. Mandler and Sarason (1952) have observed the performance of a group of college Ss classified as high in test anxiety (a personality pattern viewed in present terms as similar to system II, partly on the basis of an earlier reported relationship between manifest anxiety and system II disposition on a situational interpretation measure, Schroder and Hunt, 1957, p. 17).

They found performance disruption after *either* positive or negative evaluation by the experimenter. Optimal performance for these persons occurred when the experimenter said nothing—that is, a "no evaluation" condition. Grace (1948) studied the personality characteristics of children who performed better under a neutral condition than under either approval or disapproval and reported that such children were insecure, personally inferior, and were generally poorly adjusted at home and in school. Although the Grace study proceeds in reverse of the Mandler-Sarason study, the results attest to the relative facilitation of no evaluation upon system II functioning.

Persons disposed to system II functioning may also attempt to obtain confirmation by testing the limits and patience of the source by their irritating or irresponsible behavior until the source finally reacts in an unfriendly fashion, thus confirming the closed system II structure.

System III Functioning

Referring once more to Table 18, we would expect system III functioning to show sensitivity to the dimension that ranges from mutuality and acceptance at one pole to rejection and aloneness at the other. Events experienced as rejection will constitute refutation whereas events experienced as mutuality and dependence will constitute confirmation. Bolstering should take the form of reaffirming mutuality whereas neutralization occurs through the denial of rejection. Behavioral resolutions to system-specific refutation will involve a moving toward the other person in an effort to reinstate the bond of interpersonal acceptance.

System III Sensitization

The poles of this system indicate a sensitization to mutuality or dependence. Partly because of the more highly differentiated nature of this system, the sensitization characteristics or events to which the system is most attuned are somewhat more complicated than was true for the first two systems. Successful transition or progression to system III functioning involves a differentiation between other persons, or differentiating certain others from the generalized standard operating in system I functioning. Therefore we would expect system III functioning to be especially open to (1) the evaluative reaction of others to one's behavior and (2) the personal characteristics of the other person, especially whether he is attractive, or a potential source of approval for the individual.

SENSITIZATION TO OTHERS

In sharp contrast to the avoidance of evaluation noted in system II, the operation of system III involves an openness to the evaluation made by sources of approval since the relevant dimensions involve other people rather than the subject. In oversimplified terms, system III functioning rests on a "If you can't beat 'em, join 'em" formulation that contrasts with the "beat 'em" prevalent in system II. This system-specific sensitization is quite similar to the "other-directed" orientation described by David Riesman (1950): "What is common to all other-directeds is that their contemporaries are the source of direction for the individual . . ." (Riesman, 1950, p. 22).

In his discussion Riesman clarifies the distinction between what would presently be regarded as system III and system IV by describing what aspect is internalized in system III:

> This source [contemporaries] is of course "internalized" in the sense that dependence on it for guidance in life is implanted early. The goals toward which the other-directed person strives shift with that guidance: it is only the process of striving itself and the process of paying close attention to the signals from others that remain unaltered throughout life (Riesman, 1950, p. 22).

For system I the generalized standard rather than contemporaries provides direction. Hence, the distinction that Riesman draws between tradition-direction and other-direction is therefore applicable to distinguishing between system I and system III, respectively:

> The tradition-directed person takes his signals from others, but they come in a cultural monotone; he needs no complex receiving equipment to pick them up. The other-directed person must be able to receive signals from far and near; the sources are many, the changes rapid. What can be internalized, then, is not a code of behavior but the elaborate equipment needed to attend to such messages and occasionally to participate in their circulation. . . . This control equipment, instead of being like a gyroscope, is like a radar (Riesman, 1950, p. 26).

A recent study by Atkinson and Walker (1956) illustrates the effect of this "elaborate equipment" Riesman describes. These authors exposed a picture of a human face at subthreshold levels and studied visual awareness as a function of the strength of affiliation motive (and intensity of affiliation induction conditions). Since the stimulus of the human face was assumed to be more motivationally relevant than the impersonal control stimuli, the greater accuracy shown in identifying the face both in high affiliation Ss and under affiliation arousal was interpreted as reflecting a heightened sensitivity to motivationally relevant stimuli.

DIFFERENTIATING BETWEEN OTHERS

Persons disposed toward system III place more "weight" upon whether the other person is someone they like or dislike (Schroder and Hunt, 1958). That is, in addition to focusing on the other person more intently, system III functioning also leads to more concern with the kind of person involved. Or as Riesman puts it:

> Of course, it matters very much who these "others" are: whether they are the individual's immediate circle or a "higher" circle or the anonymous voices of the mass media; . . . acquaintances or only of those who "count" (Riesman, 1950, pp. 22–23).

In system III functioning, the subject differentiates between others by noting their differential reaction to his actions. As system III functioning becomes increasingly closed or arrested, these between-other differentiations become sharper and, although quite complex, are particularly sensitive to the dimension of source attractiveness. That persons disposed toward system III are more sensitized to the attractiveness dimension has been shown by their reaction to hypothetical criticism from liked and disliked sources (Schroder and Hunt, 1958). This sensitization is shown also in how Ss categorize others in a situation where there is a choice between the dimension of source attractiveness and other possible dimensions of categorizing (Hunt and Schroder, 1959). It has been further demonstrated through differential susceptibility to social pressure from liked versus disliked sources of influence in a conformity experiment (Wilson, 1960). System III functioning was referred to in these investigations as "social accommodation."

Conditions Producing Refutation and Confirmation in System III

For system III, refutation is represented by rejection, or events implying "aloneness." Events read as "non-mutuality" in this system are potentially refuting, in part because of the general principle that refutation is maximal when the events represent pressures toward the next highest level of functioning. Thus, part of the underlying dynamics may consist of non-supportive events that are transformed in terms of the threat implied in autonomy. In addition, these pressures toward autonomy are similar to the "negative independence" pole of system II from which the person functioning at system III has progressed.

If refutation comes from rejection, confirmation comes from approval. Riesman's comments regarding similar orientations in "other-directedness" are relevant:

It is perhaps the insatiable force of this psychological need for approval that differentiates people . . . whom we regard as other-directed, from very similar types. . . . (Riesman, 1950, p. 23).

At this level, self-definition and the evaluation of oneself are determined very largely by the effect one can produce upon others. System-specific confirmation is aptly illustrated in White's comments on the "marketing orientation" described by Fromm:

Self-esteem here depends upon conditions more or less beyond one's control. . . . Success is so heavily defined as being what others want you to be, rather than as doing certain things with effective skill, that the opinions of others become almost the sole source of self-feeling and self-esteem (White, 1956, p. 184).

Persons functioning in terms of system III will not necessarily experience refutation from poor performance or making errors provided that such responses are deemed praiseworthy by the valued other person. Stated more specifically, if confronted by negative task feedback (failure) that conflicts with positive source evaluation (praise), the person functioning in system III is more susceptible to the latter, source-mediated "channel," and thus will experience confirmation (Wells and Hunt, 1959).

Interpretive Maneuvers Associated with System III

NEUTRALIZATION

Potential loss of interpersonal support or events of potential rejection may be interpretatively avoided by two maneuvers: (1) *denial of source responsibility* and (2) *denial of rejection.*

Denial of source responsibility. If the source can be "excused" or the event reinterpreted as a special case, potential refutation can be avoided. Examples of excusing the source would include interpretations such as "He couldn't help it," or "He isn't himself today." In its aim to dissociate the source from the event, this system III–related maneuver is similar to maneuvers emanating from system I. However, a subtle, but nonetheless important, system-specific difference may be noted in that dissociation related to system I involves cultural dimensions, for example, "He did not understand what he was supposed to do," whereas dissociation related to system III involves more personalized dimensions, for example, "He may not be feeling well today."

Because this denying maneuver is more likely to be evoked by attractive sources, the study by Harvey, Kelley, and Shapiro (1957) and replication by Harvey (1958) mentioned earlier are relevant.

In studying the occurrence of three maintenance mechanisms after a negative evaluation of the self by another person (either a friend or stranger), it was found that although denial of source responsibility, or dissociation, increased sharply as the unfavorableness of the "friend's" evaluation increased, no such increase was noted to the "stranger's" evaluation. Put in current terms the evaluation from the friend is more likely to represent potential system III refutation, thus requiring an interpretive maneuver such as dissociation.

Denial of rejection. This system-specific maneuver dilutes or cancels the meaning of the event by passing it off as a joke, for example, "He's just kidding." Persons disposed toward system III functioning (based on a situational interpretation measure) are much more likely to interpret criticism from attractive sources in this fashion (Schroder and Hunt, 1959). From the viewpoint of system III relatedness, joking and "fooling around" represent modes of interaction that can foster mutuality in addition to their neutralizing function. However, as we note later, the maneuver also cuts off receptivity to information.

These two neutralizing maneuvers, denial of source responsibility and denial of rejection, may be contrasted with the system II maneuvers of denial of self-responsibility and malevolent imputation. Although in both systems the maneuvers reinterpret either responsibility or intention, the direction of the interpretation is reversed in system III functioning. The system II maneuvers excuse the self and blame the other person; the system III maneuvers excuse the other person and place the blame, if anywhere, on the self. In system III, efforts are made primarily to avoid blame on others and only secondarily of self, so that under extreme threat to the maintenance of mutuality, denial of self-blame breaks down and extreme intropunitiveness occurs (cf. extreme forms of system III functioning in Chapter 9).

BOLSTERING

Confronted by potential refutation, system III functioning should be associated with a reaffirmation of one's being accepted by others. Bolstering therefore takes the form of excessively high estimation of one's sociometric acceptance, akin to the high goal statements related to performance noted in system II. This maneuver is epitomized by the statement, "We're really the best of friends."

Behavioral Reactions to Refutation in System III

Three forms of behavioral expression are expected: (1) *excessive reliance upon others for determining self-evaluation,* (2) *submission to influence in an overgeneralized fashion,* and (3) *seeking interper-*

sonal support. In describing these system-specific reactions we distinguish between responses emanating from system I and from system III, since they are similar in many respects.

EXCESSIVE RELIANCE UPON OTHERS FOR DETERMINING SELF-EVALUATION

System III functioning consists of articulating one's self-definition primarily in terms of the effects produced in others. In some respects, therefore, it is similar to Witkin's "field dependent" mode, although as we have observed earlier, the "field dependent" mode bears a resemblance to both system I and system III.

McDavid (1959) found that, compared to a "message-oriented" group (system IV), "source-oriented" subjects (system III) were "more prone to modify their perceptions of themselves in a work situation following an interpersonal communication" (McDavid, 1959, p. 245). Similar results were obtained by Janicki (1959) who found that system III Ss (defined by a situational interpretation measure) changed their self-evaluations more after communications from an attractive source; that is, they increased their self-evaluation more following praise and decreased their self-evaluation more following criticism than did the other three groups. Such excessive dependence upon external influence is of course closely related to the next reaction pattern of submission to influence.

SUBMISSION TO INFLUENCE IN AN OVERGENERALIZED FASHION

Evidence from social influence experiments that supports the system-specific incidence of this reaction comes from several studies. Greater incidence of yielding has been reported in persons described as high in "need for social approval" (Moeller and Applezweig, 1957); in persons oriented toward pleasing others (Linton and Graham, 1959); in source-oriented persons (McDavid, 1959); and in persons placing a greater "weight" upon the attractiveness of the source (Schroder and Hunt, 1958). As will be considered in Chapter 8, in order to distinguish between systems I and III, the influencing sources must be separated in terms of power and attractiveness, respectively, because the kind of source producing overgeneralized submission differs in these two systems.

In considering the generalization of an influenced response, Schroder and Janicki (1959b) have reported that a system III group reflected greater generalization in time (less extinction) and space (change in influenced response carried over to uninfluenced responses). This latter finding is similar to Harvey's finding (1958) reported earlier, that system I Ss reflect a lack of differentiation between influenced and uninfluenced responses. Whether these similar findings represent a failure of the measuring instruments to distinguish system I from system III, or whether both systems respond identically in terms of such overgeneralization remains a matter for further investigation.

SEEKING INTERPERSONAL SUPPORT

The nature of system-specific support-seeking is illustrated by a recent report by Schacter (1959). Support-seeking was indicated by the person's preference to spend a period of time before an anxiety-arousing experience with other persons (together) or by oneself (alone). Schacter found that the preference for the "together" condition was associated with persons who were either only children or first-born. As we have noted earlier such an ordinal position is more likely to be associated with parental training that would lead to functioning arrested at system III.

Reaction to Confirmation in System III

System III functioning is associated with response facilitation under conditions of favorable evaluation from the other, such as approval. For example, McCarter and Schroder (1959) studied "learning without awareness" in response to experimenter approval ("good") in different dispositional groups. They found that persons disposed toward system III (situational interpretation measure) "learned" more rapidly than any other group under these conditions. Also, I. Sarason (1958) has reported that patients who were rated as more dependent by their therapists were more susceptible to effects of experimenter approval in a "learning without awareness" situation.

Similar system-specific facilitation is noted in a study by French (1958b), which compared the problem solving effectiveness of a group disposed toward system III (high affiliation need) with another group. Interest centered upon variations in group performance in response to two forms of feedback specifically relevant to each group: task feedback ("This group is working very efficiently") or feeling feedback ("This group works well together"). Facilitating effects occurred when the feedback was congruent with the personality organization of group members; more specifically, groups composed of what we would call system III Ss worked more effectively under conditions of feeling feedback than under task feedback.

A study by Gewirtz and Baer (1958) is also appropriate since it provided for both the induction of system III functioning and system-specific confirmation. Nursery school children underwent a brief period of social deprivation prior to experiencing social approval in relation to a particular activity, such as dropping marbles into a box. From an induction point of view they found that:

> . . . it appears that the effectiveness of a representative social reinforcer may be enhanced by an operation of deprivation, as in the case for the reinforcers of primary appetitive drives like hunger and thirst (Gewirtz and Baer, 1958, pp. 55–56).

In present terms the experience of social deprivation apparently induced system III functioning in most children. Moreover, the authors state:

> The effectiveness of this reinforcer appears enhanced particularly for Ss who typically seek it (Gewirtz and Baer, 1958, p. 56).

Again, our interpretation is that the greatest facilitating effects occurred in children disposed toward system III functioning (high in need for approval).

System IV Functioning

On the basis of Table 18, system IV functioning is associated with sensitization to the dimension that ranges from restriction of autonomy to expression of autonomy. Along this system-specific dimension, events experienced as restricting autonomy constitute refutation whereas events experienced as permitting expression of autonomy constitute confirmation. Bolstering takes the form of reaffirming the importance of autonomy and interdependence in system IV, whereas neutralization will involve a minimization of restriction in autonomy by denial of relevance of standards. Behavioral resolutions of system-specific refutation will involve an attempt to clarify one's own standards.

System IV Sensitization

System IV is characterized by openness to the individual's own standards (autonomy, multiple alternatives) and to situations favoring their expressions. We have referred to the framework of system IV organization as *ipsative,* since judgments are based on the individual's internal standards and events are transformed self-reflexively. Such openness is possible because of the operation of a mechanism similar to what Riesman (1950) has called a psychological "gyroscope," as described in the following passage:

> . . . a new psychological mechanism appropriate to the more open society is "invented": it is what I like to describe as a psychological gyroscope.

This instrument, once it is set by the parents and other authorities, keeps the inner-directed person . . . "on course" even when tradition, as responded to by his character, no longer dictates his moves. The inner-directed person becomes capable of maintaining a delicate balance between the demands upon him of his life goal and the buffetings of his external environment (Riesman, 1950, p. 16).

The highly differentiated, abstract nature of system IV organization is associated with functioning that is more sensitive to situational nuances with less defensive closedness, or restriction of information. To illustrate certain areas of sensitivity we may note three specific dimensions: (1) *openness to differences between events,* (2) *openness to differing levels of task difficulty,* and (3) *openness to variations in the competence, or information potential of sources.* These three dimensions are not intended to be exhaustive, but are all supported by empirical evidence and illustrate system IV sensitization.

OPENNESS TO DIFFERENCES BETWEEN EVENTS (GREATER DIFFERENTIATION)

In contrast to the failure to discriminate between positive and negative events noted in system II, this system is carefully attuned to the evaluative information of a communication. Thus Janicki (1959) found that, in reacting to events of approval and disapproval under varying conditions, persons disposed toward system IV (as indicated by an interpretation measure) give more "predictable" postevent evaluations in terms of a general "objective" model such as proposed by Osgood and Tannebaum (1955). Although those persons functioning in the more concrete systems may attach excessive "weight" to the source, the previous relationship between source and recipient, or to some other aspect, persons disposed toward system IV react with a minimum of such distortions, and their evaluations are accordingly closer to those predicted by the general model (which assumes all factors will be objectively weighted) than were the other three groups. System IV functioning is also associated with a differentiation between source and statement, which permits reacting to the information contained in the statement as distinct from attitudes toward the source of the statement.

OPENNESS TO DIFFERING LEVELS OF TASK DIFFICULTY

Situational variations may also involve the dimension of task difficulty. Heider (1958) points out that, if we disregard intention or "trying," a successful outcome may be seen as a function of the ability of the person and the difficulty imposed by the environment:

If the task is easy, then even a person with little ability can do it; if it is difficult, the person cannot do it unless he has greater ability. Or, we may say, if a person succeeds, then his ability must be greater than the environmental difficulty; if he fails (and has maximally exerted himself), his ability must be less than the environmental difficulty (Heider, 1958, p. 87).

System-specific sensitization to task difficulty is illustrated in the study by McDavid (1959) referred to earlier that focused on the response of two dispositional groups to social influence. He found that Ss in the system IV group ("message-oriented" according to a sentence completion measure) were affected more by variations in task difficulty than were Ss disposed toward system III.

OPENNESS TO VARIATION IN COMPETENCE, OR INFORMATION POTENTIAL, OF SOURCES

In "reading" reality in terms of potential information available, system IV functioning is more closely attuned to cues regarding the competence of the source. Postcriticism evaluations are more likely to reflect variation in the competence of criticizing sources in this system (Hunt and Wells, 1959). Wilson (1960) found that in a social influence situation the incidence of yielding by a person disposed toward system IV was determined partly by the subject's competence (intelligence level) relative to that of the influencing sources. Faced by the task of counting clicks, the person disposed to system IV utilized information from the other sources when they were considerably more competent, though not when the sources were less competent than himself. What constitutes "information" for system IV therefore is determined in part by the subject's internal standard. If the system IV S is uncertain of his judgment (and this can occur for a number of reasons, for example, difficult task, low level of competence in area, or stimulus ambiguity) he will be more likely to take account of other person's judgments as potential information.

Conditions Producing Refutation and Confirmation in System IV

Because of its more highly differentiated nature, in system IV functioning there is less likelihood of experiencing a high degree of refutation. However, refutation will be experienced in situations involving restriction of autonomy. If the person functioning in terms of system IV is certain of his judgment in a social influence experiment, he will experience social pressure or social influence as potential refutation. Under these conditions, social influence is interpreted as arbitrary, unilateral, and restrictive of opportunity for interdependent or autonomous functioning.

Confirmation is expected to occur from any events that provide the opportunity for consideration from more than one viewpoint and that permit interdependent functioning.

Interpersonal relations viewed in terms of system IV functioning will consist of a mutually respecting, tolerant atmosphere, for example, "You go to your church and I'll go to mine." Persons functioning in terms of system IV will likely be more attracted to other individuals who are flexible, informative, and autonomous, while they will avoid other individuals who are rigid, overconventional, and unspontaneous. Therefore, the sociometric choices of persons functioning in terms of system IV should theoretically be exactly opposite to the choices of persons functioning in terms of system I.

Interpretive Maneuvers Associated with System IV

The more abstract the level of functioning, the more openness to various dimensions. The more openness to various dimensions, the less is the necessity for interpretive maneuvers. Thus, although there are certain forms of interpretive maneuvers associated with system IV, we would expect the general incidence of such reinterpretations to be less frequent in this system than others because of its abstract nature.

NEUTRALIZATION–DENIAL OF RELEVANCE OF STANDARDS

Faced with potential refutation, the person functioning in terms of system IV may affirm that his standards are different from those of the (imposing) source and assert that the latter do not apply to him. This maneuver is like the little elf's retort, "I'm quite as big for me as you are big for you." The person neutralizes the potential refutation by acknowledging that, like himself, the other person has his standards, but that the standards or frames of reference are sufficiently different to obviate any necessity for the subject to take further account of the situation.

Persons disposed toward system IV (according to an interpretation measure), when confronted by criticism, were more likely to utilize the following kind of neutralizing attributions: "Something I was doing looked wrong according to his tastes or method, yet for me it was all right," or "Because what I think I was doing well, he wouldn't think it is good work" (Schroder and Hunt, 1959). We may note that such a maneuver *may* be defensive if the subject distorts the other person's standard in the interpretation. However, to the extent that such distortion occurs, we would consider the maneuver as emanating from system II functioning.

BOLSTERING

In fully articulated, well-established system IV functioning, bolstering is by definition (of the system) largely unncessary. In the development and articulation of system IV, however, bolstering could take the form of a reaffirmation of an informational orientation. Although not expected to occur frequently, such a maneuver minimizes an event because it contains no information.

Behavioral Reactions to Refutation in System IV

MAINTAINING STANDARD IN RESPONSE TO NON-INFORMATIONAL SOCIAL INFLUENCE

Results from social influence investigations described earlier (p. 231) have generally involved comparing responses of persons disposed toward system III with those disposed toward system IV. These studies (Moeller and Applezweig, 1957; Schroder and Hunt, 1959; McDavid, 1959; Linton and Graham, 1959) indicate that the system IV subject is not likely to be susceptible to generalized social pressure.

Maintenance of one's standard occurs in situations assumed to maximize system-specific refutation. However, another characteristic of system IV is a continual modification and realignment of internal organization in relation to new experiences. Janicki (1960) found that persons disposed toward system IV yielded more to a single partner than did persons disposed toward system I or III.

PROVISIONAL SELF-DEVALUATION AND SELF-CORRECTION

The effectiveness of this system in new learning situations is made possible by provisional self-devaluation and its potential consequence, self-correction. We are assuming that if a person can ascribe failure to himself, or more specifically, to some inadequacy in his response in that particular situation, he may modify his responses more effectively. The nature of this process may be seen in the following:

> Central to the present position is the assumption that, in order to adjust effectively to a situation of failure, an individual must admit that he is doing poorly, that he is in some way inadequate, or that he is, in fact, failing. We assumed that when an S interprets a failure situation by thinking "This means I'm not very good at this" that such an interpretation implies an admission of some personal *inadequacy* or *self-negation*. It should be emphasized that we are *not* using the term "inadequacy" in its usual sense which implies behavioral ineffectiveness. In contrast we mean by "inadequate" that the individual is willing to consider possible weaknesses, to admit that he *may* be wrong, thus opening the possibility for modifying his behavior (Schroder and Hunt, 1957, p. 9).

Results of this study indicated that persons who provisionally lowered self-estimates (that is, were disposed toward system IV) responded more adaptively to failure in a problem-solving task. They lowered their goals to bring them in line with their lower scores, abandoned their earlier unsatisfactory solutions, and looked for other new solutions (see below). And they persisted with continued attempts in the face of failure (Schroder and Hunt, 1957). We infer that such a constellation of responses is dependent upon provisional self-devaluation ("I may be wrong") or recognition of the need for self-correction ("I'm not very good at this") (Hunt and Schroder, 1958). This system IV-related pattern of flexibility and persistence is also based on the interdependent structure that has developed through experiences of self-competence and mastery. In order to adopt a self-corrective orientation, the person must be sufficiently confident through past successful experiences that his admission of the inadequacy will not be threatening.

Also related to this point are findings that persons disposed toward system IV functioning (as indicated by a situational measure) have the lowest score on the F scale (Schroder and Janicki, 1959a) and do not make highly extreme judgments of other people (Schroder and McCarter, 1959).

SEEKING INFORMATION (EXPLORATORY BEHAVIOR)

Implicit but highly important is our assumption that system IV functioning is associated with reactions aimed to test the highly differentiated system IV structure by trying out new differentiations in situations providing maximum feedback and subsequent structural reorganization, if necessary. System IV functioning therefore provides a paradigm of the Socratic exhortation to "Know thyself."

Persons functioning in terms of system IV are generally more likely to interpret criticism in terms of potential information, "He was showing me my mistake" or "He wants to give me some pointers" (Schroder and Hunt, 1959). System IV is therefore similar to the process of object appraisal described by Smith, Bruner, and White (1956):

> To the extent that object appraisal predominates, the person tends to react rationally, according to his lights and according to the information at his disposal. In terms of this function, his interests and values stand to be advanced by flexibility on his part in assimilating the implication of new facts (Smith, Bruner, and White, 1956, p. 277).

We mentioned above the fact that looking for alternative solutions will occur more often in this system. Furthermore, the search for further information will vary along the direct-indirect dimension within this system. This variation is illustrated by a recent study by Cohler and Kelman (1959). First, it may be noted that Kelman's concept of internalization is, in many ways, similar to our system IV, as may be seen in the following:

> Internalization can be said to occur when an individual conforms because the content of the induced behavior—the ideas and actions of which it is composed—are intrinsically rewarding. He adopts the induced behavior because he considers it useful for the solution of a problem or because it is congenial to his needs. Behavior adopted in this fashion tends to be integrated with the individual's existing values (Kelman, 1956, p. 176).

In the Cohler-Kelman study, subjects were preselected who were disposed toward internalization. Next, the Ss were subdivided into two groups, "clarifiers" and "simplifiers," and this distinction was found to be important in accounting for the degree of delayed attitude change in a controlled experiment. From the present viewpoint we would regard clarification as a more direct form of system IV behavioral expression and simplification as related to the more indirect system IV functioning.

Reactions to Confirmation in System IV

The abstract nature of system IV functioning permits the assimilation of a wide range of events without experiencing refutation. In this sense, most of system IV functioning consists of reaction to confirmation or takes confirmation for granted, and therefore such a consideration is less appropriate here than in the case of the other three systems. System IV functioning is reality-oriented and "self-actualizing." Successful interpretations of reality, adaptations to it, and the manipulation of environmental forces all contribute to confirmation in system IV. Progress toward these goals confirms and encourages the system IV orientation, and also increases the person's generalized confidence and self-respect.

Having considered the system-specific interpretive maneuvers and modes of behavioral expression it may be helpful to view them in summary form as is shown in Table 20.

Application of Other Formulations to System-Specific Interpretive Maneuvers

Heider's Levels of Attribution

In discussing the process by which an individual categorizes a situation, Heider maintains (1958, pp. 255-256) that the attributing process may proceed at one or more different levels. He considers

TABLE 20

Summary of System-Specific Maneuvers and Resolutions

System	Neutralization	Bolstering	Behavioral Resolutions
I	a. Failure to perceive b. Distortion and dissociation c. Categorical "black-white" judgments	a. Reaffirming one's obligation, duty b. Impersonalization c. Increasing evaluation of criticized aspects	a. Forming standards quickly b. Rigidity c. Overgeneralized submission to authority
II	a. Failure to perceive b. Non-commitment c. Denial of responsibility d. Imputation of malevolence	a. Reaffirming competence	a. Source devaluation b. Behavioral avoidance c. "Boomerang"
III	a. Denial of source responsibility b. Denial of rejection	a. Reaffirming social acceptance	a. Self-evaluation excessively determined by others' evaluation b. Overgeneralized submission to influence c. Seeking interpersonal support
IV	a. Assertion of difference between own and other's standard and denial that other's standard is relevant to self	a. Reaffirming concern with information	a. Maintaining standard in response to non-informational social influence b. Provisional self-devaluation and self-correction c. Exploratory information-seeking behavior

these levels in relation to the case in which a disagreeable event (x) has happened to a person (p) as follows:

> 1. What is the source of x? Did it occur by chance? Did p himself cause it? Let us assume that the source is perceived to be another person, o.
> 2. Then the question may arise as to whether the harm was intended or not. Perhaps the unpleasant occurrence was not at all intended for p. Perhaps o did it to please someone else and so did not have any personal wish to hurt p. Perhaps o's true goal was to benefit p, but his means were in error . . . (Heider, 1958, pp. 255–256).

Heider continues by discussing a third, "deeper" attributive level of responsibility and intention that provides a beginning framework to view several attributive possibilites, which will be shown to have system-specific relevance. The levels may be summarized as follows:

Diagram of Heider's Levels of Attribution

Level	Self-Responsible?		Other Responsible?	
1. Responsibility for disagreeable event	*Yes*	*No*	*Yes* ↓	*No*
2. If other responsible, what was intention?	*Negative Intention*		*Positive Intention*	

Since the questions are hierarchically organized, the question of intention is not relevant unless the other person is seen as responsible for the event. In relating this formulation to the present systems it may be noted that a "No" categorization of responsibility amounts to a neutralizing interpretation. This similarity may be seen by placing abbreviations of system referents into the Heider framework as follows:

System Referents Expressed in Terms of Attribution Levels

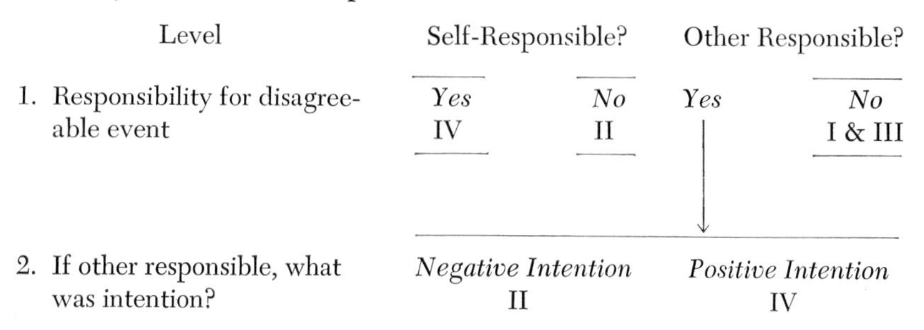

Thus, system IV is more likely to accept some self-responsibility for the event; this does not mean that system IV operation always leads to acceptance of responsibility for every event but that when circumstances are appropriate for the person accepting responsibility for the event, such an interpretation would likely be associated with system IV. Both attribution of positive intent and acceptance of responsibility may also occur to a lesser extent in system III. Placement of the other system-specific maneuvers in the diagram is based on functioning characteristics described earlier in this chapter.

Bruner, Goodnow, and Austin's "Payoff Matrix"

Bruner et al. (1956) have used the concept of the "payoff matrix" to illuminate some processes in concept attainment. If a person's judgments of an event are expressed in two categories and the event alternatives also fall into two categories, the four cells generated become the outcomes. In the present framework these outcomes may be viewed as the forms of relatedness that a particular system is attempting to avoid or to maintain, while the decision alternatives involve the "choice" of interpretation or categorization.

Outcome Values of Intention Attribution

	Source's Actual Orientation	
Subject's Interpretation	Malevolence Present	Malevolence Not Present
Malevolence imputed (II) Outcome	Protect self	Lose friendship
Malevolence denied (III) Outcome	Injury to self	Foster friendship

If the subject imputes malevolence, he protects himself (keeps his guard up) while risking the loss of friendship. In system II such risk is not only accepted but the general, often erroneous, imputation of malevolence tends to insure against friendship and confirm the oppositional orientation of the system. On the other hand if the subject denies malevolent intent ("He's just kidding"), the outcomes consist of exposure to injury versus possible facilitation of his relationship with the source. In system III, friendly, approving relations are so valued that the risk of injury through denial of actual malevolence is ignored. Failure to deal with actual malevolence may tend to reinforce the subject's dependent ties to other sources.

In the discussion above, the denial of malevolent intent involved S saying, in essence, "He's kidding." This response may be compared with an interpretation of serious intent as follows:

Outcome Values of Perceived Seriousness of Intent

	Source's Actual Orientation	
Subject's Interpretation	Kidding	Serious
Interpreted as kidding (III) Outcome	Facilitate friendship	Subject misses learning oppor- tunity
Interpreted as serious (IV) Outcome	Subject feels foolish (source may be alien- ated—scornful or angry)	Information acquired

The outcomes in this example are also system-specific. That is, in making the interpretation "He's kidding," one stands the chance of strengthening the relationship at the risk of possibly losing some information. On the other hand, to make a serious estimate of the source's intent opens the possibility of learning or acquiring information; although if "wrong," one may be judged a fool and perhaps alienate the source.

The principal advantage in applying a "payoff matrix" to the system referents or interpretation lies in its providing a basis for conceptualizing the relationship between system-specific interpretations and their potential outcomes under varying circumstances of veridicality.

Having outlined in this chapter the system-specific areas of sensitization, the interpretive maneuvers, and the modes of behavioral expression, we are now in a position to consider more specifically the interaction of dispositional and situational factors in determining system functioning, which is described in the next chapter.

8 Situational and Dispositional Determinants: Their Measurement and Effect

What factors determine the operation of conceptual systems? We consider this question in the present chapter by viewing the operation of conceptual systems in a *contemporaneous* setting as determined jointly by situational and dispositional factors. This chapter continues at the contemporaneous level used in Chapter 7, but shifts the focus from the effects of system functioning to the determinants of system functioning. *Situational determinants* of contemporaneous functioning are identical to those training conditions described in Chapter 5. If the "system pull" in a given situation is viewed as a very short-term training condition, these training conditions will serve as the basis for defining current situational determinants of system-specific functioning, which we consider in this chapter. *Dispositional determinants* of contemporaneous functioning are viewed in terms of differing thresholds of activation for the specific systems. Characteristics of system-specific functioning described in Chapter 7 therefore serve as the basis for developing dispositional measures, which are described shortly. Before turning to problems of situational and dispositional measurement, however, we need to consider briefly the interactive nature of these situational and dispositional factors.

Role of Conceptual Systems in Coordinating Situational and Dispositional Factors

A conceptual system in our view is a schema that provides the basis by which the individual relates to the environmental events he experiences. It describes, in part, how he will perceive and experience these events. Since situational and dispositional factors are viewed in the same logical fashion, the means of understanding their joint effect is "built in" to the characteristics of conceptual systems. Thus, we cannot consider the operation of a system without considering the interactive effects of both the individual and the environment confronting him. If we wish to predict what response a person will make, or to specify the conditions necessary for him to make a particular response, we approach the questions by considering both the person and the conditions in system-relevant terms. Or we may wish to answer more practical questions such as "Which of the available environmental conditions will be most likely to facilitate the functioning of a given individual?" or "Which of several individuals will function most effectively in a given environmental condition?" Since response facilitation and effective functioning are viewed as resulting from system-specific confirmation, we approach these questions in terms of the likelihood that confirmation or refutation will result from the individual-environment interaction.

As we saw in the last chapter, once a conceptual system is activated, it determines how the event will be experienced (confirmation or refutation), and the nature of this experience will in turn determine what, if any, response will occur. The present task therefore is to specify in detail the factors that determine the likelihood that a particular system or system-pattern will be activated. It is this likelihood of system activation that is viewed as jointly dependent upon situational factors (specified in terms of "pull" properties) and dispositional factors (individual activation threshold for a particular system). The nature of these effects is summarized in Table 21.

TABLE 21

The Effects of Situational and Dispositional Factors in Contemporaneous System Activation

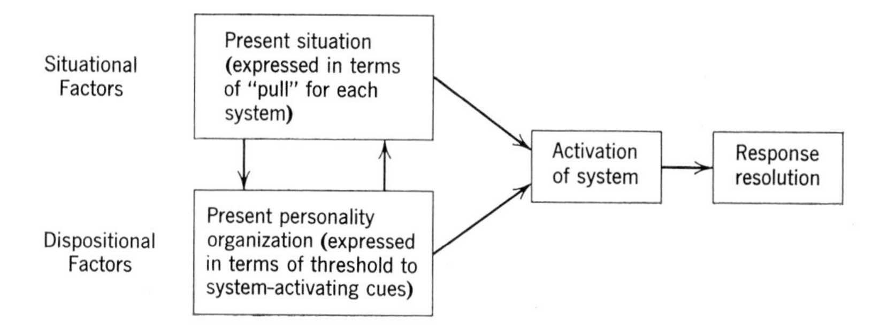

The model in Table 21, similar in many respects to a recent suggestion of Cronbach (1957), is intended to deal only with *contemporaneous* functioning. We assume that the individual's present personality organization has evolved through various stages as a result of numerous past experiences as described by the developmental model presented in Chapters 4 and 5. However, we are here concerned with the effects of this personality organization interacting with present situational factors to determine system activation. In the last chapter we assumed system activation and considered the nature of functioning; in the present chapter we consider the determinants of system activation.

In order to apply the model in Table 21, the general formulation—system activation = f (personality organization and situational "pull")—must be expressed in system-specific terms. Thus, when an individual whose personality organization shows nodal arrestation in system I is confronted by a situation high in system I "pull," the activation of system I is very likely. If this same individual were confronted by a situation weak in system I "pull," system I activation would be less likely than in the first example. However, the likelihood in the second case is higher than it would be for the person not strongly disposed toward system I. Later in this chapter we consider circumstances in which the situational-dispositional combination is either congruent or incongruent with a particular system.

It should be noted that to recognize the general principle that responses are jointly determined by situational and dispositional effects is only the first step in achieving precise prediction of behavior. Many theorists have emphasized the dual importance of situational and dispositional factors: Lewin's formula, Behavior = f (Person, Environment), is one well-known example. However, the general nature of these formulations leaves unsettled the important problem of specifying the nature of the organism in a precise fashion. For us, this specification takes the form of dimensionalizing the structural properties of systems, which are then treated as the major internal factors. Only when this is accomplished can we answer questions about what will occur when, say, a person nodally arrested at system I encounters a situation highly compelling for system IV.

Operations for System-Specific Situational Induction

The situational factors that will maximize a given system are essentially those that produce arrestation at a given stage (see Chapter 5). Thus, maximal "pull" occurs through reliable unilateral imposition, unreliable unilateral imposition, protective interdependent imposition, and informational interdependent imposition, for system I through IV, respectively.

It should be possible to determine the "pull" profile of a particular situation by exposing large numbers of persons to it, noting the kinds of responses that occur, and categorizing these responses in terms of their system relevance. McClelland and his colleagues (1953), for example, have employed this type of procedure. It is important to note, however, that such investigations study only the "main effects" of situational or conditional manipulation and therefore are necessarily gross because the results depend in part upon the nature of the sample. In studying only situational effects, the investigator implicitly assumes that he is dealing with "people-in-general," but his sample may have special characteristics that make his assumption invalid.[1]

In order to understand system-specific situational determinants it is helpful to consider some studies that employed certain situational pressures to induce system-specific functioning. These studies are reviewed here not to validate the present theory, but only to suggest some possible operation for system-specific situational determinants in the present viewpoint.

System I Induction

System I is induced by reliable unilateral conditions. Several investigations have been reported that illustrate such conditions. Perhaps most relevant is the work of Kelman (1956) who uses the concept "compliance" for one of three processes of conformity, which he defines as follows:

> Compliance can be said to occur when an individual conforms because he hopes to achieve a favorable effect from another person or group (Kelman, 1956, p. 175).

The process of compliance is induced by a source who has means-control over the subject and under conditions of limited choice behavior. The results of Kelman's experiment indicate that responses adopted through compliance are performed only under conditions of surveillance of the means-controlling source. Such surveillance by a means-controlling agent provides conditions similar to our concept of reliable unilateral training just as the resulting process of compliance appears similar to system I functioning.

[1] In addition, as recent work has shown (for example, Hardison and Purcell, 1959), situational-dispositional interactions may operate to obscure the "main effect" of the situational variable.

Jones and Thibaut (1958) have described three inferential sets, one of which, "situation-matching," appears to be similar to system I functioning as indicated in the following:

> When the perceiver decides that his goal in the interaction involves the application of social sanctions, presumably he becomes concerned with the appropriateness of the stimulus person's behavior in terms of the generalized norms which he considers to be applicable to the present behavior setting. Such a concern conditions the inference process in ways which we shall subsume under the label, *situation matching set* (Jones and Thibaut, 1958, p. 159).

Since situation matching appears quite similar to system I functioning, the procedures for inducing this inferential set should be appropriate for inducing system I functioning. In one experiment, Jones and De Charms (1958) induced situation matching by instructions that request the subject to act as if he were a member of a legal court of inquiry. Note that such instructions emphasize the sensitization aspect in contrast to Kelman's method for inducing compliance that emphasizes the behavioral expression associated with the process.

Since system I functioning is associated with perceiving people in terms of stereotypes in order to minimize changes in structure, a study by Haire and Grunes (1950) is relevant in its implicit aim to induce stereotypic thinking. These authors presented to two subject groups a list of descriptive terms, each containing the phrases "goes to union meetings" and "works in a factory," which should evoke a culturally prescribed stereotype associated with a laborer. The list contained other descriptions that with one important exception were the same for both groups. One group received a list containing the word "intelligent," which would presumably be incongruent with the stereotype of a laborer, whereas the other group did not receive this word on the list. Interest centered upon the manner in which the incongruent description was dealt with as the subject wrote his impression of the person described. Certain maneuvers by the subjects appear to be very similar to system I-related interpretations: "straight-forward denial of the existence of the disturbing element" (Haire and Grunes, 1950, p. 406). Some made statements such as "Intelligence not notable even though it is stated" or "He is intelligent but not too much so since he works in a factory" (Haire and Grunes, 1950, p. 407). Actually, this study provided two conditions, one of which (the incongruent word list) called forth "into the open" the expression of stereotypic thinking thought to be associated with system I functioning. The responses to the other list may have been based just as much on stereotypy but no resolution of incongruent data was required, so that whatever tendency to stereotypy existed in the subjects remained unrevealed.

Another example of the induction of stereotypic thinking is noted in an experiment by Thibaut and Riecken (1955) who studied subjects' explanations for why another person (a confederate of either high or low status) complied with S's request. They found that the high status person's response was accounted for in terms of "internal" reasons ("He just wanted to anyway") whereas the low status person's response was seen in terms of "external" causation ("I forced him to") (examples from Thibaut and Riecken, 1955, p. 124). The status differentials in this study constitute one set of situational conditions that evoke the categorical, unilateral, authority-oriented responses that characterize system I.

System II Induction

System II is induced by unreliable unilateral conditions. For example, James and Rotter (1958), by instructions to their subjects, induced the perception that events in a card-guessing game were caused by chance. Such instructions, when compared with "skill" instructions, which presumably induced a set favoring internal causation, led to more rapid extinction of expectancies following 100 per cent reinforcement. These chance instructions apparently call forth denial of responsibility, and thus provide an example of system II induction.

In another study (Hunt, 1957), subjects imputed less malevolent motives to a hypothetical source of criticism if they were otherwise favorably disposed toward that source, and saw the criticism more malevolently motivated (that is, increase in system II functioning) when the source was already disliked. The less attractive the source of criticism, the more likely was the occurrence of system II–related interpretations (denial of responsibility, non-commitment, and imputation of malevolent intent). Also relevant is the early classic study by Murray (1933), which indicated that the attribution of malicious characteristics to figures in a picture increased considerably after the subjects had been exposed to a fear-producing experience.

System III Induction

System III is induced by protective interdependent conditions. Induction of system III functioning as reflected by an increased use of denial of rejection is reported in a study by Schroder and Hunt (1959). When asked to account for criticism occurring from an incompetent friend, the subjects were quite likely to respond by denying rejection, for example, "He's just fooling around." Our inference is that criticism from a liked-incompetent source induces system III functioning because the friendship relationship is maximally threatened. Since to define the source as incompetent essentially rules out attributions based on potential information (validity of criticism), the likelihood that such criticism represents potential rejection is maximal.

At a more general level the conformity process that Kelman (1956) calls "identification" appears to be similar to system III functioning in many respects:

> Identification can be said to occur when an individual conforms because he wants to establish or maintain a satisfying self-defining relationship to another person or group (Kelman, 1956, p. 175).

The process of identification is induced by an attractive source, and Kelman's results suggest that responses adopted through identification are performed only when the subject's relationship to this attractive source is salient. Such induction of conformity by an attractive source is similar to protective interdependent training just as the resulting process of identification appears similar to system III functioning.

Also similar to system III functioning is the inferential set, "value maintenance," which Jones and Thibaut define as concerning a sensitivity to "what is he doing to me or for me that makes me want to approach or avoid him" (Jones and Thibaut, 1958, p. 159). In its concern with source attractiveness, value maintenance seems quite similar to system III functioning. The value maintenance set is induced by instructions, preceding S's listening to a tape recorded interview, to judge the person in terms of whether he is a "nice guy" or not (Jones and De Charms, 1958). These instructions presumably induce the heightened sensitivity to attractiveness that is characteristic of system III functioning. The success of this induction is partially indicated by results of the Jones-De Charms study: although Ss in the value maintenance induction condition heard the same recording (a military person relating the circumstances of his becoming a prisoner of war) as did Ss in the situation matching induction (see earlier), Ss receiving value maintenance induction were more likely to consider whether the object of judgment was behaving as a likeable person rather than paying attention to the offense he committed.

The "group set" proposed by Thibaut and Strickland (1956) as well as the "normative influence" sugested by Deutsch and Gerard (1955), both of which have been discussed earlier, are not only apparently similar to each other but also both provide potential operations for inducing system III functioning.

System IV Induction

System IV is induced by informational interdependent conditions. For example, Kelman's description of the induction of internalization (1956) is quite similar to operations assumed necessary for system IV functioning (cf. p. 239). He describes the antecedents of the internalization process as a communication from a highly credible source under conditions in which S is reorganizing his cognitive field. These conditions are very similar to the sensitization to source competence and willingness to modify standards in the face of new information noted in system IV. Kelman found that responses adopted through internalization are performed only when relevant to content, and will extinguish when no longer seen as useful.

Deutsch and Gerard (1955) describe informational influence in similar terms: ". . . an influence to accept information obtained from another as *evidence* of reality" (Deutsch and Gerard, 1955, p. 629). Task set, as described by Thibaut and Strickland (1956), also appears related: ". . . disposed to view others as 'mediators' of fact" (Thibaut and Strickland, 1956, p. 115). Therefore, the procedures for inducing informational influence or task set should serve as operations for inducing system IV functioning.

Measurement of System-Specific Dispositional Determinants

Assuming that the logic of measurement must flow from the logic of the theory (cf. Jessor and Hammond, 1957), we outline briefly some principles and procedures for dispositional measurement. In formulating these principles we rely on both characteristics of system *functioning* (Chapters 3 and 7) and the dimensions of system *organization* (Chapters 2 and 6). Therefore, referents for dispositional tendencies may be obtained through both functioning characteristics (nature of sensitization) and structural characteristics (degree of abstractness). Thus, a person may be classified as disposed toward system IV functioning by his sensitization to information or by the abstract nature of his functioning.

In the present view, intensive personality measurement requires describing the person in relation to each of the dimensions of personality set forth in Chapter 6: degree of abstractness, degree of openness to progression, and degree of directness of behavioral expression. For some purposes, such as the modification of conceptual systems (see Chapter 10), it is important to make quite precise measurement of the nature of each of these dimensions. Most investigations of personality factors, however, have utilized rather gross measurement, which could be viewed in present terms as classifying persons into one or another of the four generic systems. The degree of specificity of measurement required therefore depends upon the problem. Our immediate goal in this section is to derive means of measuring the dispositional tendencies toward system activation as indicated in Table 21. Therefore, we shall limit for the present the aim of dispositional measurement to the classification of persons into one of four categories: dispositions toward systems I, II, III, or IV. The principles and procedures to be described, however, should also be applicable to the more specific purposes such as classifying persons in terms of degree of transitional conflict.

Some Principles of Dispositional Measurement

Aspects of both system functioning and system structure are considered as potential sources of referents for dispositional tendencies. The following functioning characteristics may be used: sensitization, interpretation, behavior, and affective arousal. In addition, dispositional indicators may be obtained through assessing structural or organizational characteristics, for example, degree of abstractness. The operations for assessing these indicators of system-specific dispositional tendencies may be summarized as follows:

1. The presentation of controlled system-specific stimuli to subjects, the nature of the response indicating individual differences in *sensitization* to the system represented by the stimuli;
2. The presentation of relatively ambiguous stimuli, differences in *interpretation* serving to reflect the subject's systemic disposition;
3. The presentation and manipulation of system-relevant stimuli in a situation that requires some action or conflict-resolving *behavior;*
4. The presentation of stimuli, some of which are specifically relevant to one system, some to another, noting which leads to *affective arousal;*
5. The presentation of stimuli on a given dimension, the number or range of concepts generated indicating *degree of abstractness.*

SENSITIZATION

As a first principle we may restate a point made in Chapter 3: in order to infer the degree of sensitization it is necessary to observe responses to controlled stimuli. These stimuli must be ordered along a dimension specific to the system indicated in Table 18, on p. 206; for example, if system I is involved, the dimension extends from "agreement with external standards" to "violations of standards" or from culturally-derived power to the other extreme. Three general methods of measuring sensitization may be considered: (a) detection of a particular stimulus object at a lower level of stimulus intensity, (b) degree of variation in response as a function of stimulus variation, and (c) degree to which response is determined by one dimension rather than another when competing stimulus dimensions are presented.

Detection at lower level of stimulus intensity. For example, system-specific sensitization may be inferred by a lowered threshold to system-relevant stimuli. The study by Atkinson and Walker (1956) described earlier presented system-relevant stimuli, that is, the human face in this case, at subthreshold levels. S's detection of the face (by indicating in which one of the four quadrants it appeared) provided the sensitization index, which in this case related to need for affiliation. McClelland and Liberman (1949) have utilized a similar procedure for obtaining indicators of need for achievement.

Degree of variation in response as function of stimulus variation. If the person's response varies more as a function of system-relevant stimuli, system-specific sensitization can be inferred. This variation may consist of either increased or decreased response intensity indicating vigilance and defense, respectively. In other words, either negative or positive (but not zero-order) correlations of response intensity and stimulus intensity reflect sensitivity to the system. This method is similar to the procedure described in Chapter 3 for measuring the degree of response intensity at a higher level of stimulus intensity. However, in the present case, contrasting intensities of system-relevant stimuli are used to elicit variations in response. For example, the study by Roberts and Jessor (1958) described earlier indicates that persons disposed toward system I are more aggressive to low status persons, but less aggressive to high status persons than are "people-in-general." Although these authors did not use a sensitization form of analysis, it appears that the correlation between response (aggression) and stimulus dimension (status of frustrating source) was higher in persons disposed toward system I than in others. However, in order to establish such a relationship clearly it would be necessary to analyze differences in response between situations *for each individual* because sensitization is by definition an *intraindividual* process. Sensitization cannot be inferred solely on the basis of differences between mean group scores; intraindividual analysis is required.

A more precise example of this procedure is found in a study by Schroder and Hunt (1958). In this study, Ss were asked to account for criticism from sources that varied in attractiveness (liked-disliked). Some interpretations of the criticism consisted of self-negation ("This means I am doing poorly"), indicating acceptance of the criticism as valid. Since people generally are more likely to accept criticism from someone they like, the postcriticism self-negation score will ordinarily vary directly with the attractiveness of the source. However, the more a subject's acceptance of criticism is related to source attractiveness, the greater is the sensitivity to this variable. In this case the correlation between self-negation and attractiveness of criticizing source is an indicator of sensitivity to system III (mutuality) cues. From this sensitivity index we can, in turn, infer disposition to system III functioning.

Another study (Hunt and Schroder, 1957) explored the relationship between subjects' perceived self-competence (in a skill area) and their self-evaluation following criticism. Differences in how well subjects accepted the view "I lack skill in this area and therefore should learn from criticism" provided an index of system IV sensitization. The absence of such sensitization was found to be associated with school underachievement.

These three studies illustrate the way in which the dependence of response on system-specific stimulus intensities can be used as a basis for a sensitization index by which dispositional tendencies are, in turn, inferred.

Degree to which response is determined by one dimension rather than another when competing stimulus dimensions are presented. If the person, who is confronted by a stimulus complex consisting of cues for more than one system relevant dimension, responds on the basis of one stimulus, system-specific sensitization can be inferred. Of course, his response may reflect the net effect of all cues rather than being over-determined by one. This method is particularly appropriate when the purpose is that of distinguishing between two system-specific forms of sensitization. For example, Hunt and Schroder (1959) used a variation of Role Concept Repertory Test (Kelly, 1955) to tap differential system-specific sensitizations (see pp. 263–4). Ss were asked to state which two persons (of a three-person group) are most alike and different from the third, using for this comparison one of two predetermined system-specific dimensions. The task was repeated many times (offering S new three-person groups to categorize). Greater reliance by a subject upon one system-specific dimension was taken as an indicator of greater centrality of that particular system.

In considering this method it might be noted that there is a close relationship between stimulus configurations that consist of potentially competing dimensions and ambiguous stimuli. Viewed from the present position, the use of ambiguous stimuli as in some projective tests may permit sensitization inferences on the basis of a rationale very similar to that underlying the person's selecting one out of many competing dimensions as the determiner of his response (cf. interpretation below). The chief difference lies in the greater control over the system-specific stimulus intensity afforded by the use of competing dimensions.

One final comment on the measurement of sensitization: all of the illustrative procedures described above employed hypothetical stimuli or representation of actual stimuli. Although such a procedure has drawbacks, it also has two major advantages: first, it provides for more careful control of the stimuli; and second, it decreases the likelihood of sequence effects that might occur if the person were responding to actual stimuli. We have not as yet developed procedures for measuring sensitization in actual interpersonal situations, but this, though more difficult, will eventually be necessary. Our present procedures permit a simpler manipulation of system-relevant cues.

INTERPRETATION

The principle that a human response will be more heavily determined by internal factors when the external factors are ambiguous is well known (Sherif, 1935; Lazarus, 1953; Rotter, 1954). This is the implicit basis for many projective tests such as the Rorschach and the TAT. In our terms, when an individual's interpretive maneuvers are made with reference to a relatively ambiguous situation they will carry more dispositional information. Relying on this principle, numerous measures have utilized subjects' interpretations of a relatively ambiguous interpersonal stimulus to infer personality disposition (Sargent, 1944; Sherriffs, 1948; French, 1958a; Schroder and Hunt, 1957; Moeller and Applezweig, 1957). This principle also provides the rationale for the psychoanalyst's interpretation of the patient's transference manifestations, since these reactions presumably stem from an ambiguous stimulus.

In order to elicit meaningful dispositional information in the present view, however, the stimulus must also imply some potential refutation to most persons (system-specific interpretation occurs only when the system is activated). The general method is simply to confront the subject with a potentially refuting stimulus, asking him to account for or "explain" the event: the underlying system of organization is then inferred on the basis of the system-specific interpretations summarized in Table 20 on p. 240. The stimulus might hypothetically consist of a highly generalized event, "Suppose that something goes wrong." However, in practice, stimuli consisting of verbal disagreement or criticism have frequently been employed on the assumption that such a situation maximizes the occurrence of at least *some* potential refutation in each system. We discuss one form of the situational interpretation measure in more detail later in this chapter.

The nature of the interpretive process may also set limits on the appropriateness of the measure. For example, if we wish to measure a person's tendency to use the interpretive maneuver of neutralization or negation, a structured measure would probably not be appropriate.

Although a person may say or write "It's not my fault" if he is expressing himself in his own words, he is less likely to endorse a fixed alternative such as "It's not my fault" on a forced-choice test. In any case, in designing measures it is important to bear in mind that the measuring instrument should be appropriate to the variable it is intended to assess.

BEHAVIOR

Although it has been customary to think of behavioral resolutions in such terms as a "predicted response," a dependent variable, or criterion, there is no logical reason that such responses cannot serve as dispositional indicators. The major problem lies in specifying precisely a one-to-one relation between a particular behavioral resolution and a particular pattern of system operation, a difficulty we discussed earlier in a more general context. When we observe behavioral resolutions to refutation, we are dealing with the direct effects of system functioning, and therefore the observer must note very carefully the exact nature of the situation and the effect upon this situation produced by the particular behavior. Put another way, a particular system-specific behavior may occur very rapidly, producing a change in the situation so that subsequent behavior may be in response to a different situation. System-specific behavioral resolutions were summarized in Table 20 on p. 240, and are discussed in greater detail later in this chapter.

AFFECTIVE AROUSAL

Affective arousal has been considered primarily as an intervening process, but there are ways by which it can provide a means either to preselect persons or to verify certain system-specific hypotheses. One procedure, for example, is to present stimuli in a manner similar to that described in the sensitization section and measure the intensity of affective responses (pulse, blood pressure, and PGR). The rationale is identical: intensity of affective response to system-relevant stimuli indicates disposition toward that particular system.

A study by Vogel, Raymond, and Lazarus (1959) yeilded results relevant to our consideration of affective arousal. These authors preselected Ss who consistently (on a number of dispositional measures) showed a strong orientation toward achievement or social affiliation. Both groups of Ss were then exposed to achievement and affiliation stressors during which various measures of autonomic reaction were obtained (pulse rate, blood pressure, PGR). Maximum autonomic arousal was found to occur when the stressor was in the same area as the stronger motivation. We interpret these results as evidence that affective arousal is maximal when the threat is to the more central system. The study itself may be considered a prototype for the study of the interactive effects of situational-dispositional factors. In addition, such measures of susceptibility or arousal to system-specific stimuli may themselves serve as an additional means for dispositional measurement. For example, the design of the Vogel et al. study might be reversed, first selecting Ss according to differential autonomic response to the two types of stressors, using these differences to predict other indices of achievement- or affiliation-oriented behavior. As noted earlier, it would be very helpful also to have measures of the *quality* of affect, since this, too, should vary between systems, but satisfactory measures are not presently available.

CONCRETENESS-ABSTRACTNESS AND OTHER STRUCTURAL CHARACTERISTICS

Since concreteness-abstractness is the major structural dimension underlying the present systems, methods that measure degree of abstractness will also provide relevant information for dispositional classification. The methods based on functioning characteristics of systems that we have just described provide information in discontinuous terms (disposition toward one or another of four systems). In contrast, measures of abstractness yield information in continuous terms (degree of abstractness), which is less precise for purposes of dispositional classification. Put another way, the system-specific equivalence of variation in abstractness is only grossly understood (the more abstract the structure, the more likely the disposition toward system III or IV) so that the transformation of information about a given S's degree of abstractness into system-specific dispositional indicators is accordingly limited. Measures of abstractness will become increasingly useful, therefore, as their systemic equivalence is clarified, and investigations to clarify this relationship are now being conducted by the authors. For present purposes, however, we shall describe some procedures that illustrate appropriate methods for obtaining indicators of degree of abstractness.

Goldstein and Scheerer (1941) have developed several tests for measuring degree of abstractness (based on the characteristics of abstractness that we described in Chapter 2), which are relevant for present purposes, for example, object sorting test. More recently, McGaughran (1954) proposed that the concrete-abstract dimension be separated into two independent subdimensions: open versus closed and private versus public. The measures he developed on the basis of this distinction, especially the open-closed dimension, are also relevant to the present aim.

One operation for abstractness probably is the number and integration of concepts generated from a set of stimuli. Therefore, a procedure described by Bieri and Blacker (1956) for measuring "cognitive complexity" is relevant. Their method consists of E's instruction for S to write the names of six persons who meet certain descriptions, for example, closest girl friend or successful person, which is followed by E's presenting these names in groups of three to S to be sorted. As these authors put it:

> In all, 20 sorts were thus obtained, with a perception of similarity and its opposite being obtained on each sort. Essentially, then, S was confronted with a task in which he was asked to perceive a fixed number of stimuli in different combinations. The complexity of S's perceptions of others was measured in terms of the number of different perceptions . . . (Bieri and Blacker, 1956, pp. 113–114).

In present terms, the complexity of perceptions should provide an indicator of degree of abstractness.

Another operation for abstractness, we assume, is a higher degree of articulation between oneself and the environment, or as we have implied earlier in using Witkin's (1954) term, a greater "field independence." The present relevance of measures employed by Witkin et al. (1954), for example, embedded figures test, is determined by the relationship between the dimension of field dependence-independence and degree of abstractness. Although a very general relationship exists between independence and abstractness, the specific relationship is more complex because we assume that field dependence may occur at either a concrete (system I) or abstract (system III) stage, and that field independence may also occur at either a concrete (system II) or abstract (system IV) stage. Before measures of field dependence-independence can be used as system-specific indicators, therefore, we will need empirical information related to this assumption.

A study by Rudin and Stagner (1958) is relevant here in that it investigated the relationship between field independence (embedded figures test) and "personal contextual influence" (degree to which S's judgment of a given person varied according to the context, or background, in which the person was being judged). Field dependence in dealing with the non-social embedded figures was associated with reliance upon context and background in judging social stimuli. In addition, persons high on the F scale (system I) relied more upon background or context in both situations than did other groups, supporting the concrete, field dependent nature of system I functioning.

Items on the F scale are based in part on the nature of structural characteristics, in this case, the tendency to make categorical, "black-white" judgments. Although the content of F-scale items is itself relevant to system I functioning since many items are phrased in "ought" or "should" terms, it may be that S's mode of responding in obtaining a high score is an even more important indicator of system I functioning. The authors of the F scale were aware of this overdetermination of response; more recently several authors have distinguished between the content and style factors on the F scale (Chapman and Bock, 1958; Jackson and Messick, 1958). It should be possible to capitalize on stylistic modes based on structural characteristics of other systems as well (cf. Taylor, 1960). For example, a consistent "non-acquiescent" response set may indicate a disposition to system II.

We have seen that system-specific disposition may be inferred on the basis of both functional and structural characteristics. We view the methods based on system functioning, such as sensitization, and those just described based on system structure, such as degree of abstractness, as means to approach the same problem. Thus, an increase in abstractness (structure) should parallel sensitization changing from I to II, III, and IV (function). Rather than treat "cognitive" factors and "dynamic" or personality factors separately, therefore, we view them as structural and functional characteristics, respectively, which are interrelated aspects of conceptual systems.

The Importance of Multiple Measurement

Much current psychological experimentation, expecially investigation of dispositional effects, places undue reliance on a single measure or test. In contrast, the value of using multiple measurement, whenever possible, has been recently argued in diverse areas of investigation (Miller, 1956; Oppenheimer, 1956; Campbell and Fiske, 1959). We concur with these authors in advocating multiple measurement, which, in present terms, consists of obtaining referents from different systemic characteristics, for example, sensitization, interpretation, degree of abstractness, because of the numerous advantages. First, such procedures permit us to "learn more about" the phenomenon in question. Although the measures we employ should be as theory-relevant as possible, the use of multiple measurement also provides for corrective feedback in the formulation (through, for example, the absence of expected correlations, or unexpected correlations, between measures). Second, multiple measurement is congruent with the definition of a concept or a system consisting of at least *two* points in space or time. Third, and most important, such procedures increase the certainty with which we make dispositional classification. We can feel more certain that a person is disposed toward system II, for example, if we have noted system II referents from multiple measures than if based on only one measure.

Another factor that affects certainty of dispositional classification within any single measure is the extent to which the referent is a "pure" reflection of one system. There is rarely a perfect one-to-one correspondence between response and internal factor, but some responses are more construct-relevant than others. Tomkins and Miner (1957), for example, have indicated that one characteristic of a test referent is its diffuseness or non-diffuseness, terms that we infer reflect the accuracy with which one can specify the determinants of test behavior. Put in present terms, every response is assumed to emanate in part from the operation of systems or internal factors. However, knowledge is sparse concerning how well our proposals about the nature of systems fit the detailed behavioral facts of life; empirical studies must eventually provide the basis for increasingly detailed system descriptions and greater predictive precision. For now we can only estimate the most likely dispositional pattern present, realizing that error attributable both to measurement and conceptualization will occur.

System-Specific Characteristics as a Basis for Dispositional Measurement: A Working Example

In order to apply the previous principles, the measurement must always occur in relation to system-specific areas of sensitization and resolutions. Table 18 on p. 206 and Table 20 on p. 240 in Chapter 7 provide the working basis for the development of system-specific measures. Let us consider in some detail an investigation (Hunt and Schroder, 1959) that used a variety of means to assess dispositional tendencies in three of the systems (system I was not included in this particular study). In our discussion of this investigation, many of the principles and procedures just described are illustrated as we describe measurement techniques in context, as tools that serve as the means toward increasing conceptual understanding, rather than as ends in themselves. Because this investigation focused on the interrelations among system-specific interpretive maneuvers, behavioral resolutions, and areas of sensitization, it also illustrates the importance of multiple measurement.

The first phase investigated the relationship between interpretive maneuvers and behavioral resolutions in systems II, III, and IV. Viewed in terms of Table 20, the logic of methodology was quite straightforward. A paper-and-pencil measure eliciting interpretations of incongruent situations was administered, and the attributive responses of the persons (approximately 100 high school boys) were categorized according to Table 20 on p. 240. Ss were classified into dispositional groups of systems II, III, or IV, or into a general unclassified category. All persons were then exposed to differing forms of system-specific social influence. Their reactions to this situational pressure were categorized in terms of system-specific behavioral resolutions, thus providing a second, separate classification of the same persons into groupings of systems II, III, IV, or not relevant. We now have both an interpretation and a behavior measure. Therefore, if the analysis indicates that the persons are classified into the same system by these two measured aspects of system operation, the construct validity of the present viewpoint is affirmed and the utility of the measures supported. We have intentionally avoided describing this phase of the investigation in terms of a predictor (the interpretation measure) and a criterion (the behavioral resolution) because such a distinction rests only on arbitrary time sequences. Since the classification of persons into dispositional groups may be accomplished as logically from referents based upon behavior in a controlled experiment as on the basis of a paper-and-pencil measure, the order in which the two sets of referents are obtained is unimportant from a theoretical standpoint. Let us briefly consider the methods employed in this phase of the investigation and the results observed.

INTERPRETATION MEASURE

In order to evoke a sample of interpretations to situations of potential refutation, a paper-and-pencil measure that confronted S with several situations of hypothetical verbal criticism or disagreement was employed (one form of the situational interpretation measure referred to in Chapter 7). As suggested earlier, the logic underlying this measure emphasizes the importance of confronting every person with incongruity in order that his mode of accounting for its occurrence will be dispositionally relevant and can therefore be considered a system-specific interpretive maneuver (see Schroder and Hunt, 1959, for a more extensive discussion of the rationale and description of materials).

Every S then wrote down his interpretation of eight situations of verbal disagreement; these interpretations were coded by use of a manual that was nothing more than a specific version of the interpretive maneuvers in Table 20 on p. 240. For example, if a person repeatedly interpreted the various situations in terms of malevolent imputation ("He's trying to give me a hard time"), he was classified in the system II group. A person who continually interpreted events in terms of, say, denial of rejection ("He was just fooling around and didn't mean it because we're the best of friends") was classified in the system III group. Persons who made most of their interpretations along informational lines ("He wants to show me my mistake so I can improve") were placed in the system IV group. Two forms of the interpretation measure were administered. In one S wrote down the interpretation in his own words (free response form) and in the other S selected between pairs of alternatives designed to represent paradigm statements of system-specific interpretive maneuvers (forced choice form). The basis for using both approaches was to obtain a more stable set of referents for classifying persons into dispositional groups.

BEHAVIORAL MEASURE

All Ss were exposed to various forms of social influence in a conformity experiment. Their responses were categorized as: (1) yielding, (2) non-yielding, and (3) "moving away" ("boomerang") from a previously held standard in a direction opposite that of the influence. The occurrence of yielding was considered in relation to two forms of pressure: (1) normative and (2) informational. Once categorized, those responses were transformed according to the relevant system-specific behavioral resolutions in Table 20 as representing systems II, III, IV, or unclassified. Persons making an unusual number of "boomerang" responses (recoiling from influence) were classified in system II; persons yielding *only* to normative influence were classified in system III; and persons yielding *only* to informational influence were classified in system IV.

SYSTEM-SPECIFIC RELATIONSHIPS BETWEEN INTERPRETATION AND BEHAVIOR

In order to test the relationship between the two measures, only the thirty-four Ss who were classified in one of the three system groupings on both the forced-choice interpretation and the behavioral measures were considered. The analysis indicated a significant overall tendency for system-specific behavioral and interpretive groupings to be associated, as well as a significant relationship between behavioral and interpretive referents for each of the three specific systems. The relationship, however, was not perfect, which probably reflects, among other possibilities, the error of measurement in each of the techniques. In an additional analysis aimed to define more "pure" groups, Ss were categorized in a dispositional group only if their score on *both* the forced-choice and free-response measure was in the same system. Although the number of persons categorized on this more rigorous basis decreased to nine, *all* nine persons were correctly classified in terms of the expected system-specific behavioral resolution.

The next phase of the investigation extended the study of those relationships to system-specific areas of sensitization. The combined measures used in the first phase—forced-choice interpretation, free-response interpretation, and behavioral resolution measures—were employed to define dispositional groups by requiring that a person be classified in any group on the basis of at least two of the three referent measures. The system-specific sensitization of these persons was then observed as described below.

SENSITIZATION MEASURE

This phase was designed to investigate the extent of system-specific sensitization to the following interpersonal dimensions:

System II—imposition of restriction
System III—source attractiveness
System IV—source competence (information potential)

It was hypothesized that system-specific sensitization would render the individual more open to certain dimensions than to other less relevant dimensions. For example, if a person disposed toward system II is confronted by a stimulus person embodying both *restriction* (positive or negative) and *information* (positive or negative), he should be more sensitive, or alert, to the potential restriction. On the basis of this expectation, if he were requested to categorize this person, he should be more likely to utilize the potential restriction as a basis for categorizing than to use the less personally relevant dimension, information. A variation of the Kelly Role Concept Repertory Test (1955) was therefore employed in which S was confronted by names of three persons that were to be grouped. Each triad was so arranged that it could be sorted on the basis of either one of two system-specific dimensions; the dimension that each S chose was taken as evidence of his sensitization to that particular dimension.

Two studies were carried out, one comparing system II with system IV Ss, and one comparing system III with system IV Ss. In the first study, S wrote down the names of twelve persons he knew who fit various descriptions supplied by the experimenter. These descriptions varied both information potential (assumed to be relevant to system IV) and restricting potential (assumed relevant to system II), for example, "A boy who knows what he is talking about, but who makes you feel uncomfortable." Next, the names of three of these people were exposed to S, and he was asked to indicate, "which two of these people are alike and different from the third." The triads were so arranged

TABLE 22

Interrelations of Sensitization, Interpretation, and Behavior

System	Area of Sensitization	Interpretive Maneuvers	Behavior Resolutions
II	Potential restriction	Imputation of malevolence	"Boomerang" to social influence
III	Source attractiveness	Denial of rejection	Yield to normative social influence
IV	Source competence	Reaffirmation of concern with information	Yield to informational social influence

that one grouping would indicate sorting on the basis of restriction (and thus be relevant to system II) whereas another grouping would represent sorting on the basis of information potential (system IV sensitization). Sensitization indices based on several sortings were accordingly derived (each sorting permitted either grouping relevant to system II or system IV). A second study, identical in design, compared system IV with system III Ss, the system III dimension being represented by source attractiveness ("A boy whom you would like to know better").

SYSTEM-SPECIFIC RELATIONSHIPS TO SENSITIZATION

Both sensitization studies indicated significant relationships between system-specific sensitization and groups defined on the basis of interpretation and behavior. We are inclined to interpret these results as support for the construct validity of the present three systems, as outlined in Table 22.

Although system I was not explored in this particular study, such an investigation could easily be carried out using the system I characteristics described in Chapter 7. From the logic of construct validity we may note that the positive findings in these studies support the use of the present measures, which provided referents for the relationships observed. We have considered this investigation in some detail because it provides an illustration of some measures that we feel are appropriate to the present viewpoint. It is very likely that these measures could be considerably improved, or better ones devised, if the experiments were repeated. We re-emphasize that these measures are not the only tests to be used in the present viewpoint; as we have noted earlier, many other alternative methods of measurement are open. What is important, however, is to note that these results emphasize the effectiveness of multiple measurement whenever possible. Before proceeding, one aspect of this investigation, which applies to most of the studies described in the next section, should be noted: only male high school subjects were employed. Although we assume that the present systems apply equally to males and females, the behavioral expression specific to a particular stage of development or more closed system probably differs considerably.

Response to Social Incongruity as Determined by Situational and Dispositional Factors

To illustrate the role of system operation in determining responses we consider selected investigations that are presently viewed as studying system-specific effects in reaction to social influence or incongruity. The design of each investigation to be described includes variations in *both* situational and dispositional factors. Viewed in terms of Table 21, if both situation and disposition favor the same specific system, the resulting response should occur on the basis of that particular system. Most of the investigations rest on predictions of a significant *interaction* between situation and disposition. System activation is therefore expected to occur as an interactive function of system-specific situational and dispositional factors, and the resulting response to social influence (behavioral resolution) in turn should therefore emanate from the particular system activated. The emphasis is upon the *differential effects* attributable to systems.

A critical point in each investigation is the accurate specification of the relationship between system activation and the nature of response. For example, the activation of one system may result in yielding to influence whereas the activation of a different system may result in recoiling from influence as we noted in the last section. Positive results therefore depend upon both the occurrence of predicted interactive effect producing system activation and the expected relationship between system activation and response resolution.

We have selected experiments involving social influence or interpersonal disagreement partly because these experimental situations provide maximal potential refutation for all systems and also provide a wealth of response possibilities in addition to that of yielding. The major basis for citing social influence studies however is that the authors have worked in this area. These studies are grouped for review under headings that describe the major situational variations under discussion.

System-Specific Response Modification As a Function of Influencing Source

Berkowitz and Lundy (1957) studied the differential susceptibility to influence from peer sources and authority sources (Army generals). They found that Ss disposed toward system I (high F scale) were more susceptible to influence from authority figures than were others.

Wilson (1960) used a situational interpretation measure to define a system III group and a system IV group. He then compared their change in attitude in response to influencing communications conveyed by attractive and unattractive sources. He found that although system III Ss yielded significantly more than system IV Ss when the influence came from a liked source, they yielded significantly less than system IV Ss when the influence came from disliked sources. This investigation therefore provides behavioral corroboration for the hypothesized sensitization of system III Ss to source attractiveness.

System-Specific Response Modification As a Function of the Influence Procedure

McClintock (1958) compared the difference in attitude change produced in Ss disposed toward system I (high F scale) and Ss disposed toward system III (an "other-directed" subscale of the F scale) in response to two forms of influence: ethnocentric and normative. His findings that system I Ss are more susceptible to ethnocentric influence whereas system III Ss are more susceptible to normative influence indicate the system-specific effect of the two influence procedures.

When the normative-informational distinction suggested by Deutsch and Gerard (1955) is employed to describe variations in influence procedures, several studies have noted that Ss disposed to system III are more susceptible to normative influence whereas Ss disposed to system IV are more susceptible to informational influence (Schroder and Hunt, 1958; Hunt and Schroder, 1959; McDavid, 1959).

System-Specific Generalization and Extinction of Modified Response

In addition to their hypothesized role in determining the conditions under which response modification will occur, the present systems should also affect the maintenance, generalization, and extinction of modified responses under varying conditions. More specifically, if response modification occurs in system III, for example, we would expect such a change to persist as long as the attractive influencing source continues to be present (cf. Kelman, 1956), since response change mediated by system III is maintained and generalized to other stimuli when the situation remains the same. A study by Schroder and Janicki (1959b) supports this expectation. Observing the postinfluence effects upon modified responses they found that the system III group (defined by a situational interpretation measure) not only manifested greater generalization in time (that is, less extinction) than two other system groups (II and IV), but the system III group also manifested greater generalization in space (that is, change in influenced response extended to uninfluenced responses). Their findings suggest in addition that system-specific generalization over time is quite similar to system-specific generalization through space. Not only are the system III group curves of generalization in both space and time significantly different from the respective generalization curves of the other two system groups studied, but also the generalization curve of the system III group over time (maintenance of the influenced response during extinction trials) is remarkably similar in form to the generalization curve of the system III group in space (effect upon uninfluenced responses of decreasing similarity to the influenced response).

Also, as noted earlier, Harvey (1959) has observed a similar tendency of a system I group (high F scale) toward overgeneralization of influenced response.

System-Specific Maneuvers Preventing Response Modification

Because system I Ss are highly resistant to changing their evaluation of themselves, we would expect that when confronted by derogatory comments, system I Ss will utilize various maintenance mechanisms such as distortion and dissociation to prevent self-change. As described earlier, Harvey (1959) found such a heightened incidence of dissociation and distortion in Ss disposed toward system I (high F scale). He also found that the incidence of such maneuvers increased relatively more in system I Ss as the devaluing comments became increasingly negative.

Implications for Designing Investigations

All of the investigations in the preceding section employed designs that varied both situational condition and personality disposition. One valuable characteristic of such designs is that the sample of persons studied is defined in conceptually relevant terms, that is, system-specific dispositional groups. If the system-related character of the subjects is unknown and only the situational condition is varied, the investigator is forced to rely on a "random" sample, limiting his conclusions to "people-in-general." Viewed from the present position a random sample may contain a disproportionate number of persons disposed toward a particular system, thus biasing the results in an unknown fashion.

A situational-dispositional design cast in system-relevant terms avoids such unknown bias by separating the question of determining the proportion of persons disposed toward a particular system in a population from the question of studying the effect of that systemic disposition interacting with a particular situational effect. Put more specifically, the proportion of persons disposed toward any system, say system II, will likely vary considerably in different populations—for example, high school boys, housewives, college sophomores, institutionalized delinquents, immigrants, or Unitarians. Investigations to determine proportion of persons disposed toward each system in various groups (age, sex, occupation, ethnicity, or social class) is an area that we have not emphasized but which will be very valuable for the present position. However, from a systemic viewpoint, one may investigate the role of one or more system-specific dispositional factors interacting with situational factors in *any* population. If the investigator is preselecting individuals disposed toward a particular system in a population in which that systemic disposition occurs infrequently, he will face the practical problem of having a limited number of subjects available. The important point, however, is that the present view provides a basis for *studying the operation of the same conceptual processes in widely different populations.*

The major difficulty in such investigations is that although a disposition toward any system may occur in any population (assuming of course that there are no physiological limitations, as for example in a group of brain-damaged patients), the behavioral expression emanating from the same system may vary in different populations, as we noted earlier with respect to possible expressive differences in males and females. Therefore, more information is needed regarding the form of behavioral expression in various populations. As we learn more about the systemic equivalence of behavioral expression in different groups we may approach the task of replication of results by investigating the same system-relevant hypothesis in a different group rather than in another random sample.

It may be helpful to consider a study investigating three dispositional groups (of high school boys) that were exposed to three forms of situational pressure (Schroder and Hunt, 1959). Groups of persons disposed toward systems II, III, and IV were selected on the basis of a situational interpretation measure and later confronted by several hypothetical situations, each designed to elicit functioning predominantly in one of the three systems (strong situational "pull"). The design therefore is an application of the model in Table 21 to investigating system-specific effects in systems II, III, and IV. The general hypothesis was that when system disposition and situation "pull" were congruent, the operation of that system (as indicated by interpretive responses) will be greatest. The specific hypotheses stated that the occurrence of system II–related responses will be greatest when the system II group encounters strong system II "pull," the occurrence of system III–related responses will be greatest when the system III group encounters strong system III "pull," and similarly for system IV. The responses made to each of the three situations were therefore categorized as reflecting the operation of one of the three systems. The results are summarized in Figure I. The hypotheses were analyzed for each of the three systems separately in order to assess the construct

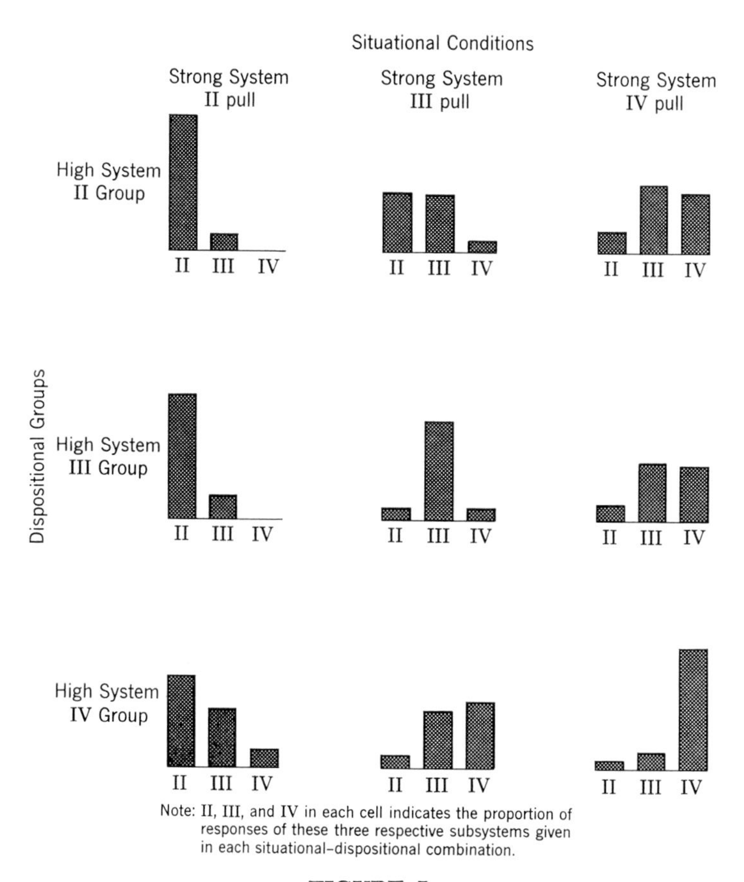

Note: II, III, and IV in each cell indicates the proportion of responses of these three respective subsystems given in each situational–dispositional combination.

FIGURE I

Occurrence of System-Specific Responses As an Interactive Function of Situational and Dispositional Factors

validity of each system. Without reviewing the results in detail it may be noted that for both systems II and IV, the hypothesis of greater occurrence of system-related responses when both disposition and situation favor that system was supported, but for system III, results were less conclusive.

The explicit aim of this investigation was to demonstrate that system operation is maximal when both disposition and situation favor that system. What happens, however, when situation and disposition favor different systems, for example, what response occurs when a person disposed to system II encounters a situation highly compelling to system IV functioning? Let us initially approach this important question from a theoretical standpoint, although Figure I provides some very tentative empirical evidence, which we consider later.

This question clearly requires an explicit formulation of the nature of the organism. As suggested earlier in this chapter, we approach this question by dimensionalizing the structural properties of systems and therefore would phrase the question, "Given this conceptual structure, how will the situational condition be dealt with?" We would hypothesize that the ease of induction of system functioning other than the system to which the person is primarily disposed will be directly related to the level of abstractness of the conceptual structure. Since progression to the organization of system IV structure requires differentiation and integration of each of the other three stages, we would assume that system IV functioning is characterized by the capacity to take on functioning at more concrete levels if the conditions require, that is, under strong situational "pull." The person disposed toward system IV can therefore adopt (or take on the closedness of) system I functioning under appropriate circumstances; however, in contrast to the person disposed toward system I, the system IV S may later become open and shift to another form of functioning. The induction of more abstract functioning will be accordingly difficult in more concrete dispositional groups. These hypotheses suggest a number of investigations that are needed, since at the moment we have sparse evidence on these questions. However, Figure I suggests that it is easier to induce system II functioning in persons disposed to system IV than it is to induce system IV functioning in persons disposed to system II, which would be expected from this view.

In order to understand how a particular individual will respond to a specific situation, we need to know more than his dispositional tendency toward one or the other system. We need to know the degree of openness, degree of transitional conflict, and degree of directness of expression since the person functioning at stage III who is open to progression will respond quite differently to a situation high in system IV "pull" than will a person whose functioning is arrested at system III, even though both may be described generally as disposed toward system III functioning. This example illustrates the difference between the gross procedure of tapping dispositional tendencies with which the present chapter has been concerned and the more precise procedure of describing personality organization along various structural dimensions, which we consider in Chapter 10 as an essential phase in the modification of conceptual systems. Before discussing the topic of modification, however, it is appropriate to consider in the next chapter the conceptual organization underlying extreme forms of functioning, or psychopathology.

9 Extreme Forms of Conceptual Functioning: Psychopathology[1]

What are the implications of the present viewpoint for psychopathology? The present chapter views the various forms of neuroses and psychoses as extreme forms of conceptual functioning. Our aim is not to enumerate all of the various diagnostic entities and then "explain" each one in terms of the current position. Rather, we attempt to derive patterns of "abnormal" functioning through the use of a few general principles. These patterns are considered in relation to the traditional descriptions of pathological syndromes as one means of evaluating the efficacy of these derivations.

Since the area of psychopathology is replete with terms, categories, and descriptions, we hope that the present use of still other terms will contribute something beyond simply proliferating the already overabundant terminology. The potential contribution of the present deductive approach is the increased generality provided. If abnormal reactions are viewed as extreme resolutions emanating from system functioning, the knowledge regarding less extreme resolutions (Chapters 7 and 8) becomes applicable. Further, if psychopathological reactions are viewed as an extreme form of conceptual functioning, therapeutic intervention procedures aimed toward modifying such extreme resolutions should be derivable from the same principles that apply to changing any system (Chapter 10). A potential disadvantage in the application of a deductive approach is that it may not come to grips with every form of disorder, since the traditional syndromes were not used as the anchors for our general formulation. Put another way, we are not attempting to set forth a comprehensive description of all

[1] Since we do not present this chapter as a definitive account of the field of psychopathology, we have drawn rather heavily on what we consider to be an excellent general source in this field. Our indebtedness to R. W. White's formulation (1956) becomes increasingly apparent as this chapter proceeds.

forms of psychopathology, but are applying our viewpoint to the area of behavior disorder as another means for evaluating the potential utility and generality of the present formulation.

In contrast to the preceding chapters, which dealt with specific systems, the unit of analysis in the present chapter is the total self-system, or the entire personality organization. Although presumably the principles derived in this chapter should be applicable to a single concept or to a circumscribed system (for example, paranoia, or the "island" psychosis), we deal with extreme resolutions emanating from the totality of conceptual systems in the total self-organization.

The organization of the present chapter revolves around the use of the concept, *threat,* which we define in terms of extreme refutation. On the basis of earlier principles the general nature and effect of threat are elaborated and related to variations along the concrete-abstract dimension. The general role of threat in nodally arrested systems and transitionally arrested systems is considered.

Introductory Considerations

Refutation, Threat, and Excessively Closed Systems

The occurrence of refutation or the experience of potential refutation depends upon both the nature of the event and the structural characteristics of the system through which the event is experienced (Chapter 3). One of the most important structural determinants is the degree of closedness of the system. Arrested systems are characterized by closedness to specific environmental events (see Table 3 on pp. 116–117). However, within arrested systems at any level, the degree of closedness varies considerably and is paralleled by variations in sensitization. Excessively closed systems are presumably extremely sensitive to potential refutation so that very slight increases in environmental pressures are interpreted as potentially refuting. We use the term, *threat* (or stress), to describe *events experienced by excessively closed systems* as well as those events that are extreme or intense in the veridical sense. In the present chapter we emphasize threat in the former sense, but it should be noted that in either case threat is equivalent to potentially intense refutation. A major portion of this chapter is devoted to the determinants and consequences of system-specific threat.

Two generic effects of excessively closed systems may be noted at this time: (1) when confronted by a single event or object, the person is more likely to make only a single interpretation without entertaining alternative interpretations (*inflexible interpretation*), and (2) the person is also more likely to apply this single interpretation over a wide range, perhaps all, of the events he encounters (*overgeneralized interpretation*). These two consequences are similar in one respect in that they involve the same underlying pattern of functioning: excessive use of a single interpretation. Whether only one or both effects occur depends on the environmental circumstances that are encountered. At a general level, therefore, we may note that these two interrelated aspects—inflexibility and overgeneralization—are the central features of what is usually referred to as psychopathological functioning.

The more any given system becomes closed to alternative evaluations or the more functioning in reference to a broad range of objects can be described in terms of a single, narrow conceptual orientation, the more pathological is the resolution syndrome. Consequently, as a conceptual system becomes increasingly closed to alternative interpretations based on other conceptual levels, the more the resolution would be expected to reflect the pure or specific characteristics of the system involved. Therefore the nodal and transitional systems represent a theoretical basis for classifying these variations in psychopathology and are summarized in Table 23. Most of the remaining portions of this chapter elaborate and clarify Table 23.

General Nature and Effect of Threat

Maximum threat to any system is defined by those situational conditions that increase pressures toward evaluations to which the system engaged is maximally closed. As we have noted earlier, arrestation at any stage and in reference to any particular set of objects results from conditions that increase the closedness of a system to those differentiations required for progression. Consequently, those conditions required for progression at any stage are the very conditions that constitute maximum threat to systems when development at that stage has been arrested.

As indicated in Table 23, maximum threat to arrested system I is produced by increased pressures toward pole B differentiations, that is, opposition to absolute standards, whereas maximum threat to system II is produced by increased pressures toward pole D differentiations, that is, dependency.

Threat may also result from increased pressures toward more concrete differentiations (see Chapters 4, 5, and 6). For example, closedness to pole D (dependency) differentiations at stage II implies an earlier failure to integrate pole A and pole B effectively during the first transitional phase. Arrestation at stage II therefore involves a concomitant progressive closedness to pole A of stage I (external control). Consequently, arrestation at stage II involves closedness to dependency in any form, including dependency on authoritative control. Similarly, arrestation at stage III represents closedness to autonomy in any form, particularly separation, but it also involves greater relative closedness to pole B (negativism) than to pole A evaluations (authoritative control).

As implied earlier, excessive closedness produces two effects: (1) extreme sensitization to conditions that increase pressures toward refuting or threatening interpretations and (2) strong tendencies to "ward off" such evaluations, which in turn results in further increasing the closedness of the system. The final result is a single interpretive schema, representing the extreme form of a given conceptual system with a minimum of checks and balances. Conversely, the more open the conceptual system to alternative differentiations the more refutation comes to be an antecedent condition for a change in the structure of conceptual linkages and progressive development.

A major assumption in the present chapter is that the more central the concept or system of concepts being threatened, the greater is the generalization of the resulting increase in closedness to other concepts in the self-system. For most individuals the level of abstractness of functioning varies across situations or areas. Threat experienced in regard to more peripheral subject-object ties may produce psychopathological functioning in a specific area, but the more central the threatening tie, the greater is the likelihood of increased closedness. *In this chapter closedness is used to refer to central ties that involve generalization to a large number of other areas.*

The extent to which "arrested systems" become increasingly closed (and in our terms increasingly psychopathological) as a result of threat, depends upon (1) the concreteness of the system and (2) the degree to which the system of subject-object relatedness is conflicting or transitional. The more abstract the system, the greater is the resistance to increasing closedness. The effect of threat on each of these systemic characteristics is considered in the next section.

Threat and the Concrete-Abstract Dimension

Arrestation of development implies that the differentiations required for progression become increasingly threatening. When such threat is intense the result is "warding off," "subjectivity," and "defensiveness," which we refer to as *extreme* resolutions. Because more abstract conceptual systems involve some already achieved integration of conflicting forms of conceptual structure, such systems are likely to have a greater tolerance of threat. Put another way, in abstract systems the range of threatening conditions is more limited; the concepts are less "brittle."

If a subject can differentiate his relatedness to objects along several

TABLE 23

The Nature and Effect of System-Specific Threat

Conceptual System	Pole to Which System Closed	Threat Is Produced by Increased Pressures toward	Effects of Threat	Related Psychopathological Syndrome
System I	Internal control (B)	Oppositional tendencies and ambiguity	Increased closedness to internal control (poles B and C)	(I) [a] Progressive (process) schizophrenia (D) [a] Reactive schizophrenia
Level I (A > B) [b]	Partially to A and B	Oppositional and aggressive tendencies	Avoidance of pole B and overcompensation of pole A	(D) Obsessive compulsive neurosis Multiple personality
Level I (B > A)	Partially to A and B	Control and Authority	Avoidance of pole A and overcompensation of pole B	Multiple personality (I) Negativism
System II	Various forms of dependency (D and A)	Reliance on dependency	Increased closedness to dependency (poles D and A)	(I) Psychopathic personality (D) Overt anti-social tendencies
Level II (C > D)	Partially to C and D	Reliance on dependency	Avoidance of pole D and overcompensation of pole C	(D) Asocial hysterical syndrome Dissociated states
Level II (D > C)	Partially to C and D	Anticipation of lack of protection	Avoidance of pole C and overcompensation of pole D	Dissociated states (I) Overassertiveness, fear of isolation

System III	Various forms of isolation and rejection (F and C)	Separation and autonomy	Increased closedness to autonomy (poles F and C)	(I) Passive dependency, borderline depression (D) Reactive depression
Level III (E > F)	Partially to E and F	Autonomous independence	Avoidance of pole F and overcompensation of pole E	(D) Anxiety states inadequacy Multiple standards
Level III (F > E)	Partially to E and F	Need for support	Avoidance of pole E and overcompensation of pole F	Multiple standards (I) Pseudo adequacy

[a] I and D refer to the within-system and transitional dimension of indirect and direct functioning, respectively.
[b] Refer to Table 1, p. 88.

dimensions and can integrate these into new conceptual linkages, he is more likely to initiate alternative and appropriate action to overcome or tolerate refutation (lowering his goals, provisionally devaluing himself) and thus avoid the consequences of increased system closedness. However, under certain conditions, these abstract systems (excluding system IV) may become highly closed to alternate evaluations in reference to particular situations (see Table 23). Any arrested conceptual system may become increasingly closed to alternate systems of ordering. It is the *probability* of becoming increasingly closed that decreases in more abstract systems. The relationship between such *probability* of increased closedness and the level of abstractness is shown in Table 24.

Since we are dealing with ego-involving or central concepts, the

TABLE 24

Relationship between Probability of Increasing System Closedness and Level of Abstractness of System As Reflected in Psychopathological Disorders

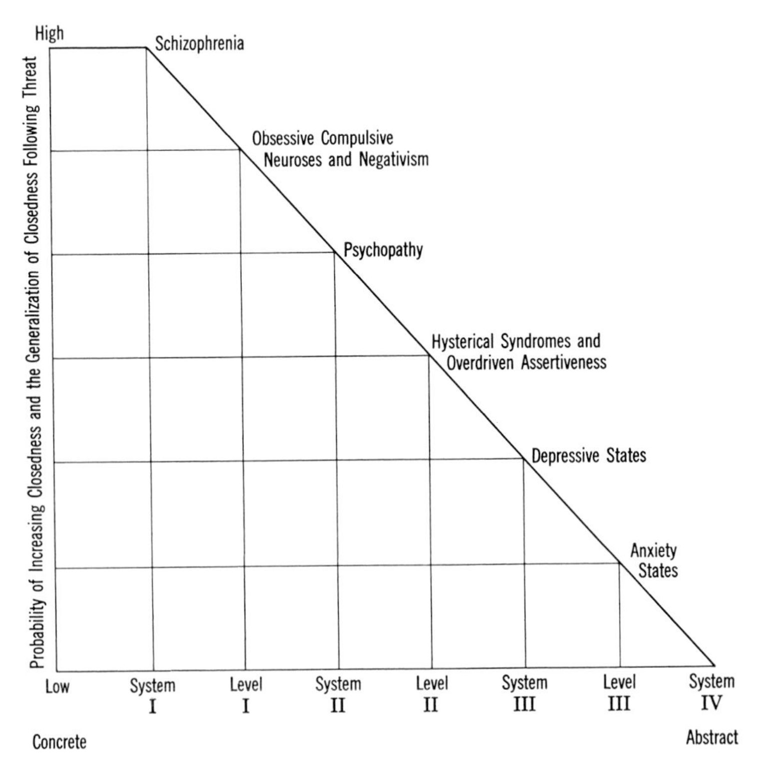

degree of closedness following threat is essentially the same as the degree to which the closedness generalizes to other areas of the life space. As Table 24 indicates, the more concrete the system, whether nodal or transitional, the more highly generalized are the effects of threat. Put in structural terms, the greater the diffuseness and absoluteness (lack of differentiation) of the system, the more generalized will be the effects of threat. To anticipate the implications of this proposition we would expect greater generalization of increasing system I closedness or increasing level I transitional conflict, than in system III closedness or level III transitional conflict. Transformed into more traditional terms, schizophrenia and obsessive-compulsive neuroses represent more diffuse effects of threat than do depressive or anxiety states. However, the relationships depicted in Table 24 are not entirely sufficient to account for the general consequences of increasing system-specific threat. A second factor to which we now turn is required.

Threat and Degree of Transitional Conflict

A second factor affects the degree of closedness resulting from threat. This factor, which operates independently from the degree of abstractness, is the extent to which the system involves conflicting forms of subject-object linkages (the extent to which the system is transitional). Since the systemic pressures involved in transitional systems operate as dynamic forces that are in opposition, it is proposed that the probability of such systems becoming completely closed, and thus generating a single interpretation of all events, is much less in transitional systems than in nodally arrested systems.

In transitional systems, conflicting differentiations tend to counteract each other so that neither becomes completely dominant. This "fulcrum-like" process may result in avoidance and overcompensatory resolutions as indicated in our discussion of transitional systems (Chapter 6), but the alternate conflicting evaluations act to prevent the more extreme degrees of closedness, which can occur in the non-conflicting, nodal systems. In the latter most conflict has been avoided; one pole is dominant. Transitional system functioning is therefore characterized by inflexible *vacillation,* which is itself also overgeneralized. The absence in non-conflicting systems of pressures toward alternate evaluations increases the probability of extreme closedness associated with a single interpretation. Thus, the simultaneous occurrence of alternating differentiations in extreme transitional systems acts as a buffer to the development of a single interpretive system.

The combined effects of level of abstractness and compartmentalization or conflict are diagrammatically presented in Table 25, which

TABLE 25

Relationship of the Probability of Increasing System Closedness As a Joint Function of Level of Abstractness and Transitional Nature of Systems As Reflected in Psychopathological Conditions

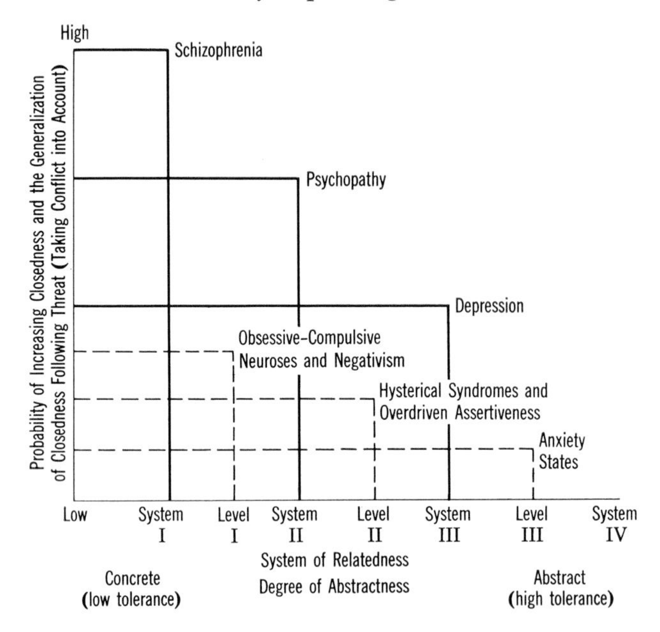

represents a combined ordering on several dimensions, as follows: First, the dimension of *tolerance for threat* (stress) is involved, in that the more abstract the system the less is the generalization of closedness following threat, and the greater is the resulting openness to new interpretations. Put in prognostic terms the more abstract the system the more positive is the prognosis under favorable training conditions (see Chapter 10). Second, the dimension of the *degree of conflict* between two forms of relatedness within a system is involved since threat to transitional systems induces greater conflict between alternate evaluations. This conflict increases avoidance and overcompensatory resolutions in order to maximize positive affect. As a consequence of threat to non-conflicting systems, closedness to alternate forms of evaluation increases, leading to a single interpretive system. This state of extreme closedness is characterized by "self-reference," "projection," and the relative inability to incorporate differentiations or evaluations generated by other systems. In this state, the extreme specific tendencies would be most clearly apparent.

The effects of system-specific threat on the more non-conflicting systems (that is, highly closed nodal systems) are, we believe, similar to what have been traditionally called "psychoses." The effects of system-specific threat on transitional systems (to highly conflicting transitional systems) are similar to the "neuroses." That is, we propose three[1] generic forms of system closedness (psychoses) and three generic forms of transitional conflict (neuroses) as outlined in Tables 24 and 25.

Implications of Within-System Dimensions

How does the indirect-direct dimension influence the effects that threat has on nodal, non-conflicting systems? We contend that the more indirect the expression of system-specific tendencies, the more progressive or evolutionary is the onset of pathological reactions. Conversely, the more direct the system of expression, the more reactive or abrupt is the onset. Direct system functioning, when not extreme, is characterized by an outgoing, overt, and apparently "successful" adjustment from a normative point of view. However, the underlying conceptual system in both forms of expression is motivationally identical at a given stage or level. Threat produces immediately apparent effects on indirect functioning in any system. The effects of threat upon direct functioning may not be immediately evident, but when threat continues over time the result is a greater refutation or discrepancy to direct systems so that extreme resolutions may appear to develop abruptly and severely.

In the traditional process-reactive distinction, we identify the extreme forms of closedness of indirect systems with progressive psychoses and the extreme forms of closedness in direct systems with the reactive psychoses. This contention receives some support from a study by Birren (1944) who found that ". . . an apathetic type of reaction in childhood is a relatively permanent type of behavior and is a forerunner of early hospitalization, poor hospital adjustment, and poor prognosis for recovery in cases developing mental disease" (Birren, 1944, p. 94).

On the basis of the principles developed in Chapter 6 regarding transition dimensions at whatever level, the following points may be derived:

1. In arrested transitional systems that are relatively more concrete at each level (level I [A > B], level II [C > D], and level III [E > F]) functioning is more direct. Since threat leads to increased conflict in these transitional systems, avoidant and overcompensatory resolutions

[1] System IV by definition is not closed to alternate forms of ordering, but remains relatively open to alternate interpretations, and is not further discussed in this chapter.

are relatively more direct, as they are an expression of a more articulated, previously established system.

2. In systems on the more abstract side of the transitional dimension (level I [B > A], level II [D > C], and level III [F > E]) expression is more indirect because these levels are dominated by a system of functioning that has been less well articulated. Such systems represent development based on the indirect avoidance of the earlier, more concrete, system of relatedness (pole A), accompanied by a lack of ability or potential to adopt the next most abstract level of functioning directly (pole B). This highly indirect expression of a poorly articulated system is contrasted with systems involving greater directness of avoidant and compensatory resolutions. Within each transitional dimension, not only does the *nature* of the dominant expression change but the degree of overall directness of expression also differs.

When conflict increases in transitional systems, the system-specific avoidant and overcompensatory resolutions become more extreme and more generalized over a wide variety of situations (increasing closedness to alternate system evaluation). One general effect of stress therefore is to produce more "pure" system-specific tendencies because of the exclusion of modifying extrasystem tendencies.

Viewed as psychopathology, those transitional systems that involve the expression of the more articulated system are referred to as the *direct neuroses*. Transitional systems that involve the expression of the less well articulated conflicting system are referred to as the *indirect neuroses* (see Table 23). The relationship between symptom or resolution syndromes and system dynamics should be more symbolic in the indirect systems.

Increasing Closedness and Regression

Since the concept of regression occupies a prominent place in many theories of psychopathology (for example, Freud, Lewin), the relation between the present conception and regression may be considered. We have emphasized the role of closedness of systems in psychopathology. In this sense closedness to alternate differentiations within a given range of objects, at any level of abstractness, represents a psychopathological reaction. From this line of reasoning psychopathology is not a regressive phenomenon since it does not represent a regression to a more concretistic level of functioning after progression to an abstract level has occurred. Therefore, we would propose that threat leads *initially* to a more extreme and overgeneralized closed system of subject-object linkages at the *same* level of abstractness. Threat presumably affects the nature of differentiations, judgments, and perceptions, but these changes occur *within* a particular stage or level. Consequently, we would expect three classes of psychosis or systems of functioning based on a single interpretative system, varying in degree of abstractness, which would correspond generally to schizophrenic (stage I) psychopathy (stage II) and depression (stage III). The psychopathological counterparts of three transitional levels would be the neurotic syndromes varying in degree of abstractness: obsessive-compulsive reactions (level I), hysterical reactions (level II), and anxiety reactions (level III).

Although we do not employ regression as an explanatory concept, we acknowledge the occurrence of reactions, which others describe as regressive. More specifically, *after the occurrence of system-specific threat to central ties the corresponding development of increasing closedness leads to two effects that may be described as regressive.* The first effect involves the generalization of the increasing closedness to other areas. The more central the threatening ties, the greater is the generalization of the effects to previously peripheral areas. At this stage the more abstract differentiations in other areas also decrease, and fewer systems of ordering in other areas of the life space are utilized. The increasing generalization of closedness to the more abstract differentiations in other areas may be viewed as regression, which is a reversal of normal developmental trends or dedifferentiation. The second effect is "cyclical" (see Chapter 4) in that closedness and generalization of closedness to other areas are likely to produce changes in the reactions of others toward the subject. In addition to this differential reaction, he may be removed to a new environment, a new job, or a hospital. His perception of a range of events changes accordingly, and therefore we would expect a "cyclical" swing toward a more concretistic orientation, relative to his past history. We emphasized in an earlier chapter that stage I functioning at age two is normatively and relatively different from stage I functioning at age five (as the child's situation changes). Similarly a return to stage I type functioning that follows changes due to increased closedness is not an exact replication of the earlier stage I behavior, owing to intervening experience and to changes in the life situation.

Therefore we view reactions described as regressive in terms of either one or both of the above two effects. Hypothetically we view psychopathological reactions as increasing closedness at any level of abstractness, but in practice secondary regressive effects are included. In this chapter we do not stress the developmental progression of a given psychopathology beyond the initial effects of increasing closedness within any system. However, we are aware of the variety of changes that occur following increasing closedness including the characteristic regressive effects that we view in terms of the generalization of system closedness.

The diagnosis and classification of psychopathology are complicated by these secondary effects of closedness (described as regression). If psychopathology, at any level of abstractness, represents the pure case of structure and function at that stage of arrestation, the psychopathologies would represent the extreme form of our descriptions of each nodal and transitional system, as indicated in Tables 24 and 25. But this simplicity is complicated by the secondary effects of closedness just described. For example, threat to central stage III systems, if quite intense, may produce a "cyclical" swing to stage I functioning and the possible intrusion of some stage I tendencies. Although these cyclical swings may occur from any level higher than system I, cyclical swings from stage II to stage I would be less probable following threat than cyclical swings from stage III to stage I for reasons we have discussed earlier. It is interesting to note, when "cyclical" effects occur in the development of extreme closedness of any system (stage I, II, or III), it is stage I tendencies that accompany psychopathological reactions. However, more important for meaningful diagnosis than these secondary effects is the primary closed system of functioning as outlined in Table 23. We suspect that the failure to distinguish primary and secondary effects may produce many of the problems in psychiatric diagnosis.

A second implication of our analysis of secondary regressive effects is that the more direct the system the greater is the "cyclical" effect and the more likely are stage I intrusions following closedness. Since direct system functioning is more "normal" from an observer's point of view, the effects of threat are likely to appear more abrupt, and in fact they are. The large discrepancy between pre- and post-threat functioning characteristic of direct systems often finds the observer relatively unprepared for the change that occurs in direct functioning. We expect increasing stage I tendencies to develop more rapidly following threat to direct systems.

We now consider in a system-specific framework the nature and effects of threat, the forms of extreme resolution, and the relationship between these resolution syndromes and more traditional descriptions of abnormal behavior. We discuss the nodal systems first, followed by a consideration of the pathological forms of transitional systems.

Threat within System I

Nature and Effect of Threat in System I

According to our theoretical expectations, the situations that are maximally threatening to system I are those that increase oppositional tendencies or are extremely ambiguous. Because system I relatedness is dependent upon external criteria, any situation that increases the tendency to abandon or to oppose such criteria threatens the subject's central ties to the world. Since independence from external control is lacking, the subject does not view what happens to him as self-determined, hence any form of failure or unfavorable evaluation of the subject is attributed to an external cause. This in turn leads the subject to experience increased aggression or resistance toward the source. However, since the system is closed to the expression of such impulses, such experiences increase anxiety.

Because the subject has not differentiated himself from the source, his internal feelings, fantasies, or impulses are therefore not well differentiated from external control. Therefore, the anxiety accompanying hostile feelings to the source is reduced by attributing these feelings to external causes ("disowning projection"). Such hostile impulse or sexual feelings, which are evaluated as being externally determined, represent transgression in system I functioning. Therefore they are likely to produce increased system closedness and in turn lead to an increasing tendency to evaluate such impulses as being caused by an external source. Threat within system I leads to increased closedness to internal control and increased openness to evaluations based on external control. Increased closedness in this system therefore not only leaves internal feeling undifferentiated from external control but also prevents the differentiation between fantasy and reality, or between thought and action.

The more closed the system, the more the subject's behavior comes to be directed toward more absolute, externally defined, depersonalized goals. In interpersonal relationships as well as other areas such as occupational goals, the subject's goal is to achieve at some absolute level. Relationships are viewed more in terms of absolute categorical or fixed characteristics. Since these external goals are beyond the control of the subject and remain unchanged, the failure to meet them does not lead to modification of the subject's behavior although he may experience tendencies toward opposition. An observer may view this inflexibility as high ambition or perhaps arrogance. The subject's dominant tendencies may increase, which widens the gap between the goal and performance, thus increasing the isolation of the subject from other people. Increasing closedness results because the experienced shortcomings lead directly to increased oppositional tendencies that are maximally threatening. *In this system shortcomings are experienced as external events, as existing in the ideas of other people, particularly in people in control.* Owing to the failure to differentiate sufficiently a system of ordering based on internal control, the subject's own thoughts, feelings, or impulses are experienced as representing either the result of external control or as identical to the thoughts of others. This tendency to assign cause to forces outside oneself is generally referred to as projection. The threat produced by increased pressure toward oppositional tendencies leads to increasing closedness to internal control, thus leaving intact the absolutistic criteria that are outside the range of self-determination.

Socially valued achievements require some degree of autonomy, independence, responsibility, and so forth for their accomplishment. As extreme system I resolutions are literally self-defacing, the individual becomes less and less able to meet the absolute goals. As the gap between absolute goal levels and performance widens, system I resolutions become more extreme and inflexible. In the final phase, the subject attributes the cause of his shortcomings directly to other persons or external forces over which he has absolutely no control and is helpless to oppose. The subject perceives the external forces as both imposing rigid, absolutistic goals and preventing their achievement by controlling and initiating the subject's actions, feelings, and urges. The net effect is an "exaggerated self-reference" and an absence of "reality testing." Although this overgeneralized delusional form of system I functioning is extreme, its systemic characteristics are essentially the same as the less extreme forms of system I functioning described earlier. Illustrating this general similarity is Jensen's finding that high F-scale (system I) Ss manifested "more primitive defenses of a compulsive, ritualistic, and schizoid nature" (Jensen, 1957, p. 310).

Before the final phase of delusional functioning occurs, immature outbursts of uncontrolled opposition may be noted. In a context of "normal" progressive development such tendencies toward negativistic opposition are integrated with other systems, which provide a basis for controlling the oppositional tendencies. In the absence of such integration, oppositional tendencies can be controlled only by external forces so that if these oppositional tendencies become sufficiently strong, they may become overt, taking on destructive and uncontrolled characteristics. However, since the expression of such opposition within system I is so extremely threatening, it is more likely that the tendency toward opposition will result in strong guilt feelings, which in turn would produce increased closedness.

Relationship of Extreme System I Functioning to Traditional Pathological Syndromes

The brief description of the more extreme forms of system I functioning is unmistakably similar to the general pathological syndrome of schizophrenia. Although many subclassifications of schizophrenia have been proposed, certain common characteristics of thought have been grouped together as characteristically schizophrenic. In addition to the work of Levy-Bruhl (1923) and Werner (1957) described in Chapter 2, Schmideberg (1930), and Lambo (1955) have studied the relationship between schizophrenic thought and the mystical and concretistic thinking of primitive man. Werner's (1957) description of the "physiognomic" content of thought, as the attribution of subjective characteristics to "things," is typical of both primitive man and of schizophrenic thought.

Werner accounts for this primitive thinking by positing a diffuse boundary between the personality and the external world. Lambo (1955) noted from his study of the Yoruba tribe, that the member:

> . . . formulates a naive psychological and epistemological attitude—a way of comprehending his social environment by identifying himself with his life soul (the "élan vital" of Bergson) even to a point of confusing its spatial relationship by regarding it as an external force. This conception of the world is pre-determined by a confused distinction between the ego and the non-ego (the external world), between the subject and the object of cognition. . . . in practice it is not always possible to delineate confidently where normal primitive beliefs cease and paranoid psychosis begins (Lambo, 1955, pp. 246–247).

Another characteristic of extreme system I functioning that is typical of schizophrenic thought is the attribution of causality to external forces, best illustrated by delusions of being controlled. In his discussion of a typical paranoid schizophrenic delusion, White (1956) states:

> To a remarkable extent he seems bent on assigning all initiative and all motives, all action of any kind, to forces outside himself, so that even his letter is being written by one of the helpless women, even his emotions originate in them (White, 1956, p. 85).

The delusion is an extreme form of projection, of experiencing one's own shortcomings in terms of external criticism. This tendency to experience real or imagined shortcomings as externally determined is typical of schizophrenic thought. White (1956) presents a case illustrating exaggerated self-reference. For example, a patient said:

"I'll tell the world!" This remark insinuates that I had been in the habit of telling the world what to do, or telling the world defiantly where to go to. This remark insinuates that in my supreme arrogance I had been telling the world some of my opinions held by me to be of more importance and consequence than the opinions of all the rest of humanity put together. . . . [And,] "He needs a woman." This is self-explanatory. It infers I am a masturbator, and that I need a woman to straighten out my sex life, but that I cannot get one (White, 1956, p. 88).

Extreme system I functioning is characterized by (1) keeping the self emotionally detached from others, (2) engaging in unilateral relationships, (3) attributing the basis for emotional feelings, including sexual urges, directly to the control of an external agent. In schizophrenic thinking, sexual urges or forces are frequently attributed to "things" rather than to internal determinants.

Developmental Antecedents of Extreme System I Functioning

Since highly closed forms of system I relatedness and certain aspects of schizophrenic thought processes appear to be related, we would expect to find a general association between reliable unilateral training (proposed as antecedent to arrestation at stage I) and the development of schizophrenic tendencies. Although studies indicate that such an association generally exists, a much more detailed analysis of the operations underlying the various methods of training is required in order to classify more complex training situations. One of the most critical questions concerns the effect of the interaction between two training agents (for example, two parents) on the training method. We need to understand the training method (from the subject's point of view) that emerges as a result of the interaction between the subject and his total training environment. This environment includes both parents and the relationship between the training method each parent utilizes (Lidz, 1958).

The major components of reliable unilateral training are: (1) external source determination of the system of ordering, (2) emphasis on ends rather than means in gaining control over behavior, and (3) extrinsic evaluation. These operations, often combined in complex ways, are reported in most investigations of the parent-rearing antecedents of schizophrenia. Generally the training environment described involves (1) the parents' compulsive requirement that the child behave in a particular fashion, (2) the parents' restriction of alternative means of behaving or thinking, (3) unilateral relationship between parent and child, which is lacking in mutuality, (4) restrictive and controlling practices, and (5) the "double bind" notion or the simultaneous demand

and prevention of a course of action, for example, "always love your mother even when she punishes you for doing something you didn't do" or "don't speak to strangers but be friendly and polite to everyone."

Lidz, Cornelison, Terry, and Fleck (1958) and Cameron (1943) view schizophrenia as a disorder of communication. Lidz (1958) stresses the etiological significance of the child's failure to assimilate the instrumentalities of parental training. These authors (Lidz et al., 1958) observed that:

> . . . The struggles of these parents to preserve their own integration led them to limit their environment markedly by rigid preconceptions of the way things must be. . . . The parents' delimitation of the environment, and their perception of events to suit their needs, result in a strange family atmosphere into which children must fit themselves and suit this dominant need or feel unwanted. . . . Their conceptualizations of the environment are neither instrumental in affording consistent understanding and mastery of events, feelings, or persons. . . . Facts are consistently being altered to suit emotionally determined needs. . . . "Masking," which also confuses communication, refers to the ability of one or both parents to conceal some very disturbing situation within the family . . . the parent being unable either to accept or to alter the situation, ignores it and acts as though the family were a harmonious and homogeneous body which filled the needs of its members (Lidz et al., 1958, pp. 310–312).

Typical of many etiological studies, Reichard and Tillman (1950), Hadju-Gimes (1940), and Tietze (1949) observed the restrictive nature of training, the artificial nature of the parents' affection, the subtly dominating features of the training practices, and the development of a symbiotic relatedness in which the ego of the child and the ego of the mother remain fused. In summary, Tietze (1949) states:

> All mothers were overanxious and obsessive, all were domineering, ten more overtly and fifteen in a more subtle fashion. All mothers were found to be restrictive with regard to the libidinal gratification of their children. Most of them were perfectionistic and oversolicitous and were more dependent on approval by others than the average mother (Tietze, 1949, pp. 64–65).

Many observers report cases of parental rejection in association with development of schizophrenic reactions. In our terms we would not expect this association unless rejection is defined in terms of a lack of mutuality, with restrictiveness and an excess of external control. It is in this sense that Reichard and Tillman (1950) described a rejecting mother of a schizophrenic as "cold and sadistically critical of her offspring, insists that the patient meet her excessive demands for neatness and cleanliness, for politeness and observance of social norms or fulfillment of her own unfulfilled ambitions" (Reichard and Tillman, 1950, p. 251).

Questionnaire responses found to differentiate between mothers of male schizophrenics and mothers of non-schizophrenics tends to support our developmental hypotheses (Mark, 1953). Mothers of male schizophrenics more often checked such items as:

> Children should be taken to and from school until the age of eight just to make sure there are no accidents. A mother should make it her business to know everything her children are thinking. If children are quiet for a little while a mother should immediately find out what they are thinking about. Children should not annoy parents with their unimportant problems. A watchful mother can keep her child out of all accidents. A parent must never make mistakes in front of the child. Parents should sacrifice everything for their children. Most children are toilet trained by 15 months of age. Children who take part in sex play become sex criminals when they grow up. A child should not plan to enter any occupation that his parents don't approve of. Some children are just naturally bad. A good way to get children to obey is by giving them presents or promising them treats. Spanking a child does more good than harm (Mark, 1953, p. 187).

Variations in Directness in Extreme System I Functioning

On the basis of our earlier assumptions we would propose (1) that the indirect expression of extreme system I functioning would be associated with a more progressive or evolutionary onset of disorder, as found in simple and/or hebephrenic forms of schizophrenia, and (2) that more direct expression of extreme system I functioning would be associated with a more reactive onset and more active forms of schizophrenia, as in the paranoid and particularly the catatonic forms of schizophrenia. The indirect pole is characterized by poor differentiation between the subject and the source or between the subject and the external world. As the gap between the child's developmental level and that of his peers increases the following progressive sequence is typical: (1) begins by being a "good" child when young, (2) progressive narrowing of interests, (3) lack of assertiveness and competitiveness, (4) gradual withdrawal from social relationships, (5) increasing tendency to perceive others as critical when this interpretation is unjustified, (6) indirect and passive forms of resistance, for example, grouchiness, (7) sporadic, immature attempts to dominate parents, and finally (8) unsystematized delusions and bizarre thoughts.

The direct systems, on the other hand, are characterized by attempts to dominate others and by greater success in striving for and reaching absolutistic goals, which together give the appearance of a more successful adjustment. However, if the perceived gap between absolute, rigid goals and performance increases, the experienced discrepancy is reacted to in a greatly exaggerated fashion. If the increased dominative attempts (which result from greater oppositional pressures in direct systems) are unsuccessful, more extreme resolution forms will result in a more active form of schizophrenia, with an "apparently" sudden onset. In these cases it is easier to point to some observable precipitating threat. Functioning is generally associated with well-developed delusions, and may involve uncontrolled oppositional tendencies, which may be destructive and/or extremely indirect and inhibited, such as various forms of catatonic reactions.

As schematized in Table 23, the catatonic reaction (peculiar gestures, stereotyped actions, immobility, and alternating states of stupor and excitement) may be viewed as midway between active system I functioning and level I transitional functioning. Catatonic reactions involve both schizophrenic process (system I) and the inhibition of negativism (level I). The onset of catatonic reactions may be exceedingly sudden. The disorder is characterized by an alternation between (1) immobility and refusal to react (the most active and direct form of resistance to external constraint without utilizing actual opposition) and (2) uncontrolled, open, violent excitement (representing the most immature, concrete, and uncontrolled form of opposition). Arrestation at this level of development produces tendencies toward opposition but prevents the control or integration of such tendencies. It seems plausible that, under high degrees of threat, this combination should produce the most severe episodes of uncontrolled violence. Systems of relatedness further along the level I transitional dimension (toward stage II systems) involve an increase in the expression and *control* of indirect oppositional tendencies.

Friedman (1953), Hemmendinger (1953), and Siegel (1953) developed a system for scoring the Rorschach Test for quality of perception. Following Werner, these authors classified responses as "genetically low" or "genetically high" on the basis of the separation of the blot areas into different parts, their hierarchic integration, and the organization of these areas into a combined whole. Fine and Zimet (1959) used this method with schizophrenic patients and found that process or evolutionary schizophrenics showed more indices of perceptual immaturity (labile and more indirect structures) than reactive schizophrenics (stable and more direct structures).

In closing this section let us acknowledge that we have ignored the genetic or biological factors that may contribute to the predisposition to extreme forms of stage I functioning. Although we can make no direct contribution to this aspect of the problem, we would like to suggest that information about the functional or systemic characteristics of behavior may help pinpoint which biological factors are likely to be relevant. In stage I systems we suggest that the most relevant predisposing biological factors should be those that limit the potential for a subject to discriminate himself from the external environment, to discriminate thought from act, fantasy from reality, and self-activation from external control. The essential nature of system I functioning, particularly when the system is highly closed, is the attribution of cause to an external agent or force. This characteristic represents, for us, a necessary operation for determining the induction (psychologically or biochemically) of extreme system I functioning as in a schizophrenic episode.

Threat within System II

Nature and Effect of Threat in System II

System-specific threat to stage II systems is produced by increasing pressures toward dependence on others or toward being controlled by them. In highly closed forms of system II, any kind of evaluation made by a source, whether positive or negative, will be threatening since the subject experiences the evaluation as potential imposition. Other system-specific threatening situations include protective or controlling pressures from distrusted sources and any situation that prevents the subject from becoming independent, such as the inability to be financially independent from such sources. Impersonal and well-defined role relationships found in gangs and institutionalized life are less threatening, and as mentioned earlier this is especially true when the intragroup structure is "in the service of" individual oppositional tendencies, as in adolescent gangs, protest groups, and so forth. The effect of threat is to close the system to source influence and dependence. This closedness is expressed by establishing greater psychological distance between the subject and other people through remaining out of reach, psychologically speaking. Like system I functioning, threat is associated with social withdrawal. However, in contrast to system I, which is characterized by withdrawal from internal control or an abandonment of the possibility of self-regulation, withdrawal within system II takes the form of attempted avoidance (through overt, negativistic tendencies) of any form of external control. Under condition of threat, the system II–related characteristics such as non-commitment, malevolent imputation, and denial of responsibility become intensified into antagonism, disobedience, and direct aggression.

In extremely closed system II functioning, the subject experiences other people's actions as interfering, interrupting, and disturbing; even minor frustrations lead to excessive oppositional reactions. The heightened sensitization to imposition is accompanied by increased defiance of authority, which assumes system-specific reward characteristics. In this sense, anti-social actions, such as stealing, can be viewed as a validation of "independence." Increased threat in system II produces inflexibility of interpretation, which is reflected by an increased tendency to view external events as interfering or malevolent and expressed via excuses, rationalization, and the externalization of blame.

Since the subject is more clearly differentiated from the source in system II, and since directionality of the relatedness (to external control) is oppositional, delusions of external control do not occur. Extreme system II functioning is characterized by (1) an absence of mutuality or empathy, (2) very little relationship between word and deed (that is, the differentiation between the self-system and the external world is sufficient for the subject to be aware of realistic goals and to be independent from external forces, but action is determined almost completely by negativistic interpretations), (3) increased restlessness, irritability, and frustration caused by minor barriers, and (4) externalization of blame.

Under appropriate conditions, extreme closedness of system II can be avoided, primarily through minimizing pressures toward dependency. For example, if such a person could obtain the necessary background for an occupation, such as writer, painter, or scientist, which minimizes dependency problems, such negativistic and critical dispositions could become assets. However, if the subject cannot utilize constructive achievement as an outward expression of negative independence, or if he cannot escape dependence on authoritative or protective interference, he is more likely to achieve the same negative ends through less socially desirable means.

Relationship of Extreme System II Functioning to Traditional Pathological Syndromes

What we have described as highly closed system II functioning is closely related to the traditional pathological syndromes of psychopathic personality and delinquency (anti-social behavior). According to White (1956) these individuals ". . . have failed to respond adequately to the process of socialization. . . ." (p. 395). Although this may be true in a value sense, from an adaptive point of view the psychopathic or delinquent individual has learned the system of functioning that would be expected from certain socialization procedures. White illustrates the adaptive significance of such functioning by quoting from Redl and Wineman (1951): "Far from being helpless, the ego of these children is suddenly a rather shrewd appraiser of that part of reality which might be dangerous to their impulsive exploits. . . ." (Redl and Wineman, 1951, p. 144). However, even from the viewpoint of social value, functioning within system II represents an attempt, albeit an immature one, to develop internal control, a circumstance with some positive significance for both development and therapy. The eventual success in handling responsibility and positive independence rests upon learning the appropriate modes of dealing with negative independence.

Compared with system I, system II functioning appears more detrimental to society by its aggressiveness and apparent lack of responsibility. System I personality organization is characterized by narrowness, rigidity, and righteousness of categorical thinking; it is accompanied by disdain for those who believe differently and who are therefore wrong, considered inferior, and destined to a role of permanent submission. From our view the human suffering and intellectual constriction that result from system I functioning (for example, Nazism and other forms of dogmatic thinking and intolerance) may be much more permanently harmful to society than system II functioning, despite society's concern with the latter.

Some of the more typical descriptions of delinquent and psychopathic behavior, summarized by White (1956), illustrate the general similarity to what we have described as closed system II functioning: destructiveness, the association between minor frustrations and temper tantrums, and overreadiness and skill for providing excuses for misconduct (externalization of blame) (Redl and Wineman, 1951); an incapacity for a consistent, organized living pattern; an alert, well-informed approach that often creates a pleasing impression; a lack of responsibility, and a lack of shame or guilt for misconduct; poor judgment about attaining well-defined realistic ends, which is illustrated by the repetition of anti-social behavior over and over again; an incapacity for real love or attachment; and although verbalization regarding self-correction may occur, it is generally nothing more than lip service without further involvement (Cleckley, 1950).

Because anti-social behavior issuing from system II represents a move toward validation of the positive conceptual pole of freedom from dependence, which in turn rests upon the unilateral negation of source control, such anti-social behavior frequently becomes public. We would expect system II anti-social behavior to be committed in the company of others; if not, we expect that the action would be communicated in a direct or distorted way in order to demonstrate freedom from controlling forces through such antagonism. Since denial of dependency is directed against external control, it must be public in order to serve its purpose.

Developmental Antecedents of Extreme System II Functioning

The developmental conditions antecedent to delinquent and psychopathic behavior syndromes found by a number of investigators generally support the association that we have suggested between unreliable unilateral training (including neglect) and system II functioning. Before considering such evidence, a brief consideration of the concept of delinquency is in order. A major shortcoming of most investigations of delinquency is the acceptance of a legal, rather than a psychological, definition. In the present view we are concerned with psychological functioning, that is, individuals whose functioning has been described in terms of system II resolutions. Therefore, we do not assume that all delinquency or anti-social behavior is based on system II relatedness. Anti-social behavior might stem from attempts to maintain relationships and to avoid rejection by peer groups (system III relatedness), in which case the social norms would be an important antecedent factor. Anti-social behavior in the form of sexual deviations, for example, sadistic or masochistic activities, may be based on feelings of worthlessness or a wish to dominate (system I relatedness). The effect of corrective, punitive, or preventive measures will therefore vary according to the system of functioning underlying the anti-social behavior. Specifically, if anti-social behavior is anchored in external control (system I) or avoidance of rejection (system III), corrective measures may be more effective. The incidence of recidivism should be higher in anti-social behavior involving system II functioning because current social controls are quite ineffective upon this system (McDavid and Schroder, 1957).

Three major sets of etiological factors have been proposed in the past as antecedent to delinquency: somatogenic, sociological, and psychological.

SOMATOGENIC

Although the evidence for theories of constitutional inferiority of delinquents is not compelling, recent studies do indicate that "delinquent" individuals show significantly more abnormal EEG records than control groups (Ellingson, 1954; Hill and Watterson, 1942; and Simons and Diethelm, 1946). However, Jenkins and Pacella (1943) found that most of the abnormal EEG records in a group of delinquents came from a small percentage of the group who were assaultive, irritable, distractible, and poorly controlled. The remaining majority of the group whose EEG patterns were normal presented typical delinquent symptoms. Central nervous system pathology may be a contributing factor (impairment of impulse control mechanisms) or a coincidental condition in delinquency as in many other forms of behavior. In general the evidence for a constitutional basis of psychopathy is not impressive.

SOCIOLOGICAL

Many studies have demonstrated a relationship between the incidence of delinquency and some form of social disorganization either in the home or in the neighborhood. From the present view, such disorganization is seen as a generic form of the unreliable unilateral training that leads to arrested system II functioning. Family and neighborhood disorganization destroys the child's trust in his parents and in the controls of society, thereby magnifying his negative "weighting" of the source and his use of aggressive resolutions.

PSYCHOLOGICAL

To consider the psychological determinants requires that we define the generic training conditions underlying system II functioning. We noted earlier that overprotective and permissive training produces overassertive, disobedient behavior; however, in such cases the counterpersonal or system II tendencies were counteracted by conflicting system III concepts, the conflict being described as a level II transitional system, in which anti-social behavior rarely occurs (Levy, 1943). However, as the training becomes more clearly unreliable (that is, more indifferent, rejecting, and neglectful) the incidence of delinquency increases sharply. In one of the most extensive studies (Glueck and Glueck, 1950) that has attempted to relate child-training practices to the incidence of delinquency, the following results were obtained: In comparison to mothers of non-delinquents, mother of delinquents were found to be less warm (45% to 80%); more overprotective (24% to 15%); much more indifferent (21% to 3%); and more hostile and rejecting (7% to 1%). A more specific analysis indicated that mothers of delinquents were much less likely to be "firm but kind" (4% to 66%); much more likely to be lax (57% to 12%); more likely to be overstrict (4% to 1%); and more likely to be erratic (34% to 21%).

It seems necessary to take the indirect-direct dimension of system II into account in considering the developmental antecedents. The more inhibitive the unreliable training (more control, less indifference and neglect), the more that distrust and negative source weighting are based on an indirectly hostile world. Arbitrary or irregular discipline or training in which control and punishment are used to demand dependency of the child on the parent leads to a strong, unconflicting tendency toward viewing the imposition of control as negative. The result is that the negativistic tendencies are indirectly expressed. In such indirect function there remains a minimum internalization of external control as absolute standards (system I) and a lack of empathic system III control.

Variation in Directness in Extreme System II Functioning

The major differences between indirect and direct system II functioning may be summarized as follows. (1) Indirect functioning involves a greater tendency to portray oneself as benevolent, that is, as not malevolent. In order to reduce pressures toward more direct forms of negativism the person expressing system II tendencies passively may assume a "mask" of conformity or respectability. However, because of the relative absence of absolutistic or empathic concepts, these interpersonal reactions are extremely tenuous, as observation of psychopathic persons attests. (2) Indirect functioning is more likely to involve passive expression of negativism such as failing to follow directions or to hold a job; minor forms of misconduct for which he blames the environment; and continual vague feelings of irritability and restlessness.

These differences indicate that we would associate the traditional description of delinquency (and the more direct forms of anti-social behavior) with the direct pole, whereas the more psychopathic and passive forms of system II functioning would be associated with the indirect pole (cf. Ausubel, 1952, for a similar distinction). It should be emphasized again that our view of anti-social behavior is not determined by a legal definition.

In system II functioning the indirect-direct dimension is not directly related to the progression of onset as was true in system I, mainly because the direct expression of system II tendencies is immediately recognized as a problem, whereas the more direct expression of system I orientations is not so readily recognized. The cultural judgment of direct system II functioning, even in its less extreme forms, is less likely to be that of "good" adjustment than is true for direct system I functioning. Consequently, the observer may be surprised by the eruption of uncontrolled violence and the increased occurrence of projection, delusions, and sadistic tendencies found in "good and obedient" people when direct system I functioning becomes extremely closed. On the other hand, the observer would not be so puzzled by extreme hostility in system II since the previous functioning was already regarded as culturally disagreeable.

By factorizing forty-five trait-ratings of 500 children, Hewitt and Jenkins (1946) isolated three factors, two of which appear relevant to system II relatedness and lend support to our indirect-direct dimension. The first factor is called "unsocialized aggressive behavior" and is comprised of traits such as assertive tendencies, initiative, fighting, and defiance of authority, which generally corresponds to direct system II functioning. The second factor was referred to as "socialized delinquent behavior" and included traits such as having bad companions, gang activities, cooperative stealing, school truancy, running away from home, and staying out late at night, which seems to be representative of the indirect pole of system II functioning. Hewitt and Jenkins also included a factorial analysis of environmental characteristics associated with each dimension of anti-social behavior. "Unsocialized aggressive behavior" was associated with unwanted pregnancy, mother unwilling to accept parent role, mother hostile to child, whereas "socialized delinquent behavior" was found to be associated with unkempt home, irregular home routine, discipline harsh, mother shielding, and so forth. As we would expect, the more direct functioning was associated with a more directly hostile or neglectful environment consisting of social and familial disorganization (less inhibition of aggression), lack of warmth, and rejection. The more indirect functioning was found to be associated with a mixture of familial irregularity and harsh, but shielding, parental attitudes. The combination of harsh and shielding training practices, representing an indirectly hostile environment, which particularly exemplifies what we have referred to as the inhibitive form of unreliable unilateral training, has also been stressed by Aichorn (1935) as an antecedent of delinquent behavior.

Threat within System III

Nature and Effect of Threat in System III

Threat within system III occurs in situations perceived as leading to increasing pressures toward autonomy, or toward separation that is interpreted as rejection. The following characteristics of system III functioning may be recapitulated: (1) closedness to autonomy, (2) sensitization to interpersonal relationships (which leads to seeking approval and support while avoiding disapproval or rejection), (3) the equating of rejection and personal failure, and (4) increasing internal causation. Increased threat produces the general effect of closing the system to alternate (non system-specific) evaluation, of increasing sensitization to rejection, and of increasing the tendency to interpret events in terms of acceptance-rejection. In the extreme case, functioning is characterized by a single interpretive schema of exaggerated self-reference, which may be seen as "psychotic." However, the effects of increasing closedness of system III are considerably different from the consequences of threat in systems I and II. Because system III functioning is more abstract, its extreme forms are less inflexible so that even extreme functioning in system III appears to be more reality-oriented and the effects of threat are less generalized than in the more concrete systems.

A major effect of threat within system III, which differentiates it from extreme forms of systems I and II, is the increased self-blame and feelings of worthlessness. Because system III operates more within a framework of internal causation, threat in the form of potential rejection is likely to lead the person to blame himself for his failure to sustain the relationship.

The tendency toward self-blame and feelings of worthlessness is especially likely to occur in indirect system III functioning. Direct resolutions more consistently include conformity operations through anticipating and adopting the standards of others, maneuvering others into a position requiring their support, and denying rejection by the outward portrayal of confidence and ability as a means of gaining support. However, if these expressions do not achieve the desired consequences, self-blame is likely to occur. Resolutions based on the more passive systems involve what may be described as "exaggerated incompetence" or helplessness in order to evoke protective reactions from others.

Since feelings of worthlessness emanating from internalizing blame may lead to suicide under extreme conditions, we would expect relatively more suicides in system III. Conversely, the occurrence of homicide would be most likely associated with system I and II functioning because of the externalization of blame. The hypothesized relationship between system III internalization and suicide as well as the relation of system I and II externalization with homicide is in essential agreement with one of the major hypotheses of Henry and Short (1954) that receives general support from their sociological studies:

> . . . the degree of legitimization of other-oriented aggression consequent to aggression varies positively with the strength of external restraint over behavior. When behavior is required to conform rigidly to the demands

and expectations of others (when external restraints are strong), the expression of aggression against others is legitimized. When external restraints are weak, other-oriented aggression consequent to frustration fails to be legitimized and the aggression is directed against the self (Henry and Short, 1954, p. 18).

Homicide is inhibited in stage III related systems by the strong orientation toward interpersonal relationships. Suicide would be inhibited in system I by the tendency to "blame the external" for perceived shortcomings and the lack of internal causation. In system II we would expect both calculated and impulsive homicides in response to generalized or intense threat. Since system IV involves a greater tolerance for stress both suicide and homicide are less likely among representatives of this system than in other systems of functioning.

In addition to these system-related expectations regarding homicide and suicide, we expect that both forms would be more likely in direct expression. Indirect systems generally involve displacement, which in system I takes the form of displaced or indirect externally-oriented hostility, and in system III takes the form of threatened or unsuccessful attempts at suicide (which implicitly demand support). In contrast, direct systems take the form of actual homicide or suicide, and in keeping with the acute or reactive nature of extreme direct functioning, such reactions occur quite suddenly. Thus, while homicide should occur relatively more frequently in direct system I functioning, suicide should occur relatively more frequently in direct system III functioning.[1]

Another effect of threat in system III is increased "jealousy." When socially accommodating efforts are unsuccessful, the individual is likely to experience some resentment toward others because of their lack of support or approval. These feelings of resentment towards others (usually observed in suicidal tendencies) will be especially strong in direct forms of system III, since socially accommodating responses have been relatively successful in the past. However, owing to the strong self-blame orientation and the tendency to maintain supportive relationships, outward expression is inhibited. The experience of resentment merely increases the threat, which in turn decreases the subject's participation and increases his withdrawal and helplessness. In contrast to more concrete systems, threat in system III is experienced as inadequacy of one's own behavior or in terms of one's failing to maintain the support of others. Increased closedness in this system is

[1] Suicide, of course, could also occur in any of the systems. For example, if absolutistic control and feelings of guilt in system I became intense, suicide might result. We are here simply maintaining which form of functioning seems most closely associated with these two destructive reactions.

associated with heightened sensitization to rejection, intensified feelings of aloneness, and greater fears of inability to cope with situations. In the extreme form of system III functioning all events are interpreted in terms of self-worthlessness.

Relationship of Extreme System III Functioning to Traditional Pathological Syndromes

The highly closed form of system described above is closely related to depressive reactions. Ausubel (1952) observes that depression is more closely related to anxiety states than are other classes of pathology. As indicated in Table 24, we would agree with this similarity since we view both disorders as extreme forms of relatively abstract systems of functioning that involve internal causation.

Although apparently withdrawn, the depressed person is more reality-oriented and integrated than the schizophrenic person. Bowman and Raymond (1931) have shown that delusions are absent in approximately 10 per cent of schizophrenic patients and about 42 per cent of depressed patients, which may reflect among other things the greater reality orientation of depressive behavior. These percentages are meaningful only if the criteria of diagnosis are clearly specified; there is often considerable confusion in distinguishing between depression and some forms of simple schizophrenia, expecially when both are characterized by extreme withdrawal. Regardless of phenotypic similarity, for example, withdrawal, we would emphasize the importance of using a more genotypic basis for differential diagnosis, or in this case, the differential locus of causality (internal versus external orientation). Projection, delusions of external control, and the diffuseness of the differentiation between the self and absolutistic control should be relatively absent in extreme system III functioning, that is, in depressive reactions.

Highly closed forms of system III functioning are characterized by (1) dependence upon others (as opposed to absolutistic concepts), (2) internal control, and (3) self-blame. A study of depressives by Schiffman (1960) using the Picture Arrangement Test (Tomkins and Miner, 1957) supports this contention. Compared to normal persons, the depressive patients were found to be (1) more sociophilic and orally dependent, (2) more self-confident that their own efforts would be causal in "winning over" a hostile or indifferent group and in winning praise from a source through their own work efforts, and (3) more pessimistic.

Although depressive and manic states generally occur alone, they may occur in alternating forms in the same patient. Our view is that the depressive and manic reactions parallel the system-specific resolutions of *exaggeration of incompetence* and *denial of rejection*, respectively. Other authors (Lewin, 1950; White, 1956) also have viewed the manic reaction as a form of denial. Many investigators have noted the similarity between mania and the elated state that may occur following bereavement. In this sense, elation or mania may be viewed as a counteraction to depression, a denial of feelings of depression. From our viewpoint both depression and mania are two different expressions of the same underlying form of relatedness (highly closed system III). An example of extreme closedness found in a depressive and manic state in the same person is given by Beers (1931). In the depressive condition any event, no matter how remote or unrelated, was interpreted pessimistically as validating his unworthiness. Precisely the opposite occurred in the manic state. According to Rado (1951):

> . . . the depressive spell is a desperate cry for love precipitated by an actual or imagined loss which the patient feels endangers his emotional (and material) security. In the simplest case the patient has lost his beloved one. . . . By blaming and punishing himself for the loss he has suffered, he now wishes to reconcile the *mother* and to reinstate himself in *her* loving care. . . .
>
> However, the patient's dominant motivation of repentance is complicated by the simultaneous presence of a strong resentment. As far as his guilty fear goes, he is humble and yearns to repent; as far as his coercive rage goes, he is resentful.
>
> In the forephase of the depressive spell the patient tends to vent his resentment on the beloved person, the one by whom he feels "let down" or deserted. He wants to force this person to love him. When the patient feels that his coercive rage is defeated, his need for repentance gains the upper hand; his rage then recoils and turns inward against him, increasing by its vehemence the severity of his self-reproaches and self-punishments. As a superlative bid for forgiveness, the patient may thus be driven to suicide (Rado, 1951, pp. 51–52).

We view the phrase, "his rage recoils and turns inward against him" (Rado, 1951, p. 52), in terms of internal causation since this rage is rarely expressed directly toward others, even in agitated forms of depression. Rado (1951) continually emphasizes the relationship between feelings of loss of affection and depression, and he views depressive behavior as an extreme effort to gain the support of others. White (1956) also observed that the "weak spot in these otherwise healthy personalities is this dependence on a high income of supporting love" (White, 1956, p. 528). An intensive study of the adjustive techniques used by manic-depressive patients complements this suggestion in its indication that these patients may skillfully utilize an ability to manipulate others into a position requiring that they provide emotional support to the subject (Cohen, Baker, Cohen, Fromm-Reichmann, and Weiger, 1954). These observations generally support our assumed similarity between the depressive syndrome and extreme forms of system III functioning.

Developmental Antecedents of Extreme System III Functioning

Unlike the extreme forms of functioning discussed in systems I and II, there is little direct evidence in the literature on the relationship between antecedent training practices and predisposition to depressive reactions. This dearth of evidence may in part be due to the fact that protective training (which we propose as antecedent to system III functioning) is less apparently negative than some other training practices. However, most investigators associate depressive reactions with training that sensitizes the subject to fear of aloneness, disapproval, and rejection. Rado (1951) describes depression as "feelings of loss of affection" and stresses the point that such exaggerated feelings are due to a reactivation of such childhood fears. Protective interdependent training emphasizes this sensitization, which may become even more severe if this training is combined with such situational factors as "separation" (see Chapter 4).

The evidence relating to the development of highly closed system III functioning or depression as here defined, comes primarily from reaction to stress in critical situations. We expect situations that lead to increased pressures toward autonomy to produce closed system III functioning (as this leads to a fear of rejection or the fear of "letting others down").

Results described by Grinker and Spiegel (1945) provide supportive evidence in their delineation of two types of personality organizations that predispose men toward depressive reactions under combat stress.

> . . . The passive-dependent person is most likely to feel depressed on separation from the group and to react with depression at home on frustration of his need for gratification. On the other hand, the compulsive-obsessive personality reacts most readily to the loss of a buddy in combat, to poor living conditions and to deviations from smooth-running performances. These men show marked repetition compulsions which force them to recreate the family circle with all their tenderness and hostility displaced to the military group. Officers become fathers, comrades are brothers, almost at first sight. Loss of these loved objects, toward whom quantities of unconscious hostility are harbored, disturbs the whole psychological equilibrium of the individual. In these cases the unconscious hostility evokes guilt and selfpunishment.

In most of these cases the mourned person is one toward whom the patient has had a great deal of repressed hostility. In every case it can be determined that the mourned person was one with whom the patient had identified, or who represented a figure to which he had been ambivalent. Depression, however, is not always based on the actual loss or death of a person (Grinker and Spiegel, 1945, pp. 304–306).

The passive-dependent persons described by Grinker and Spiegel presumably function in ways similar to extreme system III functioning, whereas the obsessive-compulsive syndrome they describe would be presently regarded as an extreme form of the level I transitional system discussed later in this chapter. As Grinker and Spiegel's observations indicate, reaction to stress is determined both by situational (nature of stress) and dispositional (personality organization) factors. The nature of stress in combat situations is apparently especially potent in inducing anxiety or depressive reactions in obsessive-compulsive and dependent individuals. However, the similarity of the behavior (depressive type responses) does not, of course, necessarily indicate a similar etiology. Grinker and Spiegel's (1945) analysis indicates that not only are the predisposing personality organizations dissimilar but also that conditions within the combat situation produce a differential effect upon these personality organizations. Contemporaneous situational factors that emphasize separation fears, aloneness, autonomy, and rejection are, in our view, just as important as the long-term effects produced by protective interdependent training that sensitizes a person to separation fears, aloneness, and rejection.

We have indicated earlier that the internal causation orientation in system III leads us to expect a higher incidence of suicide in persons with system III structures. This likelihood is enhanced when the environmental situation augments separation fear. Although direct evidence regarding such dispositional and situational information is not available, Henry and Short (1954) have presented sociological evidence showing that the incidence of suicide is highest in the unmarried, residents of cities, inhabitants of high mobility areas such as rooming houses, and homeless men.

Variation in Directness in Extreme System III Functioning

We have already indicated that indirect expression in extreme system III functioning is associated with the progressive development of milder forms of depression or passive dependency, whereas direct expression characterizes the more reactive and severe forms of depression of sudden onset. We expect indirect forms of expression to be more often associated with lower intelligence levels, greater protection during training, and inadequacies in social skills, resulting from excessive protection and isolation from peers. In extreme system III functioning, indirect reactions include: (1) increased dependency behaviors, (2) increased suggestibility to social pressures, and (3) exaggerated incompetence, including helplessness and illness as ways of avoiding aloneness. Fake attempts at suicide might be employed as attention-getting devices, and the mood would be characterized by dejection.

Direct expression is also characterized by behavior that evokes support from others, but this behavior is more outgoing and will appear superficially as more "independent." Rather than rely upon the exaggeration of inadequacies or helplessness, the person who employs direct system III concepts is more likely to enlist support from others through maneuvers that gratify or validate these other persons. In an attitude change study (Janicki, 1960) it was found that individuals predisposed to system III tended to (a) conform and (b) announce their judgments quickly, *after* they become aware of their partner's standard. Such strategies present a mask of "independence" and at the same time aim to insure acceptance. Individuals disposed toward system III may live quite successful lives, may present an outward show of responsibility and independence, and may be very "popular." However, under conditions of extreme system-specific threat, feelings of worthlessness occur. In direct "successful" system III functioning, the occurrence of extreme threat is experienced as more severe by the subject than in indirect functioning. For similar reasons, the subject's behavior appears strikingly different to an observer since the subject's expression of worthlessness, which stems from the threat, is quite disparate from the earlier behavioral baseline of accommodation and apparent "independence" in direct system III functioning.

Tentative evidence suggests that the denial of rejection (as a response on a situational interpretation measure) occurs most frequently in subjects who rate themselves as more successful than a liked person who becomes the source of disapproval (Schroder and Hunt, 1959). This relationship might be taken as very tentative evidence indicating that manic states, or the more general elated moods, would be more prevalent in the more direct stage III systems.

Certain situational and physiological factors have been noted to produce depressive reaction: bereavement, menopause, changes in estrogen cycles, retirement. and so forth. We would contend that these psychological and physiological determinants are similar in that they all produce a heightened sensitization to rejection and other system III orientations.

Nature and Effect of Threat in Transitional Systems

Threat within transitional systems increases the degree of conflict between two unintegrated and opposing systems of relatedness. However, the threat within transitional systems does not lead to increasing closedness since the conflicting influences of each form of relatedness act as a check on movement toward complete closedness (or psychosis). Threat within transitional systems increases conflict and its associated fearful anticipations, avoidance, and overcompensation, an effect we see as similar to the neuroses.

Before proceeding we shall briefly recapitulate the logic involved in deriving the extreme resolutions of the three transitional dimensions.

1. Transitional systems are characterized by conflicting forms of subject-object relatedness. Since we have argued that development progresses in a given order, the course of progression defines the nature of transitional arrestation.

2. Transitional systems represent a conflict between one stage of development and the next most abstract stage; this may be viewed as a double approach-avoidant conflict.

3. Two general modes of resolution are open: to increase the approach toward one pole or to increase the compartmentalization between poles. The former may be accomplished either by (a) avoiding or neutralizing situations that lead to the more direct expression of one pole, or by (b) adopting compensatory resolutions that bolster the more direct expression of one of the conflicting poles. These mechanisms are not mutually exclusive; either or both may occur. In either case—avoidance or overcompensation—the result is to increase the positive quality of one pole, thus maximizing positive affect.

An increase in the degree of compartmentalization may be achieved by strengthening or intensifying the boundary between the two conflicting systems until it becomes almost impermeable so that the conflict is "blocked off." In this case each system becomes tied to certain situations that provide the setting (or stimuli) for its operation. The individual thus may fluctuate between aggressive oppositional behavior and dependent obsessive responses depending on the situation but without awareness or integration of these discriminations. The more equal the centrality of the two conflicting systems, the greater is the compartmentalization.

4. Increased pressures toward expression of the less directly expressed

pole increase conflict and lead to the accompanying occurrence of avoidant and/or overcompensatory resolutions.

5. Since transitional systems involve two competing systems, the resulting resolutions differ from those emanating from either one of the two nodal systems because they represent the tempering, modifying effects of both systems. Avoidance and overcompensation are therefore viewed as the net resultant of *two* systems in conflict.

6. Avoidant and overcompensatory resolutions take different forms at different transitional levels. Overcompensatory resolutions may involve symptoms such as overcautiousness and ritualistic behavior at level I and overassertiveness at level II. It is not always possible to distinguish between avoidant and overcompensatory resolutions since both may function simultaneously, for example, compulsions enhance the avoidance of negativistic tendencies while representing an overdriven tendency toward agreement with an absolute standard.

7. Transitional arrestation may involve either a greater directness of the more concrete pole, which we refer to as *direct* expression, or greater relative overtness of the more abstract and less well articulated system, which we refer to as *indirect* expression (see Table 23 on pp. 276–277).

From the principles just summarized we derive the system-specific effects of threat at each of the three transitional levels. Before proceeding, however, we may note that at more abstract levels we would expect (1) a greater tolerance of threat, (2) less generalization of threat effects, and (3) greater self-awareness.

Threat at each transitional level is considered in terms of both the direct and indirect poles of the transitional dimensions. We also relate the resolutions of extreme transitional conflict to traditional pathological syndromes and indicate the overall nature of each transitional dimension.

Threat within Level I Systems

Direct Level I Systems (Level I [A > B] Systems)

Maximum threat within the more direct level I (level I [A > B]) systems is defined as extreme pressure toward expressing negativistic or oppositional tendencies, or pressure toward abandoning an absolute criterion (Table 26). Threat in direct level I systems is produced by ambiguity, by situations producing hostility or distrust toward relevant power sources, or by circumstances requiring the subject to rebel against absolute standards. The "anti-social" or negativistic tendencies

TABLE 26

Extreme Functioning within Level I

	Pole A		Pole B
	Level I (A > B)	Maximum Conflict	Level I (B > A)
	Direct Neuroses		*Indirect Neuroses*
Pathological form:	Obsessive-compulsive neurosis		Negativism
Maximum threat:	Pressure toward expressing opposition		Pressure toward submission to external control
Avoidant form of conflict resolution:	Avoidance or neutralization of situations producing opposition to authoritative control, leading to modified pole B expression, for example, obsessive thoughts		Avoidance or neutralization of situations producing pressure toward accepting authoritative control, leading to modified pole A expression, for example, isolation
Overcompensatory form of conflict resolution:	Overdriven pursuit or bolstering of conditions producing modified pole A expression, for example, rigidity, compulsive rituals, overkindness, and submission to "safe" criteria		Overdriven pursuit or bolstering of conditions producing modified and relatively covert pole B expressions, for example, covert expression of negativism, contrariness, anorexia nervosa, and speech and intellectual inhibition

produced by such system-specific threat are in direct conflict with the absolutistic criteria and rigid standards of right and wrong that characterize system I. Pressures toward oppositional expression are threatening in *system* I functioning also, of course, but the effect of such pressures upon *level* I functioning is to intensify the conflict rather than to close the system, as occurs in *system* I.

As Table 26 indicates, level I resolutions involve the use of phobic reactions, isolation, and withdrawal to avoid situations that produce such oppositional tendencies. These reactions are supported by the subject's feelings that others may inflict harm (fear of the consequences of oppositional impulses) or that he may harm others (oppositional or hostile tendencies). Essentially there is a fear that he may harm others and also the fear of alienating or destroying external sources of support. The latter is probably a main basis for children's anxieties about their own oppositional and hostile impulses, that is, the fear that their rage will destroy those on whom they must depend.

Conflict in level I (A > B) systems may also be expressed indirectly through obsessional wishes and behavior. Overcompensative resolutions deal with pressures toward negativism in any of the following ways: excessive kindness and politeness, suppression of anger, acceptance of tradition orientation, excessive concern about achievement, and extreme orderliness in order to avoid doubt. This pattern of resolutions is quite similar to descriptions of obsessive-compulsive neurosis. The indirect oppositional tendencies represent the obsessive wishes whereas the more direct compensatory and avoidance resolutions are represented by the compulsive symptoms. White (1956) expresses the essential nature of this functioning as follows:

> Close scrutiny of the contents of obsessive symptoms shows that they can be classified under two headings: (1) Part of the symptoms give expression to aggressive and sexual impulses. Murderous hostility, destructiveness, dirtiness, and sexual urges in a crude and violent form reveal themselves in the content of obsessional thoughts. It is as if the suppressed *antisocial impulses* returned in this guise to plague the patient. (2) The rest of the symptoms give expression to *self-corrective tendencies.* Orderliness, rituals, cleanliness, propitiatory acts, self-imposed duties, and punishments all testify to the patient's need to counteract and set right his antisocial tendencies. Guilt feelings are his almost constant companions. Perhaps he reads in the paper about a murder that was committed many miles away. So strong is his guilt that he becomes obsessed with the idea that he committed the murder and deserves terrible punishment. The division of the symptoms into these two classes, *antisocial impulses* and *self-corrective tendencies* gives an immediate insight into the nature of the underlying conflict. Nowhere is the Freudian concept of the super-ego more applicable. The childish conception

of evil joins battle with the childish conception of righteousness and punishment (White, 1956, pp. 280–281).

Indirect Level I Systems: Level I (B > A) Systems

Maximum threat within indirect level I functioning occurs in situations that increase pressure to submit to external control (Table 26). Though this control has been associated with negative consequences, it nonetheless (at indirect level I) exerts sufficient influence to prevent the direct expression of oppositional tendencies, since absolute control and opposition to external control have never been integrated. However, the expression of negativistic tendencies comes to be more dominant for a person who has never articulated internal control and fears the punishing consequences of external control. For a child to integrate poles A and B, parental behavior must include a benign form of authority emphasizing love of plus parental tolerance for the expression of oppositional exploration in the child. Parental training that is to some extent punitive and unreliable promotes oppositional tendencies that are accompanied by fear to express them directly. Such training would be expected to both prevent the direct expression of system I resolutions and promote the indirect passive-aggressive resolutions of level I (B > A).

Resolutions at this level involve the avoidance of authoritative situations and an increase in the passive, covert expression of system II tendencies. External control may be avoided by isolation and withdrawal, but, if such avoidance is impossible, compensatory activity becomes more likely. As controlling pressures increase, highly modified (covert or indirect) negativism and contrariness occur. If controlling pressures increase further, the resolutions become even more indirect and symbolic, developing to the point where they provide what may be referred to as *immunity to control.* Examples of such extreme resolutions are inhibition of eating (anorexia nervosa), inhibition of speaking, and inhibition of effective performance (underachievement).

Levy (1955) has studied a large number of cases involving such negativistic syndromes, and he views reactions or symptoms such as failure at school, anorexia nervosa, parent-child antagonisms, obesity, speech problems, and "paralysis" as protective devices against compliance. Anorexia nervosa is much more common in females than males (Levy, 1955; Rose, 1943), and according to Rose the onset is particularly associated with the beginnings of certain developmental stages, for example, entrance into school, onset of puberty. If such a transitional problem occurred in early development we would expect it to recur in the early phases (at stage II) of other developmental sequences. Levy also observed the relationship between negativistic syndromes and tendencies toward compulsive behaviors, which, as we noted in Table 26, are currently viewed as pathological reactions at about the same level of abstractness. A case quoted from Levy (1955) exemplifies what we have referred to as level I covert neuroses.

> . . . a twelve-year-old boy was referred because he was making just passing marks in school in spite of a superior intelligence. In that regard he was unusually consistent, from the first grade to the seventh. In time, he told me that it took lots of planning to manage never to fail and yet never make more than a passing mark. On occasion his parents hired a tutor to help him with his work. The patient soon learned how to dissipate the tutor's efforts by getting him to talk about certain subjects that claimed his interest.
>
> His difficulty in accepting his studies began presumably as a revolt against his mother for sending him to nursery school. At that time he put up a feeble protest, though he felt it deeply as an act of abandonment. His revenge took the special form of negativism I have described—a revenge of withholding from his mother, whose own scholastic achievement had been high, the gift of good marks in school. The boy was otherwise a dutiful son. His negativism for school work was never quite overcome. It became a system from which he could never extricate himself. He was graduated from college and a professional school, though only with passing marks. Today he is married and holds an important executive position.
>
> At the time of referral there was evidence of rather compulsive neatness, ritualistic behavior and generally an overly organized personality. He had gone through a long period of resistance in infancy. His mother had the highest standards of ethical behavior and housekeeping (Levy, 1955, pp. 220–221).

Overall Characteristics of Extreme Level I Functioning

Although we have noted several differences between direct and indirect level I transitional systems, there are also similarities. Both involve a conflict between external control and opposition to external control. In both, this conflict is generally characterized by various forms of negativism, rigidity, withdrawal, orderliness, rituals, constriction, and compulsive behavior. When conflict produces extreme compartmentalization (multiple personality), functioning alternates between system I (being obedient and proper) and system II (rebelliousness and independence).

In comparing and contrasting these two degrees of directness, we may note finally that in certain respects the direct level I system is similar to stage I functioning whereas the indirect level I system is similar to stage II (see Table 14). Thus, indirect level I functioning, like stage II functioning, may involve a lack of concern regarding achievement, repression or the avoidance of failure, excessively high self-evaluation, and a failure to assimilate cultural standards. All of these resolutions contrast sharply with those expected in relation to stage I or from direct level I functioning.

Threat within Level II Systems

Direct Level II Systems: Level II (C > D) Systems

Maximum threat in direct level II transitional systems (level II [C > D] systems) is produced by situations that increase the pressure toward highly direct expression of dependency or the need for support (Table 27). In direct level II systems the conflict is experienced and dealt with through a modified system II conceptual structure. At this level the individual tends to seek and display independent, self-sufficient resolutions and to avoid dependent situations, behavior, and appearances. These differentiated tendencies are relative, not all-or-none. Dependency or helplessness is threatening because of a distrust of dependent relationships and from an expectation that dependent hopes will not be fulfilled. The subject has experienced in development what we have referred to as the "inevitable meeting of failure" in accelerated autonomous training, and will therefore fear the consequences of the exhibition of inadequacy. In this system situations that could indicate helplessness, inadequacy, or dependency are avoided or neutralized by resolutions such as rationalization; denial of failure; repression of failure (Rosenzweig and Sarason, 1942); maintenance of an inflated image of the self; the adoption and the assertive utilization of the total role of another person (in the place of dependency). And (in very extreme forms) the denial of dependent or sexual wishes can appear in the form of organ paralysis such as conversion symptoms. Overcompensative resolutions include the excessive portrayal of independence (pseudo-independence); outgoingness; "showing off," and other extraverted characteristics. In this sense optimism is to the direct level II systems as overdriven compulsive achievement is to the direct level I systems.

This symptom syndrome closely parallels the traditional description of hysteria or hysterical personality. The histories of hysterical patients include traits such as narrow interests, sex anomalies, low energy level, lack of interest in group membership ties, and extraversion (Eysenck, 1955). In keeping with the expected relationship between direct level II systems (hysteria) and stage II tendencies, Eysenck found no tendency for hysterical patients to be suggestible and, if anything, tended to be slightly countersuggestible. Other characteristics of hysteria sum-

TABLE 27

Extreme Functioning within Level II

	Pole C		Pole D
	Level II (C > D)	Maximum Conflict	Level II (D > C)
	Direct Neuroses		*Indirect Neuroses*
Pathological form:	Asocial hysterical syndrome		Overassertiveness; fear of isolation
Maximum threat:	Pressure toward expressing dependency and need for support		Pressure indicating potential loss of support
Avoidant form of conflict resolution:	Avoidance or neutralization of situations indicating need for support, or leading to exhibition of inadequacy or dependency; denial of inadequacy through hysterical type reactions. Denial concerns dependency wishes		Avoidance or neutralization of situations indicating non-support; denial of dependence
Overcompensatory form of conflict resolution:	Overdriven pursuit or bolstering of conditions producing modified pole C expressions. Depression, rationalization, pseudo-independence, extraversion, and denial of failure		Overdriven pursuit or bolstering of conditions increasing indirect pole D expression. Indirect forms of obtaining care and support; overdriven assertiveness to insure support; to "purchase" protection

marized by White (1956) include a concern about acceptance, tendencies toward repression, impulsiveness, tendencies to dramatize, readiness to identify (diffuseness of role and taking over of the total role of another), and immaturity. White lists dependency, love, and sex as the critical issues in the hysteric's life and neurosis. Although we have not emphasized it, this view is consistent with the almost universal clinical findings that hysterics show specific conflicts over sexual behavior. These conflicts (which are similar to the oedipal-conflict situation) relate back to inadequately integrated concepts for dealing with dependence. Dependency wishes originally toward the parents and later toward others, particularly when they take the form of sexual wishes, are highly threat provoking. Finally, Erikson (1950) places the predisposition to hysteria in the same transitional stage of development that our analysis suggests, and concludes:

> In adults, where once hysteria was the usual form of pathological regression in this area, a plunge into psychosomatic disease is now common. I think that this direct attack on the organism itself can be attributed to a weakness in underlying trust which makes autonomy bothersome and facilitates a partial regression to the stage of weak homeostasis. It is as if the culture had made a man over-advertize himself and sincerely identify with his own advertisement, while he knew all along that his mother never believed in it (Erikson, 1950, p. 226).

Indirect Level II Systems: Level II (D > C) Systems

Maximum conflict and threat within indirect level II (D > C) systems occur in situations that indicate a high potentiality for the loss of support or care (Table 27). Although the conflict is between self-sufficiency versus dependency as was true in the more direct systems, in indirect systems the need to be cared for is more central. Increasing anxiety is aroused by situations that induce feelings of failure, that are interpreted either as rejection or as a limitation on the subject's capacity to "purchase" dependency. This greater anxiety leads to the more extreme forms of resolution.

Compensatory resolutions here take the form of overdriven activity directed toward eventual dependency satisfaction. The subject's aim is to insure being cared for and evaluated positively, as he was by his parents in their undifferentiated permissive training practices. Because of the modulating effects of prior dependency conflicts (system II) behavior at this level (indirect level II) and in system II does not involve the direct seeking of support. Though support is the most central goal it is sought in indirect and distorted ways. Under high degrees of threat these may include hypochondriasis and overdriven striving ("assertive" or "competitive" achievement) in which the underlying aim is to gain supportive responses from others. Other typical indirect resolutions include the "jolly good fellow" who seeks support by assertive sociality, the clown, and the Arthur Miller salesman, whose assertive—even rapacious—aggressiveness marks a desperate need for security, protection, and approval.

Unlike the more non-conflicting stage III systems, such transitional functioning is not dependent in a "personal" sense. The empathic or mutual qualities of system III are relatively lacking in indirect level II functioning; the market analogy approach to interpersonal relations is more appropriate for these transitional systems.[1] Thus, dependency is experienced at this level more in terms of a commodity that can be purchased through assertive achievement. Such individuals are overly anxious to portray themselves as successful and to demand attention, interest, and admiration.

This symptom complex has not been as explicitly classified in traditional psychopathological categories. However, many investigators have observed the expected relationship between hypochondriasis and concern about group membership (Erikson, 1950, Eysenck, 1955). Though indirect, there is evidence to suggest a relationship between overdriven, competitive activity in indirect level II systems and the incidence of peptic ulcer. Alexander (1934) reported that although peptic ulcer patients may be outwardly competitive and striving, they are nonetheless strongly motivated toward dependency and support. According to Alexander, a conditioned association is established between dependency longings and acid secretions in the stomach during early feeding experiences. Consequently, when dependent longings become intense so that most situations are experienced as non-gratifying, increasing acidity would be expected. To the extent that dependency longings and increasing acidity are related, we can expect an association between indirect level II transitional systems and peptic ulcer because these individuals are more highly sensitized toward such dependency longings.

Overall Characteristics of Extreme Level II Functioning

Both direct and indirect systems on the level II transitional dimension are characterized by some degree of conflict between independent self-sufficiency and the need for care and support. At a slightly higher level of generality, the resolutions associated with direct and indirect level II expression are similar in that both involve a concern about

[1] Fromm's "marketing orientation" referred to in Chapter 7 seems even more applicable to indirect level II functioning than to arrested system III functioning.

relationships and group membership, the consequent denial of inadequacy, and avoidance of exhibiting such inadequacy.

In the direct systems, dependent relationships have been unsatisfying or painful, and the individual is motivated to rely on independent behavior, avoiding the threat of dependency. Though there may be underlying (repressed) longings for dependency, these are too threatening for expression and have been largely abandoned. In indirect systems, the dependency motivation is stronger and is expressed, but in disguised form. The disguise has developed from experiences that associated dependency rewards (for example, parental approval) with achievement or the independent-appearing behavior. We would expect a history of sudden shift from permissive training to parental or societal emphasis on school achievement in the backgrounds of many persons whose functioning typically engages indirect level II systems. If tendencies to dependence and independence are both highly central, the most likely resolution is that of compartmentalization. In contrast to level I, compartmentalization within the level II transitional dimension will involve the denial and repression of experiences evaluated as exhibiting inadequacy. Dissociated states appear to be typical of extreme level II compartmentalization as the following case quoted by White (1956) from a report by Geleerd, Hacker, Rapaport (1945) illustrates:

> A man of twenty-nine had developed a high ideal of independence and manliness. He had been induced, however, to take work in his father-in-law's business, where he found himself dissatisfied and poorly paid. He was sometimes unable to meet family expenses and was greatly humiliated to be extricated by his father-in-law on these occasions. One day, again in difficulties, he drove with his family to the town where his father-in-law lived, but could not bring himself to ask for the needed loan and turned the car homeward. He became so preoccupied with the thought of finding a new job and making money, that by the time he reached home he no longer knew who he was nor recognized his wife and children in the car. Taken to the hospital, he spoke only of his new job. He falsified reality to the extent of interpreting everything in the hospital as though it were the operation of a business firm. Two days later he emerged spontaneously into his normal state, not remembering the amnesic episode. Shortly afterward he recalled the episode, including the suicidal despair that had filled him at the thought of asking his father-in-law for more help (White, 1956, p. 289).

Similarities between Extreme Resolutions in Level I and II Transitional Systems

Extreme resolutions emerging from indirect ($B > A$) level I and direct ($C > D$) level II transitional systems are similar in that both involve system II tendencies. However, the similarity is highly generic because the system II concepts are in conflict with different conceptual structures at the two levels (either system I or system III), so that the conflict is expressed differently in each case. There is also a less obvious and more generic similarity between direct (A > B) level I transitional systems and indirect (D > C) level II transitional systems, since both these cases involve threat from increasing negativistic or system II pressures.

Direct level I and indirect level II transitional systems both represent different forms of overdriven achievement. At level I this overdriven characteristic is associated with (1) orderliness and structure, (2) avoidance of transgressing authority and tradition, and (3) indirect forms of hostility, partially expressed by indirectly striving to be independent of others. At level II overdriven achievement is associated with (1) the need for support, (2) the avoidance of situations that would place the subject in an unfavorable light, and (3) assertive and competitive (as opposed to compulsive, safe, and ritualistic) achievement. Achievement generated by level II concepts is more often directed toward more lucrative fields where assertiveness is rewarded, and where the returns can insure the purchase of care and admiration. Level I achievement is less assertive, more cautious, more traditionally conventional, and more typical of the clichés relating to accountants and compulsive methodologists.

It is interesting that both classes of systems have been proposed as establishing a psychological link in the development of peptic ulcer. Alexander's (1934) hypothesis rests on indirect level II transitional system whereas others (Mittelman, Wolf, and Scharf, 1942; Szasz, Levin, Kirsner, and Palmer, 1947) stress the role of conflict involving hostility, resentment, and anger, which is more relevant to direct level I transitional systems. At the more generic level of conflict with system II tendencies, these two hypotheses may be almost equivalent.

Threat within Level III

Direct Level III Systems: Level III (E > F) Systems

In level III transitional systems the conflict is between autonomy and maintaining the support and mutuality of others. Level III (E > F) systems are characterized by the more direct expression of the need for mutuality and support and the more indirect expression of autonomy. Any situation evaluated as increasing pressures toward autonomous behavior is maximally threatening (see Table 28). Such situations could include (1) new situations; (2) circumstances in which being autonomous is the only means of avoiding some unpleasant outcome

TABLE 28

Extreme Functioning within Level III

	Pole E		Pole F
	Level III (E > F)	Maximum Conflict	Level III (F > E)
	Direct Neuroses		*Indirect Neuroses*
Pathological form:	Anxiety states		Pseudo-adequacy feelings
Maximum threat:	Pressure toward expressing autonomy and separation		Pressure toward expressing dependency or the need for support
Avoidant form of conflict resolution:	Avoidance or neutralization of situations in which autonomous and independent actions required, or situations that involve little support		Avoidance or neutralization of situations producing pressures toward help-seeking or reliance upon others, or of situations that cannot be handled autonomously
Overcompensatory form of conflict resolution:	Overdriven pursuit or bolstering of conditions producing modified pole E expressions. Overstriving to keep self positive in eyes of others and to avoid situations requiring autonomy		Overdriven pursuit or bolstering of conditions producing modified pole F expressions. Avoidance of conditions that would demand support and seeking highly autonomous situations

(changing jobs because of a matter of principle); and (3) other situations perceived as demanding a degree of autonomy that is beyond the subject's own estimation of confidence.

Resolutions involve the avoidance of conditions that demand excessive autonomy and overdriven, but modified, system III expressions such as exaggerated mutuality and self-blame. Avoidant reactions may include phobic-like reactions or overgeneralized fear. Overdriven tendencies emanating from direct level III functioning may involve reactions that give the appearance of autonomy (indirect expression of stage IV systems) but are directed toward avoiding autonomy through gaining social approval. Examples of these resolutions might involve overstriving, setting fairly high goals to insure shared responsibility, and enlisting the support of others in reaching the goals. Within level III transitional systems, however, the nature of avoidant and overcompensatory reaction, even in extreme functioning, is not so defensive as in levels I and II extreme functioning. The modifying effects of increased abstractness and tolerance of threat are described below.

Indirect Level III Systems: Level III ($F > E$) Systems

Threat to indirect level III functioning involves any situation that increases pressures toward seeking support or relying upon others. Resolutions include (1) the avoidance of situations that do not permit autonomous functioning, (2) lowered goals, and (3) an autonomous outlook modified by the less central tendencies toward mutuality. At this level mutuality and autonomy are in conflict, with the autonomous tendencies more dominant and with mutuality and dependence on others avoided. Individuals at this level may choose goals that are achievable through independent efforts, without the help of others.

Overall Characteristics of Extreme Level III Functioning

The most central characteristic of extreme level III functioning is the direct expression of anxiety.

The more abstract the system the greater is the tolerance for threat so that level III transitional systems should function with considerable stress tolerance. Therefore, even extreme level III functioning should be less defensive (less warding off of refutation) and, under conditions of threat, should experience more acute anxiety. The greater the tolerance for threat, the greater is the capacity to profit from the experience. In fact, it is just such capacity to tolerate at least some refutation that provides the basis for progressive development to occur. The avoidance of threat, although increasing closedness to conditions that lead to threat, is associated with some form of arrestation. Symptom-formation signifies increasing degrees of closedness to development. Ausubel (1952) makes the same point as follows:

> The ability to admit a large amount of neurotic anxiety affect to consciousness and to manage it successfully—either through intelligent resignation (learning to live with it), creating a propitious environment, or constructively lowering ego aspiration level and increasing intrinsic self-esteem—is very important in avoiding disabling psychological or psychosomatic defenses against anxiety. It is a well established clinical fact that the greater an individual's tolerance for conscious anxiety, the less likely he is to fall prey to compulsions, obsessions, phobias, hysteria, hypochondriasis or psychosomatic syndromes such as neurocirculatory asthenia or peptic ulcer. All of these latter methods of anxiety-reduction are indicative of low tolerance for anxiety and of failure in controlling it through more constructive methods (Ausubel, 1952, p. 313).

Consequently, we would associate the effects of threat within level III transitional systems with the traditional description of anxiety states. Further, we expect a higher prevalence and more severe states of anxiety to occur within the more direct level III transitional systems. The nature of anxiety at this level of functioning is illustrated by White (1956) as follows:

> Anxiety attacks can be considered to represent a partial failure of adequate defenses. Even in the face of highly disquieting fear, the patient does not produce defenses sufficient to bind and suppress his fear. . . . These take a less sweeping form: the patient is panic-stricken but not disintegrated; from time to time he is flooded by terror, but he struggles with it, brings it somehow under his control, resumes his daily life until another attack breaks through . . . (White, 1956, pp. 271–272).

When compartmentalization in this system occurs, the conflicting poles of autonomy and mutuality become more independent and alternate as a function of situational change. However, the compartmentalized structures in level III functioning are much less categorical or absolute than the massive categorization that occurs in the more concrete systems such as the obsessive-compulsive neuroses.

General Considerations

Adaptive Functions of Anxiety and Defense

Conflict resolutions are of two general types, each of which is "adaptive." A resolution that produces greater closedness is adaptive within the range of a particular system (system-specific functioning) but is maladaptive from the broader viewpoint of progressive development.

Put another way, "successful" warding off potential refutation may decrease the likelihood of progression. As we have just noted in the previous section, resolutions at more abstract levels are less likely to be defensive. At these levels, the resolutions are less likely to involve an immediate "warding off" since the tolerance for threat is greater. Threat and its associated conflicts are resolved by progressively more abstract integrations, and these resolutions are likely to be adaptive in a system-specific sense as well as in terms of potential for progression.

Following Freud, many authors have stressed the importance of distinguishing between the primary and secondary gain derived by a particular symptom. Primary gain generally refers to the degree of anxiety reduction provided by the symptom, whereas secondary gain refers to the environmental effect or "social gain" accruing from the symptom. We would consider primary gain as similar to functional adequacy of a resolution within the framework of whatever conceptual system is operating, or in terms of what we described as "successful" or "adaptive." Thus in order to estimate the degree of primary gain we would need to know the nature of the conceptual system underlying the symptom.

Since secondary gain involves social effects, we would expect symptoms related to stage III functioning (including level II transition) to be highest in secondary gain. In system III the system-specific aim is to maintain favorable interpersonal relations so that reactions such as depression, hysteria, and hypochondriasis quite obviously "pull" considerable secondary gain. In systems other than system III, particularly in system II, a resolution may accrue primary gain but no secondary gain; in system III, secondary and primary gain are more synonomous.

Relationship between Various Forms of Pathology

Which pathologies are similar? Is it possible for one form of pathology to develop into some other form of pathology? If so, what direction will the change take? In terms of our analysis, the most generic criterion for determining similarity in personality organization or pathology is the abstract-concrete dimension. For example, obsessive-compulsive neurosis would be considered more similar to schizophrenia than would negativism. Table 24 indicates the relationship of various forms of pathology to the concrete-abstract dimension, and therefore indicates those forms which would be most similar. On the basis of the order in Table 24 we would expect the following:

1. That borderline cases should occur more frequently between ad-

jacent forms of pathology, for example, a greater prevalence of borderline cases between anti-social syndromes and hysteria than between schizophrenia and hysteria.

2. That when one pathology changes to a different form, the second form will be one that is immediately adjacent on the concrete-abstract dimension. Stated generally, "syndrome choice," including a second or third "choice," is determined in part by the position of syndromes on the concrete-abstract dimension.

3. An alternate and equally testable hypothesis is that increases in pathology will be toward the more extreme resolutions associated with threat to a more concrete version of the same orientation, such as dependency. For example, if the avoidant and overcompensative resolutions at level III ($F > E$) prove inadequate, perhaps the shift in pathology may be first to level II ($C > D$) and if that doesn't work to level I ($B > A$).

4. That similarity based on symptoms or behavior may be misleading. For example, diagnosis based only on overt behavior may not distinguish between the nature of dependency strivings within system I and system III although drawing a sharp distinction between obsessive-compulsive symptoms and negativistic reactions, which, according to the present view, are quite similar.

Psychosis, Neurosis, and Normality

In the present view, psychosis is defined as an extremely closed form of system functioning that may occur at any one of the three nodal stages. Thus, schizophrenic reactions, psychopathic reactions, and depressive reactions are similar in at least one respect: all show inflexible overgeneralized interpretation or use of a single interpretative orientation. Although the content of interpretation varies between the three forms of psychosis, the inflexibility of structure is similar. We realize that to classify psychopathic reactions as psychotic is somewhat unusual although some investigators have noted the similarity (Henderson, 1939; Cleckley, 1950). The three forms of psychotic reaction do differ not only in the content of interpretation but also in the degree of closedness (or inflexibility) of the system. On the basis of the concrete-abstract hierarchy we view depressive reactions as less inflexible and less overgeneralized (that is, less loss of reality contact) than schizophrenic reactions.

In the present view, neurosis is defined as an extremely conflicting form of system functioning that may occur at any one of the three transitional levels. Obsessive-compulsive reactions, hysterical reactions, and anxiety reactions are similar in at least two respects: presence of conflicting tendencies and some degree of compartmentalization. Also, these three neurotic reactions are likely to involve much vacillation (especially when the conflicting tendencies are about equally central). They differ, however, in the degree of avoidant and/or overcompensatory maneuvers. Since the incidence of avoidance is inversely related to abstractness, anxiety reactions show less avoidance than obsessive-compulsive reactions. The more intense the transitional conflict at any level, the less likely that threat will result in extreme closedness (psychosis) because of the counterbalancing effects of the two semi-compartmentalized and conflicting system of concepts.

"Normality" may be viewed either normatively or qualitatively. The normative definition involves the establishment of arbitrary standards or rating scales in order to estimate the degree to which an individual's behavior falls within (normal) or without (neurotic or psychotic) these limits. According to this normative definition, individuals arrested at any point in development (for example, stage I, level I) may be viewed as "normal." However, if the system becomes increasingly closed or conflicting, the individual's behavior would be described as more abnormal (from the normative view). Although closedness of the more concrete systems would generally be rated more abnormal in our culture, in some of the more primitive cultures this may not always be true.

The qualitative definition of normality is based on the level of abstractness of functioning and in this sense the degree of normality is equivalent to what we would call the level of adjustment, stress tolerance, or the abstractness of the conceptual system. "Normality," defined qualitatively, characterizes what we would strive to produce in education and development, although it is by no means the goal of many training practices in current institutions or societies.

Normality is a relative matter by this definition, too, with ultimate or ideal normality represented by system IV functioning. But in the course of child development, for example, less abstract systems may constitute optimal or maximal functioning. System IV (ultimate normality) is an achievement that rests on the successful integration of societal pressures (which may themselves be conflicting) and the expression of individual autonomy. At this ideal stage the individual functions as a creative, contributing member of society-at-large, being neither bound by nor in conflict with the major pressures we have been discussing in this chapter.

Personality Organization and Neurotic Reactions

Neurotic reactions are presently viewed in terms of three complex dimensions, each leading to the evolvement of different forms of neurosis under different training conditions. Some approaches to the development of neurosis suggest a single set of antecedent conditions. For example, Dollard and Miller (1950) stress the importance of parental and environmental pressure or control in producing an excessively strong conscience, whereas Mowrer (1950) stresses a set of conditions that are almost opposite to those proposed by Dollard and Miller as underlying the development of neurosis. For Mowrer, neurosis is seen as developing from a *lack* of learning or control (as opposed to an excess), resulting in a weak conscience. Eysenck (1955) views these positions in oversimplified Freudian terms as follows: Dollard and Miller are said to maintain that superego plus ego is greater than id in neurosis, whereas Mowrer is said to view neurosis in terms of id plus ego being greater than superego. In our terms, Dollard and Miller have emphasized the development of system I tendencies and level I transitional neurosis whereas Mowrer has placed emphasis upon the conditions underlying arrestation at stage II and level II transitional neurosis. Viewed in this fashion, the apparent contradiction disappears.

In Eysenck's (1955) excellent analysis of this problem, he identifies Mowrer's position with the "hysteria" pole of Eysenck's extraversion-introversion dimension of personality and Miller and Dollard's analysis with the "disthymic" pole. The "hysteria" pole, exemplified by extraversion, degraded work history, and sex anomalies, is characteristic of active system II functioning, but the "disthymic" pole includes anxiety, depression, and obsessional characteristics. The present dimensional structure and its method of derivation are quite different from Eysenck's, which was developed by factor analysis of psychiatric ratings and other standard measures. We have proceeded on the basis of theory, observation, and experimentation, viewing factorial and other statistical approaches as means for testing the derived hypotheses.

"Normality" and Mental Health

As a final point, we would emphasize one of the direct implications of this chapter: the importance and method of utilizing "normal" functioning in order to arrive at a better understanding of malfunctioning. When defined from a normative point of view, we would expect little difference, for example, between the case histories of "normal" system I individuals and abnormal system I individuals (schizoid, withdrawn persons).

The difference between "normal" and "abnormal" functioning at any particular stage or level rests upon factors that produce what are initially *relatively small* increases in closedness or conflict but which later may produce a "snowball effect." A recent study by Schofield and Balian (1959) attests to the general similarity in case history records of schizophrenic and normal individuals drawn from populations similar in that both were referred to the hospital for diagnosis and treatment and were matched on age, sex, and marital status. We would assume even greater similarity if both groups had been functioning within the conceptual limits of system I.

Since pathological reactions are viewed in terms of overgeneralized inflexibility, the capacity for flexible adaptation is the crucial factor for distinguishing normal from pathological functioning within any arrested stage or level. The distinction is, of course, a matter of degree. To study the more "normal" individuals in each system in order to determine why the system does not become increasingly closed or conflicted is as important as studying the more closed forms of functioning, since the former provides the possibility of learning about the manner in which some individuals become "immunized" against increasing closedness. To conduct such investigations would require the selection of individuals on the basis of differences in degrees of closedness of the same system. Having selected subjects in this way, it should be possible to investigate the circumstances underlying the increased sensitivity and closedness of certain individuals compared to others whose functioning did not become more inflexible.

An alternative plan would be to select individuals functioning within the same system and at the same degree of closedness, subjecting them to different experimental conditions aimed at investigating how individuals with similar conceptual structures differ in terms of coping with potential refutation. Perhaps the most important methodological implication of these suggestions is to emphasize the importance of selecting a control group that is equivalent to the experimental group on the basis of conceptual structure. As we implied earlier, if the control population is selected on the basis of arbitrary matching, demographic variables, or on a "random" basis little useful information regarding adaptive and maladaptive functioning will be obtained.

The implications of the present viewpoint for mental health as well as for modification procedures involved in education, psychological therapy, and development are now considered in Chapter 10.

10 Modification of Conceptual Systems: Education and Psychological Therapy

The purpose of this final chapter is to describe the implications of our viewpoint for conceptual modification. We have described earlier in a context of "natural" change the conditions necessary for change or progression to occur: (1) the conceptual structure must be open to progression and (2) the training condition being experienced must provide the opportunity for differentiation and integration of new dimensions. Such knowledge of how structural development occurs should serve as the basis for how structural change can be accomplished. Therefore, we shall use the knowledge about natural change (progressive development and arrestation) to determine procedures for *induced* change (education, psychological therapy, environmental programming).

Our present purpose is to state several implications of our viewpoint for modification at a general level and to illustrate these implications by a few specific educational and therapeutic procedures currently in use. One of the most critical ultimate criteria by which a psychological theory is evaluated is its potential for producing change. The following statements represent our proposals in this direction. We feel that one of the best indications of the value of the present viewpoint will be the degree to which these proposals generate investigations and programs that will lead to a better understanding of the process of and procedures for producing change.

The General Aim of Modification Is to Produce More Abstract Conceptual Structure

As we have stated repeatedly, in earlier chapters, we believe that abstract conceptual structure and its associated creativity, stress tolerance, and flexibility is a desirable, adaptive, valuable state. The value of abstract structure is of course relative to the goals of creativity, stress tolerance, and other activities associated with system IV structure. We reaffirm this value judgment by stating that the long-term aim of every modification procedure, whether it is psychotherapy, education, milieu therapy, or whatever, should be *to produce structural change toward more abstract conceptual structure.*

Progression to a more abstract conceptual structure occurs through the processes of differentiation and integration. At any level of abstractness, therefore, the potential for progression is determined largely by the person's capacity for making new differentiations required for progression and his capacity for integrating these differentiated parts. We have used the term, *openness to progression,*[1] to describe the complex structural organization required in order for the saccadic leaps of progressive development to occur. Throughout this chapter we continue to use degree of openness to progression, along with degree of abstractness, as the two major structural properties to be considered in modification.

However, as we have noted earlier, openness to progression is a very general characteristic, which may be viewed as a composite of several interrelated structural properties.[2] We briefly recapitulate these properties in relation to their role in progression; in order for progression to occur, these three structural requirements must be met.

1. *Potential to Articulate New Differentiations*

The degree of articulation of a concept may be described by two closely similar properties, *clarity-ambiguity* or *directness-indirectness* of expression. Thus, a well-articulated concept is high in clarity and direct expression. Structural organization that is poorly articulated (ambiguous or indirect) may result from many quite differing circumstances: lack of experience, "ignorance," or extreme threat. As we shall discuss later, these differences must be considered in planning modification procedures. For now we may simply note that the poles of the more concrete stage must be articulated and differentiated before pro-

[1] Openness may also describe among other things a temporary state of receptivity toward a particular object; however, we are here concerned with relatively pervasive openness of structure toward poles at current stage of abstractness and next higher stage of abstractness.

[2] Openness, as employed here, refers to an intra-stage condition. One could speak as well of the overall openness of the total self-system, in which case the criteria for openness and abstractness would be the same. In the present case, however, variation in openness-closedness is meant to refer to a state within a given range or stage of concreteness-abstractness.

gression can occur. Conceptual clarity and direct expression are thus prerequisites for progression.

2. *Potential to Synthesize Parts*

The potential for integrating differentiated parts is indicated by the variation in *compartmentalization-interrelatedness.* Thus, a system of concepts that is either already integrated or that may be synthesized into more abstract structure is considered *interrelated.* Conversely, the greater the compartmentalization, the less is the likelihood of progression. Once the poles have been articulated and differentiated, these are synthesized and related to new, more abstract structures. Thus, a second prerequisite for progression is conceptual interrelatedness.

3. *Potential for Occurrence of Centrality with Minimum of Closedness*

Centrality-peripherality describes the intensity of affect associated with changing a particular structure. Resistance to change is very slight or non-existent in the most peripheral structure, whereas resistance is very great in the most central structure. Stated in terms of progression potential, the extremely peripheral structure is unlikely to facilitate progression because of apathy, whereas the extremely central structure is likely to prohibit progression because of resistance to change. Thus, we regard an *optimal level of centrality* to be the third prerequisite for progression.

We conclude this recapitulation by observing that the structural state, openness to progression, may be described more specifically as (1) high in clarity and (2) interrelatedness with (3) an optimal level of centrality; all three requirements must be met in order for progression to occur. Thus, to maintain openness to progression, the person should be permitted to explore, without the consequences of his explorations being unduly serious, and permitted to learn new ways of manipulating his environment. Put in terms of child development, the environment should be such that it is not too costly for the child to develop. Although some form of informational interdependent training, which permits maximum exploration with a minimum penalty, is generally conducive to progression, the specific short-term goals and procedures for accomplishing them must be planned in relation to the existing conceptual structure of the person, as we describe in the next section.

Current Conceptual Structure Determines Initial Modification Goals

The general aim of inducing more abstract structure may be stated more specifically as follows, "How can we organize the environment in such a way to permit the maximum development for this person at this time?" Given the aim of inducing more abstract structure, we must therefore know the existing conceptual structure of the person before setting initial goals because persons varying in conceptual structure will react very differently to the same environmental conditions. Those conditions that produce progression for persons at one level may produce quite a different effect for persons at another level. For example, protective interdependent training leads to progression for persons at stage II (if structure is open), but to arrestation for persons at stage III. The differential effects of the same environmental condition upon persons differing in degree of abstractness is illustrated by the following table taken from Maxwell Jones' (1953) description of the effectiveness of the "Therapeutic Community" program. The milieu therapy provided may be considered a form of protective interdependent training. The diagnostic groups have been ordered in increasing degree of abstractness. With the exception of the obsessional group (which contained only two persons) the mean adjustment scores increase as the groups approach stage III structure (depressive group), thus illustrating the differential consequence of the same environment at different levels of abstractness.[1]

TABLE 29

Mean Adjustment Scores of Various Diagnostic Groups after Therapeutic Community Program

Diagnostic group	*N*	Mean adjustment score
Schizoid character–schizophrenia	11	5.5
Obsessional features predominant	2	9.5
Inadequate psychopath	23	6.8
Aggressive psychopath	5	7.6
Hysterical features predominant	21	9.2
Predominantly depressive state	9	11.0
Anxiety features predominant	21	9.8

(From Jones, 1953, p. 136)

[1] One could argue that the results in Table 29 indicate simply that the more

Progression occurs through stages in a given order, and the person cannot leap immediately from the concrete structure of system I to the abstract structure of system IV without making the intervening differentiations and integrations that occur at the second and third stages. Therefore, in planning any modification program it is essential to know the degree of abstractness of the person.

Two persons may be similar in abstractness of structure, but they react to the same environmental condition quite differently because of differences in openness. For example, let us suppose that a person whose system III structure is closed to progression and a person whose system III structure is open to progression are both exposed to informational interdependent training. This condition will have diametrically opposite effects in that it represents intense threat for the person with closed structure whereas it will be likely to induce progression for the person with open structure. As we noted in the last section, progression can never occur unless the structure is sufficiently open to progression. Therefore, in planning any modification program we must also know the degree of openness to progression and how to increase it when necessary.

Before proceeding, one implication of these notions is in order. In the present view, the potential effectiveness or utility of a modification procedure can be evaluated *only in relation to a person with specified conceptual structure.* The "issues" of "which is better—Directive or non-directive therapy? Group or individual therapy? Foster home placement or institutionalization? Permissive versus structured educational practices?"—all disregard the structure of the person toward whom the modification is directed. The issue is not one of absolute superiority, but rather of the appropriateness of the modification effort for permitting maximum development of the particular person at a particular time. In order to choose what modification is appropriate, the conceptual structure must be simultaneously placed on the two dimensions into one of the categories in Table 30.

Table 30 summarizes the system of diagnosis or assessment that we propose as maximally relevant for modification. Although for certain purposes, it may be necessary to make finer distinctions such as those suggested in Chapter 6 (for example, level I [A $>$ B], direct expression in stage II), these distinctions are simply refinements of the two dimensions in Table 30. We now consider briefly some illustrative procedures for assessing degree of abstractness and degree of closedness.

abstract the structure the better is the prognosis, regardless of the training condition. More carefully specified investigation in which persons varying in degree of abstractness are placed in a "therapeutic environment" of a reliable unilateral nature is required before these two possibilities can be distinguished.

Assessment of Degree of Abstractness

Variations on the concrete-abstract dimension may be viewed in terms of both cognitive, structural features and in terms of dynamic, functional features. As we have stated repeatedly, the present notion of a conceptual system encompasses both structural attributes, such as degree of differentiation and integration and motivational attributes, such as mode of handling dependency relationships. Since the assessment of degree of abstractness is theoretically identical to the assessment of dispositional determinants, the procedures and examples described in Chapter 8 (pp. 257–259) provide the basis for assessing variation on this dimension. The investigator may tap structural characteristics by noting the capacity to make differentiations, flexibility in use of new interpretations of the same stimuli, and the number of dimensions that the person can employ. Abstract structure is characterized by greater differentiation, greater flexibility of interpretation, and a greater number of conceptual dimensions. Or the investigator may proceed by tapping more dynamic characteristics. Abstract functioning is presumably characterized by greater stress tolerance, greater creativity, more internal conception of causality, less absolutistic handling of external

TABLE 30

Patterns of Conceptual Structure Relevant for Modification

		Open to progression	Closed to progression
Concrete	Stage I		
	Level I		
	Stage II		
	Level II		
	Stage III		
	Level III		
Abstract	Stage IV		

control, and a more interdependent handling of dependency problems than is concrete functioning.

Ideally, the assessment of degree of abstractness occurs through a convergence of structural and dynamic referents. Thus, a particular individual might manifest difficulty both in making new differentiations and in interpreting new stimuli from a structural standpoint, and might manifest an external approach to causality, an oppositional mode of handling dependency, and a rather low level of stress tolerance. Through such a multimeasure approach, the investigator might infer from this convergence of referents that the person's conceptual structure could be placed at system II in terms of Table 30.

The recent work of Pinard (1959) in devising objective measures for some of the stages suggested by Piaget is presently relevant as the following quotation indicates:

> . . . The search for stages requires a meticulous evaluation of all test protocoles, and a classification of the various types of possible responses. This scoring implies a global assessment of the protocoles. Contrarily to what happens in most usual tests, every response, whether right or wrong, is studied and interpreted. As a matter of fact, the wrong responses are the most significant and throw more light on the real level of the child's explanations (Pinard, 1959, pp. 6–7).

In present terms the "wrong responses" may also provide indicators of the degree of abstractness. In practice the assessment of degree of abstractness will frequently proceed simultaneously with the assessment of degree of openness. However, it is helpful to consider them separately in terms of the rationale underlying each dimension.

Assessment of Openness to Progression

The more closed the structure, the more threatening will be those conditions to be synthesized at the next level of abstractness, and the more the person will rely on single interpretations emanating from the presently closed system. Thus, we must always consider openness-closedness in relation to a point on the abstractness dimension. We must specify openness to what. If we know that a person is at stage II on the abstract dimension then we need to know the degree of openness to mutuality and support since these are the relevant areas at stage III. The assessment task is to test the limits of threat, so to speak, in order to estimate how difficult it will be to induce progression.

One general procedure for assessing openness is to attempt to induce progression "in miniature." Hypnotic procedures or role-playing techniques may be employed to determine whether the person can take on provisionally the dimensions required for progression. Presumably if the person is unable to deal with progression-relevant stimuli under hypnosis or during role-playing, it would be reasonable to infer closed structure.

Although we have indicated only two points on the open-closed dimension in Table 30, it should be made clear that there is considerable variation in the degree of closedness to progression, ranging from the case of the child who is closed while he is articulating the more concrete system to the case of the psychotic person who is so excessively closed that he inflexibly interprets all events in exaggerated system-specific terms. For some purposes, it may be quite important to make finer distinctions in degree of closedness, but for present purposes we will consider broad characteristics of closedness since the general procedures for inducing openness are similar. The characteristic of inflexibility of interpretation may be used to infer excessive closedness by means of a technique such as asking the person to interpret controlled, system-specific stimuli in several ways; inability to produce alternative interpretations indicates inflexibility, hence closedness.

Another avenue of approach in assessing degree of openness is through the history of the person. We have described in detail (especially in Chapters 5 and 9) those conditions producing closedness at various levels of abstractness. The occurrence of family conditions thought to be associated with system-specific closedness may provide an indicator of closed structure (however, it should also be supported by contemporaneous indicators).

One component of openness is directness of expression, which is indicated by one or more of the following characteristics: (1) less expression in fantasy and less displacement, (2) more exploration, (3) less dependency upon environment, and (4) more capacity to delay reward. One technique for assessment of expressive directness (and hence, openness to progression) is to compare responses to so-called direct and indirect personality measures. A direct approach is to ask the subject, "How do you interpret this (real or hypothetical) situation?" A more indirect approach is to ask S how someone else would interpret the situation; or one can specifically request fantasy responses (indirect) as in the Thematic Apperception Test. An example of this direct-indirect comparative approach is the work of Leary (1957) which employed both direct and fantasy measures of dominance and submission (that is, openness within system I in our terms).

Having considered the basis for placing the conceptual structure of a person into one of the categories in Table 30 let us now consider how such placement determines the next step. Specifically, how does the current structure determine the short-term goals of modification? Two general principles govern this determination.

1. *If structure is closed, the initial goal is to induce openness.*

This first principle is simply the corollary of the by-now-familiar principle that progression cannot occur unless the system is open.

2. *If structure is open, the goal is to induce progression to next abstract stage.*

These two principles are represented diagrammatically in Table 31 so that the interrelationship between assessment of structure and initial goal is made explicit. The arrows indicate the initial goal.

Note that in using Table 31 it is always necessary to know both degree of abstractness and degree of openness. One needs to know the degree of abstractness even if the system is closed because the procedures for inducing openness vary at differing levels of abstractness. Put another way, as we describe in the next section, procedures for inducing openness are system-specific.

In the present section we are considering initial, short-term goals. Thus, Table 31 indicates that, if the structure is closed at system III, the initial goal is to induce openness. Once this has been accomplished, the next goal of inducing progression to stage IV may be undertaken. Table 31 provides a specific basis for setting intermediate goals relevant to the person's conceptual structure, which will serve the general aim of inducing more abstract structure.

TABLE 31

Relation of Conceptual Structure to Initial Modification Goals

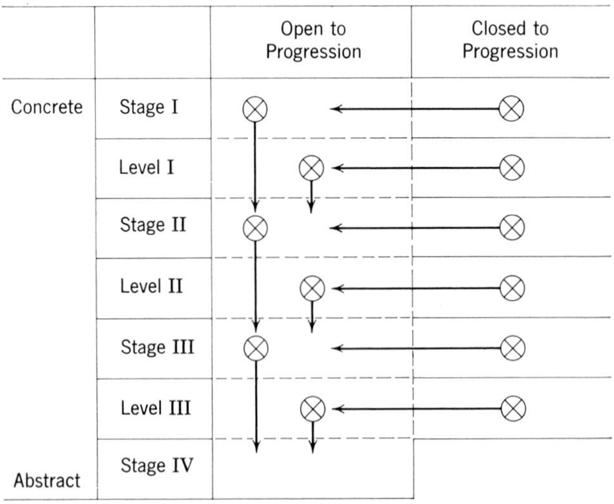

		Open to Progression	Closed to Progression
Concrete	Stage I	⊗ ↓	← ⊗
	Level I	⊗ ↓	← ⊗
	Stage II	⊗ ↓	← ⊗
	Level II	⊗ ↓	← ⊗
	Stage III	⊗ ↓	← ⊗
	Level III	⊗ ↓	← ⊗
Abstract	Stage IV		

Structural Change Is Difficult to Produce in Extremely Closed Systems

The more closed the system at any level of abstractness, the more inflexible and overgeneralized is the system-specific interpretation; therefore, the more difficult is the induction of structural change. In cases of extreme closedness this overgeneralized single interpretation may virtually prevent structural change of any kind.

Closedness to progression is a matter of degree, and a mild degree of closedness is not only "normal" but necessary in the course of development. The child must be closed to some degree during the time he is articulating and clarifying one stage of abstractness before he can progress to the next stage. A moderate degree of closedness is illustrated by the conceptual structures described in Chapter 6, which were characterized as arrested, but "normal." The relatively stable personality organization of the adult represents such a moderate degree of closedness. Extreme or excessive closedness is represented, of course, by the extreme psychopathological forms described in Chapter 9. Increasing the openness of such extremely closed structures in psychotic patients is likely to be very difficult. The degree of extreme closedness, therefore, is inversely related to prognosis.

Procedures to Reduce Extreme Closedness

Procedures aimed to decrease closedness or to reduce compartmentalization are more likely to be regarded as psychotherapeutic, whereas procedures aimed to induce progression are more likely to be regarded as educational. Although this distinction holds generally, some forms of educational procedure require the reduction of closedness, for example, remedial work in reading for a child who has become excessively closed toward those dimensions such as autonomy, which are associated with more favorable attitudes to reading.

In this section we consider briefly the general basis underlying procedures aimed to reduce closedness and indicate a few examples of specific procedures, which may be effective for reducing closedness at particular stages of abstractness. Two general principles apply. First, the procedure cannot deviate too far from the conceptual baseline of the structure of the person. Second, the determinants of the current structure provide the logical basis for selecting appropriate procedures. One must know how the structure developed in order to know how to change it.

Excessive closedness is produced by extreme pressure toward the next higher stage of abstractness; in excessively closed systems, such pressure is experienced as threat. Therefore, the general procedure in decreasing closedness is to reduce threat; since what is threatening varies between the systems, the specific procedure will consist of reducing system-specific threat. At stage I, for example, threat is epitomized by pressure toward opposition to absolute standards or ambiguity, and procedures will therefore consist of reduction of environmental ambiguity and reduction of pressure toward opposition.

Work with psychotic patients furnishes the best source of example for procedures that attempt to decrease excessive closedness. Psychological therapy or environmental programming attempt to remove those situational stimuli to which the extreme sensitization has occurred. One major difficulty in accomplishing such desensitization is that the patient may be totally unreceptive to almost all stimuli and therefore not be aware of the change. Threatening elements in the environment may be reduced markedly, but the patient may not be aware of such reduction precisely because of the operation of excessive closedness, which the reduction in threat is aimed to decrease. Therefore, the intervention procedures must include in addition to appropriate "environmental programming," a means for encouraging the patient to "test out" the environment so that he can experience this change.

One procedure aimed to decrease excessive system I closedness is to create a simpler, less ambiguous environment, and of course this is what occurs in the hospitalization of schizophrenic patients. The aim is to decrease the patient's necessity for feeling externally controlled. It is particularly apparent in dealing with excessive system I closedness that the reduction in environmental threat must be accompanied by some technique aimed to induce "reality testing" so that the patient can discover that the threatening pressure is no longer present. Interpretations by the therapist of the patient's fears of control or his inhibited aggressive wishes to control or destroy those who control him may help to make these thoughts more acceptable, less threatening, and hence more available for modification. Differences between the fantasied harshness of control and the current reality situation must be pointed out and interpreted repeatedly. But a long period of consistent acceptance is necessary as a background before interpretations may be "heard" by the patient, a point acknowledged in psychoanalytic therapy by the necessity for encouraging dependence and providing structure in the early stages of therapy. The psychotic patient is so threatened and so closed to perceptions that challenge the psychotic defense that very minor incidents or cues are interpreted in the exaggerated, distorted manner consistent with his closed system.

As the structure becomes less closed and the patient begins to "come out of his shell," he may behave in ways that place him in even more threatening circumstances. Therefore the controlled environment should be closely attuned and adjusted to changes in the structure of the patient (a procedure which is one of the operations for informational interdependent training). For example, when a patient's fear of expressing his intense hostility is reduced, there is some danger that the hostility will be expressed in all its available intensity. Attention must be paid to providing the patient with milder, relatively safe ways of expressing anger or opposition; at times it may be necessary to permit intense affective expression in a controlled situation so that the feeling can be accepted while the destructive behavior is controlled.

In excessive system II closedness, threat is represented by imposed control or pressures toward dependency. Because of the extreme sensitization to source imposition, the role of the training agent, or therapist, is extremely difficult at this stage. One means of reducing such pressure is to minimize adult control by giving responsibility to the peer group as is done in the junior republic treatment centers for delinquents. However, in extreme system II closedness, these self-governing techniques may be inappropriate since they do not reduce pressure toward dependence. For these cases what is needed is something like Bettelheim's (1951) approach in dealing with severely disturbed hyperaggressive children, which may be described as a "casual but consistent friendliness" on the part of the adult. The problem of encouraging the child to "test out" the environment is not so prominent here as in system I since system II closedness is associated with oppositional "testing out." Here, then, the training agent should permit the child to approach him, as Bettelheim suggests, and then provide a *consistent* form of acceptance. What is required is a friendliness that is not primarily based on the adult's own needs; this condition makes it more difficult for the child to maintain the view that he is merely a pawn of the (imposing) adult.

Another example of appropriate procedure for modifying excessive system II closedness is provided by the work of Goodrich and Boomer (1958). These authors list a number of procedures aimed at "supporting existing ego controls" in dealing with hyperaggressive children, as follows:

Preventive: (avoid threatening existing ego controls)

1. Therapist recognizes that he is not obligated to interpret or limit symptomatic behavior that is not disruptive or currently operating as resistance.
2. Therapist deliberately avoids mobilizing currently uncontrollable core conflict.

3. Therapist refrains from confronting child with his psychopathology when the intervention seems likely to generate a disruptive degree of anxiety.

Supportive: (help child maintain ego controls under special stress)

1. Therapist is alert to situations that are likely to overload children's ego controls and he provides clear supportive structuring.
2. Therapist helps child to maintain his ego control in a variety of situations by constantly evaluating the child's current frustration tolerance.
3. Therapist helps child to maintain or regain control by deliberate expression of positive interest.
4. Therapist firmly and clearly limits socially intolerable behavior.

Restitutive: (help child regain control after temporary failure)

1. Therapist, when setting limits to disapproved behavior, relates the intervention to an established policy.
2. In dealing with a child who is temporarily flooded by anxiety, therapist promotes recovery by:
   a. Permitting the child to regain control in his own way.
   b. Giving the child the undivided attention of a trusted adult.
   c. Permitting the child as much interpersonal distance as he needs.

(Goodrich and Boomer, 1958, p. 286)

These procedures, especially 2a and 2b, and the casual friendliness suggested earlier are all considered as similar to informational interdependent training.

System III closedness is more abstract than closedness at systems I and II; one consequence is that verbal methods are more effective in encouraging the testing of changes in the environment. Thus, in addition to reducing pressure toward autonomy, which represents maximal threat to closed structures at this stage, the training agent may interpret this change to the patient. Depressive patients (excessive system III closedness) are more amenable to such verbal techniques, and also generally have a better prognosis than persons excessively closed at less abstract stages.

We have cited examples of methods for decreasing closedness at stages I, II, and III. Procedures for reducing extreme compartmentalization in transitional levels follow the same general principle of reducing system-specific threat. In reducing closedness at transitional levels, the procedure will usually consist of reducing the threat of the more negative, concrete pole to which the structure is compartmentalized so that the person may articulate this stage and use it as a base for later progression. As was true for procedures for decreasing closedness in stages, procedures for decreasing transitional compartmentalization vary at different levels of transitional conflict.

In line with the principle that modification techniques must suit the existing personality structure, it is expected that the effectiveness of a particular type of psychotherapy will be determined by its system-relevance. For example, client-centered therapy may be especially suitable for increasing openness in cases of moderate system III closedness. The warm, receptive mutuality provided by the client-centered counselor should prove effective in encouraging the articulation and clarification of system III structure. However, client-centered procedures are poorly suited to system II problems, as Rogers (1957) observes: "The client who externalizes his problem feeling little self-responsibility is much more likely to be a failure" (Rogers, 1957, p. 101). Freud also observed that traditional psychoanalysis was not particularly effective upon what we term system II problems. Investigations are needed that focus on determining the most appropriate forms of intervention (psychotherapeutic or otherwise) for inducing openness at various stages, and the present theoretical viewpoint provides a basis for formulating such studies.

While considering psychotherapeutic procedures we would like to re-emphasize a point made in Chapter 4. Many individual and group therapists have observed that the person(s) undergoing psychotherapy evolves through stages very similar to those that we have proposed as occurring in conceptual development. Certainly the best known is Freud's observation that after the initial phase of structured dependency (first stage dependence) patients pass through a phase of negative transference (second stage opposition) and positive transference (third stage mutuality) before reaching what he considered a "successful analysis." Rotter (1954) and Rogers (1958) have also noted that the patient's reaction to psychotherapy may be considered in terms of successive stages. Many group therapists (for example, Coffey, 1954; Martin and Hill, 1957) have observed that therapeutic groups also progress through a succession of stages. Coffey (1954) notes, for example, that after the initial structure (I) groups pass through the following stages: "period of defensiveness and resistance" (II); "period of confiding" (III); and "period of integrative-prospective" (IV) (quotations from Coffey, 1954, pp. 591-592). These observations also raise many questions, which require investigation. What is the relationship between the conceptual structures of the persons in a group and the structure of the group? Does "progression" in group development generalize to the conceptual structure of the person in the group?

The aim in this section has been to indicate some of the difficulties in inducing structural change in extremely closed systems, and to suggest a few procedures for dealing with the difficult task of reducing excessive closedness. As we noted at the outset, a mild degree of closedness may be necessary during certain phases of development. We regard development as proceeding through burst-like, saccadic leaps. Preparation for these leaps requires that the person articulate the previously dimensionalized poles without becoming unduly closed or arrested so that progression can occur. The aim is not total abandonment of the earlier, more concrete orientation but a modification that permits its integration with the more abstract stage. Therefore, if parental behavior and educational procedures are to accomplish their goals, they must not only induce progressive leaps when appropriate but they must also prevent the occurrence of any too-long-sustained closedness or arrestation. Although we consider this topic in the next section primarily from the viewpoint of education (since education is intentionally *induced* change), the principles are equally applicable to parental practices as well.

The Goal of Education Is to Induce Progression to the Next Abstract Stage

The goal of education in a democratic society such as ours is (or should be) to provide the conditions to produce more abstract conceptual structure. Educational procedures therefore aim not only to induce progression to the next abstract stage, when such progressive leaps are appropriate, but also to maintain sufficient openness to progression continuously so that closedness and arrestation do not occur. If the child can be kept either in progression or in preparation for progression, the necessity for use of time-consuming, difficult procedures for decreasing closedness described in the last section is unnecessary. Thus, one goal of education is also the prevention of excessive arrestation or closedness.

In Chapter 6 we discussed the significance of achievement within the various systems and the system-relevant implications of educational practices, including the absolutistic (system I) use of educational achievement tests. We re-emphasize our contention that the role of education in our society is *not* training children to achieve higher scores on objective, machine-scored examinations. We also disagree with some prevalent views of education, especially at the college level, which emphasize placing the student in the environment that is most congruent with his existing personality structure. In our view such procedures simply promote arrestation and thereby defeat the process of growth and progression, which should be the major goal of education.

We believe that education ought to produce persons who are questioning, inventive, original, critical, creative, and if need be different.

We should not simply inculcate norms or produce the "well-adjusted" person but promote as high a degree of abstract structure as possible. If the person is to reach his maximum potentiality both in terms of social contribution and inner harmony, he must be encouraged to continue progressing to the maximum level of abstract structure. Persons who attain this goal will, in Fromm's (1941) words, think in terms of "freedom to" rather than in terms of "freedom from"; in Alper's (1946) terms, they will be "task-oriented" rather than "ego-oriented."

The view of Brogan, a British political scientist, concerning the role of the American school system expresses this point quite clearly:

> What can it do? First of all, I think, in the present crisis it should not educate the pupil "for the world he is going to live in." We don't know what kind of world he is going to live in; all that we can be certain of is that, during a normal lifetime, the world will change in ways we can't now foresee. What we can do is to suggest that the world will change, and given intellectual tools for understanding that truth, intellectual prophylaxis against the provincialism which suggests that only the most obviously current problems are the real problems. (Sputnik merely called attention to certain defects in American education; it did not create the defects.) Unless at least the more intelligent pupils are given some critical habits (including the habit of not believing all that their teachers tell them), we can be sure of one thing. They will not be at home in the world, the unknown world they are going to live in, and no textbooks, no courses, no Advice to the Lovelorn columns are going to help very much. Education would benefit in efficiency and prestige if it were more modest and more presumptuous, if it refused to claim to do so much and insisted on a hierarchy of values in what it can do (Brogan, 1960, p. 79).

The teacher's task in implementing these goals is to provide the environmental conditions that will maximize openness and induce progression. The teacher's task is not to teach the child the right and wrong responses, but to program the environment so that the child can discover things for himself. We feel that effective education is reflected not in how much the child knows but rather how he *uses* what he knows. At a general level, the teacher will provide what we have described as informational interdependent training or what Anderson and Moore (1959) call "autotelic training." The central feature of an effective educational environment is that it provides a situation in which it is not too costly for the child to develop. As Lewin (1935) put it:

> Only in a sufficiently free life-space in which the child has the possibility of choosing his goals according to his own needs and in which, at the same time, *he fully experiences the objectively conditioned difficulties in the attainment of the goal,* can a clear level of reality be formed, only thus can the ability for responsible decision develop (Lewin, 1935, p. 179, italics ours).

It follows therefore that procedures for evaluating or testing children must be separated from the procedures aimed to induce progression as completely as possible. The recent work of Sarason and his colleagues (1960) amply demonstrates the extreme concern that children experience about performing well on examinations. We view excessive "test anxiety" as a form of closedness that effectively prevents progression. As we have noted earlier one characteristic of certain stages beyond stage I, such as stage II, is that they may be associated with less effective performance on standardized achievement tests. If the child is continually confronted by such absolutistic forms of evaluation, he is likely to experience the situation as too costly to risk the difficulties involved in progression.

Current educational practices reward stage I or stage III functioning by their emphasis either upon memorization and inflexible accretion of facts or upon successful interpersonal relationships. Teachers rightly depend, initially, upon a generalization of the child's wish to please his parents by learning what he is required to learn. Although learning proceeds more smoothly when the child trusts the teacher, this bond of trust should be a means to an end rather than an end in itself. It may be too much to expect that a first- or second-grader can develop an adult-type valuation of knowledge-for-its-own-sake, though the eager curiosity of young children is remarkable. But disregarding system IV characteristics for the moment, children in the primary grades are generally discouraged from even system II functioning. Oppositional behavior in the form of argument, challenging of teacher's accuracy, curiosity in areas related to classroom subjects but outside the current "Unit," self-assertiveness beyond what is specifically structured to meet the teacher's plan—all of these are generally discouraged in our public schools. In this regard it is interesting to note that when one looks at the controversies over *the* approved method of teaching (which at any given time is very similar to *the* approved method of child-rearing) that the issue is almost always posed in terms of reliable unilateral training versus protective interdependent training. Thus, one notes references to the "pendulum swinging back from permissiveness to more discipline," as if these two training conditions were the only points on the dimensions in which educational methods vary.

In the present view environmental programming that utilizes operations of informational interdependent training provides a solution to this difficulty, and is most likely to induce progression. It may be helpful here to note briefly some possible reasons for the lack of emphasis upon informational orientation with its consequent progression to stage IV conceptual structure.

A steadfast pursuit of progression to abstract structure produces other effects, some apparently disadvantageous, at least temporarily. First, the child who is original and creative may not necessarily be popular either among his peers or his teachers (cf. Getzels and Jackson, 1959), a circumstance that runs counter to current cultural norms, which place high value on social acceptance. Second, he may be a source of embarrassment or threat to the teacher whose adequacy is challenged by questions or knowledge with which the teacher cannot cope. Third, as we have noted earlier, the child who is progressing toward stage IV may not do at all well on many achievement tests that require only a concretistic repetition of statements made in a book or by the teacher, another circumstance that runs counter to currently valued cultural norms. Fourth, in order to reach stage IV, one must go through stage II (to be inventive and creative, one must develop internal control), which may be difficult for the teacher to tolerate and to view in perspective.

Another possible reason for the dearth of informational training lies in the fact that in order for the training agent (teacher) to use informational interdependent training, he must be flexible and capable of abstract functioning himself. Training for progression requires that the training agent accept differences between students in a tolerant fashion, support and encourage the student's effort to try out new approaches, and reflect reality to the student. In addition, such training requires a keen sensitization on the teacher's part to the stage in which the child is currently functioning. How to select and prepare teachers who can provide such training is a vital area for future research. A prior problem, of course, is the way in which educational goals are valued by the culture and the teacher's role in implementing these goals. We may simply observe that it is impossible to reach some of the goals such as creativity or inventiveness, which have come to be deemed valuable in the post-Sputnik era unless there is some rather dramatic reorganization of educational procedures, which at this time are still geared to achieve different, more concrete goals.

Specific procedures for programming the environment for progression may be derived from our detailed description (Chapter 5) of training conditions for inducing progression. In the current enthusiasm for teaching machines, simulated environments, and the like, one should not lose sight of the fact that these techniques are simply more efficient procedures for accomplishing certain educational goals. Many so-called teaching machines that aim only to "train in" the concretistic occurrence of a specific response are, in our view, simply automated versions of reliable unilateral training. They are therefore as inappropriate for education as the use of standardized tests of achievement for evaluating the effectiveness of education. Put another way, one could devise automated versions of each of the four general training conditions that we have proposed. The automation is neither good nor bad, but the appropriateness of the automated technique must be considered in relation to the modification of persons with specified conceptual structure.

Although we have generally recommended procedures based on operations of informational interdependent training such as autotelic training, we again emphasize that the training condition must always be geared to the structural state of the person. Combining the observation that modification procedures are more efficient if directed toward a group of persons than toward an individual with the previous point that modification procedures are more effective when specifically geared to the conceptual structure of the person, we arrive at our final major implication described in the following section.

Modification Procedures Will Be More Effective If Directed toward Groups of Persons Similar in Their Conceptual Structure

The increased efficiency that results from directing modification efforts toward persons in groups is widely acknowledged both in educational and in psychotherapeutic circles. The problem of *how* to group persons, or the basis to use for grouping, which will not dilute the effectiveness of the modification effort remains a controversial and unanswered question as illustrated by issues of age-grading versus ability-grading in education.

We propose that the most meaningful basis for grouping (for either educational or therapeutic purposes) is classification according to conceptual structure. More specifically, we propose that if persons are placed into groups similar in terms of degree of abstractness and degree of openness, modification procedures will lose little in effectiveness due to variation among group members. Put another way, we suggest that grouping of persons into the general categories indicated in Table 30 is one of the most meaningful ways for classifying persons into modificationally relevant groups. (This contention again emphasizes the importance of developing methods for assessing these structural differences). The use of age-grading or IQ-grading are both unsatisfactory for reasons we have described earlier. Lewin's (1935) comment on the use of intelligence tests is relevant:

> One major difficulty in reasoning from the results of intelligence testing to the problem of dynamic differences is the fact that in testing procedures,

individual differences are determined by means of activities the psychological nature and general laws of which are not sufficiently known (Lewin, 1935, p. 197).

If students are grouped according to conceptual structure, the teacher may then proceed to provide the system-specific environmental conditions described in Chapter 5, which are most likely to induce progression for the particular pattern of conceptual structure that characterizes the group. We do not propose that under these conditions the teacher disregard differences between individuals in the group since these still exist, though to a lesser degree, and must be considered. However, these differences are minimized, and the likelihood that the structure-specific modification effort will be appropriate for most members in the group is maximized.

The problems in modifying structurally heterogeneous groups have been frequently described, though not in the present terms. The disruptive effects produced in a therapeutic group by only one person whose conceptual structure varies from the others have been frequently cited, and this disruption does not always occur from heterogeneity in the form of a person at stage II whose structural characteristics are associated with disruptive, oppositional tactics. One of the authors observed the disruptive effects in a group comprised primarily of aggressive delinquent boys (closed system II), which proceeded with remarkable results after several months, but which was impeded in its progress by the presence of a single boy whose personality organization might be described as closed level I structure.

When we recommend structurally homogeneous grouping it is for purposes of making maximum use of resources for environmental programming. The problem of homogeneity versus heterogeneity of conceptual structure may be considerably more complex in group therapy and to a lesser extent in some school groups, since here each group member is a part of the environment for each other. In these cases a certain degree of heterogeneity may serve a catalytic function. The question that deserves investigation here is what patterns of structural heterogeneity will be propaedeutic to progression and what patterns of structural heterogeneity will be disruptive. Again we simply suggest that the use of structural dimensions provides a basis for approaching this extremely important problem of group composition.

From the viewpoint of purposive modification, either education or psychotherapy, therefore, the procedure must be to program the environment for structurally homogeneous groups in order to achieve specific goals of structural change.

Concluding Remarks

In this chapter we have proposed several implications that the present viewpoint has for modification. The general aim of modification is to produce more abstract conceptual structure. In pursuing this aim, the current conceptual structure of the person determines the short-term goals of modification. Thus, if the system is closed, the initial goal is to induce openness, whereas if the system is open, the initial goal is to induce progression to the next more abstract stage. Structural change is very difficult to produce in extremely closed systems; however, the derivation of procedures to reduce closedness at various degrees of abstractness was described and illustrated. Because of the difficulty in inducing openness in arrested or closed systems, an important aim of educational and child-rearing procedures is to maintain openness to progression. The major aim of education is to provide appropriate environmental conditions to induce progression to the next abstract stage. In an effort to maximize the effectiveness of resources for modification we suggest that grouping persons together according to similarity in conceptual structure makes possible the use of environmental programming specifically appropriate to inducing change in the most efficient fashion.

The problems discussed in this chapter are important not only for the individual, in terms of his self-adequacy and experience of psychological well-being, but also for a culture like ours, which in the present process of increasing its valuation of creativity and inventiveness, seeks ways by which such activities can be encouraged. Every statement made in this chapter is essentially a proposal to be investigated, and should be regarded as such. We feel, however, that if the general aim of producing more abstract conceptual structure is accepted, the present viewpoint provides a potentially useful means of investigating these important problems.

Bibliography

Abelson, R. Modes of resolution of belief dilemmas. *J. Confl. Resol.,* 1959, **3,** 343–352.

Abelson, R. P., & Rosenberg, M. J. Symbolic psychologic: a model of attitude cognition. *Behav. Sci.,* 1958, **3,** 1–13.

Adorno, T. W., Frenkel-Brunswik, Else, Levinson, D. J., & Sanford, R. N. *The authoritarian personality.* New York: Harper, 1950.

Aichorn, A. *Wayward youth.* New York: Viking Press, 1935.

Alexander, F. The influence of psychological factors upon gastro-intestinal disturbances. *Psychoanal. Quart.,* 1934, **3,** 501–539.

Allport, G. W., & Postman, L. *The psychology of rumor.* New York: Holt, 1947.

Alper, Thelma G. Task-orientation vs. ego-orientation in learning and retention. *Amer. J. Psychol.,* 1946, **59,** 236–248.

Altmann, M. Adjustment problems in the adolescent moose and elk. Unpublished manuscript, University of Colorado, 1960.

Anderson, A. R., & Moore, O. K. *Autotelic folk models.* ONR Technical Report, No. 8, 1959.

Aristotle. *Aristotle's psychology,* trans. by W. A. Hammond, 1902.

Asch, S. *Social psychology.* New York: Prentice-Hall, 1952.

Atkinson, J. W. The achievement motive and recall of interrupted and completed tasks. *J. exp. Psychol.,* 1953, **46,** 381–390.

Atkinson, J. W., & Reitman, W. R. Performance as a function of motive strength and expectancy of goal attainment. *J. abnorm. soc. Psychol.,* 1956, **53,** 361–366.

Atkinson, J. W., & Walker, L. The affiliation motive and perceptual sensitivity to faces. *J. abnorm. soc. Psychol.,* 1956, **53,** 38–41.

Ausubel, D. P. *Ego development and the personality disorders.* New York: Grune & Stratton, 1952.

Ausubel, D. P. *Theory and problems of child development.* New York: Grune & Stratton, 1958.

Ausubel, D. P., Balthazar, E. E., Rosenthal, Irene, Blackman, L. S., Schpront, S. H., & Welkowitz, J. Perceived parent attitudes as determinants of children's ego structure. *Child Develpm.,* 1954, **25,** 173–183.

Ayers, E. Social attitude toward invention. *Amer. Sci.,* 1955, **43,** 521–540.

Baldwin, A. L. Difference in parent behavior toward three- and nine-year-old children. *J. Pers.,* 1946, **15,** 143–165.

Baldwin, A. L. *Behavior and development in childhood.* New York: Dryden Press, 1955.

Baldwin, A. L., Kalhorn, J., & Breese, F. H. Patterns of parent behavior. *Psychol. Monogr.,* 1945, **58,** No. 3 (Whole No. 268).

Baldwin, A. L., Kalhorn, J., & Breese, F. H. The appraisal of parent behavior. *Psychol. Monogr.,* 1949, **63,** No. 4 (Whole No. 299).

Barker, R. G. Structure of the stream of behavior. *Proceedings of the Fifteenth International Congress of Psychology, Brussels, 1957,* pp. 155–156. Amsterdam: North-Holland Publishing Co., 1957.

Bartlett, F. C. *Remembering: A study in experimental and social psychology.* London: Cambridge University Press, 1932.

Bartlett, F. C. *Thinking.* New York: Basic Books, 1958.

Beers, C. W. *A mind that found itself.* Garden City, N. Y.: Doubleday, Doran & Co., 1931.

Benedict, Ruth. Continuities and discontinuities in cultural conditioning. *Psychiatry,* 1938, **1,** 161–167.

Benedict, Ruth. *The chrysanthemum and the sword.* Boston: Houghton-Mifflin, 1946.

Bennis, W. G., & Shepard, H. A. A theory of group development. *Human Relations,* 1956, **9,** 415–437.

Berkowitz, L., & Lundy, R. M. Personality characteristics related to susceptibility to influence by peers or authority figures. *J. Pers.,* 1957, **25,** 306–316.

Bettelheim, B. Individual and mass behavior in extreme situations. *J. abnorm. soc. Psychol.,* 1943, **38,** 417–452.

Bettelheim, B. *Love is not enough.* Glencoe, Illinois: Free Press, 1950.

Bexton, W. H., Heron, W., & Scott, T. H. Effects of decreased variation in the sensory environment. *Canad. J. Psychol.,* 1954, **8,** 70–76.

Bieri, J., & Blacker, E. The generality of cognitive complexity in the perception of people and inkblots. *J. abnorm. soc. Psychol.,* 1956, **53,** 112–117.

Bird, C. The relative importance of maturation and habit in the development of an instinct. *Pedag. semin.,* 1925, **32,** 68–91.

Birren, J. Psychological examination of children who later become psychotic. *J. abnorm. soc. Psychol.,* 1944, **39,** 84–95.

Block, J., & Block, Jeanne. An investigation of the relationship between intolerance of ambiguity and ethnocentrism. *J. Pers.,* 1951, **19,** 303–311.

Block, Jeanne, & Block, J. An interpersonal experiment on reactions to authority. *Human Relations,* 1952, **5,** 91–98.

Boring, E. G. *A history of experimental psychology.* (2nd ed.) New York: Appleton-Century-Crofts, 1950.

Bowman, K. M., & Raymond, A. F. A statistical study of delusions. *Res. nerv. ment. Dis.,* 1931, **11,** 313–323.

Brogan, D. W. *America in the modern world.* New Brunswick: Rutgers University Press, 1960.

Brown, R. W. A determinant of the relationship between rigidity and authoritarianism. *J. abnorm. soc. Psychol.,* 1953, **48,** 469–476.

Brown, R. W., & Lenneberg, E. H. A study in language and cognition. *J. abnorm. soc. Psychol.,* 1954, **49,** 454–462.

Bruner, J. Going beyond the information given. In J. S. Bruner et al. *Contemporary approaches to cognition.* Cambridge: Harvard University Press, 1957.

Bruner, J. S., Goodnow, Jacqueline J., & Austin, G. A. *A study of thinking.* New York: Wiley, 1956.

Bruner, J. S., & Tagiuri, R. The perception of people. In G. Lindzey (Ed.), *Handbook of social psychology.* Cambridge: Addison-Wesley, 1954, Vol. II, pp. 634–654.

Cameron, N. The development of paranoic thinking. *Psychol. Rev.,* 1943, **50,** 219–233.

Cameron, N. *The psychology of behavior disorders: a biosocial interpretation.* Boston: Houghton-Mifflin, 1947.

Campbell, D. T. Common fate, similarity, and other indices of the status of aggregates of persons as social entities. *Behav. Sci.,* 1958, **3,** 14–25.

Campbell, D. T., & Fiske, D. W. Convergent and discriminant validation by the multitrait-multimethod matrix. *Psychol. Bull.,* 1959, **56,** 81–105.

Cantril, H. *The "why" of man's experience.* New York: Macmillan, 1950.

Cantril, H., & Bumstead, C. *Reflections on the human venture.* New York: New York University Press, 1960.

Carmichael, L. The development of behavior in vertebrates experimentally removed from influence of external stimulation. *Psychol. Rev.,* 1926, **33,** 51–58.

Carmichael, L. A further study of the development of vertebrates experimentally removed from the influence of environmental stimulation. *Psychol. Rev.,* 1927, **34,** 34–47.

Carmichael, L., & Dearborn, W. F. *Reading and visual fatigue.* London: George G. Harrap & Co., Ltd., 1948.

Carmichael, L., Hogan, H. P., & Walter, A. A. An experimental study of the effect of language on the reproduction of visually perceived form. *J. exp. Psychol.,* 1932, **15,** 73–86.

Caron, A. J., & Wallach, M. A. Personality determinants of repressive and obsessive reactions to failure stress. *J. abnorm. soc. Psychol.,* 1959, **59,** 236–245.

Cassirer, C. *An essay on man.* New Haven: Yale University Press, 1944.

Chapman, L. J., & Bock, R. D. Components of variance due to acquiescence and content in the F-scale measure of authoritarianism. *Psychol. Bull.,* 1958, **55,** 328–333.

Cherry, C. On human communication: A review, a survey, and a criticism. Published jointly by The Technology Press of Massachusetts Institute of Technology, John Wiley & Sons Inc., New York, and Chapman & Hall Limited, London, 1957.

Child, I. L. Socialization. In G. Lindzey (Ed.), *Handbook of Social Psychology.* Cambridge: Addison-Wesley, 1954, Vol. II, pp. 655–692.

Clark, K. B., & Clark, M. K. Skin color as a factor in racial identification of Negro preschool children. *J. soc. Psychol.,* 1940, **11,** 159–169.

Cleckley, H. *The mask of sanity.* (2nd ed.) St. Louis: C. V. Mosby, 1950.

Coffey, H. S. Group psychotherapy. In L. A. Pennington & I. A. Berg (Eds.), *An introduction to clinical psychology.* New York: Ronald Press, 1954, pp. 586–607.

Coffin, T. E. Some conditions of suggestion and suggestibility. *Psychol. Monogr.,* 1941, **53,** No. 4 (Whole No. 241).

Cohen, L. Level-of-aspiration behavior and feelings of adequacy and self-acceptance. *J. abnorm. soc. Psychol.,* 1954, **49,** 84–86.

Cohen, Mabel B., Baker, Grace, Cohen, R. A., Fromm-Reichmann, Frieda & Weigert, Edith V. An intensive study of twelve cases of manic depressive psychosis. *Psychiatry,* 1954, **17,** 103–139.

Cohler, J., & Kelman, H. C. Reactions to persuasive communications as a function of cognitive needs and styles. Paper read at meeting of Eastern Psychological Assn., 1959.

Cooley, C. H. *Human nature and the social order.* New York: Scribner, 1912.

Cooper, E., & Jahoda, Marie. The evasion of propaganda: how prejudiced people respond to anti-prejudice propaganda. *J. Psychol.,* 1947, **23,** 15–25.

Copple, G. E. Effective intelligence as measured by an unstructured sentence completion test. *J. consult. Psychol.,* 1956, **20,** 357–360.

Criswell, J. H. A sociometric study of race cleavages in the classroom. *Arch. Psychol.,* 1939, **33** (Whole No. 235).

Crockett, E. P. Authoritarianism and leader acceptance. ONR Technical Report No. 5, Vanderbilt University, 1958.

Cronbach, L. J. The two disciplines of scientific psychology. *Amer. Psychologist,* 1957, **12,** 671–684.

Crutchfield, R. S. Conformity and character. *Amer. Psychologist,* 1955, **10,** 191–199.

Darwin, C. R. *The origin of species.* London: 1859.

De Laguna, G. M. *Speech: Its function and development.* New Haven: Yale University Press, 1927.

Deutsch, M., & Gerard, H. B. A study of normative and informational social influences upon individual judgment. *J. abnorm. soc. Psychol.,* 1955, **51,** 629–636.

Dewey, J. The reflex arc concept in psychology. *Psychol. Rev.,* 1896, **3,** 357–370.

Dollard, J., Doob, L. W., Miller, N. E., Mowrer, O. H., & Sears, R. R. *Frustration and aggression.* New Haven: Yale University Press, 1939.

Dollard, J., & Miller, N. E. *Personality and psychotherapy.* New York: McGraw-Hill, 1950.

Durkheim, E. *Suicide,* 1897. Trans. by J. A. Spaulding & G. Simpson. London: Routledge and Kegan Paul, 1952.

Durkin, Dolores. Children's concept of justice: A comparison with the Piaget data. *Child Develpm.,* 1959, **30,** 58–67 (a).

Durkin, Dolores. Children's acceptance of reciprocity as a justice principle. *Child Develpm.,* 1959, **30,** 289–296 (b).

Ellingson, R. J. The incidence of EEG abnormality among patients with mental disorders of apparently non-organic origin: A critical review. *Amer. J. Psychiat.,* 1954, **111,** 263–275.

Ergang, R. *Europe from the Renaissance to Waterloo.* New York: Heath, 1939.

Erikson, E. H. *Childhood and society.* New York: W. W. Norton, 1950, pp. 213–220.

Escalona, Sibylle K. *An application of the level of aspiration experiment to the study of personality.* New York: Bur. of Publ., Teachers Coll., 1948.

Eysenck, H. J. *Dimensions of personality.* London: Routledge, 1948.

Eysenck, H. J. *The structure of human personality.* London: Milton & Co., 1953.

Eysenck, H. J. A dynamic theory of anxiety and hysteria. *J. ment. Sci.,* 1955, **101,** 28–51.

Festinger, L. *A theory of cognitive dissonance.* Evanston: Row Peterson, 1957.

Fine, H. J., & Zimet, C. N. Process-reactive schizophrenia and genetic levels of perception. *J. abnorm. soc. Psychol.,* 1959, **59,** 83–86.

Fischer, L. *The Life of Mahatma Gandhi.* New York: Harper, 1950.

Frank, L. K. Future possibilities in child development research. *Child Develpm.,* 1960, **31,** 189–190.

French, Elizabeth G. Development of a measure of complex motivation. In J. W. Atkinson (Ed.), *Motives in fantasy, action, and society.* Princeton, New Jersey: Van Nostrand, 1958, pp. 242–248 (a).

French, Elizabeth G. Effects of the interaction of motivation and feedback on task performance. In J. W. Atkinson (Ed.), *Motives in fantasy, action, and society.* Princeton, N.J.: D. Van Nostrand, 1958, pp. 400–408 (b).

French, Elizabeth G., & Ernest, R. R. The relation between authoritarianism and acceptance of military ideology. *J. Pers.*, 1955, **24**, 181–191.

Freud, Anna. *The ego and the mechanisms of defense.* New York: International Universities Press, 1950.

Freud, S. *Basic writings.* Trans. by A. A. Brill. New York: Modern Library, 1938.

Friedman, H. Perceptual regression in schizophrenia, a hypothesis suggested by the use of the Rorschach test. *J. proj. Tech.*, 1953, **17**, 162–170.

Fromm, E. *Escape from freedom.* New York: Rinehart, 1941.

Galton, F. *Inquiries into human faculty.* London: 1883.

Geleerd, E. R., Hacker, F. J., Rapaport, D. Contribution to the study of amnesia and allied conditions. *Psychoanal. Quart.*, 1945, **14**, 199–220.

Gesell, A. L. *First five years of life.* New York: Harper, 1940.

Gesell, A. L. *Studies in child development.* New York: Harper, 1948.

Gesell, A. L. *Youth: the years from ten to sixteen.* New York: Harper, 1956.

Gesell, A. L., & Thompson, H. Learning and growth in identical infant twins. *Genet. Psychol. Monogr.*, 1929, **6**, 1–24.

Getzels, J. W., & Guba, E. G. Role conflict and personality. *J. Pers.*, 1955, **24**, 73–85.

Getzels, J. W., & Jackson, P. W. The highly intelligent and the highly creative adolescent: a summary of some research findings. Working paper presented at University of Utah, June, 1959.

Gewirtz, J. L., & Baer, D. M. The effects of brief social deprivation on behaviors for a social reinforcer. *J. abnorm. soc. Psychol.*, 1958, **56**, 49–56.

Gewirtz, J. L., & Baer, D. M. Deprivation and satiation of social reinforcers as drive conditions. *J. abnorm. soc. Psychol.*, 1958, **57**, 165–172.

Gibson, J. J. The reproduction of visually perceived form. *J. exp. Psychol.*, 1929, **12**, 1–39.

Glueck, S., & Glueck, E. *Unraveling juvenile delinquency.* Cambridge: Harvard University Press, 1950.

Goldberg, L., & Holt, R. R. Experimental interference with reality contact: Method and group results. *J. nerv. ment. Dis.*, 1958, **127**, 99–112.

Goldstein, K., & Scheerer, M. Abstract and concrete behavior: an experimental study with special tests. *Psychol. Monogr.*, 1941, **53**, (Whole No. 239).

Goodman, M. E. *Race awareness in young children.* Cambridge: Addison-Wesley Press, 1952.

Goodrich, D. W., & Boomer, D. S. Some concepts about therapeutic intervention with hyperaggressive children. Parts I and II. *Soc. casewk.*, 1958, **39**, 207–213, 286–292.

Grace, Gloria L. The relation of personality characteristics and response to verbal approval in a learning task. *Genet. Psychol. Monogr.*, 1948, **37**, 73–103.

Grinker, R., & Spiegel, J. *Men under stress.* Philadelphia: Blakiston, 1945.

Grosslight, J. H., & Child, I. L. Persistence as a function of previous experience of failure followed by success. *Amer. J. Psychol.*, 1947, **60**, 378–387.

Gruber, S. The concept of task orientation in the analysis of play behavior of children entering kindergarten. *Amer. J. Orthopsychiat.*, 1954, **24**, 326–335.

Hadju-Gimes, L. Contributions to the etiology of schizophrenia. *Psychoanal. Rev.*, 1940, **27**, 421–438.

Haire, M., & Grunes, Willa F. Perceptual defenses: processes protecting an organized perception of another person. *Human Relat.*, 1950, **3**, 403–412.

Hallowell, A. I. Aggression in Saulteaux society. In C. M. Kluckhohn & H. A. Murray (Eds.), *Personality in nature society and culture.* New York: Knopf, 1949, 204–219.

Hallowell, A. I. Cultural factors in structuralization of perception. In J. H. Rohrer & M. Sherif (Eds.), *Social psychology at the crossroads.* New York: Harper, 1951.

Hardison, J., & Purcell, K. The effects of psychological stress as a function of need and cognitive control. *J. Pers.*, 1959, **27**, 250–258.

Harlow, H. The nature of love. *Amer. Psychologist,* 1958, **13**, 673–685.

Hart, I. Maternal child-rearing practices and authoritarian ideology. *J. abnorm. soc. Psychol.*, 1957, **55**, 232–237.

Hartley, E. L. *Problems in prejudice.* New York: Kings Crown Press, 1946.

Harvey, O. J. Reactions to negative information about the self as a function of the unfavorableness of the information, source of the evaluations, and personality characteristics of the recipients. ONR Technical Report, Vanderbilt University, 1958.

Harvey, O. J. Personality factors related to opinion change. ONR Technical Report, University of Colorado, 1959.

Harvey, O. J., & Beverly, D. Some personality correlates of concept change by entertainment of contradictory premises. ONR Technical Report No. 1, University of Colorado, 1959.

Harvey, O. J., & Caldwell, D. F. Assimilation and contrast phenomena in response to environmental variation. *J. Pers.*, 1959, **27**, 125–135.

Harvey, O. J., Kelley, H. H., & Shapiro, M. M. Reactions to unfavorable evaluations of the self made by other persons. *J. Pers.*, 1957, **25**, 393–411.

Harvey, O. J., & Rutherford, Jeanne. Gradual and absolute approaches to attitude change. *Sociometry*, 1958, **21**, 61–68.

Heathers, G. Acquired dependence and independence: a theoretical orientation. *J. genet. Psychol.*, 1955, **87**, 277–291.

Hebb, D. O. *The organization of behavior.* New York: Wiley, 1949.

Heidbreder, Edna. *Seven psychologies.* New York: Appleton-Century-Crofts, 1933.

Heider, F. *The psychology of interpersonal relations.* New York: Wiley, 1958.

Helson, H. Adaptation-level as a frame of reference for prediction of psychophysical data. *Amer. J. Psychol.*, 1947, **60**, 1–29.

Helson, H. Adaptation-level as a basis for a quantitative theory of frames of reference. *Psychol. Rev.*, 1948, **55**, 297–313.

Hemmendinger, L. Perceptual organization and development as reflected in the structure of the Rorschach test responses. *J. proj. Tech.*, 1953, **17**, 162–170.

Henderson, D. K. *Psychopathic states.* New York: Norton, 1939.

Henry, A. F., & Short, J., Jr. *Suicide and homicide: some economic, sociological and psychological aspects of aggression.* Glencoe, Ill.: Free Press, 1954.

Herbart, J. F. *A textbook in psychology,* 1834. Trans. by M. K. Smith, 1891.

Hertzer, H. Entwicklungsbedinkte Erziehungsschwirigkeiten. *Ztschr. Pädagog. Psychol.*, 1929, **30**, 77–85.

Hess, E. The relationship between imprinting and motivation. In M. R. Jones (Ed.), *Nebraska symposium on motivation, 1959.* Lincoln, Neb.: University of Nebraska Press, 1959.

Hewitt, L. E., & Jenkins, R. L. *Fundamental patterns of maladjustment. The dynamics of their origin.* Springfield, Ill.: D. H. Green, 1946.

Hill, D., & Watterson, D. Electroencephalographic studies of psychopathic personalities. *J. Neurol. Psychiat.*, 1942, **5**, 47–65.

Hoffer, E. *The true believer.* New York: Harper, 1951.

Hoffman, M. L. Conformity as a defense mechanism and a form of resistance to genuine group influence. *J. Pers.*, 1957, **25**, 412–424.

Hoijer, H. The relation of language to culture. In A. L. Kroeber (Ed.), *Anthropology today.* Chicago: University of Chicago Press, 1953.

Horney, Karen. *The neurotic personality of our time.* New York: Norton, 1937.

Horowitz, E. L. The development of attitudes toward Negroes. *Arch. Psychol.*, 1936, **28** (Whole No. 194).

Horowitz, E. L., & Horowitz, R. E. Development of social attitudes in children. *Sociometry*, 1937, **1**, 301–338.

Hovland, C. I. *The order of presentation in persuasion.* New Haven: Yale University Press, 1957.

Hovland, C. I., Harvey, O. J., & Sherif, M. Assimilation and contrast effects in reaction to communication and attitude change. *J. abnorm. soc. Psychol.*, 1957, **55**, 244–252.

Hovland, C. I., Janis, I. L., & Kelley, H. H. *Communication and persuasion.* New Haven: Yale University Press, 1953.

Hunt, D. E. Incidence of malevolent imputation as a function of situational and dispositional factors. Unpublished manuscript, 1957.

Hunt, D. E., & Schroder, H. M. Sensitization to self-competence and academic underachievement. Unpublished manuscript, 1957.

Hunt, D. E., & Schroder, H. M. Assimilation, failure-avoidance, and anxiety. *J. consult. Psychol.*, 1958, **22**, 39–44.

Hunt, D. E., & Schroder, H. M. The role of three conceptual systems in sensitization, interpretation, and behavioral expression. Unpublished manuscript, 1959.

Hunt, D. E., & Wells, H. H. Sensitization as reflected by self-negation responses. Unpublished manuscript, 1959.

Hunter, W. S. The delayed reaction in animals and children. *Behav. Monogr.*, 1913, **2**.

Ilg, Frances L., & Ames, Louise B. *Child behavior.* New York: Harper, 1955.

Jackson, D. N., & Messick, S. Content and style in personality assessment. *Psychol. Bull.*, 1958, **55**, 243–252.

James, H., & Rotter, B. Partial and 100% reinforcement under chance and skill conditions. *J. exp. Psychol.*, 1958, **55**, 397–403.

James, W. *The principles of psychology.* New York: Holt, 1890. (Dover Publications ed.).

Janicki, W. P. The effect of disposition on the prediction of resolution in a balanced situation. Unpublished manuscript, 1959.

Janicki, W. P. The effects of variation in conceptual structure on dyadic interaction. Unpublished doctoral dissertation, Princeton University, 1960.

Jenkins, R. L., & Pacella, B. L. Electroencephalographic studies of delinquent boys. *Amer. J. Orthopsychiat.*, 1943, **13**, 107–120.

Jensen, A. R. Authoritarian attitudes and personality maladjustment. *J. abnorm. soc. Psychol.*, 1957, **54**, 303–311.

Jessor, R., & Hammond, K. W. Construct validity and the Taylor anxiety scale. *Psychol. Bull.*, 1957, **54**, 161–170.

Jones, E. E., & deCharms, R. The organizing function of interaction roles in person perception. *J. abnorm. soc. Psychol.*, 1958, **57**, 155–169.

Jones, E. E., & Thibaut, J. W. Interaction goals and bases of inference in interpersonal perception. In R. Taguiri & L. Petrullo (Eds.), *Person perception and interpersonal behavior.* Stanford: Stanford University Press, 1958, pp. 151–178.

Jones, M. *The therapeutic community.* New York: Basic Books, 1953.

Jung, C. G. *Psychological types or the psychology of individuation.* New York: Harcourt Brace, 1923.

Kanner, L. Autistic disturbances of affective contact. *The Nervous Child,* 1943, **2**, 217–250.

Katz, D., Sarnoff, I., & McClintock, C. Attitude change procedures and motivating patterns. In D. Katz (Ed.), *Public opinion and propaganda.* New York: Dryden, 1954.

Kelly, G. *The psychology of personal constructs.* New York: Norton, 1955.

Kelman, H. C. Compliance, identification and internalization: three processes of attitude change. *J. Confl. Resol.*, 1958, **2**, 51–60.

Kelman, H. C. Social influence and personal belief: a theoretical and experimental approach to the study of behavior change. Unpublished manuscript, 1956.

Kennedy, J. L. Growing synthetic organisms in synthetic environments. Paper read at Eastern Psychol. Assn., April 1960.

Klein, G. S. The personal world through perception. In R. R. Blake & G. V. Ramsey (Eds.), *Perception, an approach to personality.* New York: Ronald, 1951, pp. 328–359.

Koffka, K. Perception: An introduction to Gestalt theorie. *Psychol. Bull.*, 1922, **19**, 531–585.

Kohler, W. *Gestalt psychology.* New York: Liveright, 1929.

Korzybski, A. The role of language in the perceptual processes. In R. R. Blake & G. V. Ramsey (Eds.), *Perception, an approach to personality.* New York: Ronald, 1951, pp. 170–205.

Lambert, W. W., Triandis, L. M., & Wolf, W. Some correlates of beliefs in the malevolence and benevolence of supernatural beings: cross cultural study. *J. abnorm. soc. Psychol.*, 1959, **58**, 162–169.

Lambo, T. A. The role of cultural factors in paranoid psychosis among the Yoruba Tribe. *J. ment. Sci.*, 1955, **101**, 239–266.

Lazarus, R. S. Ambiguity and nonambiguity in projective testing. *J. abnorm. soc. Psychol.*, 1953, **48**, 443–445.

Lazarus, R. S., Baker, R. W., Broverman, D. M., & Mayer, J. Personality and psychological stress. *J. Pers.*, 1957, **25**, 559–577.

Leary, T. *Interpersonal diagnosis of personality.* New York: Ronald, 1957.

Leighton, D., & Kluckhohn, C. *Children of the people.* Cambridge, Mass.: Harvard University Press, 1947.

Levin, H., & Baldwin, A. L. Pride and shame in children. In M. R. Jones (Ed.), *Nebraska symposium on motivation, 1959.* Lincoln: University of Nebraska Press, 1959.

Levy, D. M. *Maternal overprotection.* New York: Columbia University Press, 1943.

Levy, D. M. Oppositional syndromes and oppositional behavior. In P. H. Hoch & J. Zubin (Eds.), *Psychopathology of childhood.* New York: Grune and Stratton, 1955, pp. 204–226.

Levy-Bruhl, L. *Primitive mentality.* London: Allen and Unwin, Ltd., 1923.

Lewin, B. D. *The psychoanalysis of elation.* New York: Norton, 1950.

Lewin, K. *A dynamic theory of personality: selected papers.* (1st ed.) New York: McGraw-Hill, 1935.

Lewin, K. Comments concerning psychological forces and energies, and the structure of the psyche. In D. Rapaport (Ed.), *Organization and pathology of thought.* New York: Columbia University Press, 1951, pp. 76–94.

Lewin, K. Behavior and development as a function of the total situation. In L. Carmichael (Ed.), *Manual of child psychology.* (2nd ed.) New York: Wiley, 1954, pp. 238–304.

Lewin, K., Lippitt, R., & White, R. K. Patterns of aggressive behavior in experimentally created "social climates." *J. soc. Psychol.,* 1939, **10,** 271–299.

Lidz, T. Schizophrenia and the family. *Psychiatry,* 1958, **21,** 21–27.

Lidz, T., Cornelison, Alice, Terry, Dorothy, & Fleck, S. Intrafamilial environment of the schizophrenic patient: VI. The transmission of irrationality. *A.M.A. Arch. Neurol. Psychiat.,* 1958, **79,** 305–316.

Lindzey, G. An experimental examination of the scapegoat theory of prejudice. *J. abnorm. soc. Psychol.,* 1950, **45,** 296–309.

Linton, Harriet, & Graham, Elaine. Personality correlates of persuasibility. In I. L. Janis & C. I. Hovland et al. (Eds.), *Personality and persuasibility.* New Haven: Yale University Press, 1959, pp. 69–101.

Loevinger, Jane. Patterns of parenthood as theories of learning. *J. abnorm. soc. Psychol.,* 1959, **59,** 148–150.

Lowie, R. H. *The history of ethnological theory.* New York: Rinehart, 1937.

Maccoby, Eleanor E. Role taking in childhood and its consequences for social learning. *Child Develpm.,* 1959, **30,** 239–252.

Malinowski, B. *Coral gardens and their magic.* New York: American Book Co., 1935.

Mandler, G., & Sarason, S. B. A study of anxiety and learning. *J. abnorm. soc. Psychol.,* 1952, **21,** 336–341.

Mark, J. C. The attitudes of the mothers of male schizophrenics toward child behavior. *J. abnorm. soc. Psychol.,* 1953, **48,** 185–189.

Martin, E., & Hill, W. F. Toward a theory of group development: six phases of therapy group development. *Int. J. grp. Psychotherapy.* 1957, **7,** 20–30.

McArthur, C. Personality of first and second children. *Psychiatry,* 1956, **19,** 47–54.

McCarter, R., & Schroder, H. M. Dispositional effects in learning without awareness. Unpublished manuscript, 1959.

McClelland, D. C., Atkinson, J. W., Clark, R. A., & Lowell, E. L. *The achievement motive.* New York: Appleton-Century-Crofts, 1953.

McClelland, D. C., & Friedman, G. A. A cross cultural study of the relationship between child training practices and achievement motivation appearing in folk tales. In G. E. Swanson, T. M. Newcomb, & E. L. Hartley (Eds.) *Readings in social psychology.* (Rev. Ed.) New York: Holt, 1952, pp. 243–249.

McClelland, D. C., & Liberman, A. M. The effect of need for achievement on recognition of need-related words. *J. Pers.,* 1949, **18,** 236–251.

McClintock, C. G. Personality syndromes and attitude change. *J. Pers.,* 1958, **26,** 479–493.

McDavid, J. Personality and situational determinants of conformity. *J. abnorm. soc. Psychol.,* 1959, **58,** 241–246.

McDavid, J., & Schroder, H. M. The interpretation of approval and disapproval by delinquent and non-delinquent adolescents. *J. Pers.,* 1957, **25,** 539–549.

McDougall, W. *Social psychology.* London: Methuen, 1908.

McGaughran, L. S. Predicting language behavior from object sorting. *J. abnorm. soc. Psychol.,* 1954, **49,** 183–195.

Mead, G. H. *Self, mind and society.* Chicago: University of Chicago Press, 1934.

Merton, R. K. Bureaucratic structure and personality. *Social Forces,* 1940, **18,** 560–568.

Merton, R. K. *Social theory and social structure.* Glencoe, Ill.: Free Press, 1949.

Miller, J. W., & Ludwigh, E. Visual detection in a uniformly homogeneous field. *J. Aviat. Med.,* 1958, **29,** 603–608.

Miller, N E. Experiments relating Freudian displacement to generalization of conditioning. *Psychol. Bull.,* 1937, **36,** 516–517.

Miller, N. E. Effects of drugs on motivation: the value of using a variety of measures. *Ann. New York Acad. Sci.,* 1956, **65,** 318–333.

Mittelman, B., Wolff, H. G., & Scharf, M. Emotions and duodenal functions. *Psychosom. Med.,* 1942, **4,** 5–61.

Moeller, G., & Applezweig, M. H. A motivational factor in conformity. *J. abnorm. soc. Psychol.,* 1957, **55,** 114–120.

Moore, O. K., & Anderson, A. R. *Early reading and writing* (motion picture), Part I, II, and III. Guilford, Conn.: Skills Basic Education, 1960.

Mowrer, O. H. *Learning theory and personality dynamics.* New York: Ronald, 1950.

Munn, N. L. *Handbook of psychological research on the rat.* Boston: Houghton-Mifflin, 1950.

Munn, N. L. *The evolution and growth of human behavior.* Boston: Houghton-Mifflin, 1955.

Murphy, G. *Personality: A biosocial approach.* New York: Harper, 1947.

Murphy, G. *Historical introduction to modern psychology.* (Rev. ed.) New York: Harcourt Brace, 1949.

Murphy, G. *In the minds of men.* New York: Basic Books, 1953.

Murray, H. A. The effect of fear upon estimates of the maliciousness of other personalities. *J. soc. Psychol.,* 1933, **4,** 310–329.

Mussen, P. H., & Conger, J. J. *Child development and personality.* New York: Harper, 1956.

Nettler, G. A measure of alienation. *Amer. soc. Rev.,* 1957, **22,** 670–677.

Oppenheimer, R. Analogy in science. *Amer. Psychologist,* 1956, **11,** 127–135.

Osgood, C. E., & Tannenbaum, P. H. The principle of congruity in prediction of attitude change. *Psychol. Rev.,* 1955, **62,** 42–55.

Parsons, T. *Family socialization and interaction process.* Glencoe, Ill.: Free Press, 1955.

Peck, R. F. Family patterns correlated with adolescent personality structure. *J. abnorm. soc. Psychol.,* 1958, **57,** 347–350.

Phares, E. J. Expectancy changes in skill and chance situations. *J. abnorm. soc. Psychol.,* 1957, **54,** 339–342.

Piaget, J. *The language and thought of the child.* New York: Harcourt Brace, 1926.

Piaget, J. *Judgment and reasoning in the child.* New York: Harcourt Brace, 1928.

Piaget, J. *The child's conception of the world.* New York: Harcourt Brace, 1929.

Piaget, J. *The moral judgment of the child.* New York: Harcourt Brace, 1932.

Piaget, J. Principal factors determining intellectual evolution from childhood to adult life. In D. Rapaport (Ed.), *Organization and pathology of thought.* New York: Columbia University Press, 1951, pp. 154–192.

Piaget, J. *The construction of reality in the child.* New York: Basic Books, 1954.

Pinard, A. An experimental study of mental development based on Piaget's theory. Paper presented at a colloquium, Yale University, New Haven, Conn., December 1959.

Powell, E. H. Occupation, status and suicide: Toward a redefinition of anomie. *Amer. soc. Rev.,* 1958, **23,** 131–139.

Radke, M. H. The relation of parental authority to children's behavior and attitudes. *U. Minn. Inst. Child Welf. Monogr.,* Series No. 22, 1946.

Rado, S. Psychodynamics of depression from the etiological point of view. *Psychosom. Med.,* 1951, **13,** 51–55.

Redl, F., & Wineman, D. *Children who hate: the disorganization and breakdown of behavior controls.* Glencoe, Ill.: Free Press, 1951.

Reichard, Susan, & Tillman, C. Patterns of parent-child relationships in schizophrenia. *Psychiatry,* 1950, **13,** 247–257.

Riesman, D. *The lonely crowd.* (Abridged Ed.) New Haven: Yale University Press, 1950.

Roberts, A. H., & Jessor, R. Authoritarian, punitiveness and perceived social status. *J. abnorm. soc. Psychol.,* 1958, **56,** 311–314.

Rogers, C. R. *Client-centered therapy.* New York: Houghton-Mifflin, 1951.

Rogers, C. R. The necessary and sufficient conditions of therapeutic personality change. *J. consult. Psychol.,* 1957, **21,** 95–103.

Rogers, C. R. A process conception of psychotherapy. *Amer. Psychologist,* 1958, **13,** 141–149.

Rogers, S. The anchoring of absolute judgments. *Arch. Psychol.,* 1941, **37** (Whole No. 261).

Rose, J. A. Eating inhibitions in children in relation to anorexia nervosa. *Psychosom. Med.,* 1943, **5,** 117–124.

Rosenberg, M. J. Cognitive structure and attitudinal affect. *J. abnorm. soc. Psychol.,* 1956, **53,** 367–372.

Rosenzweig, S. An outline of frustration theory. In J. McV. Hunt (Ed.), *Personality and the behavior disorders,* Vol. 1. New York: Ronald, 1944, pp. 379–388.

Rosenzweig, S., & Sarason, S. An experimental study of the triadic hypothesis: reaction to frustration, ego defense and hypnotizability. *Charact. & Pers.,* 1942, **11,** 1–20.

Rotter, J. B. Level of aspiration as a method of studying personality: III. Group validity studies. *Charact. & Pers.,* 1943, **11,** 254–274.

Rotter, J. B. *Social learning and clinical psychology.* New York: Prentice-Hall, 1954.

Rotter, J. B., Seeman, M., & Liverant, S. Internal vs. external control of reinforcements: a major variable in behavior theory. Unpublished manuscript, 1958.

Rudin, S. A., & Stagner, R. Figure-ground phenomena in the perception of physical and social stimuli. *J. Psychol.,* 1958, **45,** 213–225.

Sanford, R. N., Adkins, Margaret M., Miller, R. B., & Cobb, Elizabeth. Physique, personality and scholarship. *Monogr. Soc. Res. Child Develpm.,* 1943, **8,** No. 1.

Sarason, I. G. Interrelationships among individual difference variables, behavior in psychotherapy, and verbal conditioning. *J. abnorm. soc. Psychol.*, 1958, **56,** 339–344.

Sarason, S. B., Davidson, K. S., Lighthall, F. F., Waite, R. R., & Ruebush, B. K. *Anxiety in elementary school children.* New York: Wiley, 1960.

Sarbin, T. R. Role theory. In G. Lindzey (Ed.), *Handbook of social psychology,* Vol. I. Cambridge, Mass.: Addison-Wesley, 1954, pp. 253–258.

Sargent, Helen. An experimental application of projective principles to a paper and pencil personality test. *Psychol. Monogr.*, 1944, **57** (Whole No. 5).

Schacter, S. *The psychology of affiliation.* Stanford: Stanford University Press, 1959.

Schaefer, E. S. A circumplex model for maternal behavior. *J. abnorm. soc. Psychol.*, 1959, **59,** 226–235.

Schein, E. H., Hill, W. F., Williams, H. L., & Lubin, A. Distinguishing characteristics of collaborators and resistors among American POW's. *J. abnorm. soc. Psychol.*, 1957, **55,** 197–201.

Schiffman, H. A psychological study of depressives using the Picture Arrangement Test. Paper read at Eastern Psychological Association meeting, 1960.

Schmideberg, M. The role of psychotic mechanisms in cultural development. *Int. J. Psychoanal.*, 1930, **11,** 387–418.

Schofield, W., & Balian, Lucy. A comparative study of the personal histories of psychiatric patients. *J. abnorm. soc. Psychol.*, 1959, **59,** 216–225.

Schroder, H. M. The development and maintenance of the reinforcement value of an object. *J. exp. Psychol.*, 1956, **51,** 131–141.

Schroder, H. M. Dispositional effects on reactions to the source of disapproval. ONR Technical Report No. 2. Princeton University, 1957.

Schroder, H. M., & Hunt, D. E. Failure-avoidance in situational interpretation and problem solving. *Psychol. Monogr.*, 1957, **71,** No. 3 (Whole No. 432).

Schroder, H. M., & Hunt, D. E. Dispositional effects upon conformity at different levels of discrepancy. *J. Pers.*, 1958, **26,** 243–258.

Schroder, H. M., & Hunt, D. E. The role of three processes in determining responses to interpersonal disagreement. Joint ONR & NIMH Progress Report, 1959.

Schroder, H. M., & Janicki, W. P. Conceptual systems and familial and socioeconomic conditions. Unpublished manuscript, 1959 (a).

Schroder, H. M., & Janicki, W. P. Relationship of dispositional measures to maintenance and generalization of response modification. Unpublished manuscript, 1959 (b).

Schroder, H. M., & McCarter, R. Authoritarianism and the categoricalness of attitudes. Unpublished manuscript, 1959.

Schroder, H. M., & Rotter, J. B. Rigidity as learned behavior. *J. exp. Psychol.*, 1952, **44,** 141–150.

Sears, Pauline S. Levels of aspiration in academically successful and unsuccessful children. *J. abnorm. soc. Psychol.*, 1940, **35,** 498–536.

Sears, R. R., Maccoby, Eleanor, & Levin, H. *Patterns of child rearing.* Evanston, Ill.: Row Peterson, 1957.

Sears, R. R., Whiting, J., Nowlis, V., & Sears, Pauline. Some child-rearing antecedents of aggression and dependency in young children. *Genet. Psychol., Monogr.*, 1953, **47,** 135–236.

Segal, J. Correlates of collaboration and resistance behavior among U.S. Army POW's in Korea. *J. soc. Issues,* 1957, **55,** 197–201.

Semmes, J., Weinstein, S., Ghent, L., & Teuber, H. L. Performance on complex tactual tasks after brain injury in man: analysis by locus of lesion. *Amer. J. Psychol.*, 1954, **67**, 220–240.

Shepard, J. F., & Breed, F. S. Maturation and use in the development of instinct. *J. Animal behav.*, 1913, **3**, 274–285.

Sherif, M. Some social factors in perception. *Arch. Psychol.*, 1935, **27** (Whole No. 187).

Sherif, M. Some social psychological aspects of conceptual functioning. In *The nature of concepts, their interrelation and role in social structure.* Proceedings of the Stillwater Conference, New York Foundation of Integrated Education, 1950.

Sherif, M., & Cantril, H. *The psychology of ego-involvements.* New York: Wiley, 1947.

Sherif, M., & Harvey, O. J. A study in ego functioning: elimination of stable anchorages in individual and group situations. *Sociometry,* 1952, **15**, 272–305.

Sherif, M., & Hovland, C. I. Judgmental phenomena and scales of attitude measurement: placement of items with individual choice of number of categories. *J. abnorm. soc. Psychol.*, 1953, **48**, 135–141.

Sherif, M., & Sherif, C. W. *Groups in harmony and tension.* New York: Harper, 1953.

Sherriffs, A. C. The "intuition questionnaire": a new projective test. *J. abnorm. soc. Psychol.*, 1948, **43**, 326–337.

Siegel, E. L. Genetic parallels of perceptual structurization in paranoid schizophrenia: an analysis by means of Rorschach technique. *J. proj. Tech.*, 1953, **17**, 151–161.

Simons, D. J., & Diethelm, O. Electroencephalographic studies of psychopathic personalities. *Arch. Neurol. Psychiat.*, 1946, **55**, 619–626.

Skinner, B. F. *The behavior of organisms.* New York: Appleton-Century-Crofts, 1938.

Skinner, B. F. *Science of human behavior.* New York: Macmillan, 1953.

Smith, M. B., Bruner, J. S., & White, R. W. *Opinions and personality.* New York: Wiley, 1956.

Smith, R. P. *"Where did you go?" "Out." "What did you do?" "Nothing."* New York: Norton, 1957.

Spencer, H. The principles of psychology. (Authorized Ed.) New York: Appleton-Century-Crofts, 1897.

Spitz, R. A. Anaclitic depression. *Psychoanal. Stud. Child.*, **2**, 113–117. New York: International Universities Press, 1946.

Spitz, R. A. The role of ecological factors in emotional development in infancy. *Child Develpm.*, 1949, **20**, 145–154.

Srole, L. Social integration and certain corollaries: an exploratory study. *Amer. soc. Rev.*, 1956, **21**, 709–716.

Steiner, D., & Peters, C. Conformity and the A-B-X model. *J. Pers.*, 1958, **26**, 229–242.

Stevenson, H. W., & Stuart, E. C. A developmental study of racial awareness in young children. *Child Developm.*, 1958, **29**, 399–410.

Sullivan, C., Grant, Marguerite, & Grant, D. The development of interpersonal maturity: application to delinquency. *Psychiatry,* 1957, **20**, 373–385.

Sullivan, H. S. *The interpersonal theory of psychiatry.* New York: Norton, 1953.

Sykes, G., & Matza, D. Techniques of neutralization: a theory of delinquency. *Amer. soc. Rev.*, 1957, **22**, 664–670.

Symonds, P. M. *The psychology of parent-child relationships.* New York: Appleton-Century-Crofts, 1939.

Szasz, T. S., Levin, E., Kirsner, J. B., & Palmer, W. L. The role of hostility in the pathogenesis of peptic ulcer: theoretical considerations with the report of a case. *Psychosom. Med.*, 1947, **9**, 331–336.

Taylor, I. A. Similarities in the structure of extreme social attitudes. *Psychol. Monogr.*, 1960, **74**, (Whole No. 489).

Teuber, H. L., Battersby, W. S., & Bender, M. B. Performance of complex visual tasks after cerebral lesions. *J. nerv. ment. Dis.*, 1951, **114**, 413–429.

Thibaut, J., & Kelley, H. H. *The social psychology of groups.* New York: Wiley, 1959.

Thibaut, J. W., & Riecken, H. W. Some determinants and consequences of the perception of social causality. *J. Pers.*, 1955, **24**, 113–133.

Thibaut, J. W., & Strickland, L. H. Psychological set and social conformity. *J. Pers.*, 1956, **25**, 115–129.

Thrasher, J. D. Interpersonal relations and gradations of stimulus structure as factors in judgment variations. *Sociometry*, 1954, **17**, 228–241.

Tietze, T. A study of mothers of schizophrenic patients. *Psychiatry*, 1949, **12**, 55–65.

Tinbergen, N. *The study of instinct.* London: Oxford University Press, 1951.

Tomkins, S. S., & Miner, J. B. *The Tomkins-Horn Picture Arrangement Test.* New York: Springer, 1957.

Underwood, B. J. *Experimental psychology.* New York: Appleton-Century-Crofts, 1949.

Vernon, J., & Hoffman, J. Effects of sensory deprivation on learning rate in human beings. *Science*, 1956, **123**, 1074–1075.

Vernon, M. D. The functions of schematic categories in perception. *Proceedings of the Fifteenth International Congress of Psychology, Brussels, 1957.* Amsterdam: North-Holland Publishing Co., 1957.

Vogel, W. R. S., Raymond, Susan, & Lazarus, R. S. Intrinsic motivation and psychological stress. *J. abnorm. soc. Psychol.*, 1959, **58**, 225–233.

Voltaire, F. M. *Candide*, 1759. Trans. by H. Morley. London: George Routledge.

Weiss, P. *Principles of development.* New York: Holt, 1939.

Wells, H. H., & Hunt, D. E. The role of two processes in determining reactions to two forms of failure stimulation. Unpublished manuscript, 1959.

Werner, H. *Comparative psychology of mental development.* (Rev. Ed.) New York: International Universities Press, 1957.

White, R. W. *The abnormal personality.* (2nd Ed.) New York: Ronald, 1956.

Whitehead, A. N. *Modes of thought.* New York: Capricorn Books, 1938.

Whiting, J., & Child, I. *Child training and personality: A cross-cultural study.* New Haven: Yale University Press, 1953.

Whorf, B. *Language, thought, and reality.* J. Carrol (Ed.). New York: Wiley, 1956.

Whyte, W. F. *Street corner society.* Chicago: University of Chicago Press, 1943.

Wilson, R. S. Personality patterns, source attractiveness, and conformity. *J. Pers.*, 1960, **28**, 186–199.

Winterbottom, Marian R. The relation of childhood training in independence to achievement motivation. Unpublished doctoral dissertation, University of Michigan, 1953.

Witkin, H. A., Lewis, Helen B., Hertzman, M., Machover, Karen, Meissner, Pearl B., & Wapner, S. *Personality through perception.* New York: Harper, 1954.

Wolf, Theta H. The effect of praise and competition on the persisting behavior of kindergarten children. *U. Minn. Inst. Child Welf. Monogr.,* Series, 1938, No. 15.

Wright, J. M. Extrapunitiveness and authoritarianism: changes in attitudinal correlates as a result of frustration. ONR Technical Report No. 7, Vanderbilt University, 1958.

Zelen, S. Goal-setting rigidity in an ambiguous situation. *J. consult. Psychol.,* 1955, **19,** 395–399.

Name Index

Subject Index